AF838725

Input–Output Analysis in Developing Countries

Input–Output Analysis in Developing Countries

Sources, Methods and Applications

V. Bulmer-Thomas
Queen Mary College,
London University

175 YEARS OF PUBLISHING
1807 1982

JOHN WILEY & SONS LTD
Chichester · New York · Brisbane · Toronto · Singapore

Copyright © 1982 by John Wiley & Sons Ltd.

All rights reserved.

No part of this book may be reproduced by any means, nor
transmitted, nor translated into a machine language
without the written permission of the publisher.

***Library of Congress Cataloging in Publication Data*:**

Bulmer-Thomas, V.
Input–output analysis in developing countries.

Includes bibliographical references and index.
1. Underdeveloped areas—Industries—Mathematical models.
2. Interindustry economics. I. Title.
HC59.7.B85 339.2′3′091724 81–19826

ISBN 0 471 10149 4 AACR2

***British Library Cataloguing in Publication Data*:**

Bulmer-Thomas, V.
Input–output analysis in developing countries.
1. Interindustry economics 2. Underdeveloped
areas—Economic conditions
I. Title
339.2′31′1724 HC59.7

ISBN 0 471 10149 4

Typeset by Macmillan India Ltd, Bangalore.

Printed in the United States of America.

To Barbara
and the children

Contents

Foreword

This volume offers the first comprehensive treatment of applied input–output analysis presented in systematic, handbook form.

During the fifty years that have passed since input–output was introduced, writing on various aspects of this methodology grew exponentially hand-in-hand with its applications. Except for several monographs of an essentially theoretical nature it consists, however, of articles, statistical compilation, private and public research reports and papers scattered over a great variety of specialized publications in many different fields. The author has succeeded so far as I am able to judge in incorporating in the following 288 pages most of the relevant ideas and procedures described in this literature and actually tested by experienced practitioners of input–output analysis.

Many advanced, and some of the elementary, modern economics textbooks now contain a page or two devoted to input–output. As a rule, however, it is being presented as a simple, not to say simplistic, general equilibrium theory formulated in terms of a set of linear equations. Bulmer-Thomas, on the contrary, correctly directs his reader's attention to complex and often quite sophisticated aspects of fact-finding methodology involved in the construction and analytical use of national and regional input-output tables. If economics is approached not as a speculative, primarily normative discipline, but as an empirical science, its terminological conventions as well as theoretical constructs should be understood as instrumental devices to be used to depict as concretely as possible the structure, and to analyse as accurately as possible the operational properties, of a particular economic system.

The fact that it is focused on input–output analysis as practised in the less developed countries enhances rather than restricts the usefulness of this book. The analytical problems arising in dealing with less developed countries are more complex than those encountered in the study of advanced free market economies; the greater the role of old traditional technologies and institutions and of informal non-monetary transactions in a given economy, the more difficult is the description of its structure and the more complex the analysis of its operational characteristics. In the developed, industrialized economies the input-output approach proved to be an effective tool for penetrating below the slick surface of market transactions governed by the price mechanism of a supposedly ideal competitive system. A man, capable of orienting himself under water, will have no difficulty in finding his way to the surface; an economist who has constructed an input-output table of Costa Rica and Morocco—as the author of this volume did—will find it easy to interpret the input–output table of Great Britain or the United States.

WASSILY LEONTIEF

Preface

Less developed countries (LDCs) are, almost without exception, unwilling to leave their economic destiny to be determined by the free play of market forces with no government interference. Despite the convincing evidence that producers and consumers even in the traditional sector are sensitive to price signals, there is a strong feeling on the part of policy-makers that the *laissez-faire* outcome would be less than socially optimal; the price system, in other words, can be relied on to play a *positive* role, but this is divorced from any *normative* implications.

In such a system, there is a strong case to be made for decentralized planning; by decentralizing the planning exercise, the authorities can leave decisions at the micro-economic level to those who are likely to have the best information at their disposal, while by planning the economy, they can ensure that social and economic objectives are, if not met, at least approximated.

Planning an economy requires a framework capable of answering the important questions; by its very nature, this framework must be macro-economic but—in LDCs at least—it cannot be restricted to one or two sectors. Too many important questions in LDCs call for answers at a level of detail far greater than that supplied by the usual macro-economic models.

For many countries, the correct framework can only be supplied by an input–output table with primary, secondary and tertiary activity each broken down into many further divisions; these tables, however, as many LDCs have found to their cost, are expensive and time-consuming to produce; indeed, the lags in production can be so long (up to ten years) that they become redundant by the time they are published. The result is that many tables go unused, because they were designed to fill a need which has *perforce* been met by some (inferior) substitute.

There is another reason why input–output tables produced by LDCs are often under-utilized. The main thrust of input–output research has been geared to the needs of advanced countries; much of this work is inappropriate for application to LDCs, at least not without considerable modification. Economists working in the Third World are aware of this, but usually lack the resources or support to carry out the necessary adaptations.

Developing countries can ill afford to make such poor use of their scarce resources. Their input–output tables need to be produced more quickly, while familiarity with a range of input–output techniques, suitable for application to LDCs, needs to be increased. The aim of this book is to make a modest contribution to both these objectives; at the same time, the book should be useful to professional economists and students of input–output analysis and development economics interested in a more detailed account of the input–output model than is available elsewhere.

The book is in two parts; in the first eleven chapters, the sources and methods used in the construction of input-tables are discussed at some length. The author's ambition in this part is to lay down the general principles which act as a guide to the resolution of the innumerable problems which occur every time a table is constructed, while at the same time giving the economist interested in working with input–output techniques greater insight into the mechanics of an input–output table. In the second part (Chapters 12 to 17), the book concentrates on a range of applications which should prove suitable for most LDCs. Inevitably, this part of the book will be criticized for omissions, but it is not possible to include all possible applications and some very attractive uses of the input–output model, e.g. in the study of pollution problems, have had to be excluded.

Chapter 1 is on the social accounting framework for input–output tables, while Chapter 2 considers the production accounts—the basis for input–output tables—in more detail. The reason for giving so much prominence to the accounting aspects of input–output work is, first, that the framework in which the input–output table is set provides an effective limit on the uses to which the table can be put and, secondly, because the work of constructing a national input–output table often acts as a check on other aspects of the accounting process, in particular the national accounts.

In Chapter 3, the task of sampling and surveying in the construction of input–output tables is examined. This is in general a very neglected side of input–output research and all sorts of *ad hoc* procedures have been adopted by input–output workers—some with less statistical justification than others. The aim of this chapter is to show how optimal sampling techniques can in fact be applied to input–output work and, where this is impossible, what the most appropriate procedures might be.

The subsequent chapters of the book assume a basic understanding of matrix algebra and the input–output model, so Chapter 4 is devoted to these questions. The most elementary input–output model is first presented and this is followed by some simple extensions, based largely on the accounting framework in Chapter 1.

Chapter 5 is concerned with the problems of classification and aggregation: the first problem arises *before* the construction of the table and determines its maximum size, while the second arises *after* construction and determines the minimum number of sectors to which the table can be sensibly reduced. Aggregation is often necessary, because the input–output model is buried in a larger econometric model, the solution to which presupposes only a small number of sectors.

Because sales and purchases data are usually denominated in different prices, a choice has to be made over the valuation convention in input–output work. This is considered in Chapter 6, where the author takes issue with the usual resolution of this problem and proposes instead a new valuation convention.

Perhaps because of the early association of input–output analysis with the United States and the Soviet Union, both relatively closed economies, foreign trade entries—particularly imports—have not received sufficient attention in the input–output literature. An attempt is made to remedy this deficiency in Chapter 7, which also considers the most appropriate way of valuing trade entries. Chapter 8 is then concerned with reconciling inconsistencies in the commodity balances—the most usual method by which input–output tables are constructed.

Because of the absence of a one-to-one relationship between commodities and industries/activities, the construction of symmetric input–output tables (i.e. industry × industry or commodity × commodity) requires decisions on the treatment of secondary products. This problem is considered in Chapter 9, by the end of which all the work needed to produce a base year input–output table will have been reviewed. For many purposes, however, the table needs to be updated and projected and the literature concerned with these problems is reviewed in Chapter 10.

In Chapter 11 a number of special problems which arise in the construction of tables are considered; the subheadings of this chapter are in general self-explanatory, but students of development economics may be particularly interested in the proposed treatment of the informal sector, which has traditionally been neglected in input–output work.

The next chapters are all concerned with applications of the input–output table. Chapter 12 examines multipliers and linkage analysis, while Chapter 13 takes as its theme employment and income distribution. The adaptation in recent years of the input–output model to handle questions of income distribution is a major achievement and the most significant contributions are considered in some depth.

In Chapter 14, a number of extensions of the basic input–output model relevant to LDCs are considered. These include the inter-regional model and the price model; the latter is still a neglected source of input–output research and many developments can still be expected in this field. Even so, the current state of the art offers LDCs an excellent opportunity to study the mechanics of, for example, the inflationary process.

The input–output model has sometimes been attacked for its neglect of questions of choice and efficiency. In Chapters 15 and 16, an effort is made to show how the model can be adapted to consider these matters; Chapter 15 looks at models concerned with the choice between home production and imports, while Chapter 16 takes as its theme the measurement of inefficiency using input–output tables. These two chapters should prove particularly useful to those concerned with development planning in the broadest sense.

The best known use of input–output analysis to the public is perhaps as a forecasting tool. This use is considered in Chapter 17, where the role of the input–output model in a general planning exercise is shown to be limited mainly to the sector stage. No planning exercise, however, is complete without such a stage and the input–output model is well suited to its elucidation.

I first became interested in input–output analysis while a graduate student at Oxford University. My doctoral thesis involved construction of an input–output table for Costa Rica, and my first academic post (at the Fraser of Allander Institute, Strathclyde University) was linked to the construction of an input–output table for Scotland. This in turn led to participation in a joint venture with the Moroccan government for construction of an input–output table for Morocco. These three exercises in applied input–output work have convinced me of the need for a book such as this, although whether this book fills that need will have to be determined by the readers themselves.

I owe a special debt of gratitude to those many people, too numerous to mention by name, who have read parts of this book in draft form. I am, however, particularly indebted to Professor Sir Richard Stone for his encouragement over the years and to my former colleagues, Professors David Simpson and James MacGilvray, for providing such a stimulating atmosphere at the Fraser of Allander Institute for research into input–output problems. To my typist Lydia Foreman, I can only say how glad I am that she managed to finish the manuscript without permanently damaging her eyesight; I know few people who would continue to struggle with such illegible script with such unfailing good humour.

CHAPTER 1

The Social Accounting Framework for Input–Output Tables

1.1 INTRODUCTION

This book is about input–output tables: how to construct them and how to derive from them models which will be of relevance to less developed countries (LDCs). In itself, however, an input–output table is simply a double-entry system of accounting for transactions between producers; an input–output table is not a model nor does it provide any detail on many of the stocks and flows which occur within an economy.

The reason why an input–output table is a worthwhile system of accounting is that, by simple assumptions, a powerful model can be derived from it. Nevertheless, even the simplest model requires that we adopt some point of view about transactions other than those between producers. For this reason, it is essential that the input–output table is set in a wider accounting framework.

Such a framework requires a Social Accounting Matrix (SAM). This matrix provides an accounting record for a whole economy (not just transactions among producers), although not all entries will be considered in the same detail. The way in which SAM is drawn up will be determined by the class of models we wish to build, and so it follows that the scope of model-building is constrained by the form of SAM. Consequently, it is imperative that the SAM we work with is capable of answering the kind of questions which are regarded as important by LDCs.

A great deal of work has been done on SAMs in the last two decades and progress has been made on the important question of international standardization (United Nations, 1968). It is undoubtedly the case, however, that most of this work stems from the data availability and model-building requirements of developed countries (DCs). Although much of this work is still pertinent to the case of LDCs, the latter need to modify their own SAMs in a number of ways.

SAMs are useful in their own right, not just as a guide to model-building. In this chapter, we shall show how it is possible to develop a SAM suited to the requirements of LDCs which provides useful insights even without the need for formal model-building.

1.2 A SIMPLE SAM

The simplest possible economy cannot exist without producing and consuming, so clearly we need accounts for these two fundamental activities. Even a very primitive economy, however, needs to set aside some of its current production for future requirements, so we also need an account for the activity of accumulation. Finally, we must recognize the fact that virtually no economy can supply all its needs from its own resources, so we need one other account for the activity of foreign trade.

This simple four-account matrix is set out schematically in Table 1.1. An entry in a row records an incoming or credit, while that in a column records an outgoing or debit. Since every entry appears in both a row and column, we can see it from two different angles; for example, the entry C in the row for production means that producers were credited for the sale of consumer goods (500 units in this example) to the consumption accounts. From the point of view of consumers, however, this same entry represents a debit, which is why it appears in the column for the activity of consumption.

The other entries in this table can be quickly described, because they correspond closely to well-known macro-economic aggregates. Continuing along the production row, we find I, which stands for gross capital formation, and EX which represents exports. Exports represent an incoming for the production account, but an outgoing for the rest of the world. Consequently, the trade column represents debits as seen from abroad, while the trade row records the rest of the world's incomings.

In the row for consumption, we find Y which represents the income of consumers, although from the point of view of producers this is an outgoing. The other entry in the row (F) represents net factor and transfer payments from abroad; examples are gifts and remittances, dividends and the wages and salaries of non-residents. The figure is given net, so there is no corresponding entry at the intersection of the consumption column and trade row.

From their income of 650 units ($Y+F$), consumers spend only 500 units in Table 1.1, leaving them savings of 150 units. This accounts for the entry S in the accumulation row, but it is not quite sufficient to finance gross capital formation ($I > S$); the balance has to be obtained from abroad through foreign borrowing

Table 1.1 Four-account SAM without disaggregation

	Production	Consumption	Accumulation	Trade	Total
Production		(C) 500	(I) 200	(EX) 300	1000
Consumption	(Y) 600		—	(F) 50	650
Accumulation	—	(S) 150		(B) 50	200
Trade	(IM) 400	—	—		400
Total	1000	650	200	400	2250

Note: An entry in the table represents a credit to the row account and a debit to the column account.

(B). Finally, in the trade row, we observe imports (IM) which are absorbed into the production account and distributed along with home output to the consumption and accumulation accounts. At 400 units, imports exceed the value of exports and net factor receipts ($IM > EX + F$), so that B represents not only the net borrowing requirement, but also the deficit on the current account of the balance of payments.

Although simple, Table 1.1 is still sufficient to provide the basis for a number of macro-economic models. For example, since the row and column for any account must balance, we can write for the production account the identity:

$$Y + IM \equiv C + I + EX \tag{1.1}$$

or

$$Y \equiv C + I + (EX - IM) \tag{1.2}$$

which is the familiar national income identity stating that Gross Domestic Product (Y) and Gross Domestic Expenditure are equal. If we now make two behavioural assumptions, namely that consumption and imports are linear functions of income and can be written:

$$C = a + cY \tag{1.3}$$

$$IM = b + mY \tag{1.4}$$

and that the sum of exports and investment is autonomous and can be written as A, then we get:

$$Y = a + cY - (b + mY) + A \tag{1.5}$$

or

$$Y = \left[\frac{1}{1 - c + m}\right] A^* \qquad A^* = A + (a - b) \tag{1.6}$$

where $1/(1 - c + m)$ is the Keynesian income multiplier for the case of an open economy. Thus, even in this simplest possible case, our SAM has provided enough information on certain important transactions between accounts for us to develop a workable model of the economy.

The deficiencies, however, of Table 1.1 are readily apparent. First, it will be noticed that there are no entries on the diagonal of the matrix. This happens because all transactions within an account disappear on consolidation; if, for example, we were to provide separate accounts for different classes of producers and consumers, we would be forced to recognize the interdependence of sectors within an account. This, therefore, is what is attempted in Table 1.2.

In Table 1.2, the trade account is not broken down any further (as, of course, it could have been. There could, for example, be separate accounts for each of the country's main trading partners as well as a separate account for tourists). The row for the accumulation account is also the same, but in the column recognition is given to the difference between gross fixed capital formation and investment in inventories (stock change). In the consumption accounts, two sectors are now

Table 1.2 Four-account SAM with some disaggregation

	Production 1, . . . , n	Consumption		Accumulation		Trade	Total
		Private	Public	Gross fixed capital formation	Change in inventories		
Production	$\Sigma_i \Sigma_j W_{ij}$ 1000	Σc_i 400	Σgx_i 100	Σj_i 150	$\Sigma \Delta s_i$ 50	Σe_i 300	Σz_i 2000
Consumption (private)	Σv_j 450		TR_{pg} 50	—	—	F 50	550
Consumption (public)	Σt_j 150	TR_{gp} 50		—	—	—	200
Accumulation	—	S_p 100	S_g 50			B 50	200
Trade	Σm_j 400	—	—	—	—		400
Total	Σz_j 2000	550	200	150	50	400	3350

Note: An entry in the table represents a credit to the row account and a debit to the column account.

identified—private and public—and this applies to the row as well as the column, while in the production accounts, we recognize the existence of n different sectors.

With our disaggregated production account, we are obliged to acknowledge the interdependence between sectors. The aggregate value of all these transactions between producers are recorded in the matrix by the term $\Sigma_i \Sigma_j W_{ij}$ with a gross value of 1000 units, so that a purchase from the ith sector by the jth sector is denoted by W_{ij}. This entry in the matrix, when filled out in detail, represents an input–output table and it is, of course, the subject matter of this book. Much more will be said about it later, but for present purposes it is sufficient to notice how it fits into the rest of the social accounts.

Because there are now n sectors of production, each column entry corresponding to the row for production will have n entries. The sum of private consumption is therefore given by $\Sigma_i c_i$, while public or government consumption is given by $\Sigma_i gx_i$. The other entries in the row are straightforward, and the gross value of supply (i.e. home production plus imports), when taken across all sectors, is 2000 units ($\Sigma_i z_i$).

In the rows for consumption, the 600 units of income have been broken down into $2n$ entries. Factor payments to the private sector ($\Sigma_j v_j$) account for n of these entries while the rest are represented by net indirect tax payments to the government ($\Sigma_j t_j$). As there are now two consuming sectors, we need also to take into account *their* interdependence. Thus, we can see that the public sector transferred 50 units (TR_{pg}) to the private sector, representing such things as social security benefits, while the private sector paid 50 units of direct taxation (TR_{gp}) to the government.

The row for accumulation is much the same as before, except that we now acknowledge that both the private (S_p) and the public sector (S_g) contribute to domestic savings. The row for trade is the same except that imports are now absorbed into the n different production accounts. The column sum for each production account (z_i) gives the gross value of supply in each sector and when summed across all sectors its value is again 2000 units.

By making a number of simple assumptions, it is possible to derive a new class of models, including input–output models, from Table 1.2. However, we would be anticipating the argument of later chapters if we did so here and the input–output model in its simplest form will not be introduced until Chapter 4. At this point, it is more important to point out what classes of transactions are ignored by Table 1.2, since it is what is left out or suppressed which restricts the range of models we can apply.

The first thing to notice is that Table 1.2 refers only to flows over a specific time period (usually a year). Stocks are not mentioned, so that the capital or accumulation accounts refer only to *changes* in the stock of assets held. The absence of information on stocks means that in our model-building work we have to by-pass those developments in the literature which stress the importance of stock levels or wealth in determining such things as consumption and investment.

The second omission has to do with the financing of capital formation. The plethora of transactions which in the real world link households, corporations, banks, the government and the rest of the world in financing investment are reduced to the three net flows in the row for the accumulation account in Table 1.2. The instruments of savings and the capital transfers between sectors are completely ignored. Thus, the results of our models will tell us nothing about how the financial system must adapt to match the developments in the real economy.

Table 1.2 also tells us nothing about the distribution of income; this is true whether we are interested in the functional, institutional or size distribution of income. (The functional distribution records the division of income between a country's factors of production, e.g. (i) wages; (ii) property income. The institutional distribution shows the division of income by sector, e.g. (i) rural; (ii) urban, while the size distribution records the percentage share of income accruing to a percentage share of the population starting with the poorest.) Consequently our models will tell us nothing about the effect of various autonomous changes on income distribution, so that the model will be incomplete in its treatment of such things as domestic savings, which are usually assumed to be influenced by the distribution of income.

Many other features of a real economy are ignored by Table 1.2, such as the regional dimension of production, but this need not be of any consequence. Any system of social accounting and model-building must ignore or suppress detail about many economic transactions, if it is to operate efficiently. However, it is legitimate to demand of any SAM that it be capable of providing answers to the kind of questions which are regarded as important. In this respect, Table 1.2 must be classed as a failure since it could not, for example, provide any information on the distribution of income which is regarded by most countries, particularly LDCs, as being of great significance. In the next section, therefore, we shall review the attempt made by the United Nations to provide a standard SAM, which is sufficiently detailed and flexible to answer all relevant questions.

1.3 THE REVISED SYSTEM OF NATIONAL ACCOUNTS (SNA)

While international guidelines for national income accounting were first laid down by the United Nations in 1953, it was not until 1968 that international recommendations for a complete system of social accounts were presented (United Nations, 1968). This revised system of national accounts (SNA) is far-reaching and ambitious, but continues to be based on the four fundamental accounts that were identified above: production, consumption, accumulation and trade.

The major advance in the SNA is the inclusion of data on opening and closing stocks in the accounts. At any one time, the following balance sheet identity holds:

> Written-down value of tangible assets held plus excess of financial claims held as assets over financial claims issued as liabilities equals Net Worth.

To pass from the opening to the closing balance sheet, our SAM must be able to identify the flows which affect the values of stocks over time, but if we return to Table 1.2, it is clear that very little information on the link between opening and closing stocks by sector is provided. What is required is a breakdown of the capital formation data by sector, deduction of depreciation from the sectoral savings data, deconsolidation of the diagonal of the accumulation account to provide data on capital transfers between sectors and a new subset of accounts within the activity of accumulation to record dealings in financial claims.

In the production account, the most important innovation of the SNA is the distinction between commodities and activities. The distinction is in recognition of the fact that there is not a one-to-one correspondence between the output of a commodity and the output of an industry producing that commodity as principal product; it is unusual for the output of an industry to fall completely within one commodity group, while conversely the total output of a commodity group may be drawn from several different industries. This means that our Table 1.2 may be in error in one important respect, because we have assumed that we can, for example, allocate household purchases of commodities to the *n* industries without ambiguity.

In the SNA, industries sell their output to the commodity accounts in the proportions in which they make the different commodity groups. The commodity accounts then distribute their output to industrial users as intermediate purchases and to final users as final demand. The United Nations also recommends that entries in the commodity accounts be recorded net of indirect taxes, trade and transport margins, a recommendation we shall return to in Chapter 6.

In the consumption accounts, the SNA begins with a breakdown of expenditure between households and government (not unlike Table 1.2), but then recommends a further breakdown by purpose (e.g. health and education in the case of government). Industry, however, does not make factor payments by purpose, so the rest of the consumption account is quite complicated: industry is shown as paying income to the owners of factors of production, which is then broken down by institutional sector of origin. This income is then shown by form, e.g. wages, salaries, employers' contributions, so that it can be summed and broken down by institutional sector of receipt. The circle is now complete, because the income received by each sector can then be paid out by purpose to the commodity accounts, while the balance is accounted for by transfers and savings.

The consumption accounts in the SNA therefore require much more detail than is provided by Table 1.2 and some of this information, such as the form of income table, is likely to be extremely difficult for LDCs to provide. Furthermore, despite the wealth of detail demanded by the SNA, it is still not sufficient to explore the distribution of income, since the household sector remains aggregated. We shall return to this point below.

The final account to be mentioned concerns the rest of the world, where the only division is between current and capital transactions. The latter is needed, because the SNA identifies flows of funds data which involve the capital account of the balance of payments. Apart from that, the trade account is treated similarly to the trade account in Table 1.2.

This description of the SNA is very brief, but it is sufficient to show its main features. Its data requirements are quite advanced and the range of models which can be derived from it is much broader than can be obtained from Table 1.2. Nevertheless, two questions can be posed in relation to any SAM: first, whether the models which can be obtained from it permit us to tackle the most vital problems facing a country and, secondly, whether the data requirements are realistic in the light of scarce statistical resources. There is a third and more subtle question, which involves our asking whether the benefit from the increased flow of information outweighs the cost of collecting it, but this exercise in applied cost–benefit analysis will not be attempted here.

As far as the SNA's emphasis on stocks and balance sheets is concerned, this is certainly a good idea. Nevertheless, for most LDCs the data problems are likely to prove too great; apart from the question of valuing opening stocks correctly, it is very difficult to account correctly for depreciation and revaluations in inflationary economies. Although LDCs often can provide data on financial claims, it is not clear whether it is really worth the effort in the light of their relatively simple financial markets, and even in the case of DCs attempts to build models of financial systems using flow of funds data have not proved particularly successful. Finally, the institutional division for the stock data proposed by the SNA is not very helpful for LDCs where financial and non-financial enterprises are closely interlocked and where the major institutional division is between foreign and domestic control. Since there is no hard and fast line between firms by form of control, it would be very difficult to rearrange the stock data to conform to this division.

The treatment of the production accounts in the SNA is sensible and within the capacities of most countries, but the divisions within the consumption accounts do not appear to conform to the realities of LDCs. Most serious is the absence of any framework for analysing the institutional and size distribution of income; there is no separation of the rural from urban areas and no division of the household sector by size of income. Furthermore, the form of income table, which links income by institutional sector of origin with income by institutional sector of receipt, is more appropriate for countries where wage labour is the predominant form of factor payment.

Discussion of the accumulation accounts has already been anticipated to some extent by the discussion of the stock and balance sheet data above. In LDCs, one of the most important financial features of any sector is its net lending/borrowing requirement, i.e. the difference between its capital expenditure and savings after allowing for transfers. Although this information can be read off the SNA, it is not immediately obvious because it emerges as the difference between changes in financial claims held as assets and issued as liabilities. If the flow of funds data are suppressed, then it becomes necessary to account for each sector's net lending/borrowing directly.

In one important area, the trade accounts, the SNA asks for too little information, not too much. In LDCs, where the pattern of trade is still changing rapidly, it is essential to provide detailed information on imports not only by use (as the SNA proposes) but also by source (i.e. their commodity composition). This requires a *matrix* of import flows rather than a *vector*. Furthermore, studies of import substitution possibilities require the separation of imports in intermediate and final expenditure from expenditure on domestically produced goods. Because of the recurrence of balance of payments difficulties and associated restrictions on trade, many LDCs have the statistics to provide such data.

1.4 A PROPOSED SAM FOR LDCS

There is no objection in principle to expanding the SNA to take account of the above criticisms; the system is flexible and could easily be adapted. In practice, however, such an expansion is likely to be unfruitful, because the system already demands too much of LDCs in terms of data requirements. In this section, therefore, a SAM for LDCs is proposed which is designed to fit both their model-building needs and their data limitations.

The proposed SAM is set out in Table 1.3; no accounts are presented for stocks, so the system begins with a three-fold division of production into commodities, activities and factors. Consumption is divided into private and public and the latter is then further subdivided by responsibility, e.g. Central and Local Government. Private consumption is first divided into rural and urban and then further subdivided by institutional sector, e.g. rich and poor households. The accumulation accounts are similarly divided with a further subdivision corresponding to fixed capital formation and inventory change, while there are two additional accounts for land and finance. The trade account column is divided into tourism and commodity exports, although the latter could be broken down by area of sale (e.g. North America, EEC), while the trade account row has m accounts for imports by source (e.g. rubber, plastics, processed food).

This idealized system works as follows: activities deliver their output net of indirect taxes[1] to the commodity accounts (M). The latter then distribute this domestic output[2] to activities as intermediate purchases (W), to consumers (c_r, c_u, gx) and to the capital accounts ($j_r+\Delta s_r$, $j_u+\Delta s_u$, and $j_g+\Delta s_g$). The entry in the land column represents the transfer costs of land and buildings ($TCLB$), i.e. that part of land purchases which is not matched by land sales. The only other source of demand for commodity output comes from tourists (e_t) and the rest of the world (e_o).

The balance of activity output not consumed by purchases of domestic commodities (W) is spent on imported materials (M_I) and payments to the f factors of production (V). The latter also receive income from the consumption accounts (e.g. household payments to domestic servants) and from abroad (F_o). Factor income is then distributed pre-tax to the institutional sectors in rural and urban areas (Y_r, Y_u). The institutional sectors receive current transfers from one another (TR_{ij}) as well as from abroad (TR_{io}). Their outgoings consist of purchases of home-produced commodities, purchases of imports (m_r, m_u, m_g), transfers, direct and indirect taxes (T_r, T_u, T_g) and new savings including

Table 1.3 Proposed SAM for LDCs

	Production			Consumption			Accumulation					Trade		Total
	Commodities	Activities	Factors	Private		Public	Private		Public	Land	Finance	Tourism	Other	
	$1, \ldots, n$	$1, \ldots, n$	$1, \ldots, f$	Rural $1, \ldots, r$	Urban $1, \ldots, u$	$1, \ldots, g$	Rural $1, \ldots, r$	Urban $1, \ldots, u$	$1, \ldots, g$					
Production														
Commodities $1, \ldots, n$	—	W	—	c_r	c_u	gx	$j_r + \Delta s_r$	$j_u + \Delta s_u$	$j_g + \Delta s_g$	$TCLB$	—	e_t	e_o	t_1
Activities $1, \ldots, n$	M	—	—	—	—	—	—	—	—	—	—	—	—	t_2
Factors $1, \ldots, f$	—	V	—	F_r	F_u	F_g	—	—	—	—	—	—	F_o	t_3
Consumption														
Private														
Rural $1, \ldots, r$	—	—	Y_r	TR_{rr}	TR_{ru}	TR_{rg}	—	—	—	—	—	—	TR_{ro}	t_4
Urban $1, \ldots, u$	—	—	Y_u	TR_{ur}	TR_{uu}	TR_{ug}	—	—	—	—	—	—	TR_{uo}	t_5
Public $1, \ldots, g$	—	—	—	T_r	T_u	T_g	—	—	—	—	—	—	T_o	t_6
Accumulation														
Private														
Rural $1, \ldots, r$	—	—	—	S_r	—	—	KTR_{rr}	KTR_{ru}	KTR_{rg}	—	—	—	—	t_7
Urban $1, \ldots, u$	—	—	—	—	S_u	—	KTR_{ur}	KTR_{uu}	KTR_{ug}	—	—	—	—	t_8
Public $1, \ldots, g$	—	—	—	—	—	S_g	KTR_{gr}	KTR_{gu}	KTR_{gg}	—	—	—	—	t_9
Land	—	—	—	—	—	—	L_r	L_u	L_g	—	—	—	—	t_{10}
Finance	—	—	—	—	—	—	B_r	B_u	B_g	—	—	—	B_o	0
Trade $1, \ldots, m$	—	M_I	—	m_r	m_u	m_g	—	—	—	—	—	—	—	t_{11}
Total	t_1	t_2	t_3	t_4	t_5	t_6	t_7	t_8	t_9	t_{10}		t_{11}		

depreciation (S_r, S_u, S_g). The only source of government revenue not yet mentioned is taxes on exports and transfers from abroad (T_o).

The institutional sectors supplement their savings with capital transfers amongst one another (KTR_{ij}). These sources of funds are then disbursed either as new capital expenditure, capital transfers or net purchases of land (L_r, L_u, L_g). The balancing item is then net lending/borrowing (B_r, B_u, B_g). In the trade accounts, the only entry not yet mentioned is the balancing item (B_o), which can be interpreted (if imports exceed exports) either as the deficit on the current account of the balance of payments, or the net borrowing requirement from abroad. B_o is therefore equal to the sum of the net lending/borrowing requirements of the institutional sectors, so that the row sum for the finance account is zero and there are no entries in the column.

The proposed SAM is therefore very simple, but it highlights the main features of LDCs. Trade data are provided in some detail and it is possible to identify the distribution of income in a meaningful way. In the next sections, we shall examine some actual examples of social accounting which use a format similar to Table 1.3 to derive interesting results even without the need for formal model-building.

Case I—SAM for Sri Lanka

The first example of social accounting in practice comes from Sri Lanka and is derived from a SAM prepared for 1970 (Pyatt, 1977). Sri Lanka comes quite close to the typical idea of an LDC with a predominantly agricultural economy, which combines traditional subsistence farming with the raising of cash crops for export by modern commercial means; in particular, the commodities tea, rubber and coconuts are raised on estates which are virtually isolated from the rest of the economy.

The SAM for Sri Lanka is presented in Table 1.4. Unlike Table 1.3, there is no disaggregation of the accumulation accounts nor is there any distinction between commodities and activities, but in all other respects it corresponds closely to the scheme proposed above. In the account for factors of production, three types of labour are identified as well as three types of capital, of which one refers to the owners of housing. The latter draws its income from the production accounts partly by imputation, which is given by the rental value of owner-occupation.

The first thing to note about the table is the way factors of production receive factor income not only from the production accounts, but also from the institutional sectors; most of these payments are accounted for by the hire of domestic servants and the wages and salaries of civil servants. Another interesting feature of the table is the breakdown of factor payments by institutional sector of receipt; while all labour income is paid into the corresponding household account, both housing and private capital income benefit all the private sectors, although in very different proportions. Finally, we can see how the income of the institutional sectors is affected by transfers to and from the government, firms and the rest of the world; for example, while rural households receive transfers

Table 1.4 SAM for Sri Lanka, 1970 (Rs million)

	Production							Consumption					Accumulation	Trade	Total
	Activities	Factors						Firms	Urban households	Rural households	Estate households	Government			
		Urban labour	Rural labour	Estate labour	Housing	Public capital	Private capital								
Production															
Activities	4358	—	—	—	—	—	—	—	1871	5103	627	302	1962	2113	16336
Factors															
Urban labour	1112	—	—	—	—	—	—	—	38	—	—	523	—	—	1673
Rural labour	2386	—	—	—	—	—	—	—	—	56	—	742	—	—	3184
Estate labour	695	—	—	—	—	—	—	—	—	—	6	10	—	—	711
Housing	633	—	—	—	—	—	—	—	—	—	—	—	—	—	633
Public capital	175	—	—	—	—	—	—	—	—	—	—	—	—	—	175
Private capital	5098	—	—	—	—	—	—	—	—	—	—	—	—	−113	4985
Consumption															
Firms	—	—	—	—	135	175	1266	—	—	—	—	294	—	—	1869
Urban households	—	1673	—	—	137	—	662	434	—	—	—	91	—	6	3004
Rural households	—	—	3184	—	330	—	3026	203	—	—	—	151	—	6	6902
Estate households	—	—	—	711	31	—	30	7	—	—	—	6	—	6	791
Government	856	—	—	—	—	—	—	376	368	195	4	104	313	130	2346
Accmulation	—	—	—	—	—	—	—	833	520	808	11	43	—	425	2640
Trade	1023	—	—	—	—	—	—	16	207	741	143	79	364	—	2573
Total	16336	1673	3184	711	633	175	4985	1869	3004	6902	791	2346	2640	2573	

Source: Derived from Table 3.11 in Pyatt, 1977.

worth 360 units of account they pay out only 195. The estate households, however, receive a mere 19 units and pay out 4.

The row or column sums of the consumption accounts give the total income of the institutional sectors. Since tax payments are also recorded, it is possible to calculate the distribution of income before and after tax by institutional sector. The results are as follows:

Distribution of Institutional Income (%)

	Pre-Tax	*Post-Tax*
Firms	14.9	15.5
Urban households	23.9	22.0
Rural households	54.9	55.9
Estate households	6.3	6.6
Total	100.0	100.0

which enables us to observe the dominance of rural incomes and the relative impotence (in Sri Lanka at least) of the tax system in redistributing income between households and firms and among households.

At the intersection of the row for the capital account and the column for the consumption accounts can be found the savings of the institutional sectors. The saving ratio before and after tax can then be calculated as follows:

Saving Ratio (%)

	Pre-Tax	*Post-Tax*
Firms	44.6	55.8
Urban households	19.3	19.7
Rural households	11.7	12.0
Estate households	1.4	1.4
Government	1.8	1.9

which shows that the estate household and government sectors hardly make any contribution to domestic savings while rural households, whose savings were much more important in absolute terms, had a much lower saving ratio than urban households.

In the complete disaggregated SAM for Sri Lanka, one can observe how expenditure patterns for each commodity vary with income and by type of household. These results are not discussed here, because the information cannot be obtained from Table 1.4, but they represent another use to which SAM can be put without the aid of formal model-building.

One final point—concerning the enclave or estate household sector—will be mentioned. Although receiving income from a number of different sources, virtually all of it is accounted for by receipts from estate labour. Similarly, almost no money is transferred to other sectors by estate households and savings are negligible. The bulk of income is therefore consumed, but is not spent on commodities requiring estate labour directly (although this is not shown in Table 1.4) and the activities upon which estate income is spent also have very few links with the estate sectors. Thus, the estate households form a virtual enclave in the economy and, if they are to benefit from progress elsewhere, some means has to be found for integrating them into the national economy.

Case II—SAM for Taiwan

The second case study comes from Taiwan and is derived from a study of capital flows between agriculture and the rest of the economy (Lee, 1971). When a traditional agricultural economy seeks to transform itself into a modern industrial one, it is inevitable that the resources for this development must come mainly from the agricultural sector. These resources consist of real flows (e.g. the consumer goods needed from agriculture as a wages fund for urban workers), financial flows consisting of the net lending of the agricultural sector and factor flows, which are provided predominantly by rural–urban migration.

The purpose of the study referred to here is to make more precise the nature of this resource transfer. In real terms, the agricultural sector produces output, part of which is held back for its own needs as intermediate and final consumption; in addition, the agricultural sector requires intermediate inputs from the non-agricultural sector as well as consumer and capital goods which it cannot produce itself. (In terms of an open economy this means that all imports are routed through this non-agricultural economy.) The balance of these commodity flows represents the net contribution in real terms of the agricultural sector to the non-agricultural or urban economy.

For every real flow there is a financial flow in the opposite direction. Consequently, if there is a net commodity outflow from agriculture, there must be a net financial inflow. This finance must then be transferred or lent out to other sectors, so there are two methods of arriving at the resource transfer from agriculture which should give identical results.

In Table 1.5, a SAM for Taiwan is presented which is similar in form to Table 1.3 and which identifies the flows necessary to measure the resource transfer from agriculture. The production activity has two accounts, agriculture and non-agriculture, while the consumption accounts add a third row and column for government. The accumulation accounts are organized in the same way, but there is no row or column for finance because capital transfers this time include net lending/borrowing as well as gross flows of funds.

The table is not complete, because the original data were not set up in matrix form, but it does permit us to identify the relevant flows since the production, consumption and accumulation accounts for agriculture are given in full detail. Identified flows are given in absolute values (millions of Taiwanese dollars) and the notation follows that in Table 1.3 as closely as possible.

The commodity outflow from agriculture consists of sales to non-agricultural sectors. In the notation of Table 1.5 this is ($W_{an} + C_{an} + E_a$). The commodity flow into agriculture consists of intermediate purchases from non-agriculture (W_{na}), consumer goods bought from non-agriculture (C_{na}) and capital goods from the

Table 1.5 SAM for Taiwan, 1956–60 (T$ million)

	Production		Consumption			Accumulation			Trade	Total
	A	Non-A	A	Non-A	G	A	Non-A	G		
Production										
A	—	4926 (W_{an})	6363 (C_{aa})	4177 (C_{an})	—	—	—	—	562 (E_a)	16028
Non-A	2594 (W_{na})		4926 (C_{na})	(C_{nn})	(C_{ng})	1196 (I_a)	(I_n)	—	(E_n)	—
Consumption										
A	13434 (Y_a)	— —		1552 (TR_{an})	71 (TR_{ag})	—	—	—	—	15057
Non-A	—	(Y_n)	739 (TR_{na})		—	—	—	—	—	—
G	—	—	1453 (TR_{ga})	—		—	—	—	—	—
Accumulation										
A	—	—	1576 (S_a)	—	—		44 (KTR_{an})		—	1620
Non-A	—	—	—	(S_u)	—	425 (KTR_{na})		—		—
G	—	—	—	—	(S_g)	—	—		—	—
Trade	—	(M)	—	—	—	—	—	—		
Total	16028	—	15057	—	—	1620	—	—	—	—

A = Agriculture; Non-A = Non-Agriculture; G = Government.
Source: Based on Table 2 in Lee, 1971.

same source (I_a). The commodity balance (B) is therefore given by:

(1.7) $$B = (W_{an} + C_{an} + E_a) - (W_{na} + C_{na} + I_a)$$

The financial outflow on current account for agriculture consists of income paid to non-agricultural sectors as land rent, interest, etc. (TR_{na}) and taxes paid to the government (TR_{ga}), while the financial inflow consists of income received from non-agricultural sectors (TR_{an}) and various government subsidies (TR_{ag}). On capital account, the financial inflow consists of capital transfers from the non-agricultural sectors (KTR_{an}), while the outflow represents the flow of funds transferred to other sectors through financial intermediaries (KTR_{na}). Thus, the resource transfer from agriculture can also be written:

(1.8) $$B = [(TR_{na} + TR_{ga}) - (TR_{an} + TR_{ag})] + [KTR_{na} - KTR_{an}]$$

Whether estimated by equations (1.7) or (1.8) the resource transfer comes out as 950 units of account, which represents about 10% of total sales of agricultural products to non-agricultural sectors for the year in question. Thus, SAM has enabled us to make more precise the role of agriculture in economic transformation by quantifying its contribution. Furthermore, with a series of SAMs for different years it is possible to chart the resource transfer through time.

NOTES

1 In Table 1.2, output and supply were valued *inclusive* of net indirect taxes. In Table 1.3, we follow the SNA proposal and value these flows *exclusive* of net indirect taxes; this difference in treatment means that indirect taxes appear to be paid by consumers in Table 1.3, while in Table 1.2 they appear to be paid by producers. The valuation convention adopted may seem trivial, but it becomes important when considering the stability of input–output coefficients (see Chapter 6).

2 This implies another important distinction between Tables 1.2 and 1.3. In the former, home output and imports were distributed together along the row of the production account; in the latter, home production and imports are ruthlessly separated, so that the row for the production account refers to home output only.

CHAPTER 2

The Basis of Input–Output Tables—Accounts for Producers

2.1 INTRODUCTION

Although the need for a complete social-accounting framework as the basis for input–output work has been stressed in the previous chapter, the accounts for producers occupy a special place in the accounting hierarchy, because no input–output table or model can be completed without them. The production accounts include two matrices which are indispensable for input–output work; the first is the matrix recording the commodities made by all activities in the economy, which is usually called a *make* matrix (M in Table 1.3); the second is the matrix showing the purchases or absorption of commodities by all activities, which is usually called an *absorption* matrix (W in Table 1.3). When supplemented by purchases of primary inputs in the columns for activities and by sales to final demand accounts in the rows for commodities, the absorption matrix becomes an input–output table.

The proposed SAM for LDCs in Chapter 1 divided production into three accounts for factors, commodities and activities—a word we shall use interchangeably with industries. Activities sell their many products to the commodity accounts (the make matrix), which then distribute them to intermediate users (the absorption matrix) and to final users (final demand accounts). Factors of production, on the other hand, receive their income mainly from activities as well as through transfers from the rest of the economy and from abroad, which they then pay out as shown in Table 1.3 (factor accounts). The production accounts are thus closed and each of these sets of transactions will now be considered in detail.

2.2 THE MAKE MATRIX

The number of commodities made even in LDCs is huge and it is impossible in practice to organize separate accounts for each one. Instead, commodities are formed into groups usually linked either by the nature of the materials used (e.g. all plastic-based products) or by the nature of their final use (e.g. all household shoes regardless of material). For purposes of input–output analysis, the first kind of grouping is most desirable (for reasons which will be discussed in Chapter 5) but whatever the nature of the grouping it is unlikely that the whole output of an industry can be neatly allocated to one and only one commodity group.[1] Thus, the first problem we encounter is that industrial output may need to be allocated to more than one commodity group, while the overall output of any one commodity group may come from more than one activity.

The reason why industrial output may involve a mix of commodity groups is that it is typically organized in units which are flexible and large enough to produce more than a very narrow range of products. As we examine smaller and smaller industrial units—first the enterprise, then the firm, the plant and finally the establishment—the degree of product homogeneity tends to increase; it never becomes perfect, however, because the establishment is by definition the smallest unit on which it is possible to collect industrial statistics and it is frequently impossible to carry this to the point of product homogeneity, because of the difficulty of allocating overhead expenditure and other items of an indivisible nature. Although most input–output workers, *ceteris paribus*, would favour a reduction in the size of the industrial reporting unit, one would soon reach a point where the advantages of more specialized production statistics were outweighed by the arbitrary nature of the allocation of indivisible outlays. Thus, it has to be accepted that product heterogeneity and the absence of a one-to-one relationship between commodities and industries is a fact of input–output life.

In principle, the number of commodities or commodity groups—terms we can now use interchangeably—need not be the same as the number of activities. In practice, however, it is much easier to carry out input–output analysis if the number is the same, because there is then much less ambiguity about determining the activity whose output is stimulated by any increase in final expenditure. Furthermore, many schemes of industrial statistics define an industry in terms of all those establishments producing as principal product a unique commodity or set of commodities, so that this will automatically bring about the equality of commodities and activities, if the commodity classification is drawn up according to principal products.[2]

Equality in the number of industries and commodities means that the make matrix (M) in Table 1.3 showing the distribution of industrial output by commodity group will be square; the matrix will be dominated by the elements on the diagonal, because these represent the principal product output of each industry, which by definition will be the most important. The remaining, or off-diagonal, elements represent production of secondary products.

An example of a make matrix for Brazil in 1970 is given in Table 2.1. The table has been reduced from a much larger number of rows and columns in order to save space, but it should always be remembered that the importance of off-diagonal elements shrinks as the number of sectors declines; with fewer sectors, the definition of principal production becomes broader so that many secondary products are swallowed into the main production of the industry. Even so, there are a number of unallocated products in Table 2.1 which explains why there is one more column than there are rows.

Activities are recorded in the rows of Table 2.1 and commodities in the columns

Table 2.1 Make matrix for Brazil, 1970 (millions of cruzeiros)

Activities	Commodities										
	Agricultural products	Mineral products	Metal goods	Chemical products	Agro-industrial products	Other manufacturing products	Construction	Transport and distribution	Services	Unallocated products	Totals
Agriculture	25956	—	—	48	2388	—	—	—	—	20	28412
Mining	—	1862	19	1	—	10	—	—	3	30	1924
Metal Industries	—	—	35617	.69	6	95	—	17	13	1695	37512
Chemicals	—	—	30	19786	55	41	—	11	62	1082	21066
Agro industries	3	—	53	501	44349	250	—	31	6	1992	47185
Other manufacturing industries	—	289	90	50	303	14377	—	15	23	471	15618
Construction	—	—	—	—	—	—	27455	—	—	—	27455
Transport and distribution	—	—	262	—	—	—	—	46408	795	—	47466
Services	—	—	—	—	—	—	—	217	28940	—	29157
Total	25960	2151	36070	20455	47102	14773	27455	46701	29842	5288	255796

Note: Components may not sum to total due to rounding.
Source: Derived from IBGE, 1979.

and the first point to note is that total commodity output is never quite the same as total activity output. Thus, we find that metal industries (row 3) produce not only metal goods (35, 617) but also chemical products (69), other manufacturing products (95) and other minor items. On the other hand, metal goods (column 3) are produced not only by the metal industries, but also by other activities, e.g. transport and distribution (262).

The next point to note about Table 2.1 is the dominance of the diagonal; nearly all commodity output is accounted for by the principal production of the relevant industry, while the latter also contributes the lion's share of activity output. Indeed, in the case of one activity—construction—this share is 100% because in the sample used, construction firms (i.e. the industry) were defined as producing only construction services.

Innumerable problems arise in the construction of make matrices, but these can be more easily resolved if certain general principles are observed. The first principle concerns the determination of gross output. The gross output of an activity or industry represents the sum of its 'make' of commodities, i.e. the row of the make matrix in Table 2.1 summed column-wise. Consequently, gross output should represent all additions to the supply of goods and services during a period of account.

This definition is certainly a useful starting point. For example, we can immediately exclude from gross output sales of second hand goods and income received by firms as dividends on financial investments; on the other hand it encourages us (correctly) to include non-marketed production for own use and any increase in inventories of finished goods and work-in-progress.[3] The definition, however, is still a little loose, because it suggests we include all those household activities, such as making bread, which add to the supply of goods and services, but are normally treated as being outside the production boundary.

The production boundary is usually drawn in each country by statistical offices long before input–output tables are prepared. The input–output worker may well be tempted to accept the division between what is inside and outside the production boundary on the grounds that his task is to disaggregate production statistics in the national accounts rather than revise the national income figures. One of the most useful purposes fulfilled by the construction of input–output tables, however, is to act as a check on the national accounts; in the case of the three tables which the author has helped to prepare (Costa Rica, Scotland, Morocco), work on the input–output tables has produced a number of modifications and revisions to the national accounts. For this reason, the input–output worker should not necessarily accept the inherited production boundary and this means he needs a satisfactory definition of what activities to include inside it.

As stated above, whatever is inside the production boundary contributes to gross output. An input–output model, as opposed to a table, assumes a unique relationship between inputs and gross output, such that additional requirements of gross output from any source will stimulate the requirement of inputs (see Chapter 4). Consequently, a more precise definition of gross output for input–output purposes is that, in addition to adding to the supply of goods and services, it is also possible to identify a set of unique inputs associated with the production of that output. That is why household activities need, in practice, to be excluded from the production boundary. Although it might be possible to determine the 'output' of bread made by households, it is virtually impossible to determine the inputs associated with its production without resorting to arbitrary devices.

The second principle involved in constructing a make matrix is as follows: whatever is delivered to the commodity accounts by activities becomes the supply of commodities; the dual entry character of SAMs requires that this supply be matched by demand, i.e. absorptions by intermediate and final users. Consequently, whatever enters on the supply side must be capable of being identified and absorbed on the demand side.[4]

A good example of the application of this principle concerns non-marketed output; this is a widespread form of production in LDCs, particularly in agriculture, and there is no reason why we should exclude it from the commodity accounts, since the latter provide a record of real flows. Indeed, exclusion of non-marketed output can produce very strange results, if the mix of subsistence and cash crop farming changes sharply. However, there is no point in recording non-marketed output on the supply side, unless it is possible to identify its user on the demand side.

In most sectors, the definition of gross output can be derived from the above principles in a straightforward manner. In the case of financial institutions, however, a number of special problems are encountered; these institutions are usually very profitable, but most of their income comes from the difference between interest received and interest paid. In the national accounts, interest is usually treated as a factor payment (receipt) and if the gross output of financial institutions is calculated exclusive of net interest receipts, it is often insufficient to cover operating costs so that the financial sector appears to make a loss.

In the SNA (United Nations, 1968, pp. 97–8), a proposal has been made for introducing a dummy account, which preserves the 'profitability' of financial institutions without disturbing the value and sectoral distribution of Gross Domestic Product (GDP). This procedure, however, leaves as the contribution on production account of non-financial sectors to financial institutions payment for commissions and service charges only. Our second principle of commodity accounting requires us to identify the source of demand for any addition to commodity supply, but it is not possible to distinguish on the demand side the value of this service charge separately from net interest payments.

In the case of insurance companies, the SNA recommends that the 'service' of insuring be measured by the difference between premiums received and claims paid. This addition to commodity supply is matched on the demand side by intermediate consumption (absorptions by firms) and final expenditure (mainly households). If it is desirable to measure in this way the output of insurance companies, it would seem reasonable to measure the service provided by financial institutions in the same way, i.e. as the difference between interest paid and interest received inclusive of all commissions and service charges. Financial institutions would then be seen as dealing in claims on which they earn a 'margin' (just as retailers earn a margin on dealing in commodities). The margin measures the service provided and is associated with a unique set of inputs; the service is then sold to firms (intermediate consumption) or final demand.

This treatment of financial institutions is unconventional, but is certainly feasible and was the method adopted in Scotland (Fraser, 1978) and in Costa Rica (Bulmer–Thomas, 1977a). If the treatment of interest in the national accounts is the conventional one, then certain modifications will need to be made to GDP, but these usually affect the distribution of sectoral value added more than the total itself. As far as the make matrix is concerned, however, the 'make' of financial services will be the same whether the United Nations system or the above proposals are adopted.

There are many activities which add to the supply of goods and services and with which a unique set of inputs is associated—suggesting that they should be included inside the production boundary—but for which little or no charge is made, so that costs of production are not covered by revenue received. Examples are provided by government services, such as defence, health and education, and by private non-profit-making services assumed to be rendered to households such as religious institutions, charities and trade unions.

It is customary in such cases to value the service at the costs of production, although a good deal of thought has gone into ways of avoiding this unsatisfactory treatment (United Nations, 1975). Nonetheless, even valuation at cost does not resolve the question of whether the activity should be inside or outside the production boundary, as the following example makes clear: if we consider state education, we can either create an activity inside the production boundary which 'sells' its output valued at cost to the Government consumption account or we can eliminate the activity from the production boundary and have a division of Government expenditure which absorbs all the costs of state education as part of final demand.

From an accounting point of view, both treatments are satisfactory; all transactions are accounted for and final expenditure does not change in either case. Problems arise, however, when some charge, however notional, is made for the service. For example, it might be the case that users of a national health service contribute something directly to its costs; in this case, if the service is inside the production boundary, it will sell its output to many users, not just Government final expenditure. If, however, the service is outside the production boundary, there will be no way of accounting for expenditure by private users.

If the service in question is a 'pure' public good such that no private expenditure on the service is possible (e.g. defence) or if it is a private non-profit-making service rendered exclusively to households (e.g. pension funds where the service charge is equivalent to administrative expenses), then its exclusion from the production boundary is acceptable. However, this assumes that the 'output' of the service will never be measured independently of the inputs: given developments in this field, it seems preferable to include as many of these services as possible within the production boundary so that the different sources of demand can be identified.

There still remain a number of difficulties encountered in constructing make matrices. One of these concerns the treatment of factoring, i.e. the purchase of goods for resale, by establishments whose principal product is neither wholesaling nor retailing.

Provided that the system of purchasers' prices is *not* adopted (see Chapter 6), the contribution of factoring to the gross output of an establishment is the sales of factored goods (SF) less the value of purchases (PUR) adjusted for stock change (ΔS); this contribution (XF) is then transferred to the distribution column for commodities in the make matrix, since factoring is the principal product of the activity distribution. Thus, we have:

$$XF = SF - [PUR + \Delta S] \tag{2.1}$$

but equation (2.1) is not always easy to apply, because while purchases and sales are usually denominated in prices which represent some sort of weighted average for the mid-point of the time period (a year, for example), stocks are denominated in end-period prices. In inflationary times, therefore, the value of the change in stocks may be due mainly to stock appreciation and it may not be possible to extract this element from the value change. Mechanical application of equation (2.1) can then produce absurd results, such as a negative contribution to gross output from factoring.

One way to resolve this problem is to apply our second principle of commodity accounting. Factoring by firms represents an addition to the supply of the commodity distribution; the corresponding demand is represented by the margin on purchases by intermediate and final users. If the 'mark-down' on sales is known (r), then a much easier way of calculating the contribution of factoring to gross output is:

$$XF = r \, . \, SF \tag{2.2}$$

i.e. the value of sales multipled by the mark-down. These two approaches, of course, will give exactly the same results when the mark-down is calculated from the formula:

$$r = \frac{SF - [PUR + \Delta S]}{SF} \tag{2.3}$$

but mark-downs are often obtained by other means than equation (2.3). Thus, whatever method has been used to calculate mark-downs, equation (2.2) will ensure equality between supply and demand in the commodity accounts and satisfy our second principle.

Most off-diagonal elements in the make matrix represent secondary products, whose treatment is straightforward. A few, however, raise special problems; the main point about secondary products is that decisions over their level of production are taken independently of the principal product. Some products, however, are by-products, e.g. animal feedstuffs from distilleries, and their level of output cannot be chosen independently, so that special treatment is required.

A by-product refers to a commodity produced as principal product by another industry; there are some products, however, whose production is dependent on the output of the principal product, but which do not correspond to the main output of any activity. Examples are hides from cattle and wool from sheep. Such products are known as joint-products and like by-products they require special treatment. Both will be discussed in more detail in Chapter 9.

Many firms use their own transport for the delivery of goods; this is a secondary product of the relevant activity and, in general, the value of such undertakings should appear in the column for the commodity transport in the make matrix. Where flows in the input–output table, however, are valued inclusive of transport margins, it may be preferable to value the entries in the make matrix at delivered prices (see Chapter 6). In this case, the value of own transport undertakings ceases to be a secondary product and is absorbed into the other entries of the make matrix. This was the procedure adopted in Scotland (see Fraser, 1978, pp. 5–6). The problem of own electricity generation, however, although similar in some respects to own transport undertakings, is discussed in the appendix to this chapter.

The value of work done by establishments in installing capital equipment, erecting or improving buildings should be treated as a secondary production of the commodity construction, although it is often exceedingly difficult to establish from questionnaires the value of this work; in LDCs, however, the practice of own construction is widespread and every effort should be made to establish its value in order to avoid distortion of both the capital and production accounts. In this respect, Table 2.1 must be regarded as deficient because secondary production of construction has been ignored.

Those waste products, which contribute to the gross output of an industry, can be treated either as by-products or joint-products. In some cases, however, the amounts involved are so small that it is not worth the trouble of setting up a dummy account (see Chapter 9) and in this case it may be admissible to add the value of the products sold to principal production, even though this offends our second principle of commodity accounting.[5] Sales of second-hand goods do not contribute to gross output and should not therefore appear in the make matrix. Their treatment will be discussed below. Royalty and patent receipts should also be excluded, because they represent payment for factor services rather than work done on production account.

2.3 THE ABSORPTION MATRIX

Having completed our discussion of the make matrix, we may now turn to the absorption matrix; this entry in SAM records all inputs absorbed by activities in production and it provides the basic data frame from which an input–output coefficient matrix can be obtained. In order to derive the basic principles involved in its construction, therefore, we must make a slight digression into input–output theory.

If an input–output table is to be turned into an input–output model, it is necessary to make some assumptions about the relationship between inputs and outputs. Clearly, this relationship will refer to the value of inputs *used up* in the value of output; the absorption matrix, therefore, should refer to uses not purchases and all purchases must be adjusted for any deviation from uses. Secondly, it is assumed in input–output work that additional inputs of any commodity can only be met by increasing their supply. Consequently, all entries in the absorption matrix must occur opposite the commodity group whose output is expected to rise when inputs are increased. Thirdly, an increase in expenditure should have the same effect on output whatever its source and this will only be the case if the entries in each row of the commodity accounts are valued at a common set of prices.[6]

Applying these principles will resolve most difficulties encountered in filling the commodity rows; purchases must clearly be adjusted for any element of stock change in order to reflect uses. If stocks, for example, have been built up in expectation of a price rise, this will distort the underlying relationship between inputs and output, but deducting the value of stock increase from purchases will restore the relationship. Stocks, however, are assumed to be valued at constant (mid-period) prices; if it is not possible to deduct the element of stock appreciation from the value of the change, the adjustment of purchases to absorptions will be seriously affected.

We can now see why, in calculating the gross output of an activity through the make matrix, it was so important to include all work done—not just marketed output. The underlying relationship between inputs and output is distorted if purchases are not adjusted for stock change, but the same thing will happen if 'output' is not measured to take account of all uses to which absorptions are put. A good example of this is own construction by farmers; in the farm accounts, various entries will record the absorption of construction materials. If the output is not adjusted to include the value of own construction, it will appear from the accounts as if there is a production function linking the input of cement, bricks, etc. to the output of such crops as wheat, maize and barley!

Not all entries in the absorption matrix correspond to transactions at market prices. An example is provided by subsistence farming; even subsistence output requires certain non-factor inputs; the most important of these is seed, which should appear on the diagonal of the absorption matrix. Thus, in the case of corn raised by subsistence farmers, the output should be valued at a price which corresponds to the other entries in the row for corn; part of the value of this output will then be sold to the activity itself (as seed or animal feedstuffs), while the balance will be sold to final demand as household consumption.

There are other examples of transactions which do not take place at market prices. In LDCs, for example, where the activities of multinational companies (MNCs) can account for a large share of transactions between industries, one encounters the problem of transfer pricing (Lall, 1973). When the price used in valuing quantities is not a market price, there is a danger that the same product will be valued differently by different users; although revision to market price is desirable, it may necessitate a number of changes in the national accounts, particularly the distribution of sectoral value added. Transfer pricing will be discussed again in Chapter 6 as part of the general problem of valuation of transactions, but the author knows of no input–output tables where these internal corporate accounting prices have been adjusted.

If the absorption matrix is built up from a questionnaire on purchases, the problem of unallocated entries will inevitably arise. These are purchases which individually are so small that establishments do not find it worthwhile to list them separately. Difficult as it is, these entries somehow have to be distributed across the rows of the absorption matrix. Much can be done to avoid this problem if it is anticipated when designing the questionnaire and some suggestions will be offered in this direction in Chapter 11. The general rule, however, is that the earlier in the construction of tables the allocation is made, the more accurate will be the final product.

In general, most establishment inputs fall neatly into one of two classes: intermediate and primary. Since primary inputs include profits, these are usually treated as a residual to ensure consistency between inputs and outputs, but this practice should be resisted as far as possible because non-cancelling errors and omissions will be absorbed into profits. Sometimes, it is possible to check on the profitability of an activity from independent sources, but in any case the share of profits in gross output can give a rough indication of how accurate the residual is. As far as intermediate inputs are concerned, the general rule is that they must form part of the output of the supplying commodity. Royalty payments and purchases of second-hand goods, therefore, should not be treated as intermediate inputs, while purchases of waste products may count as intermediate inputs, because they often contribute to the gross output of supplying activities.

Purchases of second-hand goods must, however, be accounted for in our SAM. One of the distinguishing features of most second-hand goods is their durability; these are goods which, when new, tend to be purchased on capital account. Later they are bought and sold either within the capital accounts (in which case the entry cancels on consolidation)[7] or between the capital accounts and the production accounts or other final demand accounts. Since sales on capital account represent a decrease in assets, they can be treated as negative entries, while purchases on production or other final demand accounts must be given a positive sign. Positive and negative entries will then cancel out and so it is possible to account for second-hand purchases and sales using one row only which is sometimes labelled Sales by Final Buyers. Examples of entries in this row are sales of second-hand capital equipment as scrap to the iron and steel industries and sales of second-hand cars by businesses (which sell them on capital account) to households (which buy them on consumption account).

So far, it has been assumed that the absorption matrix refers to domestic flows only;[4] intermediate imports, for example, are then dealt with in the matrix M_I in Table 1.3 along similar lines to intermediate domestic transactions in the absorption matrix. Sometimes, however, it is not possible to distinguish the imported part of absorptions from the part accruing to domestic producers.

When this happens the balance between supply and demand in the commodity accounts can be retained if imports are treated as a column of negative entries in the trade accounts corresponding to the commodity rows. Imports, however, play such an important part in input–output work that a separate chapter has been reserved for their discussion (Chapter 7).

The case of smuggled goods or illegal production raises a number of problems in the absorption matrix; in constructing an input–output table for Morocco, for example, the first attempt to balance supply and demand for cement produced a huge shortfall on the side of supply. The explanation was provided by cement smuggled in from abroad; in such situations one has only two choices: either to reduce demand to the level 'permitted' by official statistics or adjust supply to the observed level of demand. The latter is clearly preferable, although it may disturb such sensitive official figures as the balance of trade.

2.4 THE FINAL DEMAND ACCOUNTS

That part of commodity supply which is not absorbed on production account as intermediate consumption is sold to the final demand columns; these cover all expenditures on commodities by the consumption, capital and trade accounts. Within the consumption accounts, the expenditure of households is usually the most important; most of the entries in this column represent straightforward purchases of new goods and services from producers, but others present complications.

One frequent problem encountered in the household expenditure column is the need for imputed values where market prices are either unavailable or inappropriate. Some of these, such as consumption of own-account production by farmers, have already been discussed; others, such as the imputed rental value of owner-occupied housing, will be determined by the treatment given to ownership of dwellings in the national accounts.

In many firms, it is a frequent practice for the workers to receive commodities for which no charge is made. Where the workers are the principal beneficiaries, it would clearly be wrong to treat the commodities as intermediate consumption of the firms involved; instead, the commodities should be valued at appropriate prices[8] and entered in the final demand columns as household expenditure. This addition to household expenditure, however, must be matched by an addition to household income, i.e. the wages and salaries paid by firms. Since this income in kind is quite different from the more usual monetary remuneration, it should be entered in a separate row in value added; in Scotland, for example, all such imputations were initially embedded in a row entitled 'wages in kind' (Fraser, 1978, p. 12). In LDCs, this treatment could prove a useful method of handling firms which pay wages and salaries partly in the form of coupons redeemable at company stores.

Another problem encountered in the household column is consumption of food and drink which is not purchased by households. There are many occasions when food and drink are purchased by firms, but the employees are the beneficiary; this is also true of educational establishments where the 'employees' are schoolchildren. Input–output tables littered with minor entries for food and drink absorbed by activities (but which are not subject to further transformation) are most unattractive and can be misleading, although in a strict accounting sense they are not wrong. It is preferable to pass the expenditure forward to the household column; thus, in the case of salesmen's allowances, an entry can be included for wages in kind which covers expenditure by salesmen (in the household column) on food, drink and accommodation, while in the case of educational establishments, any fees (actual or imputed) paid for this service should be net of catering expenses, which can then be directly absorbed by households.

Most purchases of second-hand goods by households occur within the household sector, so that on consolidation they cancel out leaving only the dealers' margin. Sometimes, however, purchases are matched by sales from the government and businesses (on current or capital account). Provided all purchases (net of dealers' margins) are entered as a positive entry in the row Sales by Final Buyers and all sales as a negative entry, no difficulties need be encountered.

Households consist of residents and non-residents; expenditures by the latter represent a credit in the balance of payments current account and since SAM is a record not just of production, it is desirable to separate out the two types of households. Non-resident expenditure will then be treated in the trade accounts along with commodity exports and foreign tourist expenditure as discussed in Chapter 7. Resident households, however, must be defined to include diplomatic and military personnel abroad, as well as those workers seasonally employed in other countries; expenditure by such groups as well as tourist expenditure abroad by resident households represents a purchase of non-commodity imports and should be entered against a row for imports of services in the import matrix. This was the procedure adopted in constructing the Costa Rican input–output table and is consistent with the recommendations of the SNA.

The arrangement of Government current expenditure in the consumption accounts has been outlined briefly above. Two important distinctions, however, need to be made; the first is between production of commodities and production of services by Government, while the second is between current and capital expenditure.

Production of commodities by activities within the public sector is in principle no different from the same activities carried out by the private sector. The precise treatment of such activities will depend on the nature of the classification scheme (see Chapter 5), but without doubt these activities should be firmly planted within the production boundary; their output is then absorbed by other activities and by final demand. Production of services, however, involves the provision of public goods and non-marketed output, for which little or no charge is made. It was suggested above that such services be treated as production activities whose imputed output, net of any private expenditure on the service, is absorbed by the Government current account.

The second distinction (between current and capital expenditure) is normally carried out by the office responsible for the national accounts, but in the author's experience there is frequently a confusion between the two types of expenditure. The need in input–output work for a balance between commodity supply and demand is often sufficient to weed out these confusions and results in appropriate modifications to national accounts methodology. The precise nature of the distinction between the two types of expenditure is very competently discussed in the SNA (United Nations, 1968, pp. 110–11).

Apart from the trade accounts (to be dealt with in Chapter 7), the only entries in final demand not yet discussed are the absorptions on capital account. These are of two kinds: changes in stocks and gross fixed capital formation; dealings in non-reproducible tangible assets, such as land and mineral deposits, are excluded, because they do not represent payment for new production of goods and services, although such transactions do appear elsewhere in the capital accounts (see Table 1.3).

Stock change represents the difference between the value of opening and closing stocks at constant (mid-year) prices. Any entry in the stock change column represents the row summation of a matrix with activities in the columns and commodities in the rows, because some commodities may be held in stock by more than one activity. Indeed, there will normally be two such matrices: one for opening stocks and one for closing stocks.

The diagonal of each stock matrix represents the holdings of stocks of any commodity by the industry producing it as principal product, i.e. stocks of finished goods and work-in-progress. Since any element of stock appreciation in the diagonal of the stock change matrix will appear on both the supply and demand sides of the commodity accounts, its removal is not too serious a problem. This does not apply, however, to the off-diagonal elements where failure to remove stock appreciation will cause commodity demand to exceed commodity supply: thus, great efforts need to be made to put the value of stocks on a common price basis.

Where gross fixed capital formation is derived from the purchases data in the capital accounts of establishments, it is customary to build up the column in the same way as for stock change, i.e. as the row sum of an investment matrix, whose columns record purchases of capital goods by each activity. In many LDCs, however, the production of capital goods is so limited that the major source of capital equipment is provided by imports. In this case, it is possible to build up the column directly from sales or supply—side data—a method which has the advantage of preserving a common price basis between supply and demand. A large entry in the investment column—construction—is provided by a non-traded activity, so import data are of no assistance, but the whole output of the construction industry, net of repair and maintenance work, is absorbed by the capital accounts so that gross fixed capital formation is often quite easy to estimate.

This completes our discussion of the commodity and industry accounts; the principal problems encountered in allocating commodities by use have been discussed and the main problems associated with industrial absorption of commodities, but not primary inputs (see next section), have been mentioned. It is now possible, therefore, to show how these ideas work out in practice by presenting in Table 2.2 a simple input–output table.[9]

In Table 2.2 each activity's absorptions are recorded in the columns; we may note, for example, that the construction industry (column 4) absorbed £55.4 million of the commodity 'metal goods' (row 2) during the year in question; this amount covers domestic absorptions only and does not include imports of metal goods. All imported commodities are recorded in row 8 which tells us that household purchases, for example, from outside the region, were £1033 million. The entries in the Sales by Final Buyers row are dominated by the purchases of scrap by the metal industries (£19.2 million), and by household purchases of second-hand goods (£63.3 million), while the source of supply is mainly sales on capital account (£75 million). The total for the row is zero, because sales and purchases cancel.

All industry output is accounted for by absorptions of commodities or purchases of primary inputs, while commodity output is sold either to industries as intermediate absorptions or to final demand; the treatment of primary inputs, however, in Table 2.2 is highly aggregated and calls for further discussion.

2.5 ACCOUNTS FOR FACTORS OF PRODUCTION

Factors of production receive income from activities as a reward for their contribution to the productive process. These factors are often described in textbooks as land, labour and capital, but this classification is not particularly appropriate for LDCs. First, the ownership of land is rarely divorced from the ownership of capital improvements to the land so that it is virtually impossible to separate out the rental on land from the return to capital. Secondly, neither capital nor labour is homogeneous and many of the most powerful applications gifts, etc.; (3) returned exports; (4) errors in bills of lading. Clearly some decision

There are at least three classes of capital which it is worth trying to distinguish: publicly-owned, foreign-owned and privately- (other than foreign) owned. In practice these three forms of capital are likely to be restricted to corporate bodies, because the return to capital in unincorporated enterprises cannot be distinguished from the return to labour. Joint ventures, sometimes involving all three types of capital, can be handled quite easily in this accounting scheme by apportioning the return to each class according to its share in paid-up capital.

Labour divides naturally in LDCs into wage labour and the self-employed, although a possible further subdivision of the latter would involve unpaid family workers on the one hand and workers on own account on the other. Furthermore, each class of labour has many subdivisions by occupation and it is only at this occupational level that a satisfactory employment programme can be worked out. Entries in the factor accounts are in values, but in the case of labour it is important to know both the price and the quantity content of this value.

Factors of production receive income not only from industries. In certain cases,

Table 2.2 Input–Output table for Scotland, 1973 (£ million)

Commodities	Activities											
	Primary industries	Metal industries	Other industries	Construction	Utilities	Services	Private consumption	Public consumption	Gross fixed capital formation	Stock change	Exports	Total
Primary goods	80.2	6.1	288.3	18.3	45.1	17.3	66.2	0.7	8.8	54.6	135.6	721.1
Metal goods	11.9	208.5	48.7	55.4	5.0	25.4	11.0	7.2	37.3	136.3	1568.9	2115.8
Other manufactured goods	87.4	38.4	334.7	121.3	14.4	77.3	441.7	6.6	67.5	21.7	1824.1	3035.2
Construction	19.9	15.1	12.4	295.5	6.2	56.2	20.6	33.5	773.3	10.4	—	1243.1
Gas, electricity and water	9.9	28.3	31.6	2.9	16.9	44.1	149.5	7.6	11.1	−2.3	2.1	301.6
Services	95.9	132.4	299.2	31.2	13.6	306.6	1214.0	687.5	79.4	8.1	335.1	3202.9
Sales by final buyers	—	19.2	—	—	—	—	63.3	−7.5	−75.0	—	—	0.0
Imported goods	82.4	742.4	959.5	183.9	34.5	306.2	1033.0	103.0	619.1	119.3	12.7	4196.0
Other primary inputs	337.0	948.9	1104.7	525.0	172.8	2301.6	857.1	340.1	25.1	−300.0	64.9	6377.3
Total	724.5	2139.2	3079.1	1233.7	308.5	3134.7	3856.4	1178.8	1546.6	48.1	3943.5	21193.0

Note: Components may not sum to total due to rounding.
Source: Derived from Figure A6 in Burdekin, 1978a.

they will be paid directly by the institutional sectors, e.g. wages and salaries paid by public administration and payments to domestic servants by households. (If domestic and administrative services, however, have been treated as productive activities, these factor payments will appear in the activities columns.) The only other entry in the factor rows is net factor payments by the rest of the world (see Table 1.3). In the case of labour, for example, this will consist of the earnings of seasonal and border workers in other countries net of any flows in the opposite direction, while in the case of capital it consists of such things as the return to (local) capitalists earned abroad (a positive entry) and the return at home to foreign capital (a negative entry), as well as royalty payments. These entries, of course, form the bridge between the gross domestic product and the gross national product.

All income received by factors of production is paid to the institutional sectors on current account. In certain cases there will be a one-for-one mapping; a factor of production such as rural labour, for example, will pay all its income to rural households (gifts to relatives in urban areas are transfers and are shown elsewhere in SAM). In the case of income earned by capital, however, the mapping is more complicated because households receive part of the income as dividends while firms retain only undistributed profits; again, it is worthwhile distinguishing in the institutional accounts between public, private and foreign-owned firms.

This completes our discussion of the production accounts; similar treatment could be given to other entries in SAM, but this would be inappropriate in a book whose primary purpose is input–output analysis and these other entries are dealt with very thoroughly in the SNA. Although it has been lengthy, this description of the production accounts is necessary because much confusion in the preparation and interpretation of input–output tables can be avoided if the principles laid down in this chapter are followed.

The major omissions of this chapter concern the system of valuation, the classification scheme and the treatment of imports and exports and these will all be discussed later. Furthermore, we have not yet said anything about the sources to be used in the preparation of input–output tables and this, therefore, is the province of our next chapter.

APPENDIX SECONDARY PRODUCTION OF ELECTRICITY

The production of electricity by establishments whose principal product is something else is widespread in LDCs. This applies as much to the agricultural as non-agricultural sectors of the economy, since many farms generate their own electricity supply. Some establishments purchase all their electricity requirements from the national grid, others produce all or some of their needs, while some others may produce more than is needed and sell the balance to other users. These different practices make the treatment of this secondary product particularly complicated.

The case of a shoe manufacturer (Establishment 1) who buys in all his electricity supply is illustrated in Case 1 of Table 2.1a. In Case 2, however, we illustrate the example of a similar shoe-producing establishment which generates its own electricity and sells 100 units to other users (Establishment 2). Clearly, if these two establishments were aggregated together to form the column of an input–output table, the result would be very odd leading to aggregation bias (see Chapter 5). The impact on the economy of an increase in final demand for shoes will be wrongly measured, unless the increment in output is met by the two establishments in the same proportions as their initial output levels.

Table 2.1a Alternative treatments of own electricity generation

	Establishment 1	Establishment 2			
	Case 1	Case 2	Case 3	Case 4	Case 5
Inputs					
Materials	300	500	460	500	300
Electricity	200	0	0	200	200
Wages	400	450	420	450	400
Profits	100	150	120	150	100
Total	1000	1100	1000	1300	1000
Outputs					
Shoes	1000	1000	1000	1000	1000
Electricity	–	100	–	300	–
Total	1000	1100	1000	1300	1000

In Case 3, therefore, the inputs associated with the 100 units of electricity sold by Establishment 2 have been 'hived off', leaving an account for the production of shoes only. This would still give odd results, however, after aggregation because the second firm is producing its own electricity, while the first is buying it in; although the impact on the economy would not necessarily be biased when the indirect as well as direct impact is taken into account, there seems to be no justification for treating the electricity produced for own use differently from sales of electricity. If we therefore impute a value to all the electricity produced, we reach the position in Case 4 where 'sales' of electricity by Establishment 2 are now 300 units; to balance the account we now need a 'purchase' of electricity to the value of 200 units.

In Case 4, we are treating as a secondary product all electricity produced. This is then delivered to the commodity account for electricity; if both the output of this secondary product and the inputs associated with it are 'hived off', we reach the position in Case 5. This is now identical to Case 1, so we have succeeded in putting the two establishments on the same accounting basis, although their electricity supply is obtained by different means.

The choice between these different accounting schemes depends on industrial practice; if establishments typically produce, but do not sell electricity, the treatment in Case 3 is probably most appropriate. In this treatment the costs of producing electricity are not distinguished from other costs of production. If sales of electricity are widespread, the treatment in Cases 4 and 5 is most appropriate, while if electricity is 'bought-in' the treatment in Case 1 is clearly sufficient. The treatment proposed here for electricity would apply equally well to the provision of gas, water supply and other such services.

NOTES

1 There is a useful discussion of the problem of commodity grouping in the SNA (United Nations, 1968, pp. 99–100).

2 The most recent input–output table for Brazil, however (for 1970), contains many more commodities (160) than activities (88). This difference arises because the Brazilian industry is defined not in terms of one principal product, but in terms of a series of related products. The glass-making industry, for example, is defined as containing all firms making one of the following as principal product: plate and sheet glass, glass containers and other glass objects (see IBGE, 1979).

3 It is important to remember that the make matrix refers to the *output* of commodities by activities. This means that any change in the real value of stocks of finished goods and work-in-progress must be added to sales to give output. Two problems can be encountered here; first, it may be difficult to remove the stock appreciation element from the value of the change in stocks so as to put sales and stock change on a common price basis; secondly, the primary data may not disaggregate stock change by commodity. Neither of these problems is very serious in practice; an increase in stocks of finished goods, for example, represents an addition to commodity supply, but the source of demand is simply the capital account of the establishment itself. Consequently, whatever method is used to resolve these problems should result in a balance between supply and demand and a common price basis.

4 In Table 1.3, the commodity accounts are presented net of imports so that commodity supply refers to home output only and commodity demand to expenditure on home produced goods only. This convention is also adopted in this chapter, so that 'demand' is assumed to be net of imports. The problems that arise from not being able to separate demand into a 'domestic' and 'imported' component are discussed more fully in Chapter 7.

5 This is the practice adopted in the input–output tables for the United Kingdom (CSO, 1973, p. 18).

6 A formal statement of this proposition is given in the appendix to Chapter 6.

7 Except for the dealers' margins which should appear at the intersection of the commodity row for distribution and the appropriate column of the capital accounts.

8 These prices should be the same as those used for other entries in the commodity row.

9 Although Scotland is not a LDC, its input–output table has been selected for Table 2.2 because it illustrates very clearly the main points made in this chapter.

CHAPTER 3

Methods of Surveying–Censuses and Samples

3.1 INTRODUCTION: CENSUSES *v.* SAMPLES

In the previous chapter, we dealt at length with the elements of the production account—in particular the make and absorption matrices. In this chapter we focus on the most appropriate methods for collecting the data which enter these accounts. In order to do this, we assume that some preliminary sectorization scheme for production (and therefore the input–output tables) has already been chosen; the considerations which enter into such a scheme will then be discussed in Chapter 5.[1]

The units which provide us with most of the data for constructing input–output tables are those establishments in each sector chosen for census or sampling purposes. If establishments within each sector vary enormously by size, choice of technique and products made, then sampling is unlikely to be a reliable way of preparing input–output tables.

Some input–output workers, sensitive to this problem, are tempted to categorize each establishment (at least in manufacturing) as heterogeneous. In other words, not even multiple stratification (by sector, size, region, etc.) can overcome the need for a census or 100 % sample; historically, indeed, this has been the most common way of preparing an input–output table, starting with Leontief's pioneering work for 1919, and it is therefore impossible to ignore the question of whether sample error in *any* input–output sample is likely to prove unacceptably large, so that the census method is the only reliable way of preparing tables.

The advantage of the census method is that a complete enumeration of the population (assuming full response) reduces sample error towards zero. So much is obvious. The disadvantages of the method, however (apart from cost), may not be so obvious, but are nonetheless important. First, in practice the census method is very rarely a complete enumeration; small firms (e.g. less than 25 employees in Great Britain, less than five in Central America and Morocco) are omitted and since these firms form a separate stratum with characteristics often quite unlike larger firms, the estimates derived from the census will be biased. Secondly, the census method is, as far as the author is aware, always adopted primarily for reasons other than input–output work. The questionnaire, therefore, is not designed specifically with the construction of input–output tables in mind, and it may be difficult to extract from it the information necessary to complete the tables. In Costa Rica, for example, where a census had been taken, the author came across entries such as 'payments for work or services of an industrial character' which are ambiguous in input–output terms where one needs to know the actual supplying sector. A third problem sometimes met with is that the government departments taking the census and preparing the input–output table may not be the same. In this case, the input–output team may be given only a point estimate from which to construct the tables; there is then no possibility of determining the precision of the table nor of attaching confidence intervals to the results of using it. Furthermore, some of the domains used in sample work, such as classification of establishments by region and by size, may be of interest in their own right and this dimension will be lost if only a point estimate is furnished.

We see, therefore, that the census method is not intrinsically superior; if a good census is available, with a questionnaire adapted to input–output needs, it is clearly foolish not to take advantage of it, when this is permitted, but there are times when a well-drawn sample can be just as good. Furthermore, it is only in certain sectors that a real choice exists; in services, for example, censuses are very rare, do not usually provide the kind of information needed by the input–output worker and only by chance correspond with the year of the census of manufacturing.[2] It is only in the case of mining, manufacturing and public utilities that one can expect to have to choose between the two methods; many of the remaining activities, however, such as retailing and non-financial services consist of a large number of small, relatively homogeneous establishments where random sampling may be appropriate.

If the input–output table is constructed from a census, the need for statistical inference is avoided and the problems are reduced to such things as the questionnaire, non-response and data processing. Consequently, it will be assumed in what follows that a sample is being taken, since we have still not resolved many of the choices that need to be made in sampling work. (The problems of designing a questionnaire and data processing will be returned to in Chapter 8.)

Sampling is one of the most neglected parts of input-output work. The insights of sampling theory on optimal overall sample size, within stratum sample size, precision of estimators and confidence intervals for population estimates have been ignored almost without exception in the preparation of input–output tables. The problems of sampling in the input–output context are formidable, but much more can be done to incorporate scientific methods of sampling, as we shall see below, into input–output work.

3.2 PROBLEMS OF SAMPLING IN THE INPUT–OUTPUT CONTEXT

One of the biggest problems is the (usually) defective nature of the sampling frame. In a well-known text on sampling theory (Yates, 1960), the various types of defects to which a frame can be subject are listed as: (1) inaccurate; (2) incomplete; (3) subject to duplication; (4) inadequate; (5) out of date. It is fair to say that a listing of establishments—the normal frame in input–output work—in most LDCs will be defective in all these ways. In preparing input–output tables for Costa Rica, Scotland and Morocco, the author has come across examples of all these problems; in Scotland, for example, the listing of establishments was inaccurate, because establishments were frequently assigned to sectors which did not correspond to their principal product. When such establishments are drawn in the sample, it is easy to reclassify them, but unless the degree of inaccuracy in the population is known, the sample fractions will necessarily be sub-optimal. In Morocco, on the other hand, the problems of incompleteness and inadequacy were encountered, since many establishments were omitted from the listing either because their principal production was not known or because they had failed to respond to previous questionnaires. Completion of the frame is necessarily a time-consuming and often arbitrary task and is one reason why input–output workers are frequently content to use *ad hoc* procedures in drawing samples.

A second difficulty is provided by the sampling unit. Where the frame is provided by a listing of establishments, the sampling unit will clearly be the establishment, but use of the inverse of the implied sampling fraction in grossing up to estimates of the population will involve considerable inaccuracies if there are large differences in size between establishments. Suppose, for example, we are interested in estimating the total input of textiles ($\tilde{X}$) to the clothing industry; there are N establishments in the sector and we have elected to sample n. Thus, the population estimate ($\tilde{X}$) is provided by:

$$\tilde{X} = \left(\frac{N}{n}\right)\Sigma x_i \tag{3.1}$$

where x_i is purchases of textiles by ith sampled establishment or

$$\tilde{X} = N\left(\frac{\Sigma x_i}{n}\right) = N\bar{x} \tag{3.2}$$

where $\bar{x}$ is average purchases in the sample or

$$\tilde{X} = N\left[\left(\frac{1}{n}\right)x_1 + \left(\frac{1}{n}\right)x_2 + \cdots + \left(\frac{1}{n}\right)x_n\right] \tag{3.3}$$

In other words, each establishment sampled has been given the same weight $(1/n)$, although the largest may be many times bigger than the smallest. In the extreme case, where $N = 3$, $n = 2$ and $x_1 = 990$ while $x_2 = 10$ (and the unknown $x_3 = 800$) one can see how poor the results obtained by equation (3.3) will be; in place of a (true) population value of 1800, we find that the population estimate is 1500.

Although the *frame* is provided by a listing of establishments, the control total is usually provided by employment, sales or work done. The grossing-up factor is therefore not the same as the inverse of the sampling fraction; in technical terms, although the sampling unit is the establishment, the 'elementary unit' (Yamane, 1967, p. 48) is the worker or unit of sales, so that input–output work involves a form of cluster sampling. If the control total is employment (E), for example, and sample employment is given by e, then:

$$\tilde{X} = E\bar{x} = E\left(\frac{\Sigma x_i}{e}\right) = \left(\frac{E}{e}\right)\Sigma x_i \tag{3.4}$$

and in our previous example if $e_1 = 600$, $e_2 = 10$ and $E = 1000$, then the population estimate is $(100/61) \times 1000 = 1639.3$, which is a considerable improvement on our previous effort.

A problem sometimes encountered with the sampling unit is provided by multi-establishment firms. Some firms can only furnish data for the whole of their operations, and this may include establishments which fall within different sectors (strata). (In the case of regional input–output tables, the problem can be further exacerbated if some of these establishments are located outside the region of interest.) From a scientific point of view, optimal allocation of the sample among the different strata (see Appendix) depends on the population of establishments in each stratum and the listing of establishments will need to be revised where multi-establishment firms are discovered, so that strictly speaking the sample should be redrawn.

A third difficulty met within input–output samples is non-response; the extent of non-response to voluntary questionnaires is often very great and many input–output workers feel disinclined to go to considerable lengths to draw a 'scientific' sample when the results can be invalidated by a low response rate. As has been said elsewhere (Yates, 1960, p. 59): 'Unless non-response is confined to a small proportion of the whole sample the results cannot claim any general validity.'

In Table 3.1 the response rate for the Scottish input–output table is given. The most interesting row perhaps is that for manufacturing, where it can be seen that non-response was 47% of firms sampled. Non-response as a proportion of firms *approached* was considerably higher, since many of them made it clear at the preliminary stages that they were not interested in participating; furthermore, the non-response rate would have been higher had it not been for the labour-intensive system of interviews employed in sampling. (A postal questionnaire carried out consecutively yielded a non-response rate as high as 90% in some sectors.)

One of the problems with non-response is that it can lead to bias, i.e. the expected value of the statistic used as an estimator is not equal to the population parameter to be estimated. This can arise either through failure to do anything about the non-respondents or through attempts to substitute other firms (Yates, 1960, p. 10). Bias, however, can arise from other sources in input–output work; for example, the extreme difficulty of getting usable responses from tiny establishments (less than five employees) means that this stratum is often completely ignored in input–output sampling, so that bias will arise unless the ignored stratum is homogeneous with the others.

Table 3.1 Data sources and coverage for 1973 Scottish input–Output table

Sector	No. of columns	Source	Firms asked	Response	Employment	% Employment covered	Type of processing
Agriculture, forestry and fishing	4	*E*	—	—	52000	100%	*M*
Extraction	3	2*S* 1*E*	25	48%	35000	92%	*C*
Manufacturing	54	*S*	750	53%	670000	40%	*C*
Construction	1	*S*	100	32%	160000	7%	*M*
Utilities	3	*S*	10	90%	32000	90%	*C*
Transport and communications	5	*S*	100	52%	139000	66%	*C*
Distribution	1	*S*	160	41%	243000	2%	*C*
Services	6	3*S* 3*E*	180	38%	580000	5%	*C*
Final demand	9	6*S* 3*E*	—	—	—	—	*M* and *C*

S = Sample survey. *E* = External data. *M* = Manually processed. *C* = Computer processed.
Source: Burdekin, 1978a, p. 9.

The other component of the total sampling error, i.e. apart from the error due to bias, is the random sampling error. This component of sampling error is inversely proportional to the square root of sample size, so that we can reduce it by taking larger and larger samples. It may be, however, that to achieve a certain precision with a given reliability (say 99 %), the sample size has to be almost as large as the sample frame ($n \doteq N$). This will be the case where the elements of the population are so heterogeneous that—short of a full census of 100 % sample—any sample will exhibit a large standard deviation.

We shall see below how sample error and sample standard deviation can be reduced by further stratification within sectors. Nonetheless, the reader should be aware of the powerful forces contributing to a high standard deviation in input–output sampling.

3.3 OBJECTIVES OF THE SAMPLE AND METHODS OF SAMPLING

The objectives of an input–output sample are basically thee-fold: to obtain good 'coverage' in each sector, to collect data on the different domains of interest within each sector, and to draw the sample in a way which enables the science of statistical inference to be applied. Unfortunately, input–output practice often produces an inconsistency between these objectives; for example, the objective of maximum coverage suggests non-probability sampling in order to incorporate all large firms, which rules out the possibility of statistical inference. Another frequent occurrence is the use of a stratified random sampling procedure to draw the sample together with a method of estimating the population variables from the sample which is inconsistent with the structural principles of random stratification.[3]

The first problem, therefore, is to select a sampling method which is consistent with all three objectives. If we ignore the fact that each sector is already a stratum and instead think of each sector as a separate population, then the simplest method is random sampling; if, however, we take a random sample of the sample units (i.e. establishments), then a very large firm only has the same probability of being drawn as a very small one. Coverage, therefore, may be low and sample error high. Although we can always obtain the desired precision by increasing the sample size, the latter may be unacceptably high involving many small firms which are costly to interview. The method of random sampling, therefore, is unlikely to be our first choice, unless there is little difference in size among the sampling units in the sector.

A second possible method of sampling is random stratification; provided there is some between strata variance,[4] this method will provide more efficient estimates than random sampling. Furthermore, if there are enough strata, the problem of elementary and sample units may disappear since within each stratum, the former may be approximately proportional to the latter. This idea will now be explained further.

There are many ways each input–output sector can be stratified: by ownership, region, size, factor-intensity and so on. Given the comparatively small number of firms, however, in many—particularly manufacturing—sectors, multiple stratification is unrealistic; we therefore need to think in terms of one type of stratification. The ideal type will serve all three objectives listed above and the closest approximation to this type is stratification by size. The latter will enable us to achieve good coverage, it is a domain of interest and the principles of statistical inference will not be violated; none of the other forms of stratification are likely to achieve the same degree of coverage.

If we stratify by size and assume for the moment that this is measured by employment, then firms with a large number of employees will be grouped in one stratum, firms with very few employees in another and so on. In the extreme case, where the stratum width is one employee, all firms within it will have the same number of employees; in that case, a random sample chosen from the sampling units within each stratum will give each elementary unit the same probability of being selected. Of course, the stratum width is in practice much wider than one employee, but as long as it is not too broad, we can afford to ignore the difference between sampling and elementary units.

One stratum will be all establishments with more than k employees. In the manufacturing sectors, which tend to dominate the input–output aggregation scheme, these firms often account for the bulk of sector employment and output. In Morocco, for example, a sample of 15 % of all establishments (i.e. all those with more than 50 employees) was sufficient to 'cover' nearly 75 % of all employment; in no sector did coverage fall below 30 % and in one sector (coal and oil extraction) one establishment gave 97 % coverage.

Since maximum coverage is one of our objectives, we can take advantage of the concentration found in industry to take a 100 % sample from the largest stratum. Since all the large firms need to be sampled (at least in manufacturing), it follows that k is a relative measure. In the USA, $k = 100$ would produce an impossibly large sample, while in Costa Rica $k = 1000$ would yield about three firms; k should therefore be selected with an eye to the maximum sample size which is likely to be feasible. In Scotland, for example, we set $k = 500$ and in Morocco $k = 50$.

We assumed above that establishments would be stratified by emloyment size. Employment, however, may not be a good measure of size; two firms, for example, can produce the same output with quite different labour inputs if they employ different technologies; the same criticism applies equally to capital assets as a measure of size. Since it is output we are interested in, the best measure of size is sales, but where it is impossible to draw up the sample frame on this basis, employment has to be used instead.

As so often happens in input–output work, our discussion of sampling has tended to think of manufacturing as the paradigm. It is therefore important to remind ourselves that there are many other sectors entering into an input–output table. In some of these, stratified random sampling will also be appropriate (e.g. agriculture, construction), while in others (personal services, commerce), simple random sampling is usually sufficient. The choice of the sampling method should, however, be easily resolved in terms of the arguments presented above.

3.4 STRATIFIED RANDOM SAMPLING: AN EXAMPLE

Using the method of stratified random sampling, we can now show how entries in the make and absorption matrices may be estimated. (Since subscripts can become cumbersome, variables will refer to the i, jth element of these matrices unless otherwise specified.) What we are interested in is the estimate of the population total ($\tilde{X}$) for each cell and this can be written:

$$\tilde{X} = \sum_h N_h \bar{x}_h \tag{3.5}$$

where h is the number of strata in each sector, N_h is the number of *elementary* units in the hth stratum and $\bar{x}_h$ is the sample stratum mean. The latter can be written:

$$\bar{x}_h = \left(\frac{1}{n_k}\right) \sum_k x_{kh} \tag{3.6}$$

where $\Sigma_k x_{kh}$ is the sum of all sample unit values in the stratum and n_k is the number of elementary units sampled in the stratum.

In Table 3.2, simulated primary data for the population of firms in the clothing sector is given along with the number of sampling units and the corresponding number of elementary units (assumed to be workers). All information except the input of textiles and the output of principal and secondary products has been suppressed. The sector is divided into three strata—large, medium and small—according to the number of employees, and numbered one, two, three respectively. As suggested above, all firms in the largest stratum will be sampled, but we assume that in the second stratum only establishments (1) and (3) are sampled along with their corresponding elementary units, while in the third stratum, establishments (1), (3) and (5) are taken.[5]

Applying formula (3.6), we obtain for the input of textiles (x_i):

$$\bar{x}_1 = \left(\frac{1}{1100}\right)1050, \qquad \bar{x}_2 = \left(\frac{1}{200}\right)190, \qquad \bar{x}_3 = \left(\frac{1}{40}\right)40 \tag{3.7}$$

while for the output of principal production (${}_pq_i$), we obtain by application of the same formula:

$${}_p\bar{q}_1 = \left(\frac{1}{1100}\right)1950, \qquad {}_p\bar{q}_2 = \left(\frac{1}{200}\right)400, \qquad {}_p\bar{q}_3 = \left(\frac{1}{40}\right)80 \tag{3.8}$$

and for secondary products (${}_sq_i$):

$${}_s\bar{q}_1 = \left(\frac{1}{1100}\right)150, \qquad {}_s\bar{q}_2 = \left(\frac{1}{200}\right)0, \qquad {}_s\bar{q}_3 = \left(\frac{1}{40}\right)10 \tag{3.9}$$

which gives the following estimates for population values (see equation 3.5):

$$\tilde{X} = \left[1100 \times \frac{1050}{1100}\right] + \left[400 \times \frac{190}{200}\right] + \left[100 \times \frac{40}{40}\right] \tag{3.10}$$

therefore $\tilde{X} = 1530$, while $X = 1510$.

Table 3.2 Primary data for estimating population values using a stratified random sample

Clothing sector

Strata	Large (1) (>500 employees)		Medium (2) (100 – 500 employees)				Small (3) (<100 employees)						Total
Sampling Units	1*	2*	1*	2	3*	4	1*	2	3*	4	5*	6	12
Elementary Units	1–500	501–1100	1101–1200	1201–1275	1276–1375	1376–1500	1501–1520	1521–1550	1551–1560	1561–1580	1581–1590	1591–1600	1600
Absorptions													
.													
.													
.													
Textiles	500	550	100	80	90	100	15	25	10	20	15	5	1510 (X)
.													
.													
.													
Sales													
1. Principal products	950	1000	200	180	200	180	30	45	25	40	25	15	2890 $_{p}Q$
2. Secondary products	50	100	—	10	—	—	5	—	—	5	5	—	175 $_{s}Q$

* Selected for sampling.

$$(3.11) \qquad {}_p\tilde{Q} = \left[1100 \times \frac{1950}{1100}\right] + \left[400 \times \frac{400}{200}\right] + \left[100 \times \frac{80}{40}\right]$$

therefore ${}_p\tilde{Q} = 2950$, while ${}_pQ = 2890$.

$$(3.12) \qquad {}_s\tilde{Q} = \left[1100 \times \frac{150}{1100}\right] + \left[400 \times 0\right] + \left[100 \times \frac{10}{40}\right]$$

therefore ${}_s\tilde{Q} = 175$, while ${}_sQ = 175$.

By comparing the estimated population values in equations (3.10) to (3.12) with the actual totals (as given by the last column of Table 3.2), we can see that the precision of the estimators is quite high, which is not surprising since the two largest firms give us approximately two-thirds coverage. The 'worst' performance is provided by the estimate of principal production (${}_p\tilde{Q}$) and this is mainly due to sampling firms in the middle stratum which had no secondary production. The estimator of secondary production (${}_s\tilde{Q}$) is the same as the true population value (${}_sQ$) because errors in the second and third strata cancel out.

3.5 NON-SURVEY TECHNIQUES

In principle, sampling can be applied to all sectors and all strata, including final demand. In practice, however, considerations of time and cost will necessitate the use of non-sampling techniques in certain areas. In preparing the Scottish input–output tables, for example, sampling techniques were used to estimate the columns of the make and absorption matrices corresponding to manufacturing, construction, public utilities, transport and communications, distribution and parts of mining, services and final demand; in Morocco, sampling techniques were used only for mining, manufacturing, public utilities, construction and commerce, while in preparing a table for Costa Rica, the author did not have to use sampling techniques at all.

The organization of an efficient sample involves a number of related tasks such as coding, storing, data processing, which—as anyone who has experienced it will know—is immensely complicated. It is inevitable, therefore, that input–output workers should constantly be searching for reliable non-survey techniques. The most obvious of these is to use secondary sources, of which the most important are official statistics. It is extremely unlikely, for example, that the entries in final demand corresponding to public expenditure cannot be obtained from secondary sources; similarly, most governments carry out family expenditure surveys at sufficiently regular intervals to enable this information to be used to prepare an estimate of private consumption in the absorption matrix, while all nations publish trade figures which can be used to prepare columns for imports and exports.

Sometimes, secondary sources can be used to even greater effect; in countries where the bulk of plant and machinery is imported, most of the column for gross fixed capital formation can usually be prepared from trade data; nationalized industries, too, often publish their accounts in a form which can be used directly by the input–output worker without the need for additional survey work. Similarly, the worksheets involved in preparing the national accounts may carry enough information on such things as inventory change to enable the relevant column of the absorption matrix to be constructed.

The reasons why the author was able to eschew the use of samples in preparing an input–output table for Costa Rica are also instructive. First, he was given access to the worksheets of the most recent industrial census; although all establishments with more than four employees were surveyed, this still only amounted to 750 establishments, so that the work of data processing was quite manageable. Secondly, the national accounts in Costa Rica are prepared on a sectoral value added basis, i.e. value added in each sector is estimated as the difference between gross output and intermediate inputs. To estimate outputs and inputs, the Central Bank each year takes a sample of establishments in commerce, transport, services, etc., and in the worksheets the intermediate absorptions of each sector are articulated in sufficient detail for an input–output column to be constructed.

Official statistics are only one kind of secondary source; chambers of commerce often publish information which can be used by input–output workers, while in Costa Rica the author used agronomists' reports to prepare the estimates for the agricultural sectors. Furthermore, the shelves of most government departments are littered with the reports of private consultancy groups on particular sectors, which are often ideal material for input–output work.

There is one area where neither sampling techniques nor secondary sources are likely to be of much assistance; this area is firms with very few employees (an arbitrary cut-off point is five employees). Firms with less than five employees, often called the artisan or informal sector, usually find it extremely difficult to answer a questionnaire since they may not keep records of purchases and sales, while secondary sources cannot normally provide more than a very rough estimate of employment.[6] What often happens, therefore, is that these small firms are ignored in sampling, but included when 'grossing-up' by the inverse of the sampling fraction.

The main problems with this procedure are that it implicitly assumes that the small firms are similar to the larger ones in their pattern of purchases and sales and it becomes impossible at a later stage to distinguish errors of estimation due to inclusion of the small firms from other errors. In preparing the Moroccan input–output tables, therefore, the small establishments in each manufacturing sector were treated as a separate stratum; the stratum was not sampled, but the input–output coefficients for each stratum were approximated by reference to 'similar' firms among those with more than five employees. The informal sector is so important in many LDCs, however, that a further discussion of its treatment in input–output tables is reserved until later (see Chapter 11).

APPENDIX CHOOSING THE SAMPLE SIZE

3.1A OPTIMAL SAMPLE SELECTION

In section (3.4) dealing with stratified random sampling, it was assumed that the stratum sample size was known. However, the size of the sample is not a simple matter; first, there are limited resources available and, secondly, the size of the sample will depend on the precision which is considered acceptable in the population estimators. Now with each sample that is drawn there will be associated a sample variance ($V(\bar{x}) = \sigma_{\bar{x}}^2$) and an obvious way of resolving the problem of choice is to minimize this variance subject to the budget constraint. This is known as the method of optimal allocation. Assuming the budget constraint can be written as a simple linear function of the number of sampled units in each stratum, the sample variance in the optimal solution can be written (Yamane, 1967, p. 140):

(3.1a) $$V(\bar{x}_{\text{opt}}) = \left(\frac{1}{N^2}\right)\left(\frac{1}{n}\right)(\Sigma N_h S_h \sqrt{c_h})\left(\frac{\Sigma N_h S_h}{\sqrt{c_h}}\right) - [1/N^2 \Sigma N_h S_h^2]$$

where c_h is the unit cost of sampling in the hth stratum, S_h is the stratum standard deviation, n is the number of elementary units in the sample, N_h is the population of elementary units in the hth stratum, N the total population of elementary units.

$V(\bar{x}_{\text{opt}})$ is the value of the sample variance in the optimal solution. Both $V(\bar{x}_{\text{opt}})$ and n—the sample size—are unknowns, but if we knew one, we could determine the other (provided, of course, we knew S_h and c_h). Fortunately, we can develop another expression for $V(\bar{x})$ which enables us to solve for n.

The distribution of the sample mean can be assumed normal; consequently, we can use the Central Limit theorem to work out the probability of the sample mean falling within a particular interval. In particular, for the case of a 95% confidence interval, we can write:

(3.2a) $$P(\bar{x} - 1.96\sigma_{\bar{x}} < \bar{X} < \bar{x} + 1.96\sigma_{\bar{x}}) = 0.95$$

or

(3.3a) $$P(-1.96\sigma_{\bar{x}} < \bar{x} - \bar{X} < 1.96\sigma_{\bar{x}}) = 0.95$$

which simply means that 95 times out of 100, the sample mean will be within nearly two standard deviations of the true mean. However, another way of explaining this is to say that there is a 95% probability that the sample mean will differ from the true mean approximately by less than two standard deviations, so that the maximum value which this divergence can assume is $1.96_{\sigma\bar{x}}$, i.e.

(3.4a) $$|\bar{x} - \bar{X}| = d = 1.96\sigma_{\bar{x}}$$

where d is sometimes called the precision of the estimator.

We can rewrite the formula for precision, after squaring, in general terms as:

(3.5a) $$d^2 = z^2 \sigma_{\bar{x}}^2$$

where z is a measure of confidence[7] or

(3.6a) $$\sigma_{\bar{x}}^2 = \left(\frac{d^2}{z^2}\right)$$

Now $\sigma_{\bar{x}}^2$ is the sample variance which is *desired* to achieve the required precision (d), so if we set the desired variance (which we now call D^2) equal to the optimal variance ($v(\bar{x}_{\text{opt}})$), we will obtain an expression in which the only unknown is n—the sample size.

Before doing this, however, we need to make one minor adjustment. In selecting the desired variance, we set d and z to the appropriate values; there is no problem with z, but d in equation (3.4a) measures absolute precision. Often, we prefer to specify precision in relative terms (e.g. ± 5%). Consequently, relative precision (d') can be written:

(3.7a) $$d' = \left(\frac{d}{\bar{X}}\right) = \frac{z \, . \, \sigma_{\bar{x}}}{\bar{X}}$$

so that

(3.8a) $$(d')^2 = \frac{z^2 \, . \, \sigma_{\bar{x}}^2}{(\bar{X})^2}$$

and

(3.9a) $$D^2 = \frac{(d')^2 (\bar{X})^2}{z^2}$$

With this minor adjustment, we can now derive the solution for n by setting equations (3.1a) and (3.9a) equal to each other. The result is:

(3.10a) $$n = \frac{(\Sigma N_h S_h \sqrt{c_h})(\Sigma N_h S_h / \sqrt{c_h})}{N^2 D^2 + \Sigma N_h S_h^2}$$

Using the data in Table 3.2, from which the stratum variance can be derived,[8] assuming sampling costs per elementary unit in the three strata of \$4, 9, and 16 respectively,[9] specifying relative precision at 5% ($d' = 0.05$) and demanding 'virtual certainty' ($z = 3$), we obtain an optimal sample size of 1225 elementary units. This compares with an 'actual' sample size of 1340, which was not based on optimal considerations.

Having settled on overall sample size, the next thing is to distribute it by stratum. Now the definition of sample variance, where random stratification is used (see Yamane, 1967, p. 116), is:

(3.11a) $$V(\bar{x}) = \frac{1}{N^2} \sum N_h^2 \left(\frac{N_h - n_h}{N_h}\right)\left(\frac{S^2 h}{n_h}\right)$$

and the cost function can be written:

(3.12a) $$C = \sum c_h \, . \, n_h$$

Minimizing equation (3.11a) subject to this budget constraint gives the optimal solution. Provided n is known, the only unknowns are n_h which is what we want to determine. Each n_h can therefore be written:

(3.13a)
$$n_h = \left[\frac{N_h S_h / \sqrt{c_h}}{\Sigma (N_h S_h / \sqrt{c_h})} \right] . n$$

Applying this formula to the data of Table 3.2 gives the following optimal sample sizes ('actual' sample sizes in brackets) in terms of elementary units (i.e. employees):

1st stratum	975 (1100)
2nd stratum	184 (200)
3rd stratum	66 (40)

so it appears that only the first two strata were actually oversampled, while the third stratum was undersampled.

The formulae for the optimal sample and stratum size make use of a formidable range of variables, whose values are assumed to be known in advance; the only troublesome one of these, however, is S_h^2, the stratum variance, and it will be discussed below. The cost parameters c_h may also present difficulties, although it is sufficient to know the ratio of costs in the different strata rather than the absolute value. (Each parameter should represent cost per elementary unit rather than cost per establishment, but it is a simple matter to move from one to the other.)

In one other respect, the move from sample to elementary units is not so simple. Suppose, for example, that the elementary unit is represented by an employee; application of the formulae might suggest that sample variance can be minimized with the selection of n_h elementary units from the hth stratum. This is not an easy matter. If a table of random numbers is used, the chances are that only some employees of an establishment will be selected; since it is impossible to sample less than the whole of an establishment, this procedure would be wasteful.

There are a number of possible solutions to this problem; first, we could select an elementary unit from a table of random numbers, find the establishment to which it belongs and sample all elementary units; then select another elementary unit using random numbers and—provided it does not belong to the first establishment—proceed as above until the sample quota of elementary units has been filled. Another possibility is to select stratum sizes with only a small standard deviation in the number of elementary units (e.g. 20–30 employees).[10] Then the number of elementary units to be selected (n_h) can be divided by the average number of elementary units per establishment in the stratum to give the number of establishments (sampling units) which need to be selected. If these establishments are chosen from a table of random numbers, it will give a close correspondence to the desired number of elementary units.

Another problem encountered in sampling work is that the formulae derived for n_h and n assume that each stratum will be sampled. If, however, the largest stratum is to be sampled exhaustively, we already know its size and its cost (approximately) so that these variables should not enter into the problem of optimal allocation as unknowns. This requires some slight modifications in the formulae, which can then be reapplied to the example in Table 3.2. Assuming that all 1100 employees in the first stratum are sampled, we then obtain $n = 215$, $n_2 = 158$, $n_3 = 57$. The two samples are set out below:

	First sample	*Cost* ($)	*Second sample*	*Cost* ($)
n_1	975	3900	1100	4400
n_2	184	1656	158	1422
n_3	66	1056	57	912
n	1225	6612	1314	6734

where it will be noticed that sample size in the two smaller strata has been reduced to accommodate the larger sample in the first stratum.

In all our discussion so far, it has been assumed that we have only stratified within sectors, so that n and N are sector-specific. If this were the case, sampling would be unnecessarily complicated since the calculations would need to be repeated for each sector. There is nothing to stop us, however, treating each sector as a stratum so that summation signs are taken across the size-groupings in *all* sectors. N will now refer to the population of elementary units in all sectors and n to the overall sample size. Optimal allocation will select the sample size for each size-group and this will then define the sector sample size.

3.2A THE STRATUM STANDARD DEVIATION

In order to derive n_h and n in equations (3.10a) and (3.13a), it was assumed that the stratum standard deviation (S_h) or its estimate (s_h) was known. The difficulties involved in estimating S_h (which represent the main reason why the science of statistical inference is not used in input–output work) are of two kinds; the first is a general sampling problem, while the second is specific to input–output analysis. We will consider the second difficulty first.

In the case of input–output work it is not immediately obvious what is meant by a stratum variance or a stratum standard deviation. The sample is used to estimate a large number of stocks and flows each of which will be subject to error; one of the most important estimates is inputs per elementary unit. Where the elementary unit is a dollar of sales, this becomes $\tilde{a}_{ij}$ for the jth sector, i.e. an input–output coefficient representing the average requirement from the ith sector per unit of output in the jth sector.[11] Each $\tilde{a}_{ij}$ will be subject to error and its variance can be written $V(\tilde{a}_{ij})$.

There will be several $V(\tilde{a}_{ij})$ in the jth sector or stratum, so that S_j^2—stratum variance—is not a simple matter to define and it could be a very costly and cumbersome parameter to estimate. It is therefore worth demonstrating a method of estimating S_j^2 which emerges as a by-product of estimating the input–output coefficients themselves.

In a notable contribution to input–output analysis (Gerking, 1976), a method was developed for estimating input–output coefficients stochastically. One of the basic equations used by Gerking is:

(3.14a) $$X_{ij}^{(v)} = a_{ij}X_j^{(v)} + \theta_{ij}^{(v)}$$

where v refers to establishments, X_{ij} is the purchases from the ith sector by the jth sector, X_j is the output of the jth sector, so that $\theta_{ij}^{(v)}$ is the error involved in using the input–output relationship for the vth firm. Two-stage least squares (TSLS) is used to estimate a_{ij}, and its estimated variance ($V(\tilde{a}_{ij})$) is given by:

(3.15a) $$V(\tilde{a}_{ij}) = \sigma^2_{\theta_{ij}} . \beta_j / n_j$$

where $\sigma^2_{\theta_{ij}}$ is the variance of θ_{ij}, β_j is a non-stochastic scalar which is a function of sample size, output and value added in the jth sector and n_j is the number of establishments in the jth sector.

For each sector (stratum) we want to minimize $\Sigma_i V(\tilde{a}_{ij})$, but this will vary from stratum to stratum. Assuming the cost function can be written as in equation (3.12a), the optimal allocation of the sample will result from minimizing total sectoral (stratum) variances subject to a budget constraint in the following Lagrangian expression:

(3.16a) $$\min \phi = \Sigma_j \Sigma_i \sigma^2_{\theta_{ij}} . \beta_j / n_j + \lambda (\Sigma c_j n_j - C)$$

from which the following first-order conditions can be derived:

(3.17a) $$\partial \phi / \partial n_j = -\frac{\sum_i \sigma^2_{\theta_{ij}} . \beta_j}{n_j^2} + \lambda c_j = 0$$

If we are interested only in the *ratios* of sample size, this becomes:[12]

(3.18a) $$\left(\frac{n_j}{n_i}\right) = \left[\frac{c_i \beta_j \sum_{ij} \sigma^2_{\theta_{ij}}}{c_j \beta_i \sum_h \sigma^2_{\theta_{hi}}}\right]^{\frac{1}{2}}$$

At first glance, this looks unlike the formula used above for sample size, but if equation (3.13a) is expressed in a comparable way, it becomes:

(3.19a) $$\left(\frac{n_j}{n_i}\right) = \left[\frac{N_j S_j / \sqrt{c_j}}{N_i S_i / \sqrt{c_i}}\right] = \left[\frac{c_i N_j^2 S_j^2}{c_j N_i^2 S_i^2}\right]^{\frac{1}{2}}$$

so that N_j has been replaced in Gerking's equation by $\beta_j^{1/2}$ and S_j^2 by $\Sigma_i \sigma^2_{\theta_{ij}}$. Since both β_j and $\sigma^2_{\theta_{ij}}$ emerge as by-products of the TSLS estimation process, equation (3.18a) can be used to estimate the optimal sample size in each sector once the sample size in any one sector has been chosen.

Gerking used equation (3.18a) to estimate optimal sample size ratios for the West Virginia input–output table (see Miernyk, 1970), to whose data base he had access, and then compares these optimal with actual ratios. The ratios proved to be radically different, which confirms the view that *ad hoc* procedures for drawing input–output samples may not serve to minimize variance for a given budget and LDCs would do well to remember this.

Although the TSLS estimation process yields estimates of stratum variance which can in principle be used to select an optimal sample size, it suffers from a logical difficulty which its critics have been quick to point out: the estimate of $\sigma^2_{\theta_{ij}}$ can only be provided after the sample has been drawn.

If a country is preparing its first input–output table, there is clearly no way around this logical difficulty: if, however, the data base for a previous input–output table survives, TSLS can be applied to yield estimates of stratum variance which in turn make it possible to apply the formulae for optimal sample selection.

Even when TSLS cannot be applied to a previous data base, it is still possible to furnish reasonable approximations to the standard deviation in each stratum; for example, the variance of sales or capital stock per worker may be quite a good approximation to the variance in purchasing patterns and would be a simple matter to estimate stratum by stratum from an earlier input–output table.

The main sources of stratum variance in input–output work are differences in technology and product mix. Since these tend to vary more by stratum than by country (the engineering sectors will have a high variance wherever located), there is a strong case to be made for building up a master sample which all input–output workers can draw on. Once S_h or $\Sigma\sigma^2_{\theta_{ij}}$ has been established for this master sample, sample size can be determined very quickly from a knowledge of desired precision, costs and the sample frame.

3.3A NON-OPTIMAL SAMPLE SELECTION

As was stated above, input–output samples have not usually been drawn by methods involving optimal allocations. In practice, simpler methods are used and an attempt has been made to justify these as follows: if we take the formula for n_h in equation (3.13a) and divide by n_j, we get:

$$\left(\frac{n_h}{n_j}\right) = \left[\frac{N_h S_h/\sqrt{c_h}}{N_j S_j/\sqrt{c_j}}\right] \tag{3.20a}$$

If costs per unit between strata do not vary and if there is no reason to believe that stratum variance changes between strata, this becomes:

$$\left(\frac{n_h}{N_h}\right) = \left(\frac{n_j}{N_j}\right) = \cdots = \left(\frac{n}{N}\right) = k \tag{3.21a}$$

where k is the sampling fraction, which is the same for all strata and is proportional to sample size.

A variant of this method was adopted in Morocco to draw the sample for the 1975 input–output table (Dar Al-Handasah, 1979). In this study, a decision had already been taken to sample all large firms (50 + employees) exhaustively,[13] so the problem of allocation was restricted to the small firms; furthermore, the maximum number of small establishments which it was felt could be sampled was arbitrarily set at 500.

If N were known, setting n to 500 would determine the sampling fraction;

however, there were two problems with N. If it referred to all establishments, large and small, it would have resulted in an allocative procedure which ignored the number of large firms in a sector already selected. Secondly, knowledge of N does not help one to determine those sectors where product mix and technology differences suggest that a larger than proportional sample should be taken.

Bearing this in mind, N was restricted to small firms and the number of small firms in each sector was adjusted for product mix and technology differences on the one hand and the weight of large firms in the sector on the other by the formula:

$$\tilde{N}_h = N_h(1 + g_h + v_h) \tag{3.22a}$$

where $g_h = (0, 1, 2)$ = weight to account for the degree to which large establishments are represented in sector h, and $v_h = (0, 1, 2)$ = weight to account for the expected range of product mix and technology differences in sector h. A sector, therefore, with 10 small establishments where no large firms had been sampled ($g_h = 2$) and where product mix was very large ($v_h = 2$) would therefore be estimated to have 50 establishments. The sample frame was then obtained as $\tilde{N} = \Sigma_h \tilde{N}_h$ and so the sample fraction became $k = 500/N$.

3.4A CONCLUSIONS

Sample selection in input–output work according to optimal considerations is, as far as the author is aware, a fairly novel suggestion; it is not applied widely in developed countries and is ignored almost completely by LDCs. The alternatives to optimal sample selection, however, such as that outlined in the previous section, are somewhat crude and arbitrary and they raise the possibility, confirmed by the author's experience, that scarce resources may be wasted through over-sampling in some sectors, while other sectors are left largely neglected.

The only serious objection to optimal sampling is the difficulty of obtaining prior estimates of stratum standard deviations. As this appendix has shown, however, these estimates can be obtained with effort and imagination, particularly when the data base for a previous input–output table survives. Where the data base is held in machine-readable form, it is neither difficult nor time-consuming to prepare estimates of stratum standard deviations, which can be used to select an optimal sample for the next input–output table, provided that the problem is anticipated sufficiently far in advance.

When a country is preparing an input–output table for the first time (and several of the smaller LDCs are in this position), it is reasonable to eschew optimal sampling techniques in favour of simpler methods. Many LDCs, however, have had some experience in input–output work and for them the problem is one of improving the quality of the product; in this respect, optimal sampling has an important part to play.

NOTES

1 The reason why the sectorization or aggregation scheme cannot be discussed immediately after this chapter is that it requires prior knowledge of the input–output model; the latter is therefore discussed first in Chapter 4.

2 Manufacturing is always treated as *primus inter pares* in input–output work because its purchases from and sales to other sectors tend to dominate the entries in an input–output table.

3 For example 'grossing up' is often done by the formula $\tilde{X} = gx$ where $x = \Sigma_i x_i$ is the sum of all sample values and g is the inverse of the sampling fraction. This, however, is an unbiased estimator only in the case of a random, not stratified random sample.

4 In a random stratified sample, sampling variance has two components: variation *within* each stratum and variation *between* strata. If each stratum consists of very similar units, then the former will be small and the latter large; however, when within stratum variance is small, the variance of the whole sample is also small. Thus, random *stratified* sampling is more efficient than random sampling when the population can be broken down into strata exhibiting homogeneity *within* each stratum (see Yamane, 1967, pp. 109–119).

5 The considerations which affect the choice of establishments within each stratum are discussed in the Appendix.

6 'Employment' in small establishments is in any case ambiguous, because of the use of part-time labour, unpaid family labour, the extent of self-employment, and the absence of a division between the owner and the workers.

7 $z = 2$ means 95% confidence, $z = 3$ means 99% confidence, i.e. virtual certainty.

8 The stratum variance has been calculated with individual observations on purchases of textiles by *establishments* while averaging through by *elementary* units, i.e. $S_h^2 = (1/n_h - 1)\,\Sigma_i(x_{hi} - \bar{x}_h)^2$, where x_{hi} refers to the ith establishment in the hth stratum and n_h refers to the number of elementary units in the hth stratum. This 'mixed' approach to calculating standard deviations gives $S_1 = 1.0665$, $S_2 = 0.8309$ and $S_3 = 1.5813$. These standard deviations are much higher than would be obtained if x_{hi} referred to the ith elementary unit in the hth stratum and account for the high sampling proportion. The justification for this procedure is that, first, it is the relative standard deviation between strata which is most important in calculating optimal sample size and, secondly, a low standard deviation suggests that only a small number of elementary units be sampled, which is impracticable since all elementary units in each sampled establishment must be taken.

9 The largest stratum has the lowest cost, because there are substantial economies of scale where costs are calculated per elementary unit.

10 This procedure is not possible for the largest stratum size (e.g. 500 + employees), but it has been suggested above that this stratum should be sampled exhaustively.

11 The estimation of input–output coefficients will be discussed in detail in Chapter 4. For the moment, however, it is sufficient to think of each coefficient as being obtained by dividing the estimate of the population input ($\tilde{X}_{ij}$) by the estimate of the population output ($\tilde{X}_j$), i.e. $\tilde{a}_{ij} = \tilde{X}_{ij}/\tilde{X}_j$.

12 Gerking chose to solve for ratios, because he wanted to apply the method of optimal allocation to a particular case study (the West Virginia input–output table) and 'a numeraire had to be chosen since the sampling budget in West Virginia was not known, and as a consequence, the Lagrange multiplier, λ, could not be eliminated'. (Gerking, 1976, p. 56.) In fact, this is not quite correct since knowledge only of the *ratio* of sample costs is required. The solution for n_j can in fact be written:

$$n_j = \left(\frac{[\Sigma_i \sigma^2_{\theta_{ij}} \beta_j / c_j]}{[\Sigma_j \Sigma_i \sigma^2_{\theta_{ij}} \beta_j / c_j]}\right)^{1/2} . n$$

13 All large firms in the *industrial* sector; most of the non-industrial sectors were estimated by non-survey methods.

CHAPTER 4

Linear Algebra and the Input–Output Model

4.1 INTRODUCTION

The procedures suggested in the last chapter are designed to furnish a set of 'grossed-up' columns for an absorption and make matrix. This is still a long way from a complete input–output table, but it is impossible in the chapters which follow not to assume some understanding of the input–output models derived from input–output tables; simple input–output models, however, are strictly linear and the structure of such models lends itself to treatment by matrix algebra, so that it is also necessary to review the principal characteristics of this branch of mathematics (see Appendix A to this chapter).

In this chapter, we shall ignore the difference between commodity and industry output; we can either assume that the work necessary to prepare 'symmetric' tables (commodity × commodity or industry × industry) has been completed (see Chapter 9) or that there is no secondary production; in the second case, the production account in Table 1.3 will no longer be subdivided between commodities and activities and we can therefore write the supply–demand balance equations for the nation's productive system as:[1]

$$
(4.1) \qquad
\begin{array}{ccccccccc}
x_1 \equiv w_{11} & + & w_{12} & + & w_{13} & + & \dots & + w_{1n} & + f_1 \\
x_2 \equiv w_{21} & + & w_{22} & + & w_{23} & + & \dots & + w_{2n} & + f_2 \\
\vdots & & \vdots & & \vdots & & & \vdots & \vdots \\
x_n \equiv w_{n1} & + & w_{n2} & + & w_{n3} & + & \dots & + w_{nn} & + f_n
\end{array}
$$

where x_i is the output of the ith sector, w_{ij} represents the value of absorptions by the jth sector from the ith sector and f_i is final demand for the ith sector; assuming an open economy, f_i includes exports of the ith commodity as a positive entry and imports of the ith commodity as a negative entry; thus w_{ij} is *total* absorptions of the ith commodity by the jth sector inclusive of imports and the entries in final demand referring to private and public consumption, investment and stock change are also inclusive of imports.

Equations (4.1) are written as identities, because the relationship between supply (x_i) and demand ($\Sigma_j w_{ij} + f_i$) must always be satisfied; this identity can be achieved through unintended rises or falls in stocks or through a change in imports, so that it is not necessary to assume an equilibrium relationship between the demand for the ith commodity and its output. Despite this limitation, the equations (4.1) will still prove a useful starting point.

4.2 THE SIMPLE INPUT–OUTPUT MODEL

Leontief's great achievement was to provide us with an empirically implementable general equilibrium system. In the Leontief system each w_{ij} is a function of x_j alone (prices being ignored) and we can write the relationship as:

$$w_{ij} = f_{ij}(x_j) \tag{4.2}$$

and substitution of (4.2) into (4.1) now gives us a determinate system of n equations in the n unknown x_js, provided that final demand is given exogenously.

The elimination of prices from equation (4.2) can be justified in a number of ways. First, if there is only one scarce factor of production (e.g. labour), then there is only one thing on which to economize; with everything reduced to its value in terms of labour time, relative prices cannot change, because numerator and denominator will always move in the same proportion; there is, therefore, no need to include them in equation (4.2). This is often called the 'no-substitution' theorem (Samuelson, 1951), but it breaks down where more than one scarce factor (e.g. labour *and* capital) can be identified.

The second justification, preferred by Leontief, deals with the limited scope for substitution between inputs at the firm level; plant of given size, it is argued, embodies equipment and machinery which require specific inputs and these requirements cannot be altered in the short run. It should be noted that while the no-substitution theorem implies inter-temporal stability in the relationship between inputs and outputs, Leontief's justification does not. Furthermore, if different firms within a sector have different input requirements (as a reflection, perhaps, of the capital stocks of different vintages) then the relationship between inputs and output in equation (4.2) will only be stable, even in the short-run, if all firms expand at the same rate.

The original Leontief formulation assumed not only that relative prices could be ignored; it also assumed that the relationships in equations (4.1) and (4.2) are expressed in physical terms, so that f_{ij} in equation (4.2) has a quantity dimension; thus the underlying relationship links the physical requirements of the input from the ith sector (e.g. tons of iron ore) to the physical output of the jth sector (e.g. yards of steel plate). Physical measures, however, are very difficult to collect for many sectors and impossible for others, such as services, but by choosing our quantity unit in the base year such that its price equals the country's unit of account, we can use value data in the base year *as if* they referred to physical quantities.

With the Leontief formulation, the future relationship between the value of inputs and outputs is equal to the physical relationship in the base year adjusted for relative price changes; we said above, however, that the Leontief formulation does not necessarily imply inter-temporal stability and it is possible therefore that, in response to relative price changes, the underlying physical relationship is changing. A third justification for eliminating prices from equation (4.2) therefore arises, if all cross-price elasticities are zero while the own-price elasticity of demand is unity, for in that case an $x\%$ change in price will produce an $x\%$ change in quantity purchased and the relationship between inputs and output will be stable in value terms.[2]

Although we have discussed various reasons for determining each intermediate absorption by reference to the value (volume) of output alone, equation (4.2) is only a functional form; the relationship still needs to be specified and, despite the linearity assumption which rules out quadratic or log-linear forms, there are still a number of possibilities. The most important of these are:

(4.3) $$w_{ij} = a_{ij}x_j$$

(4.4) $$w_{ij} = b_{ij} + m_{ij}x_j$$

In equation (4.3), the relationship between inputs and outputs is assumed to be linear proportional, i.e. constant returns to scale; in equation (4.4), we allow for the possibility of non-constant returns to scale, since a doubling of x_j—b_{ij} and m_{ij} constant—can produce a less than or more than doubling of w_{ij}. Each m_{ij} is therefore a *marginal* input–output coefficient, whereas a_{ij} is an *average* input–output coefficient.

It should be clear that substitution of equations (4.3) or (4.4) in equations (4.1) will produce a determinate system of n equations in the n unknown xs. The choice between them will therefore depend on data availability; equation (4.3) requires only one observation for its estimation and this is the minimum provided by an input–output table, which records both w_{ij} and x_j for a single year. However, more information may be available either on a time-series (input–output tables for different years) or on a cross-section basis (detailed survey or census data for firms of different size within a sector) so that it may be possible to estimate equation (4.4), for which at least two observations on w_{ij} and x_j are required.[3] Estimation of equation (4.4) is clearly preferable, since if constant returns to scale in fact prevail, the estimate of b_{ij} will not be significantly different from zero, while if non-constant returns prevail, the use of marginal rather than average coefficients will offer great gains in efficiency in applied work.[4]

4.3 THE INPUT–OUTPUT MODEL AND ITS MATRIX PRESENTATION

Many LDCs are unlikely to be in a position to make their choice over estimation procedures on the basis of full information; for various reasons the only estimate is likely to be a point one of average input–output coefficients implying the non-stochastic relationship:

(4.3) $$w_{ij} = a_{ij}x_j$$

If we now substitute this relationship into equation (4.1), we get the input–output system:

$$
\begin{aligned}
x_1 &= a_{11}x_1 + a_{12}x_2 + a_{13}x_3 + \quad \ldots \quad + a_{1n}x_n + f_1 \\
x_2 &= a_{21}x_1 + a_{22}x_2 + a_{23}x_3 + \quad \ldots \quad + a_{2n}x_n + f_2 \\
x_3 &= a_{31}x_1 + a_{32}x_2 + a_{33}x_3 + \quad \ldots \quad + a_{3n}x_n + f_3 \\
&\vdots \\
x_n &= a_{n1}x_1 + a_{n2}x_2 + a_{n3}x_3 + \quad \ldots \quad + a_{nn}x_n + f_n
\end{aligned} \tag{4.5}
$$

where the output of each sector is seen to depend on final demand for that sector and the output of all other sectors.

Equations (4.5) can be written much more easily in matrix terms.[5] If we isolate all the input–output coefficients (a_{ij}), we can form them in a two-dimensional array or matrix (A), i.e.

$$
\begin{bmatrix}
a_{11} & a_{12} & a_{13} & \ldots & a_{1n} \\
a_{21} & a_{22} & a_{23} & \ldots & a_{2n} \\
a_{31} & a_{32} & a_{33} & \ldots & a_{3n} \\
\vdots & \vdots & \vdots & & \vdots \\
a_{n1} & a_{n2} & a_{n3} & \ldots & a_{nn}
\end{bmatrix} = A \tag{4.6}
$$

where the first subscript on a coefficient determines its row and the second its column. As there are n rows and columns in this matrix, it is square, of order n and of type ($n \times n$). We can also form the output of each sector into a column vector (x) and the final demand for each sector into a column vector (f). This means that equation (4.5) can now be rewritten in matrix terms:

$$x = Ax + f \tag{4.7}$$

or

$$[I - A]x = f \tag{4.8}$$

where I is the unit matrix (see Appendix A). Assuming the inverse of $[I - A]$ exists, we can write:

$$[I - A]^{-1}[I - A]x = [I - A]^{-1}f \tag{4.9}$$

therefore

$$Ix = [I - A]^{-1}f \tag{4.10}$$

therefore

$$x = [I - A]^{-1}f \tag{4.11}$$

Thus, given f, we can solve for the vector of gross outputs.

Equation (4.11) 'translates' a given final bill of goods into a vector of gross outputs. If, however, there are any negative entries in the matrix $[I-A]^{-1}$—the 'Leontief inverse', as it is usually called—there would be an economically meaningless result implying that some final demands have negative impact on gross output. It is worth considering, therefore, what restrictions need to be put on the input–output coefficients to ensure a sensible interpretation.

Fortunately, the restrictions are not at all severe; known as the Hawkins–Simon conditions (Hawkins, 1949), the restrictions are: first, that the diagonal of the $[I-A]$ matrix should be strictly positive (i.e. $1-a_{jj}>0$) and, secondly, that all principal minors of the $[I-A]$ matrix be positive. It is possible to give both these conditions a simple economic interpretation.

Consider a three-sector input–output system. The principal minor of $(1-a_{33})$ is:

$$\begin{vmatrix} (1-a_{11}) & -a_{12} \\ -a_{21} & (1-a_{22}) \end{vmatrix} = (1-a_{11})(1-a_{22})-a_{12}a_{21}$$

We require that each principal minor is positive, which in this case means $(1-a_{11})(1-a_{22})>a_{12}a_{21}$. If we give the coefficients a physical interpretation, $(1-a_{11})$ denotes the quantity available from the first sector for distribution to other sectors after satisfying its needs for its own output as an intermediate input; if this is not positive, it means, for example, that it takes more than a ton of steel to make a ton of steel, which is not a viable proposition. Thus, the first condition—$(1-a_{jj})>0$—will always be met and $(1-a_{11})(1-a_{22})$ will be positive. Now the net output of the two sectors is available for distribution elsewhere, and what the second condition states is that these two sectors must be capable of supplying more than their own needs for the products produced by this group of two sectors. In our three-sector example, given the demands made by the third sector and by final demand, it is not difficult to believe that this condition will be met in practice, so we can have great confidence in the existence of a solution to equation (4.11).[6]

4.4 THE ECONOMIC INTERPRETATION OF THE LEONTIEF INVERSE

The Leontief inverse is a most useful and powerful tool, but we have yet to show its economic significance. The matrix $[I-A]^{-1}$ is a complicated expression whose elements capture both the direct and indirect effects of any change in the exogenous vector f; it would therefore help us in our economic interpretation of this inverse if we could separate out the direct from the indirect effects. Fortunately, we can do this by making use of the approximation to the inverse of a power-series expansion (Waugh, 1950).

In the simplest Keynesian model, the multiplier $1/(1-c)$, where c is the marginal propensity to consume, can be approximated by the infinite series:

$$\left(\frac{1}{1-c}\right) \approx 1+c+c^2+c^3+\cdots$$

provided that $c < 1$. The matrix equivalent of this scalar expression is:

$$[I-A]^{-1} \approx I+A+A^2+A^3+\cdots \tag{4.12}$$

provided that each column sum of A is less than one. We may also note that the power-series expression itself can be written as:

$$I+A+A^2+A^3+\ldots = [I+A+A^2+\cdots+A^{k-1}] \times [I+A^k+(A^k)^2+(A^k)^3+\cdots] \tag{4.13}$$

or

$$I+A+A^2+A^3+\cdots = [I+A+A^2+\cdots+A^{k-1}][I-A^k]^{-1} \tag{4.14}$$

which will prove useful later on.

If we now insert the power-series approximation of equation (4.12) in the solution—equation (4.11)—we get the expression:

$$x = [I+A+A^2+A^3+\cdots]f \tag{4.15}$$

or

$$x = f+Af+A^2f+A^3f+\cdots \tag{4.16}$$

Equation (4.16) shows us how the gross output of any sector is built up 'round' by 'round'; in the first round (f) are the deliveries to final demand itself. In order to meet these deliveries, each sector makes direct demands on the other sectors for intermediate inputs (Af), which can only be satisfied if further demands are made on the productive system ($\Sigma_{\theta=2}^{n} A^{\theta} f$). Because in any 'round' some of the requirements are met from outside the productive system through factor inputs or imports, for example, the terms on the right-hand side of equation (4.16) diminish in importance; indeed, tests for one developing country (see, for example, Bulmer–Thomas, 1977a, Chapter 7) have shown that all the elements of the Leontief inverse are approximated within 95% after six iterations or rounds.

The economic significance of the Leontief inverse can be illustrated in another way; let us define this inverse as:

$$[I-A]^{-1} = R = \{r_{ij}\} \tag{4.17}$$

where r_{ij} is the i,jth element of the Leontief inverse. Because of the strict linearity of equation (4.11):

$$r_{ij} = \delta x_i / \delta f_j \tag{4.18}$$

i.e. the i, jth element of the Leontief inverse is the partial derivative of x_i with respect to f_j. If, therefore, f_j increases by one unit—all other final demands unchanged—the total effect on the productive system, or the increase in the gross output of all sectors, is captured by the expression $\Sigma_i r_{ij}$. Thus, the column sum of the Leontief inverse shows the direct and indirect effects on the economy of a unit change in final demand for the sector shown at the head of column. Similarly, $\Sigma_j r_{ij}$, i.e. the row sum of the Leontief inverse, shows the total effect on the ith sector when each final demand increases by unity.[7]

In the derivation of the input–output model, we have made only one assumption, namely that there are fixed coefficients of production ($w_{ij} = f_{ij}x_j$). If constant returns to scale are also assumed, we get the relationship $w_{ij} = a_{ij}x_j$, although this additional assumption is not strictly necessary. However, by interpreting the Leontief inverse in the way suggested above, we have in fact made two further assumptions, which warrant discussion.

First, we have assumed that when the jth final demand increases, only the jth sector's output is affected in the first instance. This will only be the case if there are no joint products, so that the principal product of the jth sector must not be produced elsewhere as a secondary or by-product; in fact, such cases of joint production are quite common in the real world and input–output workers have to resort to a series of devices (see Chapter 9) in order to bring the input–output table into harmony with the assumptions of the model.

Secondly, we have to assume that there are no external economies or diseconomies associated with the production process. The production function for the jth sector is therefore of the form:

(4.19) $$x_j = F(w_{1j}, w_{2j}, \ldots, w_{nj}, v_{1j}, v_{2j}, \ldots, v_{mj})$$

where v_{ij} is the input of the ith primary factor of production. If, on the other hand, technological external (dis)economies are present (Meade, 1952) such that the output of the jth sector depends also upon the output and input utilization of the kth sector, then our simple linear system of equations breaks down.

Fortunately, technological external economies are quite rare; pecuniary external economies (Scitovsky, 1954), which refer to the interdependence among producers through the market mechanism, are generally thought to be much more common—particularly in developing countries—but the input–output system is effectively isolated from such external (dis)economies by the absence of price effects. Thus, the impact of capacity expansion in sector k on the output of sector j via the change in the price of the kth input is ignored in the input–output model, but this is not a new assumption as it is embodied in that of fixed coefficients of production.

4.5 SOME EXTENSIONS OF THE INPUT–OUTPUT MODEL

The input–output model in its simplest form—equation (4.11)—is a means for predicting the vector of gross outputs from a given bill of final goods (f). No welfare significance whatsoever can be attached to the volume or value of gross output, so it is worth pondering whether the input–output model can yield solutions for such variables as net output, value added, factor payments, incomes, employment and so on, to which welfare significance can be attached.

Fortunately, the answer is in the affirmative; for example, let us denote the matrix of factor payments per unit of gross output by V, where V is a matrix of type $(m \times n)$ corresponding to the m separate factors of production. The vector of factor receipts (v) can then be written:

(4.20) $$v = Vx$$

so that

(4.21) $$v = V[I-A]^{-1}f$$

A similar interpretation can be given to the matrix product $V[I-A]^{-1} = C = \{c_{ij}\}$ as was given to the Leontief inverse. Each c_{ij} represents the direct and indirect increase in the payments to the ith factor when final demand for the jth sector increases by unity.

An assumption required by equation (4.20) is that of constant returns to scale, i.e. a doubling of output requires a doubling in payments to all factors. While constant returns to scale may be a tolerable approximation to reality in the use of intermediate products (Ozaki, 1970), it is unlikely to be so for factor inputs; for example, in the case of physical labour inputs, substantial evidence of economies of scale exists suggesting the relationship:

(4.22) $$l_j = \alpha_j x_j^{\beta j}$$

where l_j is employment in the jth sector and β_j is the elasticity of employment with respect to changes in output, which we assume to be less than unity. The parameters of this expression can be estimated in the log-linear form:

(4.23) $$\log l_j = \log \alpha_j + \beta_j \log x_j$$

so that equations (4.22) and (4.23) can be used to predict employment once the gross output of the jth sector is known. Since the latter is obtained from equation (4.11), there is no reason why the unrealistic assumption of constant returns to scale need be imposed on the employment and other primary input functions.[8]

So far, we have shown how a final bill of goods is translated into a vector of gross outputs from which factor demands can be derived. Factor incomes, however (see Table 1.3), are supplemented by various transfer payments before being distributed to the household accounts, where they are to a large extent spent on consumption. This additional expenditure will provide a further stimulus to output, which will provide additional employment, incomes, etc., so that the picture we have so far described is far from complete.

In Table 4.1, the social accounts for a country have been set out in schematic form. The whole arrangement can be thought of as a partitioned matrix with each submatrix denoted by $T_{i,j}$.[9] Thus, $T_{2,1}$ represents payments to factors of production by activities, while $T_{1,3}$ represents payments to producers for goods and services by households. The balance equations for activities—we ignore for the present the distinction between commodities and industries—are given by:

(4.24) $$x = q_1 = T_{1,1}i + T_{1,3}i + T_{1,4}i + T_{1,5}i$$

In the simplest input–output model, $T_{1,1}$ is related to q_1 through the input–output coefficient matrix ($A = T_{1,1}\hat{q}_1^{-1}$) while the other terms on the right-hand side of equation (4.24) are gathered into the exogenous vector of final demand. However, it seems reasonable to extend the assumption of fixed coefficients to $T_{1,3}$ by assuming that households distribute their income over consumption goods in fixed proportions.

Table 4.1 Schematic social accounting matrix

	Production		Consumption	Accumulation	Trade	Total
	Activities	Factors				
Production						
Activities	$T_{1,1}$	0	$T_{1,3}$	$T_{1,4}$	$T_{1,5}$	q_1
Factors	$T_{2,1}$	0	$T_{2,3}$	0	$T_{2,5}$	q_2
Consumption	0	$T_{3,2}$	$T_{3,3}$	0	$T_{3,5}$	q_3
Accumulation	0	0	$T_{4,3}$	$T_{4,4}$	$T_{4,5}$	q_4
Trade	$T_{5,1}$	0	$T_{5,2}$	0	0	q_5
Total	q'_1	q'_2	q'_3	q'_4	q'_5	

The assumption of fixed coefficients is a strong one and is clearly not appropriate for all submatrices in Table 4.1. However, we can limit ourselves to the transactions amongst the accounts for producers, factors and consumers and form the coefficient matrices:

(4.25) $$B_{ij} = T_{ij}\hat{q}_j^{-1} \qquad i, j = 1, 2, 3$$

so that total incomings for each account (q_j) are distributed in fixed proportions, and B_{11} is the familiar input–output coefficient matrix (A).

In terms of partitioned matrices, we can now write the balance equations for activities, factors and consumers as:

(4.26) $$\begin{bmatrix} q_1 \\ q_2 \\ q_3 \end{bmatrix} = \begin{bmatrix} B_{11} & 0 & B_{13} \\ B_{21} & 0 & B_{23} \\ 0 & B_{32} & B_{33} \end{bmatrix} \begin{bmatrix} q_1 \\ q_2 \\ q_3 \end{bmatrix} + \begin{bmatrix} e_1 \\ e_2 \\ e_3 \end{bmatrix}$$

where the exogenous component of demand for each account is given by the vector e_j.

The above system of equations, if written as:

(4.27) $$q = Bq + e$$

can be seen to have a solution as:

(4.28) $$q = [1 - B]^{-1}e$$

so that the i, jth element of the inverse matrix—$[1 - B]^{-1}$—can be interpreted as the direct and indirect requirements for the ith activity/factor/consumer group per unit of exogenous demand for the jth activity/factor/consumer group. Such an interpretation, however, is somewhat clumsy and in particular fails to separate out a number of different effects.

Consider an exogenous increase for a sector in the activities account (e.g. textile exports). This will result in a stimulus to other sectors, which will require complementary increases in output; this is the conventional multiplier effect of input–output analysis and—following Stone (1978)—we may call it the intra-group effect. In our extended system, however, the impact of the increase in textile exports will be felt also by the accounts for factors and consumers and their efforts to spend their extra income according to equation (4.25) will result in a further stimulus to the activities' account, which we may call the inter-group effect; finally, some of the stimulus to the activities' account will end up in the other accounts and this we may call the extra-group effect.

These three effects, therefore, are contained in the extended inverse $[I-B]^{-1}$, but fortunately the technique of matrix partitioning enables us to separate them out. We may begin by writing the B matrix as:

$$B = \begin{bmatrix} B_{11} & 0 & 0 \\ 0 & 0 & 0 \\ 0 & 0 & B_{33} \end{bmatrix} + \begin{bmatrix} 0 & 0 & B_{13} \\ B_{21} & 0 & B_{23} \\ 0 & B_{32} & 0 \end{bmatrix} \tag{4.29}$$

or

$$B = \tilde{B} + B' \quad \text{(say)} \tag{4.30}$$

which enables us to rewrite equation (4.27) as:

$$q = [B-\tilde{B}]q + \tilde{B}q + e \tag{4.31}$$

or

$$q = [I-\tilde{B}]^{-1}[B-\tilde{B}]q + [I-\tilde{B}]^{-1}e = B^{*}q + [I-\tilde{B}]^{-1}e \tag{4.32}$$

Multiplying both sides of equation (4.32) by B^* gives:

$$B^{*}q = B^{*2}q + B^{*}[I-\tilde{B}]^{-1}e \tag{4.33}$$

and substituting for B^*q in equation (4.32) gives:

$$q = B^{*2}q + [I+B^{*}][I-\tilde{B}]^{-1}e \tag{4.34}$$

Now multiplying both sides of equation (4.32) by B^{*2} and substituting for $B^{*2}q$ from equation (4.34) gives:[10]

$$q = B^{*3}q + [I+B^{*}+B^{*2}][I-\tilde{B}]^{-1}e \tag{4.35}$$

so that

$$q = [I-B^{*3}]^{-1}[I+B^{*}+B^{*2}][I-\tilde{B}]^{-1}e = M_3 M_2 M_1 e = Me \tag{4.36}$$

where

$$M_1 = [I-\tilde{B}]^{-1} = \left[\begin{array}{c|c|c} [I-B_{11}]^{-1} & 0 & 0 \\ \hline 0 & I & 0 \\ \hline 0 & 0 & [I-B_{33}]^{-1} \end{array}\right]$$

$$M_2 = [I + B^* + B^{*2}]$$

$$= \left[\begin{array}{c|c|c} I & \{[I-B_{11}]^{-1}B_{13}\}\{[I-B_{33}]^{-1}B_{32}\} & 0 \\ \hline B_{21} & I & B_{21}[I-B_{11}]^{-1}B_{13} \\ \hline [1-B_{33}]^{-1}B_{32}B_{21} & [I-B_{33}]^{-1}B_{32} & I \end{array}\right]$$

and

$$M_3 = [I - B^{*3}]^{-1}$$

$$= \left[\begin{array}{c|c|c} [I-B^*_{13}B^*_{32}B^*_{21}]^{-1} & 0 & 0 \\ \hline 0 & [I-B^*_{21}B^*_{13}B^*_{32}]^{-1} & 0 \\ \hline 0 & 0 & [I-B^*_{32}B^*_{21}B^*_{13}]^{-1} \end{array}\right]$$

If we now return to equation (4.36), we can see that the total impact of any change in the jth element of the exogenous vector (e) on the ith member of the endogenous vector (q) is measured by the i, jth element of the matrix M. The latter, however, consists of three parts (M_3, M_2, M_1) which combine multiplicatively to give the final result; the first and third parts (M_3, M_1) are block-diagonal[11] and this gives them a straightforward interpretation. M_1, for example, has only three entries, one of which is the unit matrix while another is the Leontief inverse $(I - B_{11})^{-1}$. This matrix, therefore, measures the intra-group or transfer multiplier effects, i.e. those effects which remain within the subsystem where the 'shock' was first introduced; it follows that there can only be intra-group effects when there are diagonal elements in the B matrix; since factors do not make transfers to each other in Table 4.1, the element of M_1 corresponding to factors is just unity, so the total intra-group effect in this case is the same as the exogenous change.

M_3 is also block diagonal, but its interpretation is more complicated; it measures the inter-group or closed-loop multiplier effects, i.e. the impact of the initial injection on the group where it first entered after it has 'toured' through all the other groups; for example, when exogenous payments to an institution such as households rise, they are induced to spend more on consumption, which then enters the production account as a credit; producers then pay factors of production, some of which accrues to households; the 'inter-group' effect in this case therefore measures the total impact on households when exogenous payments to households rise.

From our description of M_1 and M_3, it follows that M_2 captures the extra-group effects, i.e. the impact on one group when exogenous payments for another group change. (In the above example for households, the impact on producers would be an extra-group effect.) We shall return in Chapters 12 and 13 to this extension of the basic input–output model, as it proves a fruitful way of looking at various applications of input–output analysis.

APPENDIX A MATRIX ALGEBRA

Matrix algebra is an indispensable part of input–output analysis and familiarity with its basic principles will be assumed throughout the rest of this book. This appendix, therefore, reviews the main elements of matrix algebra, although readers looking for a more detailed treatment than can be given here would do well to consult one of the many texts on the subject (e.g. Hadley, 1961).

Matrices in input–output work are two-dimensional arrays such as that shown in equation (4.6) of the main text of this chapter. The number of rows of a matrix (m) and the number of columns (n) determine its *type* ($m \times n$) and when the number of rows and columns are the same ($m = n$) the matrix is said to be square and of order n. A vector, on the other hand, is a one-dimensional array of type ($n \times 1$) in the case of a column vector and of type ($1 \times n$) in the case of a row vector.

A very common operation in matrix algebra, much used in input–output work, is that of forming a diagonal matrix from a vector; the latter, when of type ($n \times 1$) for example, can be formed into a matrix of order n by setting the vector on the diagonal of the matrix with zeros everywhere else; such a matrix is known as a diagonal matrix and is denoted by a hat (^). Thus, the diagonal matrix formed from x is $\hat{x}$ of order n and type ($n \times n$).

Now consider the vector (i) whose elements are all equal to unity, i.e.

$$i = \begin{bmatrix} 1 \\ 1 \\ \vdots \\ 1 \end{bmatrix} = \{1 \;\; 1 \;\; \ldots \;\; 1\}$$

This unit vector, when diagonalized, yields the unit matrix (I) with unity on the diagonal and zeros elsewhere. This unit matrix is very important in input–output work since it appears in the solution to the input–output model.

Matrix algebra comprises a set of rules which make it possible to manipulate a series of matrices and vectors arranged in mathematical form. The principal operations performed are addition, subtraction, multiplication, inversion and partitioning; these operations will be used frequently in the rest of this book and each will now be discussed in turn.

1 Matrix Addition and Subtraction

This is possible where two matrices are of the same type (i.e. they have the same number of rows and columns); matrices can be added by adding corresponding elements, and subtracted by subtracting corresponding elements.

2 Matrix Multiplication

If two matrices are to be multiplied, the number of columns in the first (A) must be the same as the number of rows in the second (B). The size of the matrix product (C), however, is given by the number of rows in the first matrix (A) and the number of columns in the second (B). Thus, if A is $(m \times n)$ and B is $(n \times l)$, C will be $(m \times l)$. The rule for matrix multiplication is:

$$c_{ik} = \sum_j a_{ij} b_{jk}$$

where c_{ik}, a_{ij} and b_{jk} are elements of the C, A, B matrices respectively, so that the i,kth element of the new matrix (C) is obtained by multiplying the ith row of A by the kth column of B. It should be noted that, unlike scalar algebra, matrix multiplication is not commutative so that in general $AB \neq BA$.

3 Matrix Division

This operation is roughly equivalent to division in scalar algebra, but it is a much more complicated operation and cannot be properly understood without first discussing the notions of a determinant and matrix inversion.

(i) *The determinant of a matrix.* Consider the matrix A of order n; if we remove the elements in row r and column s, we obtain a smaller matrix of order $(n-1)$. The determinant of this smaller matrix is called the *minor* of a_{rs} in A and is denoted $|A_{rs}|$. When multiplied by $(-1)^{r+s}$, the minor becomes the *co-factor* of a_{rs} in A and the determinant of A can then be written:

$$\text{Det. } A = |A| = \sum_{s}^{n} a_{rs}^{(-1)^{r+s}} |A_{rs}|$$

This still leaves us with the n determinants $|A_{rs}|$ of order $(n-1)$, but 'application of the cofactor expansion method to the cofactors reduces the task of evaluating each cofactor of order $(n-1)$ to that of evaluating $(n-1)$ determinants of order $(n-2)$ etc.' (Hadley, 1961, p. 92). Eventually, the problem can be reduced to finding the determinant of a matrix of type (2×2). In the case of

$$A = \begin{bmatrix} a_{11} & a_{12} \\ a_{21} & a_{22} \end{bmatrix}$$

the determinant is simple det. $A = |A| = (a_{11}a_{22} - a_{12}a_{21})$.

It is not practicable to solve the determinants of matrices with $n > 3$ by hand, but fortunately many computer programmes are available to carry out this work. It should be noted at this stage that the determinant of a matrix is a number or scalar and that only the determinants of square matrices can be found. Furthermore, the determinant of a square matrix can be zero; this will arise when two columns or rows of a matrix are identical or related to each other by a scalar. In this case, the matrix is said to be singular.

(ii) *Matrix inversion.* In scalar algebra, any real number (a) has an inverse (a^{-1}) such that $a^{-1}a = aa^{-1} = 1$. The matrix equivalent of this would be a matrix (B), such that $AB = BA = I$. Fortunately, such a matrix (denoted A^{-1}) can be found under certain circumstances and is called the inverse of (A), i.e.

$$AA^{-1} = A^{-1}A = I$$

Advanced texts (see, for example, Hadley, 1961) have shown that the inverse matrix, here A^{-1}, is formed by the expression:

$$A^{-1} = \frac{1}{|A|}A^{+} \tag{4.1a}$$

where (A^{+}) is called the adjoint of matrix (A) and is the transpose of the matrix obtained from (A) by replacing each element a_{ij} by its cofactor. Although looking formidable, equation (4.1a) does not in fact involve any new concept that of a transposed matrix. This is simply obtained by interchanging rows and columns of a matrix. Thus the transpose of

$$A = \begin{bmatrix} a_{11} & a_{12} \\ a_{21} & a_{22} \end{bmatrix} \quad \text{denoted } A' \text{ is} \quad \begin{bmatrix} a_{11} & a_{21} \\ a_{12} & a_{22} \end{bmatrix}$$

From an examination of equation (4.1a), it should be clear that it will only be possible to form the inverse of a square, non-singular matrix. A rectangular matrix cannot have a determinant, while the determinant of a singular matrix is zero; fortunately, it is almost always possible to derive an A matrix from an input–output table which satisfies both these reqirements.

4 Matrix Partitioning

Suppose we have a square matrix C of the fourth order (i.e. of type 4×4), and let us imagine that it partitions conveniently into the arrangement given by the dotted lines, i.e.

$$C = \left[\begin{array}{c|ccc} c_{11} & c_{12} & c_{13} & c_{14} \\ c_{21} & c_{22} & c_{23} & c_{24} \\ c_{31} & c_{32} & c_{33} & c_{34} \\ \hline c_{41} & c_{42} & c_{43} & c_{44} \end{array}\right] = \begin{bmatrix} C_{11} & C_{12} \\ C_{21} & C_{22} \end{bmatrix} \tag{4.2a}$$

where

$$C_{11} = \begin{bmatrix} c_{11} \\ c_{21} \\ c_{31} \end{bmatrix}, C_{12} = \begin{bmatrix} c_{12} & c_{13} & c_{14} \\ c_{22} & c_{23} & c_{24} \\ c_{32} & c_{33} & c_{34} \end{bmatrix}$$

$$C_{21} = c_{41} \text{ and } C_{22} = [c_{42} \quad c_{43} \quad c_{44}]$$

Each C_{ij} is a submatrix of C, which itself is called a partitioned matrix. The usual rules of matrix algebra apply to matrices in partitioned form; thus, if there exists a matrix D partitioned in the same way as C, we can write:

$$C + D = \begin{bmatrix} C_{11} + D_{11} & C_{12} + D_{12} \\ C_{21} + D_{21} & C_{22} + D_{22} \end{bmatrix} \tag{4.3a}$$

and similarly for subtraction. We can also form the matrix product (CD) provided each submatrix is conformable for multiplication, i.e. there must be as many columns in the i, jth submatrix of C as there are rows in the j, kth submatrix of D. It is also possible to form the inverse of a non-singular partitioned matrix (see, for example, Hadley, 1961).

APPENDIX B STOCHASTIC INPUT–OUTPUT MODELS

The vast majority of input–output models have estimated input–output relationships from one observation assuming constant returns to scale. Although frequently inevitable, this method of estimation has a number of undesirable features; first, the relationship between inputs and output is assumed to be exact or deterministic, so that it is not possible to estimate standard errors for the coefficients and confidence intervals for the predicted values of the xs. Secondly, if the single observation on w_{ij} and x_j is obtained from a series of observations on firms in the jth sector, which may be subject to measurement errors, the estimate of a_{ij} in equation (4.3) will be biased.

We can see this more clearly if we write the observations on the rth firm as:

(4.1b) $$w_{ij}^{(r)} = wt_{ij}^{(r)} + u_{ij}^{(r)}$$

and

(4.2b) $$x_j^{(r)} = xt_j^{(r)} + v_j^{(r)}$$

where $wt_{ij}^{(r)}$, $xt_j^{(r)}$ refer to the true, but unobservable intermediate purchases and output respectively of the rth firm in the jth sector and $u_{ij}^{(r)}$, $v_j^{(r)}$ are the measurement errors assumed to be random with zero mean and constant variance. Assuming the production function is the same for each firm in the sector, we can write the true input–output coefficient as:

(4.3b) $$a_{ij} = \frac{\sum_r wt_{ij}^{(r)}}{\sum_r xt_j^{(r)}}$$

Unfortunately, a_{ij} in equation (4.3b) cannot be estimated; instead we have its estimator $(\hat{a}_{ij})$ given by:

(4.4b) $$\hat{a}_{ij} = \frac{\sum_r wt_{ij}^{(r)} + \sum_r u_{ij}^{(r)}}{\sum_r xt_j^{(r)} + \sum_r v_j^{(r)}}$$

It can be shown (Gerking, 1976, pp. 23–4) that the relationship between these two is given by:

$$(4.5b) \qquad \hat{a}_{ij} = a_{ij} + \left\{ \frac{\sum_r u_{ij}^{(r)} - \dfrac{\sum_r wt_{ij}^{(r)} \sum v_j^{(r)}}{\sum_r xt_j^{(r)}}}{\left[\sum_r xt_j^{(r)} + \sum_r v_j^{(r)} \right]} \right\}$$

and, in general, the expected value of $(\hat{a}_{ij})$ is not equal to a_{ij}, because the second term in equation (4.5b) is not a random variable with zero mean.

For many purposes, these weaknesses of the simple deterministic input–output model will not matter and in the chapters of this book dealing with applications of input–output analysis, models based on equation (4.3) will be frequently used. Readers of this book should be aware, however, of developments in this field and other methods of estimation have been proposed: such estimates require either observations over time or across establishments at a point in time (or both). We shall discuss time-series estimates first.

The most obvious method of estimation for time-series analysis is:

$$(4.6b) \qquad w_{ij}^{(t)} = a_{ij} x_j^{(t)} + \theta_{ij}^{(t)}$$

$$(4.7b) \qquad w_{ij}^{(t)} = b_{ij} + m_{ij} x_j^{(t)} + \varepsilon_{ij}^{(t)}$$

where the superscript t refers to time and θ_{ij}, ε_{ij} are random variables with zero mean. However, the requirement of a set of input–output tables giving comparable data over time on w_{ij} and x_j has proved a most severe obstacle; furthermore, the method assumes inter-temporal stability in input–output coefficients and this is consistent neither with Leontief's theoretical formulation (see above) nor with the facts (see Chapter 10). We shall therefore ignore the time-series approach in the following discussion.

In cross-section analysis, the appropriate estimating equation is either:

$$(4.8b) \qquad w_{ij}^{(r)} = a_{ij} x_j^{(r)} + \theta_{ij}^{(r)}$$

or

$$(4.9b) \qquad w_{ij}^{(r)} = b_{ij} + m_{ij} x_j^{(r)} + \varepsilon_{ij}^{(r)}$$

where the superscript, r refers (as before) to the rth firm and we may begin by considering the more ambitious equation (4.9b). If ordinary least squares (OLS) is used, the method will yield estimates of both the constant (b_{ij}) and the marginal input–output coefficient (m_{ij}), but the estimates will be biased and inconsistent, if $x_j^{(r)}$ and $\varepsilon_{ij}^{(r)}$ are not independent. It is easy to show (Gerking, 1976, p. 26) that this independence is unlikely to be satisfied, so that OLS is not a very satisfactory technique.

Bias and inconsistency in OLS estimators can arise when there are errors in variables (cf. equations (4.1b) and (4.2b) or where there are errors in the way the equations are specified. In both cases, an alternative to OLS which yields consistent estimators is Two-Stage Least Squares (TSLS) and an application of

TSLS using cross-section data from a West Virginia input–output study has been made (Gerking, 1976).

Since Gerking's TSLS estimators are biased (although consistent), it may be asked whether they confer any great advantage over the simple 'ratio' method (see equation (4.4b)), which although biased is also consistent. The answer is that by using an econometric technique, one is immediately supplied with estimates of standard errors which can be used to construct confidence intervals and to choose optimal sample sizes (see appendix to Chapter 3). In turn, confidence intervals are likely to be important when forecasting is a major use to which input–output tables are put.

The TSLS method of estimation is still not widely established in input–output work and a number of criticisms have been voiced (e.g. Brown, 1979). Some of these points have been successfully answered (cf. Gerking, 1979), while others remain; the 'identification' problem, for example (see Kmenta, 1971, pp. 539–46), means that TSLS cannot be applied to equations with a constant term, such as (4.9b), so that only *average* input–output coefficients can be derived. For these reasons, most LDCs are likely to fall back on simpler methods, although this need not prevent them from using the TSLS technique to help in sampling problems, as was shown in the appendix to the previous chapter.

NOTES

1 Throughout this book, x_i will refer to the output of the ith sector when it is not necessary or possible to distinguish between commodity and industry output.

2 This argument has been put more formally elsewhere (de Boer, 1976); it is there shown that the assumption of constant value shares can be supported within the neoclassical framework of cost minimization subject to a production function provided that the latter is of the linear-homogeneous Cobb–Douglas type. Indeed, starting with Diewert (1971), there have been in recent years a series of attempts to derive the Leontief input demand functions from within a neoclassical framework. In the most recent and thorough of these efforts (de Boer, 1979), it is shown that both the 'volume' and 'value' versions of the input demand functions can be derived from cost minimization subject to a two-level CES production function; relative prices, however, appear explicitly in these functions and therefore the validity of the Leontief assumption (in either a value or volume form) is something which can be tested empirically using the more general functions.

3 Where there are several observations on w_{ij} and x_j, it becomes possible to estimate input–output relationships stochastically using econometric techniques. This method is still largely experimental and many LDCs will be prevented from making use of it through data deficiencies; it is likely to become more important in the future, however, and reference was made to this technique in the appendix to the previous chapter dealing with optimal sampling. For both these reasons, there is a brief discussion of stochastic input–output models in Appendix B to this chapter.

4 The evidence on marginal *v.* average coefficients is somewhat confusing; in a study of The Netherlands (Middlehoek, 1970), two-thirds of all non-zero marginal coefficients differed from the equivalent average coefficient at the 95% level, while in a study of Japan (Ozaki, 1970) the assumption of constant returns to scale was found adequate for material inputs, but not for primary inputs.

5 Readers not familiar with matrices and the principal operations of matrix algebra should turn to Appendix A to this chapter.

6 For an interesting two-sector geometric interpretation of the Hawkins–Simon conditions, see Dorfman (1958, p. 213).

7 We can now see the importance of the Hawkins–Simon condition. If any element of the Leontief inverse is negative, at least one r_{ij} is negative and an increase in the final demand for the jth sector would require a fall in the output of the ith sector, which is economically meaningless.

8 Not all primary input functions can be treated in this way, because this could lead to an 'adding-up' problem. However, provided one factor input—profits or other value added—is treated as a residual, this is not a problem.

9 In Table 4.1 we introduce the null matrix 0, whose elements consist entirely of zeros.

10 Clearly this process of multiplication could go on indefinitely; the decision to stop it at B^{*2} corresponds to mathematical convenience and economic logic (see Pyatt, 1979).

11 A block-diagonal matrix is a square matrix with all non-zero entries confined to blocks along the diagonal.

CHAPTER 5

Problems of Classification and Aggregation

5.1 INTRODUCTION

Whether the make and absorption matrices are assembled from sample or census data, as discussed in Chapter 3, some preliminary classification scheme will be needed. The more detailed the scheme, the greater the freedom of choice over the final size of the table; more detail, however, requires more effort at each stage in the preparation of input–output tables so that the *problem of classification* is essentially one of balancing the convenience of flexibility against the inconvenience of extra work.[1]

If the initial completed table is very large, it may for many purposes be necessary to reduce it by aggregating certain sectors. The results obtained, however, from using the input–output model based on the smaller table may not be the same as those obtained by using the larger table and then aggregating; this is known as the *problem of aggregation.*

The input–output literature has been dominated by a concern with the aggregation problem to the almost total neglect of the classification problem. This is understandable, given that the former lends itself to mathematical formulation, but it is nonetheless most unfortunate, particularly in LDCs, where data and resource constraints determine maximum size from an earlier stage in the preparation of tables and this size is often small enough to make the question of aggregation irrelevant. This position is likely to change as the quality of statistics and other resources improve in LDCs, so that a consideration of the aggregation problem in a book such as this is still justified.

The most obvious reason for restrictions on the classification scheme is to avoid 'unnecessary' effort. Data collection and processing is a most time-consuming exercise and the compilation of input–output tables can be accelerated considerably if a smaller rather than a larger table is aimed for initially. On the other hand, input–output tables should be designed with their potential uses in mind. If it is known that the sole use of the input–output table is to provide some disaggregation, say, of the results of a macro-model, then no great harm is done (and a great deal of effort is saved) by opting for a small table right from the start. Tables do, however, and should become public goods on completion;

consequently, the potential uses of the tables are limited only by the imagination of their users, and some of these applications require a very great deal of detail. For example, practitioners of cost–benefit analysis now use input–output tables to calculate the accounting ratios for project appraisal and these ratios are more useful the bigger the size of the table. Marketing applications, too, using input–output tables are of little use on small tables, so there is a strong case for not reducing the classification scheme below what is strictly necessary (see below). For many applications, a small table will suffice, but this can be derived from the larger table by aggregation as suggested below.

Concern with the problem of aggregation started in the early 1950s (Hatanaka, 1952), when a major constraint on the size of the table was computing machine capability. Most uses of input–output models require inversion of matrices, a process which requires a good deal of computer time and core space. As the price of computing comes down, machine capability is a constraint for fewer and fewer LDCs, but it can still impose an upper limit on the size of tables which is low enough to influence the classification scheme.[2]

Sometimes, the construction of an input–output table is simply the first stage in a planning process, which may be based on a dynamic model. If the latter is run over ten years, the model will yield results for each intervening year, so that there will be ten output, employment, income, etc. vectors in the solution. This amount of information is often confusing, rather than illuminating, so there is a very reasonable desire in the case of dynamic modelling to reduce the number of sectors to manageable proportions. If the latter is twenty, while the initial table has 100 sectors, there are clearly a large number of ways in which the table can be aggregated and it is only natural that we should want a method of choosing between them which is in some sense optimal.

The problem of aggregation has often been discussed in terms of the conditions necessary to reduce aggregation bias to zero. Since these conditions are virtually never met in practice, this literature has not been of much operational significance. Fortunately, the emphasis is now shifting towards determining the conditions for *minimizing* aggregation bias; the latter is clearly of much more relevance where problems of input–output construction are in question.[3] The literature on aggregation can clearly be of relevance when we start from a large completed table and wish to reduce it for modelling or computational purposes. It can also be of use, however, where a different problem is faced, namely how to prepare a single table from dissimilar elementary or sampling units. In other words, it may be possible to avoid or reduce aggregation bias even at the *classification* stage by paying attention to the conditions for minimizing bias at the *aggregation* stage. We shall return to this problem below, but first what is needed is consideration of the classification problem in more depth.

5.2 THE PROBLEM OF CLASSIFICATION

As stated above, data limitations are sometimes so powerful as to remove any element of choice over the classification scheme. The most important of these restrictions is provided by the 'control' total; if sample data are used,[4] there must always be some point of correspondence with the population and this is provided either by the elementary (number of employees, dollars of sales, etc.) or sampling unit (the establishment or firm). The population data, or sampling frame, come from official statistics so that the latter provide the first effective restraint on classification.[5]

In this context, the Moroccan input–output table for 1975 is instructive; the elementary unit was the employee and the greatest level of detail at which official statistics list employees is the *sous-branche*; as there were some 150 of these, of which 103 were in mining and manufacturing, this gave a preliminary restriction on the classification scheme. In the Scottish input–output table the elementary unit was also the employee, which is provided by official statistics at Minimum List Heading (MLH) level; with 181 MLHs, this again provided a preliminary restriction on table size. In Costa Rica, on the other hand, the elementary unit was a dollar of sales, which gave a maximum initial table size of nearly 100 sectors.

Without revisions in the methodology of official statistics, therefore, it is impossible to present tables in excess of the size thereby imposed. Although tables with more than 100 sectors appear large even by today's standards, there are a number of reasons for dissatisfaction with the constraints provided by official statistics. First, they often do not conform to the conditions required (see below) for eliminating aggregation bias; even at the maximum level of disaggregation, therefore, some aggregation bias may be built in. Official classifications of the engineering sectors, for example, usually refer to a large number of different products with a variety of uses, while every official classification always includes the rubrics 'other manufacturing', 'other services', etc. which are very difficult to reconcile with the conditions for zero aggregation bias. Although official statistics try to furnish information on 'units which are relatively homogeneous in respect of the character, cost-structure and technology of production' (United Nations, 1968), it is clear that this aim is far from fulfilment. Nonetheless, without a 100% sample, there is very little the input–output worker can do about it.[6]

The second problem with official statistics is that they ignore activities which are about to come into existence. Fortunately, this problem is easily overcome by allocating a row and column in the absorption and make matrices to the relevant activity; in the base period used for the construction of the tables, all elements of these vectors will be zero except in the case of the row of the absorption matrix which then refers to imports. (This was the treatment adopted in Scotland in the 1973 table for the activity of producing crude oil, which it was known would become important in the years ahead.) In fact, any activity can be 'slotted in' to the table at a later date, but it is easier if the decision is made at the construction stage so that absorptions can be separately identified.

Apart from these problems of official statistics, there are further considerations which affect the classification scheme, the first two of which can be taken together as they are rather similar. The first concerns the problems encountered in identifying the supplier of a purchase and the second that of identifying the user of a sale. The first problem arises where the columns of the absorption matrix are built up from purchases data, while the second occurs when the rows of the absorption and/or make matrices are constructed from sales or production data.

Where purchases data are used, each input recorded in the questionnaire must be allocated to one and one only supplying sector; ignoring the special problem of unallocated purchases (see Chapter 11), this raises difficulties because the product description may be insufficient to identify the commodity of supply; in Scotland, for example, the initial classification scheme for commodities was based on a five-digit code, which gave fifteen divisions alone for the commodity grouping 'iron and steel products'. Establishments, however, tended to describe their inputs at a three-digit level, which reduced our fifteen-fold classification to a single one. Questionnaire response, therefore, determined the treatment of this group of products in the classification scheme, and a great deal of unnecessary work could have been avoided if this problem had been anticipated.[7]

The rows of a make matrix are constructed from information on sales or production by establishments and any inadequacies in the description of products made can result in restrictions on the size of the classification scheme; sometimes, however, absorption matrices also are prepared from sales data, although this technique will not be discussed in detail until Chapter 11. In the author's Costa Rican tables, for example, the imported component of absorptions was calculated from trade data, i.e. total imports in each commodity group were first calculated and then distributed across the rows of an 'import absorption' matrix according to user. The distribution was done using a two-digit code, which put very severe restrictions on the classification scheme. Indeed if a column vector rather than a matrix of imports had been adopted, the classification scheme could have been increased from 41 to 65 sectors (Bulmer-Thomas, 1977a).

Other considerations also will affect the classification scheme. The confidentiality of individual questionnaire returns must usually be preserved so that certain industries represented by one establishment may have to be aggregated with others; this can be a source of great difficulty where the industrial base is small or characterized by monopolistic features and there is no simple solution of how to aggregate the single-firm sectors with others. The best solution, if this is practical, is to retain the one-firm industries in the classification scheme for working purposes and then use one of the criteria for minimizing aggregation bias (see below) to determine the classification scheme for publication purposes.

The factors influencing the classification scheme may affect the rows and columns of the make and absorption matrices differently. Indeed, two cases must be considered where the number of identifiable activities is less than the number of identifiable commodities and vice versa. The first case gives rise to more rows than columns in the matrices, but no special difficulties are produced by this and it avoids the waste of useful information. In the most recent Brazilian tables, for example (IBGE, 1979), 90 activities and 165 commodities are separately identified in the make and absorption matrices. Although the final input–output table itself needs to be square if inversion is to be carried out, there is no reason why greater detail should not be preserved in the primary matrices.

The second case occurs where the number of identifiable rows or commodities is less than the number of columns or activities. At one time, this was thought to be such a widespread occurrence in LDCs that it became the basis of a modified input–output model (Seers, 1966). In this Seers model, there is no possibility of matrix inversion so that the range of applications of the model is severely restricted. Some work has been done on extending the Seers model so that matrix inversion can be performed, but it involves a number of arbitrary assumptions and it is therefore preferable to make every effort at the data processing stage to see that the number of commodities is at least as great as the number of activities.

So far, we have considered restrictions on the classification scheme over which the input–output worker has little or no control. Any further restrictions will therefore be self-imposed and should depend on the conditions for minimizing aggregation bias; we shall therefore return to the classification scheme below after discussing aggregation bias.

5.3 THE PROBLEM OF AGGREGATION—ZERO BIAS

From now on it will be assumed that a 'large' input–output table has been completed from which we wish to derive a 'small' one by aggregation. Although the large or micro-table will not be free of errors, we can distinguish between those errors in the aggregated or macro-table which have simply been transferred from the micro-table and those which arise as a result of aggregation. It is the latter type of error which concerns us here.

It is assumed that the coefficients of the micro-table (A) are obtained from the absorption matrix (W) by dividing each element in the jth column by the appropriate gross output (x_j) and that a similar process is used to obtain the coefficients of the macro-table (A^*), i.e.

$$A = {}_0W_0\hat{x}^{-1} \tag{5.1}$$

Where the subscript 0 refers to the base period and the hat denotes a diagonal matrix.

$$A^* = {}_0W^*{}_0\hat{x}^{*-1} \tag{5.2}$$

The two input–output tables are linked by a grouping matrix (S) which has as many rows (m) as the aggregated table and as many columns (n) as the micro-table, i.e.

$${}_0W^* = S_0WS' \tag{5.3}$$

where a prime (′) denotes a transposed matrix and

$$S = \begin{array}{c} \\ 1 \\ 2 \\ \vdots \\ m \end{array} \begin{array}{c} 1\ 2\ 3 \qquad \ldots \qquad\qquad n \\ \begin{bmatrix} 1, & \ldots & 1;0 & \ldots & & & 0 \\ 0, & \ldots, & 0;1 & \ldots & 1;0 & \ldots & 0 \\ & & \vdots & & & \vdots & \\ 0 & & & \ldots, & 0;1 & \ldots & 1 \end{bmatrix} \end{array}$$

We want to find out the relationship between (A) and (A^*). Let us therefore write:

$$A^*{}_0\hat{x}^* = {}_0W^* = S_0WS' = SA_0\hat{x}S' \tag{5.4}$$

therefore

$$A^* = SA[{}_0\hat{x}S'{}_0\hat{x}^{*-1}] \tag{5.5}$$

The term in brackets on the right-hand side of equation (5.5) is a weighting matrix (Morimoto, 1970) whose elements record the base year weights within each aggregated sector in terms of the micro-sectors. If we call this matrix Z, we have:

$$Z = {}_0\hat{x}S'{}_0\hat{x}^{*-1}$$

where

$$Z = \begin{bmatrix} Z_1 & 0 & \dots & 0 \\ 0 & Z_2 & & \vdots \\ \vdots & \vdots & \ddots & \\ 0 & 0 & \dots & Z_m \end{bmatrix}$$

and Z_J is a column vector, whose elements z_j record the share of the jth micro-sector in the Jth macro-sector's gross output in the base period and $\Sigma z_j = 1$ for each Z_J.

If we now return to equation (5.5)—written in the form $A^* = SAZ$—we may note that we have found a way of writing (A^*) in terms of (A). The elements of (Z), however, are base year weights; if these should change, (A^*) will need to change even if there is no change in (A). It follows that aggregation bias will arise, if the base year weights change or if we cannot anticipate the change in weight for the forecast period. Since the latter is very difficult, we must assume that one condition for avoiding aggregation bias is to group sectors in such a way that the base year weights do *not* change and this will only be the case where the products of grouped industries are distributed in the same way to all users (Malinvaud, 1956).

We can see from equation (5.5) that any element of the macro-table can be written as a weighted average of the elements of the micro-table. Consequently, there may be certain configurations among the micro-coefficients which make the weights irrelevant. In order to explain this possibility, let us write the solution to the micro-model[8] as:

$$x = [I - A]^{-1} f \tag{5.6}$$

where f is a $(n \times 1)$ vector of final demands and $[I - A]^{-1}$ is the Leontief inverse, so that the 'true' solution to the macro-model is given by:

$$x^* = Sx \tag{5.7}$$

The 'approximate' solution to the macro-model, however, is given by:

$$x_e^* = [I - A^*]^{-1} f^* \tag{5.8}$$

where the subscript e denotes an estimated value, so that the vector of aggregation bias (b) is defined as:

$$b = x_e^* - x^* = [I - A^*]^{-1} f^* - S[I - A]^{-1} f \tag{5.9}$$

or

$$b = \{[I - A^*]^{-1} S - S[I - A]^{-1}\} f \tag{5.10}$$

Now the Leontief inverse matrices can be approximated by power-series expansions (see Chapter 4), so we can rewrite equation (5.10) as:

$$b = \{[I + A^* + A^{*2} + \dots]S - S[I + A + A^2 + \dots]\} f \tag{5.11}$$

i.e.

$$b = \{[A^*S - SA] + [A^{*2}S - SA^2] + \dots\} f \tag{5.12}$$

since $IS = SI$.

We have now broken down the bias into a series of terms involving powers of (A) and (A^*). The first term $[A^*S - SA]$ is therefore known as *first-order* bias (Theil, 1957), the second as *second-order* bias and the whole expression is known as total aggregation bias. Because of the way equation (5.12) is written, it is possible to work out the conditions not only for zero total bias, but also for zero first-order bias. (The latter, of course, is not a sufficient condition for $b = 0$.)

If we look at equation (5.12) we can see instantly that one condition for zero bias (both total and first-order) is $A^*S = SA$. What does this condition mean in practice? Let us assume that the micro-table is of size (3×3) and that it is planned to aggregate sectors two and three. Then:

$$A^*S = \begin{bmatrix} a_{11}^* & a_{12}^* \\ a_{21}^* & a_{22}^* \end{bmatrix} \begin{bmatrix} 1 & 0 & 0 \\ 0 & 1 & 1 \end{bmatrix} = \begin{bmatrix} a_{11}^* & a_{12}^* & a_{12}^* \\ a_{21}^* & a_{22}^* & a_{22}^* \end{bmatrix}$$

and

$$SA = \begin{bmatrix} 1 & 0 & 0 \\ 0 & 1 & 1 \end{bmatrix} \begin{bmatrix} a_{11} & a_{12} & a_{13} \\ a_{21} & a_{22} & a_{23} \\ a_{31} & a_{32} & a_{33} \end{bmatrix} = \begin{bmatrix} a_{11} & a_{12} & a_{13} \\ (a_{21} + a_{31}) & (a_{22} + a_{32}) & (a_{23} + a_{33}) \end{bmatrix}$$

The conditions for $b = 0$ are therefore $a_{11} = a_{11}^*$; $a_{12} = a_{12}^*$; $a_{13} = a_{12}^*$; $(a_{21} + a_{31}) = a_{21}^*$; $(a_{22} + a_{32}) = a_{22}^*$; $(a_{23} + a_{33}) = a_{22}^*$ so that we require for the micro-table $a_{12} = a_{13}$ and $(a_{22} + a_{32}) = (a_{23} + a_{33})$, since the other conditions are already met.

This requirement is known as the condition of homogeneous input structures (Theil, 1957 and Ara, 1959) and it has often been misunderstood. It does not mean that for zero bias the activities forming the aggregated sector must have identical input coefficients; it does mean, however, that each activity in an aggregate sector (J) requires the same inputs per unit of output from the aggregate sector (I). In our simple example, the aggregate sector comprises activities 2 and 3; the former's call on the aggregate sector per unit of output is $(a_{22} + a_{32})$, while the latter's is

$(a_{23}+a_{33})$; as long as these composite coefficients are equal, the condition of homogeneous input structures is fulfilled.[9]

So far, we have assumed that the grouping matrix (S) consists of a series of unit vectors. Such a matrix corresponds to a special case of weighted aggregation where unit weights are attached to each original sector (Morimoto, 1971). It may be the case, however, that a more general weighted aggregation scheme is preferred so that each micro-sector can receive more or less than unit weight in the macro-table. Let us call such a grouping matrix G; then, as before, the condition for zero aggregation bias can be shown to be $GA = A^*G$ (Morimoto, 1971). Since the elements of G are now free to take on any values, however, the conditions for zero aggregation bias are less rigid. Indeed, a necessary condition for zero bias is that the A matrix should now be either (1) indecomposable[10] or (2) completely decomposable or (3) cyclic.[11,12]

None of these matrix structures are very common in practice and there is no obvious way of choosing the weights which will provide zero bias, so that the fruits of this mathematical labour are somewhat thin.[13] If we return to equation (5.12), however, we may note that bias is not only a function of the coefficient matrix, but also of the vector of final demand. It is therefore worth considering what restrictions have to be met by this vector if bias is to be avoided, since this may prove a more rewarding line of attack in practice.

Several cases have been identified where restrictions on the final demand vector will produce zero aggregation bias regardless of the structure of the A matrix. They are stated here without proof as:

1 All components of final demand in the micro-table are proportional to the corresponding component of final demand in the base period, i.e. $f = k\,{}_0f$ where k is the scalar of proportionality (Theil, 1957, p. 120).

2 In the more realistic case, where the factor of proportionality is the same *within* each aggregated sector, but differs *between* aggregated sectors, then this *may* result in zero first-order bias, but even that is not certain.[14]

3 First-order aggregation bias will be zero if the structure of final demand *within* each aggregated sector is the same as the structure of the corresponding outputs in the base period (Morimoto, 1970): i.e. $f_j/f_J^* = {}_0x_j/{}_0x_J^*$ for all $j \in J$.

4 First-order aggregation bias will be zero, if some sectors are not aggregated and any change in final demand from the base period occurs only in the unaggregated sectors (Morimoto, 1970): i.e. $f_I^* = {}_0f_I^*$ for all aggregated sectors and $f_i = {}_0f_i + \Delta f_i$ for all unaggregated sectors.

Three of the four restrictions on final demand only ensure zero first-order bias, but this is likely to be the most important component of total bias. It appears then that the structure of the f vector offers more hope than the A matrix for selecting an aggregation scheme from our micro-table which avoids bias and we shall return to this important point below. Since, however, these restrictions are never likely to be completely fulfilled, we must now look at methods which are designed simply to *minimize* aggregation bias.

5.4 THE PROBLEM OF AGGREGATION—MINIMUM BIAS

It will be recalled that the vector of aggregation bias can be written as $b = x^*_e - x^*$. We now want to select an aggregation scheme so as to minimize this bias;[15] as it stands, however, b is an inappropriate criterion, because positive and negative deviations will cancel out. It has therefore been suggested (Fisher, 1958) that we take as our criterion minimization of the trace[16] of the second moment around zero of the aggregation bias,[17] i.e.

$$\text{(5.13)} \qquad \text{Min. } C = \text{tr } E(x^*_e - x^*)(x^*_e - x^*)'$$

where E denotes an expected value and C is a scalar.

This is not yet an operational expression, because x^*_e depends on A^*, S and f. However, we can make use of equation (5.10) and rewrite equation (5.13) as:

$$\text{(5.14)} \qquad \text{Min. } C = \text{tr } E\{[(I^* - A^*)^{-1}S - S(I - A)^{-1}]f\} \times \{[(I^* - A^*)^{-1}S - S(I - A)^{-1}]f\}'$$

where the criterion (C) for minimizing bias is now a function of the coefficient matrices, the aggregation matrix and the final demand vector. A can be assumed stable, and S will depend on what aggregation scheme we want to implement. We can therefore minimize C with respect to A^* *provided* we can simplify equation (5.14) by imposing certain restrictions on the final demand vector.

Fisher (1958) suggests the following restrictions. He assumes that each final demand in the micro-table (f_j) is a random variable with mean equal to its base year value, with variance proportional to the mean and all covariances zero, i.e.

$$E(f_j) = {}_0f_j; \text{ Var } (f_j) = v({}_0f_j) \text{ and } (\text{Cov } f_j f_k) = 0$$

Making use of these restrictions we can then write equation (5.14) (see Neudecker, 1970) as:

$$\text{(5.15)} \quad C = \text{tr } [(I - A^*)^{-1}S - S(I - A)^{-1}]\, {}^{00}\hat{f}\, [(I - A^*)^{-1}S - S(I - A)^{-1}]'$$

where ${}^{00}\hat{f} = v{}_0\hat{f} + {}_0f{}_0f'$, i.e. the second moment around zero of the micro-vector of final demand.

Equation (5.15) is now operational: for a *given* aggregation scheme (S), it can be minimized with respect to (A^*). If different schemes are tried, we can then choose that one which yields the smallest value for C. Minimizing equation (5.15) leads to the solution:

$$\text{(5.16)} \qquad [I - A^*]^{-1} = S[I - A]^{-1}\, {}^{00}\hat{f}S'(S\, {}^{00}\hat{f}S')^{-1}$$

from which we can obtain the optimal value of (A^*) corresponding to any specific aggregation scheme (see Neudecker, 1970, p. 923). These values of (A^*) can then be inserted in equation (5.15) to see which gives minimum bias.

At first sight, Fisher's method (as we shall call it) looks attractive. For example, if we have three or four aggregation schemes between which we are undecided, we can apply equation (5.16) for each S and use the solution for $[I - A^*]^{-1}$ in equation (5.15) to find the scheme which gives minimum bias. Unfortunately, we will never know whether the resulting bias is greater or less than the bias associated with some *other* scheme with which we did not experiment. In his original paper, Fisher (1958) experimented with the reduction of an 18×18 matrix for the USA to an 8×8 table. With such a small 'micro-table', the number of realistic permutations for S is not prohibitive, but where the micro-table is of order 100 or more, this will not be the case; an arbitrary selection of a handful of aggregation schemes cannot guarantee us minimum bias. It seems, therefore, that unless the choice of aggregation scheme is for some reason severely restricted, we need to try an alternative approach.[18]

Let us now return to the vector of aggregation bias defined by equation (5.12). It can be seen from this equation that the input–output coefficients of the macro- and micro-tables play a crucial role in determining aggregation bias. The more 'similar' the input structures of two activities in the micro-table, the less danger of introducing bias by aggregating them. 'Similarity', however, is a rather loose criterion to adopt for minimizing bias and it needs to be replaced by something more precise.

In a recent work (van Driel, 1980), aggregation bias is minimized according to the criterion of 'highly correlated input structures'. This criterion then lends itself to the method of factor analysis which seeks out the number of common factors from among the micro-sectors; these common factors then become the macro-sectors of the aggregated table, so that there is no need to list the alternative aggregation schemes in advance.

This method has been applied with some success to the 55-sector micro-tables of various EEC countries and the number of common factors (i.e. macro-sectors) is almost uniform (between 14 and 16 for all countries). Factor analysis, therefore, represents a distinct advance on the somewhat *ad hoc* procedures often adopted in aggregation of input–output tables. Apart from formidable computational problems, however, it suffers from the difficulty that we have little or no control over the aggregation scheme. Furthermore, even though we can decree the number of macro-sectors, we cannot be sure that the groupings of the micro-sectors will make much economic sense.

It is therefore worth showing one other method, which has been developed recently to cope with the problem of aggregation. As before, it is assumed that the criterion for grouping the micro-sectors should be the notion of technological similarity; if each group is thought of as a 'cluster', then the object is to make the members of the cluster as 'similar' as possible and as 'dissimilar' as possible from non-members.

As in any clustering problem, we need to find m clusters from n objects defined by q attributes. In input–output analysis, the n objects are the column vectors $(a_1, a_2, \ldots, a_n)$ of the micro-table. The q attributes for the jth object are the jth column's input–output elements $(a_{1j}, a_{2j}, \ldots, a_{qj})$. If we now join any micro-sector to the first micro-sector, we need a measure of dissimilarity so that we can compare it with the result achieved when some other sector is added instead. If this measure is provided by Euclidian distance, it can be written for the pth cluster as:

$$E_p = \sum_{j=1}^{n_p} \sum_{i=1}^{q} (a_{ij(p)} - \bar{a}_{i(p)})^2 \tag{5.17}$$

where $\bar{a}_{i(p)}$ is the mean value for the i,jth coefficient in the pth cluster (i.e. $1/n_p \Sigma_j a_{ij}$), $a_{ij(p)}$ is the i,jth coefficient in the pth cluster and there are n_p sectors in the pth cluster. In the simplest case where the pth cluster consists of micro-sectors 1 and 2, and each sector has three inputs—(a_{11}, a_{21}, a_{31}) (a_{12}, a_{22}, a_{32}) respectively—we get the following expression:

$$\begin{aligned} E_p = {} & (a_{11(p)} - a_{1(p)})^2 + (a_{21(p)} - \bar{a}_{2(p)})^2 + (a_{31(p)} - \bar{a}_{3(p)})^2 \\ & + (a_{12(p)} - \bar{a}_{1(p)})^2 + a_{22(p)} - \bar{a}_{2(p)})^2 + (a_{32(p)} - \bar{a}_{3(p)})^2 \end{aligned} \tag{5.18}$$

which will be zero, when the two sectors have identical input structures because $a_{ij(p)} = \bar{a}_{i(p)}$. Now E_p is a measure of dissimilarity for one cluster and if we sum across all p we get:

$$E = \sum_{p=1}^{m} E_p \tag{5.19}$$

which is the total within-group-error-sum-of-squares. Consequently, one criterion for the fusion of micro-sectors into clusters and small clusters into large clusters is to choose that fusion which produces the least increase in E.

This approach has been applied by Blin and Cohen (1977) to the 1967 input–output table for the USA which is of order 83. The clustering algorithm they chose continues to fuse clusters until only one is left; at each step in the fusion process, however, two values are determined: first is the number of clusters (i.e. macro-sectors) and second is the aggregation bias. We can therefore stop the fusion process either when we have reached a given level of aggregation or when we reach the limit of acceptable aggregation bias. The method, therefore, gives greater control over the aggregation scheme than is provided by factor analysis.

For implementation in the case of input–output tables two problems have to be resolved; the first is whether to standardize the elements of the A matrix and the second is whether to make the similarity test dependent on the columns of the A matrix or the Leontief inverse. As far as the first point is concerned, Blin and Cohen take an agnostic viewpoint; since differences in value added per unit of output are dimensions of dissimilarity between production functions, they experiment with excluding and including the value added coefficient, and they found that inclusion increases the number of macro-sectors which need to be distinguished, when a given level of dissimilarity is chosen. In the second case, they also experiment, but there can be little doubt that basing the similarity test on the Leontief inverse is more consistent with the conditions for zero aggregation bias.

5.5 CONCLUSIONS

It appears, then, that there is no lack of methods for optimal aggregation of a large input–output table. For the success of these methods, however, it is necessary in general to have the inverse of the micro-table and to have the time and resources required for the considerable amount of computational work involved. Two questions therefore suggest themselves for LDCs: (1) Are there any short-cuts to the optimal aggregation? (2) What procedure must be adopted if we want to reduce the classification scheme before inversion of the micro-table?

The conditions for zero aggregation bias can be summarized as follows:

1 The products of grouped industries must be distributed in the same way to all users.

2 Homogeneous Input Structures.

3 When the weight of the grouping matrix can take on any values, the input–output coefficient matrix must be indecomposable, completely decomposable or cyclic.

4 The micro-bill of final demands must be proportional to the base year.

5 If the factor of proportionality is the same within each macro-sector, then first-order bias *may* be avoided.

6 First-order bias *will* be avoided if the structure of final demand, *within* each aggregated sector, is the same as the structure of the corresponding outputs in the base period.

7 First-order bias will be zero, if some sectors are not aggregated and any change in final demand occurs only in the unaggregated sectors.

Each of these conditions may help to answer question (2) above. For example, there are often micro-sectors whose outputs are sold only to final demand (processed foods are a good example) and for which the income elasticity of demand is similar; Condition (1) would therefore be met by aggregating such sectors. Conditions (2) and (3) are unlikely to be much help in practice, and Condition (4) is too restrictive, but condition (5) looks helpful, although it depends on the vanishing of the M^2 covariances (see Note 14). Condition (6) may be satisfied in certain cases and can be tested by reference to simple time-series analysis.

Condition (7) is in many ways the most useful of all; a large number of experiments with input–output tables involve simulations for one industry, i.e. assessing the direct and indirect effects of a change in final demand for the industry in question on the rest of the economy. It has been known for a long time (Balderston, 1954) that the results of these experiments are remarkably insensitive to the level of aggregation and Condition (7) provides the theoretical underpinning for this insensitivity.[19] Consequently, if the applications of the input–output tables are to be restricted to these kinds of simulations, we can afford to aggregate all those sectors which are not candidates for final demand change. In the Moroccan input–output study, for example, as its name implies,[20] the mining and manufacturing sectors were singled out for special attention and that is one reason why it was possible to give a very aggregated treatment to other sectors.

Thus, in answer to Question (2), there is much that can be done to reduce the size of the classification scheme without the need for inverting a micro-table. Whether or not these procedures are consistent with optimal aggregation, however, depends on the criterion of optimality adopted: all the criteria we have examined make reference to similarities in the structure of the A matrix, whereas only two of the seven conditions listed above do so. In providing an answer to Question (1), therefore, it is necessary to look elsewhere.

The most promising short-cuts to optimal aggregation are provided by the methods of factor and cluster analysis. We noted above how similar the number of common factors appeared to be for the members of the EEC. This suggests that other countries with similar economic structures could use the results of the factor analysis without the need to apply the method itself. In the case of LDCs, this could prove most advantageous; suppose, for example, factor analysis had revealed 25 common factors in the case of the Brazilian input–output table. Then this aggregation scheme could be used by other large Latin American countries (Mexico, Argentina, Venezuela) in the knowledge that the result is likely to be close to optimality.

In the case of cluster analysis, a similar procedure suggests itself. Suppose, for example, results were available for an LDC (X) whose economic structure is 'similar' to another (Y). If the results are presented in detail, so that the fusion process is recorded right back to the micro-table, then, Y can select its aggregation scheme simply by reference to the scale of dissimilarity or to the required number of macro-sectors. For example, if Y wants to run experiments on an input–output model in which more than ten sectors is inconvenient, it can select that lowest level of dissimilarity in the fusion process which leaves only ten sectors in Xs input–output table.

These 'short-cuts', unfortunately, cannot yet be applied in LDCs, because even the complete methods of optimal aggregation are still in the experimental stage and have only been applied to developed countries. There is every reason to believe, however, that the methods will be more generally applied in the future.

NOTES

1 There is an asymmetry in the construction of input–output tables, since it is a simple matter to reduce the size of an initial table through aggregation, but a very difficult one to increase it through disaggregation.

2 The computer belonging to the Statistics Office imposed a limit on the size of the 1975 Moroccan table of about 60 sectors. Since the final table was (70 × 70) and since for working purposes a 100-sector table was used, computations had to be carried out elsewhere.

3 Aggregation from a larger to a smaller table is normally carried out on a completed input–output table. By discussing the problem of aggregation in this chapter, we therefore anticipate the argument of the next few chapters, but it seems most natural to discuss the problems of classification and aggregation together.

4 If census data are used, the correspondence between sample data and sample frame should, of course, be perfect, but in practice (see Chapter 3) some units are usually omitted from the census so that 'grossing up' is necessary and the above remarks on samples therefore apply equally to a census.

5 There is one exception; where a 100% sample is taken by the input–output team (with no omission for small or artisan firms), then the data can be presented at a finer level of detail than official statistics.

6 Even with a 100% sample, difficulties remain because updating the input–output table will have to rely on official statistics unless another 100% sample is taken.

7 The problem of over-ambitious classification schemes is particularly acute in textiles, wood products and chemicals. It can be avoided to some extent by using a 'structured' questionnaire (see Chapter 11) or by letting firms know at what level of detail absorptions should be described.

8 It is assumed that readers are now familiar with the solution to the input–output model (see Chapter 4) and know what is meant by the Leontief inverse and power-series expansions.

9 In our three activity case, it turned out that we also required $a_{12} = a_{13}$. The reason for this is that the first activity is transferred unchanged to the macro-table, so that there is only one input for the aggregated sector to draw on from the first sector in the macro-table and that is why we require $a_{12} = a_{13}$.

10 An indecomposable matrix is one where it is *not* possible to rearrange rows and columns so that all non-zero elements appear either above or on the main diagonal, where the latter consists of blocks of square submatrices. A decomposable matrix is one where it *is* possible to arrange the rows and columns in this way and a *completely* decomposable matrix is one where all non-zero elements are on the block-diagonal and each block is indecomposable.

11 For the definition of a cyclic matrix, see Morimoto, 1971, p. 146.

12 But not sufficient in the cases of (1) and (3), since in the first case we also require aggregation into one all-inclusive sector, while in the third there are further restrictions on the products of the partitioned (cyclic) matrix (Morimoto, 1971, p. 141).

13 If the coefficients of the micro-table are estimated by cross-section regression analysis (Gerking, 1976), it turns out that there are still more circumstances under which the structure of the A matrix can yield zero bias, but the practical importance of these structures is very small.

14 First-order bias will be zero if the following M^2 covariances are zero (see Theil, 1957, p. 119):

$$\sum_{j \in J} z_j \left(a^*_{IJ} - \sum_{i \in I} a_{ij} \right) \frac{f_j}{z_j} \qquad (I, J = 1, \ldots, M)$$

15 It is assumed that some kind of prediction or forecast model is involved. If the analysis is confined to the base year, ${}_0x^*_e = {}_0x^*$ and the bias is zero. Bias can only arise when we wish to predict future values for the aggregated output vector using the short-cut equation (5.8), so that it is 'prediction error' which we want to minimize.

16 The trace of a square matrix A is defined as the sum of its diagonal elements and is denoted by TrA.

17 In what follows we make use of a paper by Neudecker (1970), which has extended Fisher's pioneering work in a number of directions.

18 A further criticism of the Fisher method concerns the restrictions on the final demand vector, in particular the vanishing of the covariances, since this implies that there are no complementarities in final demand.

19 Although Condition (7) only generates the absence of first-order bias, this is likely to be the most important source.

20 'Etude d'identification et d'évaluation des possibilites d'investissements *industriels.*' See Dar Al-Handasah (1979).

CHAPTER 6

The Valuation of Transactions

6.1 INTRODUCTION

In this chapter, we assume that preliminary versions of the make and absorption matrices are available. The column sums of the make matrix represent the supply of commodities, while the row sums of the absorption matrix (including final demand) represent the demand for commodities. The accounting identities discussed in Chapters 1 and 2 require supply and demand for each commodity to be equal, but this is unlikely to be the case at this stage.

Part of the reason for the imbalance is simple enough. As explained in Chapter 3, the absorption matrix is usually built up column by column on the basis of purchases; the make matrix, however, is based on sales or production data. Quite apart from sampling and other errors, therefore, supply of any commodity is unlikely to equal demand, because the former reflects the prices received by producers, while the latter reflects the prices paid by purchasers.

There are many different ways in which the supply of and demand for commodities can be reconciled to take account of the different prices used. The choice between these different methods is an important one, since it will affect many aspects of input–output table construction, as well as the stability of input–output coefficients themselves. In this chapter, an effort is made to identify the principal ways in which transactions in input–output tables can be valued to achieve consistency between commodity supply and demand and to lay down criteria for choosing between them.

6.2 METHODS OF VALUATION

We may begin by assuming that a preliminary version of the input–output table has been prepared from absorption and make matrices with columns added for final demand. This table would normally have commodities in the rows and industries in the columns and this is the table on which valuation adjustments should be carried out; we shall make things simpler for ourselves, however, by assuming that there is no secondary production so that commodity and industry output are the same and we will also assume that the gap between the supply of and demand for commodities (industries) is accounted for by the use of different valuation conventions.[1]

With two sectors producing commodities, a transport industry and a distribution network, the input–output table might look like the one described in Figure 6.1. Commodity supply (taken from the make matrix) is shown on the left-hand side of the table while the demand for commodities, which is simply the sum of intermediate and final demand, is shown on the right-hand side. The first point to note about the table, therefore, is that supply and demand do not balance in any of the rows and that demand for transport and distribution services is zero.

Commodity supply	1	2	*T*	*D*	Final demand	Commodity demand	
100	36	35	12	12	27	122	Sector 1
100	24	35	—	—	63	122	Sector 2
15	—	—	—	—	—	0	Transport (*T*)
29	—	—	—	—	—	0	Distribution (*D*)
	40	30	3	17			Value added
	100	100	15	29			Industry output

Figure 6.1 Unbalanced input–output table (Purchasers' prices)

The reason why the transport and distribution rows of the table are empty is that entries in each column of the table are assumed to be denominated in the prices paid by purchasers (purchasers' prices), while commodity (industry) supply is assumed to be at the prices received by producers at the farm or factory gate (producers' prices). What the purchaser pays includes any transport or distribution margins which must be added to the price of goods when they leave the farm or factory; these margins appear in the table *as if* they were paid to the producers of the goods and that is why the table is unbalanced.

As stated in the introduction to this chapter, there are many ways in which the table could be made to balance. A necessary condition for a balanced table is that commodity supply and demand must be equal; since there are many components of demand (five in Figure 6.1), but only one of supply (assuming that imports are treated as negative demand), the easiest way of satisfying the accounting constraint for commodities would seem to be to add to supply the estimated difference between the two valuations.

This technique is known as the method of *purchasers' prices*, because entries in the input–output table remain denominated in the price paid by purchasers. Commodity supply, however, must now be valued to include transport and distribution margins and this will affect the valuation of industry output (by an equal amount in our simple example, because we have assumed commodity and industry output to be the same). Industry is then seen as 'purchasing' transport and distribution services in the absorption matrix from the transport and distribution sectors and the entries in the jth industry's column will be the same as the amount by which the jth commodity supply was raised to take account of these margins.

The position is now as set out in Figure 6.2. Commodity supply in Sector 1, for example, is now valued at 122 which ensures equality with commodity demand. The increase of 22 units on commodity supply at producers' prices is assumed to come partly from transport margins (8 units) and partly from distributors' margins (14 units); these margins are then entered in the column for industry (1) and a similar treatment is given to Sector 2. No adjustments have to be made to the columns for transport and distribution and the demand for the services of these two sectors has now been raised to equality with the supply. It should also be noted that it is not necessary to make any changes to final demand, which remains denominated at purchasers' prices.

Commodity supply	1	2	*T*	*D*	Final demand	Commodity demand	
122	36	35	12	12	27	122	Sector 1
122	24	35	—	—	63	122	Sector 2
15	8	7	—	—	—	15	Transport (*T*)
29	14	15	—	—	—	29	Distribution (*D*)
	40	30	3	17			Value added
	122	122	15	29			Industry output

Figure 6.2 Balanced input–output table (purchasers' prices)

The additional data requirements needed to move from Figure 6.1 to Figure 6.2 are very modest and this must be considered a distinct advantage of the method of purchasers' prices despite its drawbacks (see below). All we need is an estimate of the *average* mark-up for transport and distribution costs on each commodity. (In Figure 6.2, for example, the average transport mark-up was assumed to be 8% in Sector 1—8 units on commodity supply of 100 units.) These average mark-ups can usually be obtained from surveys of the transport and distribution sectors or from regular trade sources.

Unfortunately, although it is so simple, the method of purchasers' prices suffers from a serious weakness. Although the adjustment of commodity and industry output to purchasers' prices can be achieved through the use of average mark-ups, it does not follow that all users of a commodity are subject to this average margin.

In the case of distributive margins, for example, some buyers (e.g. households) purchase goods inclusive of a retail mark-up, while others (e.g. businesses) do not. When this happens, the entries in each row of the input–output table will not be denominated in the same prices.

When different prices are found in the same row of the table, a bias is introduced into the results of the input–output model; the reasons for this are formally set out in Appendix A to this chapter, but an intuitive explanation can easily be given; in order to work out the impact on output of any change in final demand, the input–output model must deduct from each 'dose' of demand the margin owed to the distributors. With the method of purchasers' prices, the model has only one margin (the average mark-up) to work with, so that the results will be biased if the particular demand change we wish to study does not carry with it the 'average' margin used in the method (see also United Nations, 1968, p. 51). It follows that we must look at alternative methods of valuation, even if these are more complicated, in order to achieve a uniform valuation of entries in each row.

Let us assume to start with that only distribution margins vary according to the user. This means that we must deduct from each entry in the input–output table of Figure 6.1 the estimated margin paid to distributors; in the case of final demand, for example, this will include retail as well as wholesale margins, while in the case of intermediate demand it will refer only to the latter. The deducted margins must then be credited to the distribution row, so that all buyers are shown as purchasing distributors' margins directly. The entries in the input–output table will now be at purchasers' prices less distribution margins and therefore still inclusive of transport costs; these transport costs must then be included in the value of commodity and industry supply, just as in Figure 6.2, so that transport margins appear to be borne by the seller. For that reason this method of valuation is known as *delivered prices*.

The position is now as set out in Figure 6.3; the final demand column has been changed substantially, because the entries in this column carry retail margins which are normally quite high. The intermediate demand entries have also

Commodity supply	1	2	*T*	*D*	Final demand	Commodity demand	
108	33	32	11	11	21	108	Sector 1
107	22	32	—	—	53	107	Sector 2
15	8	7	—	—	—	15	Transport (*T*)
29	5	6	1	1	16	29	Distribution (*D*)
	40	30	3	17			Value added
	108	107	15	29			Industry output

Figure 6.3 Balanced input–output table (delivered prices)

changed as a result of removing the wholesale margin, and distributors' margins now all appear to be borne by the buyer. The data requirements for the method of delivered prices are quite demanding, because it is necessary to know the distribution margin paid by each user and a survey of the distribution sector would not normally be sufficient to determine this.

In terms of valuing the entries in each row of the table uniformly, delivered prices represent a distinct advance on purchasers' prices. Nonetheless, delivered prices will still not give a uniform valuation if transport margins on each commodity differ according to the user; such an occurrence is very common, since transport rates normally vary according to the distance commodities are carried so that the *average* mark-up for transport costs in Figure 6.3 conceals a high variance among different users. By deducting transport as well as distribution margins from the entries in the input–output table of Figure 6.1, it should be possible to improve the uniformity of valuation in each row; removal of both sets of margins will leave the entries in the table denominated in the same prices as are used to value commodity supply, which is why this technique is known as the method of *producers' prices.*

The position is now as set out in Figure 6.4. The only differences from Figure 6.3 are that commodity supply is given in producers' prices (as in Figure 6.1), while transport margins are deducted from the purchases of commodities and credited directly to the transport row. The data requirements for producers' prices, however, are very demanding, as it is now necessary to know the transport costs as a percentage of purchases in each cell of the table and this information is unlikely to be obtained from a survey of the transport sector. We find, therefore, that although delivered and *a fortiori* producers' prices hold out the prospect of an improvement in the uniformity of valuation for the entries in each row of the table, it may be difficult to find the information necessary to implement the methods. We shall return to this important point in the next section.

Unfortunately, sellers' or producers' prices are not a guarantee of uniform row valuation either, since they usually include net indirect taxes (i.e. they are at market prices). These taxes and subsidies also differ according to user, so the

Commodity supply	1	2	*T*	*D*	Final demand	Commodity demand	
100	30	30	10	10	20	100	Sector 1
100	20	30	—	—	50	100	Sector 2
15	5	4	1	1	4	15	Transport (*T*)
29	5	6	1	1	16	29	Distriution (*D*)
	40	30	3	17			Value added
	100	100	15	29			Industry ouput

Figure 6.4 Balanced input–output table (producers' prices)

uniformity of each row can be improved by deducting indirect taxes (adding them in the case of subsidies) from the producers' prices and crediting them to the appropriate row in value added.

Assuming that there are no subsidies and that indirect taxes are levied only on final expenditure, the position will be as summarized in Figure 6.5. The table will now be expressed at factor cost, since the price of each commodity can be completely decomposed into its accumulated factor costs.[2] For this reason, the treatment of transactions in Figure 6.5 is known as the method of *basic prices*, i.e. the price of each commodity is reduced to its basic (factor) constituents. In a régime of basic prices, transport and commercial margins as well as net indirect taxes are paid by the buyer and this is the method of valuation recommended by the United Nations (see United Nations, 1968, Chapter 3). The additional data requirements associated with basic prices are information on indirect taxes paid by each user for each commodity and information on subsidies received on each commodity by user. These additional requirements, however, are usually straightforward, as data on indirect taxes and subsidies are normally well documented.

Commodity supply	1	2	*T*	*D*	Final demand	Commodity demand	
90	30	30	10	10	10	90	Sector 1
80	20	30	—	—	30	80	Sector 2
15	5	4	1	1	4	15	Transport (*T*)
29	5	6	1	1	16	29	Distribution (*D*)
	—	—	—	—	30		Indirect taxes
	30	10	3	17			Factor costs
	90	80	15	29			Industry output

Figure 6.5 Balanced input–output table (basic prices)

6.3 PROBLEMS OF UNIFORM ROW VALUATION

It might appear from the above that the case in favour of basic prices and a uniform row valuation (URV) is overwhelming. This in fact is not so. URV raises a number of difficulties, some of which are practical, some conceptual. For the moment, let us assume that basic prices do give a URV. Then the problem can be reduced to a discussion of distributors' margins, transport margins and net indirect taxes. Later, we can relax this assumption.

The element of distributors' margins which differs most among users of the same product is the retail margin. It is usually assumed in input-output work that payment of this margin is limited to households and tourists, but this is not always the case; significant amounts of office expenditure may come through retailers, although it is usually impossible to estimate this. Similarly, not all household or tourist expenditure on goods comes through retailers; certain amounts of food, DIY materials etc. are bought direct or through wholesalers.

It is also extremely difficult to determine *the* retail margin in input-output work. At the level of the single commodity, there is a spread of margins corresponding to the organization of the retail sector (hypermarkets, supermarkets, co-operatives, independents, etc.) and to obtain a weighted average we require knowledge of the portion of sales coming through each of these organizational types. At the level of the commodity group, in which input-output tables are usually expressed, there is the problem of obtaining weighted averages of these weighted averages. Finally, the results will differ depending on whether retailers are asked to estimate their margins directly (as a percentage mark-up or mark-down) or whether the input–output worker calculates them from data on purchases, sales and stocks. In the latter case, the margin will include an element of stock appreciation (assuming rising prices) whereas in the former it will not (see Chapter 2).

The wholesale margin also poses serious problems, because the use of this service varies enormously between activities, countries and over time. It is customary, for example, for larger retailers to bypass wholesalers and purchase direct from factories; consequently, when estimating the wholesale margin paid by, say, households, we need to know the proportion of purchases passing through wholesalers. Within industry, the use of wholesalers at times appears to be entirely random: some firms buy the same commodity partly through wholesalers and partly direct from other manufacturers. If the input–output worker uses census returns, he is likely to be presented with the data in a form in which this information, even if available, is lost; he then assumes either that the commodity passes through a wholesaler or that it is bought direct. If he uses survey data, he can adjust each establishment for the proportion passing through wholesalers, but he has little grounds for assuming these proportions apply to the non-sampled part of the population.

We may now turn to the problems encountered when trying to adjust purchases for transport margins. Transport rates are quoted as so many units of domestic currency per unit of weight per unit of distance, so that transport margins in input-output tables can only be calculated accurately if we have information per user per commodity on quantities bought and distance travelled. This is virtually never available (and is never available for all commodities), so input–output workers use a series of devices or tricks which are hardly ever written down because of their arbitrary character. In practice, what usually happens, is that one rate per commodity group is chosen; this does not improve URV at all, since all purchases are adjusted by the same proportional amount.

A further problem is the multiplicity of transport margins. In the case of imports, for example, there is the difference between the f.o.b. and c.i.f. price (which also includes insurance); there are port handling charges and transport costs from the port to the first wholesaler (the problem of import duties is considered below); there are transport costs from the wholesaler to other wholesalers or from the first wholesaler to retailers or factories/offices. It is never clear who pays these transport margins; they may be paid by the buyer or the seller or be contracted to an independent transport firm. Talk of *the* transport margin only makes sense in the case of purchases by one factory directly from another.

There are also cases where deducting transport margins may reduce the URV. Some companies, for example, charge distributors the same price whether they are one or 400 miles from the factory. If these (different) transport margins were deducted, we would no longer have URV. Similarly, the theory of location suggests that what is equalized by competition is the *delivered* unit price. A firm may compete at a distance with a congested local market, because it can offset the distance factor by lower overhead costs.

It might seem that at least with indirect taxes and subsidies we would be on firmer ground. This is not so, however, although we can dispense with a discussion of those taxes or subsidies which affect all classes of users equally. The taxes and subsidies to be considered are those which affect the price at which goods and services are marketed. Many taxes and subsidies, however, such as investment grants, subsidized rates of interest, credit on easy terms, etc. are excluded from input–output tables at basic prices, even though they *both* affect the marketed price *and* affect different classes of users differently.

For some commodity groups, hydrocarbons for example, the aggregation problem is formidable; we need to know how each user distributes his purchases over each commodity since each bears a different rate of tax. For some taxes or subsidies, it will be known that there is no incidence for certain users, but considerable ambiguity about the users on whom the tax or subsidy falls; the support given to marginal transport undertakings, for example, will not affect the price charged to industry, but may affect the price charged to agriculture, services, households and tourists.

The assumption that basic prices give a URV now needs to be examined. URV will be satisfied when the prices used to convert quantities to values in the ith row of the table are the same in all cells. However, price is often an inverse function of quantity sold with firms granting cash discounts in proportion to the quantity bought and this introduces different prices into each row of the table which need to be adjusted if URV is to be satisfied.

We have also assumed that the quality of any quantity is the same. This is not so and quality differences will create different prices in each row of the input–output table. Similarly, some firms buy and sell at transfer prices and this will upset URV, since any one row will tend to be a mixture of transfer and market prices, i.e. a weighted average of both. There are cases, too, where the row of the input–output table describes the activities of a price discriminating monopolist, e.g. public utilities, and this too will create a set of prices in each row which deviate from the requirement of URV.

It would not be hard to continue with such a list, but it should by now be clear that the commitment to URV is an open-ended one. It is possible to argue, of course, that we learn by doing so that each input-output table over time will tend more and more to URV. The input-output model, however, would then become like the vintage capital model with each vintage corresponding to the introduction of a new technique and where trends in coefficients over time may be due as much to the techniques of valuation used as to changes in the technology of production.

There are three areas, however, where putting flows on a URV is not simply a question of introducing new techniques. First, there is the problem of goods whose time rate of production is different in different uses. Alcohol, for example, sold to stock is often immature and several years younger than the same product sold to final demand. The unit prices, of course, differ substantially when the time rate of production is different,[3] and it is very difficult to see how one would adjust for these different prices without introducing a dynamic model of considerable complexity.

Secondly, there is the problem of imports. It might seem that URV requires that imports be valued c.i.f. plus duties, since the price of home produced importables in most LDCs is assumed to be determined by world prices plus tariffs. However, there are many countries where the rate of duty on a commodity differs according to user,[4] so that strictly URV requires that imports be valued c.i.f. and domestic output and purchases be adjusted for the implicit tariff. This would, however, virtually require the abandonment of market prices as the standard in input-output tables. (In view of their importance, however, a more extended discussion of imports is reserved for the next chapter.)

Thirdly, there are many sectors for which it is meaningless to talk of URV. In the service sectors, it is usually unclear what the 'price' is which is supposed to be equalized across users, while in agriculture and, indeed, many industrial sectors the number of commodities aggregated makes it quite impossible to talk about a unique price.

6.4 INTERNATIONAL PRACTICE

There is a pitiful gap between theory and practice in the construction of input–output tables. In Table 6.1, a brief description of sources and methods is given for a number of input–output tables. Where purchases have been adjusted for margins, one cannot be sure that the final results will be more accurate since the sources used have a high probability of introducing errors. In the tables the author prepared for Costa Rica, for example (Bulmer-Thomas, 1977a), Central Bank estimates of distributors' margins were available for only twenty commodity groups and these did not even distinguish between retail and wholesale margins.

The construction of the United Kingdom (UK) input–output table in this context is particularly interesting, since the UK is a developed country with a wealth of available statistics. Intermediate purchases are adjusted to producers' prices by assuming that the whole difference between intermediate supply and demand is due to distributive margins. This means that any errors of observation,

Table 6.1 Valuation in practice in some input–output tables

Country	Year	Valuation	Retail margins	Wholesale margins	Transport margins	Net indirect taxes
United Kingdom	1968	Basic prices	Source not given in official publications	For intermediate sectors, estimated as the difference between purchases and sales in each row and allocated between industries in proportion to purchases (see CSO, 1973)		Estimated from official sources for excise duties and some subsidies
Scotland	1973	Delivered prices	Estimated using a sample survey of retailers	Estimated using a sample study of wholesalers	Supply assumed to be at delivered prices with costs borne by seller so no adjustment made (see Fraser, 1978)	Estimated from official sources for excise duties and some subsidies
Costa Rica	1968	Basic prices	All intermediate and final demand expenditures adjusted using Central Bank annual estimates of mark-ups for 20 commodity groups (see Bulmer-Thomas, 1977a)		Estimated from data on transport rates constrained by total freight earnings	Sales taxes assumed to be limited to consumers' expenditure, which was estimated as a residual and is therefore at basic prices. Duties charged to user
Morocco	1969	Purchasers price	Method not given in official publications but supply in each row adjusted for estimated difference between supply price and demand price using data on margins from surveys of distribution in 1968 and 1969		No adjustment made as costs are assumed to be borne by seller	No adjustment made as net indirect taxes are assumed to be included in sellers price

measurement or estimation, may have been carried over into distribution margins. We are not told how the gross margin is broken down between transport and wholesaling, but we are expected to believe that 'analysing total commodity supply in this way ensured that the rows had a homogeneous valuation'. (CSO, 1973, p. 21).

If international practice bore some relation to supposed theoretical requirements, one would feel more hesitant about advocating a change in the conventions governing the valuation of input–output tables. However, the state of practice is such that almost any change is likely to be for the better. If even the developed countries—rich in statistical sources—have to use techniques with a high probability of introducing error, the position for the developing countries is grim indeed.

6.5 CONSTRAINED MINIMIZATION

URV is pursued as a means to greater accuracy in the use of the input–output table. Each change involves an adjustment to the original data which in theory brings the etimated values in the solution to the input–output model (see Appendix A) closer to the true values. However, it also brings the possibility of introducing errors and, as URV is pushed further, the probability of the potential gain being swamped by the potential loss from introducing errors increases. The problem of URV is therefore one of constrained minimization.

Let us denote the true output of the ith sector using the jth method of valuation by x_i^j. This (true) output is by assumption never observed; it is approximated by the use of the jth method of valuation. This gives an estimated value for the ith output of $\tilde{x}_i^j$, where j can represent the use of purchasers' prices, delivered prices

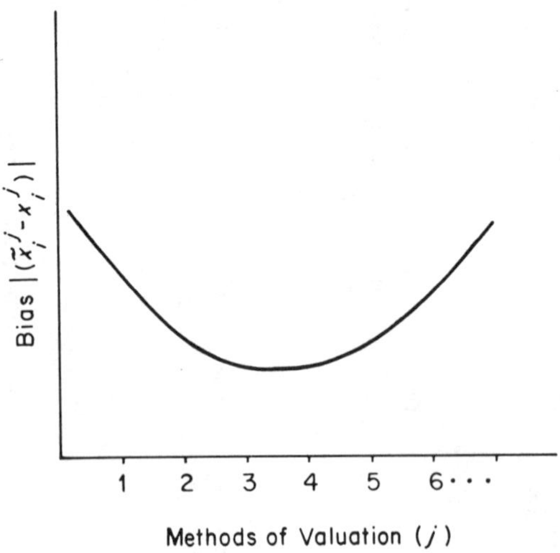

Figure 6.6 Relationship of bias $|(\tilde{x}_i^j - x_i^j)|$ to method of valuation

etc. The deviation of this (estimated) output from the (true) output $(\tilde{x}_i^j - x_i^j)$ reflects both the potential gain from a more uniform row valuation and the potential loss from the probability of introducing errors.

The objective is to minimize the gap $(\tilde{x}_i^j - x_i^j)$. The position is shown in Figure 6.6, where the relatively most 'successful' methods of valuation are shown first. For example, at $j = 0$ we might assume purchasers' prices which would give a large deviation of $\tilde{x}_i^0$ from x_i^0. If retail margins were deducted ($j = 1$, say), there would be a considerable improvement. A further absolute improvement might be made if indirect taxes ($j = 2$) and subsidies ($j = 3$) were removed, although the rate of improvement would be declining. If wholesale margins ($j = 4$) and transport margins ($j = 5$) were removed, it is conceivable that the position might actually deteriorate, and as we move to more and more sophisticated valuation conventions (e.g. allowing for transfer prices), the probability of finding ourselves on the rising part of the curve increases.

Choosing the point at which the curve in Figure 6.6 is at a minimum is not easy. The main conclusion, however, to be drawn is that such a curve may have a minimum and need not necessarily approach the j axis asymptotically, as has conventionally been supposed.

6.6 A METHOD OF VALUATION FOR LDCS

The United Nations has recommended basic prices as the method of valuation to be adopted by all countries in preparing input–output tables (see United Nations, 1968, Chapters 3 and 4). It is, of course, highly desirable that all countries should adopt the same valuation convention, since it increases the possibility of making international comparisons; nevertheless, many LDCs have great difficulty in adopting basic prices as the basis for their input–output tables, while others (in an effort to conform to international recommendations) introduce distortions into their tables which reduce the utility of input–output models based on them.

It should be recognized, therefore, that some LDCs would do better not to adopt basic prices at present; for such countries, a less rigorous valuation convention is needed and the author elsewhere (Bulmer-Thomas, 1978b) has proposed the use of *standard prices*. According to this method, entries in the unbalanced input–output table (e.g. Figure 6.1) should be adjusted for retail margins, indirect taxes and subsidies only; entries would therefore continue to be valued, inclusive of wholesale and transport margins, so that commodity supply and industry output have to be adjusted to reflect this (as in Figures 6.2 and 6.3).

Reverting to our original simple example (see Figure 6.1), the position with standard prices is now as set out in Figure 6.7. Retail margins have been deducted from the entries in final demand (4 units in the case of Commodity 1 and 7 units in the case of Commodity 2), but the intermediate demand entries for commodities in Figure 6.7 are carried over unchanged from Figure 6.1, because standard prices include wholesale margins. Indirect taxes, which we have assumed apply only to final demand, have been deducted and credited to the indirect tax row and value added for each sector is therefore the same as in Figure 6.5. Commodity supply is

Commodity supply	1	2	T	D	Final demand	Commodity demand	
108	36	35	12	12	13	108	Sector 1
95	24	35	—	—	36	95	Sector 2
15	8	7	—	—	—	15	Transport (*T*)
29	10	8	—	—	11	29	Distribution (*D*)
	—	—	—	—	30		Indirect taxes
	30	10	3	17			Factor costs
	108	95	15	29			Industry output

Figure 6.7 Balanced input–output table (standard prices)

now valued inclusive of transport and wholesale margins, but exclusive of (net) indirect taxes and retail margins.

The justification for standard prices is as follows: since the accuracy of the solution to the input–output model depends on the entries in each row of the input–output table being valued uniformly, it is essential to remove those margins which differ substantially among users. Retail margins, indirect taxes and subsidies fall into this category, because they are usually quite large and are paid by some users, but not at all by others. Transport margins, on the other hand, are normally quite modest (except for cement, bricks, etc.) and do not differ very much by user, while the same can be said of wholesale margins. LDCs which have prepared input–output tables at standard prices can therefore have confidence in the solution to the models derived from them—at least as far as the valuation convention is concerned.

The data requirements for standard prices are minimal and this is a further justification for their adoption by LDCs deficient in statistical resources. Information is needed on retail margins by commodity, which can normally be obtained from a retail survey or trade sources, and on indirect taxes and subsidies by commodity and user, which in the author's experience is always well documented. Commodity supply needs to be adjusted to take account of the *average* wholesale margin to which sales are subject and this, again, is something which can normally be obtained from a distribution survey; commodity supply must also be adjusted for the *average* mark-up due to transport costs, but this is often easier than it sounds because firms frequently report the value of sales at delivered prices, i.e. inclusive of transport costs.

APPENDIX A CONDITIONS FOR NO VALUATION BIAS[5]

At purchasers' prices, the incremental output vector can be written:

(6.1a) $$\Delta x^* = [I - A^*]^{-1} \Delta f^*$$

where Δx^* is the incremental output vector at purchasers' prices, $[I - A^*]^{-1}$ is the Leontief inverse matrix calculated at purchasers' prices, and Δf^* is the incremental final demand vector at purchasers' prices.

We can also write:

(6.2a) $$\Delta \tilde{x} = [I - \hat{R}] \Delta x^*$$

where $\Delta \tilde{x}$ is the estimate of the incremental output vector at producers' prices, I is the identity matrix and $\hat{R}$ is a diagonal matrix whose ith element shows the proportion by which purchasers' prices must be deflated *on average* to match demand at sellers' prices.

Using producers' prices, we can write:

(6.3a) $$\Delta x = [I - A]^{-1} \Delta f$$

where the absence of asterisks denotes the use of producers' prices and:

(6.4a) $$\Delta x = [I - A]^{-1} [I - \hat{\pi}] \Delta f^*$$

where $\hat{\pi}$ is a diagonal matrix whose ith element shows the margin on the ith good paid by final demand. The condition for no valuation bias is therefore:

(6.5a) $$\Delta \tilde{x} - \Delta x = [I - \hat{R}][I - A^*]^{-1} \Delta f^* - [I - A]^{-1} [I - \hat{\pi}] \Delta f^* = 0$$

where 0 is a null vector.

Let us now assume that the margin on the ith good is the same for all *intermediate* use, i.e. industrial user j pays the same margin as user k. Then it can be shown that the matrix A is related to the matrix A^* by the relationship:

(6.6a) $$A = \hat{B} A^* \hat{K}^{-1}$$

where A^*, A are the input–output coefficient matrices at purchasers' and producers' prices respectively, $\hat{B}$ is a diagonal matrix $(I - \hat{P})$, whose ith element can be defined as $(1 - p_i)$ where p_i is the margin on the ith good in intermediate use and $\hat{K}$ is $(I - \hat{R})$.

Now the Leontief inverse can be written in matrix multiplier form as:

(6.7a) $$[I - A^*]^{-1} = I + A^* + A^{*2} + \ldots$$

and

(6.8a) $$[I - A]^{-1} = I + \hat{B} A^* \hat{K}^{-1} + [\hat{B} A^* \hat{K}^{-1}]^2 + \ldots$$

so that equation (6.5a) can now be written:

(6.9a) $$\{I - \hat{R}\} [I + A^* + A^{*2} + \ldots] \Delta f^* - [I + \hat{B} A^* \hat{K}^{-1} + \{\hat{B} A^* \hat{K}^{-1}\}^2 + \ldots][I - \hat{\pi}] \Delta f^* = 0$$

Writing $\hat{K}$ for $(I-\hat{R})$ and $\hat{L}$ for $(I-\hat{\pi})$ this becomes:

(6.10a)
$$\{[\hat{K}-\hat{L}]+[\hat{K}A^{*}-\hat{B}A^{*}\hat{K}^{-1}\hat{L}] + [\hat{K}A^{*2}-\{\hat{B}A^{*}\hat{K}^{-1}\}^{2}\hat{L}]+\ldots\}\Delta f^{*}=0$$

For this condition to be satisfied, each of the terms in square brackets must be a null matrix. In this case the first term $(\hat{K}-\hat{L})$ shows us we require $\hat{K}=\hat{L}$. With $\hat{K}=\hat{L}$, we have $\hat{K}^{-1}\hat{L}=I$ and the second term becomes $(\hat{K}A^{*}-\hat{B}A^{*})$ which will be a null matrix when $\hat{K}=\hat{B}$.

The third term is more complicated but with $\hat{K}=\hat{L}=\hat{B}$ it can be written:

$$[\hat{K}A^{*2}-\{\hat{K}A^{*}\hat{K}^{-1}\}^{2}\hat{K}]$$

or

$$[\hat{K}A^{*2}-\hat{K}A^{*}\hat{K}^{-1}\hat{K}A^{*}\hat{K}^{-1}\hat{K}]$$

but $\hat{K}^{-1}\hat{K}=I$, so this reduces to $\{\hat{K}A^{*2}-\hat{K}A^{*2}\}$, which is of course equal to a null matrix.

The requirement for no valuation bias is therefore $\hat{K}=\hat{L}=\hat{B}$ or $\hat{R}=\hat{\pi}=\hat{P}$. This states that the margin on the ith good must be the same in all uses, so that bias will only be avoided completely in the method of purchasers' prices when the margin applied to *all* users of the commodity is equal.

APPENDIX B THE STABILITY OF COEFFICIENTS

An input–output table is used to forecast changes over scale as well as over time. Over scale, relative prices cannot change because of the assumption of constant returns, so the input–output coefficients will be stable whatever the method of valuation.

If the input–output table is used to forecast changes in output over time, there is the possibility that the relative prices of trade and industry will change and this has implications for the method of valuation which need to be examined.

Let us now assume that the i,jth input–output coefficient expressed at producers' prices, does not change over time, so that $a_{ij}^{0}=a_{ij}^{1}$, where the superscript refers to the time interval. At purchasers' prices we can write:

(6.1b)
$$a_{ij}^{0*}=a_{ij}^{0}\frac{(1+p_i^{0})}{(1+r_j^{0})}$$

where p_i is the margin on ith commodity paid by intermediate sectors, and r_j is the proportion by which sellers' prices must be raised on average to match demand at purchasers' prices. Similarly,

(6.2b)
$$a_{ij}^{1*}=a_{ij}^{0}\frac{(1+p_i^{1})}{(1+r_j^{1})}$$

so the condition for stability over time is:

$$\left(\frac{a_{ij}^{1*} - a_{ij}^{0*}}{a_{ij}^{1*}}\right) = 1 - \left[\frac{(1+p_i^0)}{(1+p_i^1)} \times \frac{(1+r_j^1)}{(1+r_j^0)}\right] = 0 \tag{6.3b}$$

which means that instability will be avoided if the margin paid by intermediate sectors on the ith good and the average mark-up on the jth sellers' price move in the same proportions over time. The condition for stability is therefore less restrictive than the condition for no valuation bias.

NOTES

1 The problems which arise when the imbalance is due to something other than valuation are discussed in Chapters 8 and 9.

2 Approximate factor cost only, because the table will not have been adjusted for the accumulated net indirect taxes on inputs (see United Nations, 1968, Appendix to Chapter 3).

3 For a more detailed discussion of this point, although in a different context, see Oswald (1977).

4 As, for example, in Central America. See Bulmer-Thomas (1976).

5 The author is grateful to his former colleague Frank Harrigan for comments on an earlier version of this Appendix.

CHAPTER 7

Foreign Trade Entries in Input–Output Tables

7.1 INTRODUCTION

Transactions with the rest of the world involve a great many difficulties in input–output analysis and therefore deserve a special chapter to themselves. First, as was pointed out in the previous chapter, such transactions have to be adjusted to a valuation basis consistent with that chosen for other entries in the input–output table; secondly, there are sometimes conceptual and statistical problems associated with the trade entries in the production accounts which can produce large imbalances when the time comes to reconcile the supply of with the demand for resources. Finally, even when imports and exports have been appropriately estimated and valued, there remains the problem of their incorporation as endogenous or exogenous variables in input–output models.

If we return to Table 1.3, we may note that the construction of a complete SAM requires that all balance of payments entries be included. In input–output analysis, at the very least, we require a record of all transactions with the rest of the world on production account. This will include trade in commodities (visible trade), but it will also include payments for non-factor services such as travel, tourism, shipping and insurance. Thus, the 'balance' of all entries in the production accounts, where debits are set against credits, refers to the balance of trade in goods and services.[1] It is therefore more comprehensive than the balance of visible trade, but less so than the balance on current account, which includes transfers and factor payments.

7.2 EXPORTS IN INPUT–OUTPUT TABLES

Our discussion of exports will begin with their valuation in input–output tables, which is relatively straightforward; the choice of valuation will depend on the system adopted for the input–output table and if basic prices are adopted, for example, the free on board (f.o.b.) value of exports in the trade statistics must be adjusted for export taxes, transport costs involved in the transfer from farm or factory to port and distribution margins if the goods have passed through a wholesaler; in the case of standard prices, the only adjustment needed to f.o.b. values is for export taxes, which are usually well documented and therefore present few problems. By contrast, adjustment of f.o.b. values for trade and transport margins can be quite difficult.

Although trade statistics, with exports valued f.o.b., will normally be used, there are occasions—as in the construction of input–output tables for a single region—where the only source is provided by the records of producers themselves. It is possible for producers to value their exports at anything from ex-works' prices to the landed price at the foreign country's port, and great care has to be taken in drafting questionnaires to try to ensure a homogeneous price response. In general, however, where the system of pricing goods inclusive of delivery costs prevails, the valuation basis used by firms will correspond to f.o.b.[2]

The main source used for commodity exports is a country's trade statistics (in the case of a region without such statistics, see Chapter 11). These statistics are valued f.o.b.[3] and can be thought of as representing demand for home production by the rest of the world. It is quite possible, however, that a 'supply-side' estimate also exists, based on sample data or a census of production, and the two are unlikely to be equal.

The imbalance between the two estimates can have a number of causes. First is the difference in classification; trade data are normally classified according to an internationally accepted trade nomenclature, from which it is then necessary to build a bridge to the industrial or commodity classifications used in the organization of production statistics. It is possible for errors to creep in at various points in this process; for example, in Costa Rica where a nine-digit trade classification had been used, the 'bridge' to the industry classification involved such palpable errors as classifying exports of second-hand goods to the industry which might have supplied them if they had been new. Another problem is that goods can be invoiced to the wrong trade classification, so that the bridge to the industry classification will also allocate them to the wrong producing sector. There is no simple answer to the classification problem, and the solution may well vary from country to country, but it is usually possible by careful analysis to eliminate the worst excesses.

A second source of imbalance between supply and demand is differences in valuation, since the f.o.b. price can include transport and wholesale margins as well as export taxes, while the supply-side estimate of exports from production statistics may be at other prices. This problem, however, has been discussed fully above; the method of reconciling the two estimates will depend on the chosen basis of valuation.

A third reason for a difference can arise from the timing of transactions. In general, where annual data are used, the timing problem can be ignored, but in the case of exports—where goods can often be stored for months or even years before shipment—it can be acute. A good example is provided by exports of coffee, since the latter can be stored for five years and most coffee-exporting countries have institutes whose function is to store the commodity and release it only when prices are most favourable. The solution to this problem is simple enough in principle; the production function of the input–output model assumes that inputs in the columns of the table refer to outputs in the rows and this will not be the case if the 'output' entry (in this case exports) refers to a previous year. In practice, it may be difficult to make the adjustment and often there is an understandable reluctance on the part of input–output workers to alter official balance of payments figures.[4]

If the supply-side estimate of exports comes not from a census of production, but from a sample, an additional source of imbalance is provided by sample error in the population estimates. It is a simple matter to calculate the standard error of the population estimate for exports of a particular sector, and if the demand-side estimate falls within the standard error, the former can safely be used. If the two estimates are wildly different, however, the supply-side figure is most likely to be suspect, because there are no theoretical grounds for assuming that the export performance of the sampled establishments is representative of the population (see Chapter 11).

There is one final problem faced by input–output workers in treating commodity exports. Trade statistics are compiled before the full balance of payments presentation for a country is completed and the latter often involves a number of minor adjustments to the f.o.b. valuation of exports in the trade statistics. This can arise from such things as the discovery of invoice errors, but is usually due to 'classification, coverage, timing, and valuation adjustments . . . in order to bring the data on to a balance of payments basis' (IMF, 1979, p. viii). In principle, the input–output worker would like to follow these adjustments in order that input–output exports may be consistent with the balance of payments, but it is frequently impossible to do so with any accuracy; in Costa Rica, for example, the balance of payments contains the following adjustments to merchandise exports: (1) repair works on boats and aircraft; (2) postal packets, gifts, etc.; (3) returned exports; (4) errors in bills of lading. Clearly some decision has to be taken on these entries, but they cannot be accounted for at the sectoral level with much accuracy.

Exports of services are, in general, much more difficult to handle than commodity exports. In one respect, however, they can be easier, because there is no supply-side estimate; tourist expenditure, for example, is usually only estimated from the side of demand, since many establishments would be unable to estimate sales to tourists.

Tourist sales are only a subset of sales of services to non-residents, all of which count as service exports. Other examples are provided by the expenditure of foreign students and businessmen, as well as outlays by foreign embassies. In view of its importance to many LDCs, it is sensible to record tourist expenditure separately rather than aggregating it with commodity exports, and the breakdown of this expenditure by commodity group usually relies on sample surveys. The other sales to non-residents are usually small enough to be 'buried' with commodity exports, although there are LDCs where the expenditure of non-resident workers (e.g. seasonal migrant labour) is sufficiently important to receive separate treatment. The author knows of no surveys of expenditure by students, embassies, etc. and the breakdown of this balance of payments entry has to be somewhat arbitrary.

Exports of transport and insurance services are usually straightforward and can be assigned directly to the appropriate row of the absorption matrix from the balance of payments statistics. More difficult is the entry 'port disbursements', which represents purchases by foreign vessels (airlines, ships, etc.) on such things as bunker fuel, provisions, water supply and for which sample surveys rarely exist. The input–output worker has to take some view on the commodity breakdown of these disbursements, but of necessity it cannot be very accurate. Sales of patent rights and royalties abroad should not be counted as exports of services in the input–output table, because these represent factor income.

We may conclude our discussion of exports by considering possible forms of presentation. In vector notation, total exports (e) can be written:

$$e = \sum_i c_i + \sum_i t_i + \sum_i o_i + \sum_i s_i \tag{7.1}$$

where c_i is the vector of commodity exports sold to region i, t_i is the vector of expenditure by tourists from region i, o_i is the vector of expenditure by other non-residents from region i, and s_i is other service exports to region i. With two regions,[5] this implies eight export vectors, which is probably excessive for presentation (but not working) purposes and may be impossible to achieve if o, s or t cannot be broken down by region. It is usually necessary, therefore, to adopt a presentation which distinguishes either by region ($e = \Sigma_i [c_i + t_i + o_i + s_i]$) or by type of export ($e = c + t + o + s$), but compromise solutions (e.g. $e = \Sigma c_i + [t + o + s]$) are of course possible. The final choice will depend on the uses to which the input–output table is to be put.

The tourist expenditure vector(s) can be treated either as final or intermediate expenditure. In the latter case, there will be an entry in one of the other export columns representing aggregate tourist expenditure which is credited to the tourist row in the input–output table; the tourist column then contains the details of tourist expenditure by commodity group. The choice between these two methods of presentation is entirely a matter of taste.[6]

7.3 IMPORTS IN INPUT–OUTPUT TABLES

Although the valuation of exports in input–output tables is a comparatively simple matter, the same cannot be said of imports. In the previous chapter, the case for valuing uniformly entries in each row of the input–output table was made at some length and it was suggested that either basic prices or standard prices will give a tolerable approximation to uniform row valuation (URV). The important question, therefore, is what valuation for imports comes closest to each of these types of price.

Suppose, for example, that basic prices have been adopted for the absorption matrix; the value of imports which corresponds most closely is c.i.f. dollar values converted to home currency units at the appropriate exchange rate with the addition of protective, but not revenue,[7] duties. Apart from the difficulty of distinguishing protective from revenue duties, this system of valuation will involve a non-uniform valuation of the same commodity if different users pay different rates of duty and can convert dollars at different rates of exchange. In the author's experience, this is quite a common situation in LDCs (cf. Bhagwati, 1978).

We can illustrate this problem formally by means of a simple example. Let the c.i.f. dollar value of one unit of commodity i be M_i which is the same regardless of the user (i.e. $M_{ij} = M_{ik}$). If the exchange and tariff rates for the ith commodity applied to the jth user are r_{ij} and t_{ij} respectively, then the unit price in the home currency for the jth user (p_{ij}) is:

$$p_{ij} = M_i\{(1+r_{ij})(1+t_{ij})\} \tag{7.2}$$

while for the kth user, it is:

$$p_{ik} = M_i\{(1+r_{ik})(1+t_{ik})\} \tag{7.3}$$

Uniform row valuation requires $p_{ij} = p_{ik}$ for all $j \neq k$, which will in general only be the case where:

$$\begin{aligned} r_{ij} &= r_{ik} \qquad \text{for all } j \neq k \\ t_{ij} &= t_{ik} \qquad \text{for all } j \neq k \end{aligned} \tag{7.4}$$

which is precisely what *cannot* be automatically assumed.

In Chapter 6 it was pointed out that, in this situation, the only way to achieve URV strictly is to value imports c.i.f. with dollar values converted at the official or lowest rate of exchange; domestic prices must then be deflated for the implicit protection given both by protective duties and by the multiple exchange rate system. This procedure is far too complicated, however, and, if implemented, is likely to introduce substantial errors into otherwise satisfactory data.

If standard prices are chosen for the input–output table, the value of imports which corresponds most closely is c.i.f. dollar values converted to home currency units at the appropriate rate of exchange plus protective duties, transport and distribution costs up to the first point of use. Standard prices, therefore, raise much the same problems as basic prices and our discussion of both sets of prices suggests that the solution to the valuation of imports must be less than perfect.[8]

The United Nations now recommends that imports be valued c.i.f. plus protective duties (United Nations, 1973, pp. 54–5).[9] As we have seen, this is the valuation convention implied by the use of basic prices; where the latter has been adopted as the basis for preparing the input–output table, it seems sensible—despite the imperfections mentioned above—to adopt the UN recommendation.[10] There is a small accounting problem associated with this valuation of imports, however, since not all the c.i.f. price represents payments to foreigners; a part of it—at a maximum equal to the difference between the c.i.f. (home port) and f.o.b. (foreign port) price—represents payments to *domestic* shipping and insurance companies and should not therefore appear as an import.

Fortunately, this problem is discussed very competently elsewhere (United

Nations, 1973, p. 55) and only the proposed solution need be mentioned; the overestimate of imports can be matched by entries in the export column corresponding to the rows for shipping and insurance in the absorption matrix. The net balance between total exports and imports is then left unaffected and all service output is accounted for. It should be pointed out, however, that for many LDCs that part of the difference between c.i.f. and f.o.b. values accruing to domestic firms is negligible.

There is still one small problem to clear up before we can leave the question of valuation, namely the problem of distinguishing between protective and revenue duties; this is a distinction to which the United Nations refers, but it must be remembered that although a tariff may be imposed for revenue purposes, it still functions as a protective duty unless there is a countervailing excise tax on home production. Where there is such a tax, the use of standard prices or basic prices would result in its removal from the entries in the absorption matrix and it is therefore desirable to make a corresponding adjustment to imports; where there is no countervailing tax on home production, however, revenue duties should be included with protective duties in the valuation of imports.

The main data source for imports in the case of a country is again its trade statistics, but this time the trade data represent a supply-side estimate. This supply is distributed to producers as intermediate absorptions or sold to final demand; on the demand side, it may be possible to estimate intermediate absorptions of imports from census or sample survey data on purchases, while final demand for imports can sometimes be obtained from survey work on such things as the division of household expenditure between home and imported goods.

It may therefore be possible to build up an estimate of imports by commodity group from the demand side, but it is usually highly inaccurate; many firms purchase commodities through wholesalers and cannot furnish a breakdown by area of origin, while those who can may not be representative, and a demand-side estimate of the import content of final expenditure is the exception rather than the rule. It follows that, although most of the problems associated with reconciling supply and demand estimates in the case of exports reoccur in the case of imports, reconciliation nearly always has to be achieved in favour of the supply-side or trade statistics estimate.

Trade statistics are normally valued c.i.f. in foreign currency, although duties paid (denominated in home currency) are often included in the statistics as well. Valuation in home currency, therefore, requires that foreign currency payments be converted at the appropriate exchange rate, and with some of the complicated multiple exchange rate systems operating in LDCs, this can be difficult. For example, in constructing the Costa Rican table, the author had to distinguish between trade which took place at the official rate of exchange and trade at the free rate; since the latter moved during the year, one problem was to determine the 'average' free rate; another problem was that the same commodity at the nine-digit level in the trade statistics entered at the official rate if it came from Central America, but might enter at the free rate if it came from the rest of the world; an even greater difficulty arose because the government source listing the relevant exchange rate for imports was sometimes more detailed than the nine-digit trade classification, so that it was possible for the latter to be affected by two rates of exchange. With patience, all these problems can be resolved, although it can be very tedious; the use of short-cuts, however, such as an 'average' exchange rate for all imports, is likely to produce serious errors.

In constructing estimates of import supply, it is inevitable that the input–output worker will come up against the problem of imports for which no corresponding domestic production exists; these imports (e.g. coffee beans purchased by the United Kingdom) are sometimes known as complementary and their treatment is discussed more fully below. However, it is worth noting at this stage that there is no difficulty involved in identifying more commodity groups among import supply than there are among home supply. For example, with n domestic sectors and two groups of complementary imports, the balance equations might look as follows:

(7.5)

$$\begin{bmatrix} x_1 \\ x_2 \\ \vdots \\ x_n \\ 0 \\ 0 \end{bmatrix} + \begin{bmatrix} m_1 \\ m_2 \\ \vdots \\ m_n \\ m_{n+1} \\ m_{n+2} \end{bmatrix} = \begin{array}{c} \begin{array}{cccc} 1 & 2 & \cdots & n \end{array} \\ \begin{bmatrix} W_{11} & W_{12} & \cdots & W_{1n} \\ W_{21} & W_{22} & \cdots & W_{2n} \\ \vdots & \vdots & & \vdots \\ W_{n1} & W_{n2} & \cdots & W_{nn} \\ W_{n+1,1} & W_{n+1,2} & \cdots & W_{n+1,n} \\ W_{n+2,1} & W_{n+2,2} & \cdots & W_{n+2,n} \end{bmatrix} \end{array} + \begin{bmatrix} f_1 \\ f_2 \\ \vdots \\ f_n \\ f_{n+1} \\ f_{n+2} \end{bmatrix}$$

where x_i, m_i and f_i are home output, imports and final demand for the ith sector respectively, and W_{ij} is absorptions of sector i by sector j; the last two rows therefore refer only to the supply of and demand for complementary imports.

As with exports, the balance of payments statement of a country makes a number of adjustments to the value of merchandise imports in the trade statistics. In general, it is not difficult to make allowances for such adjustments, unless an attempt is being made to identify each user of an import. In this case, the adjustment may affect not just the estimates of supply, but also each use to which supply is put. In Costa Rica, for example, fish bought from foreign vessels is included in the balance of payments statement, but excluded from the trade statistics and, as a matrix treatment of imports had been adopted (see below), each sector to which the fish was sold had to be separately identified.

If imports are valued c.i.f. plus protective duties, imports of services are quite straightforward. The freight and insurance entries are assumed to be included in the c.i.f. price and any underestimation of home earnings is allowed for by an overestimate of service exports. Most other service imports require that the input–output worker makes use of at least one 'import of services' row; for example, expenditure abroad by households, businesses, students and the country's embassies, consulates, etc. can be dealt with by this means, since it is unnecessary to have a commodity breakdown of the expenditure. The same is true of port disbursements abroad by the country's vessels and even airline tickets bought from foreign companies.

There are a large number of minor entries in the balance of payments statement which affect a country's production account either as debits or credits, but the input–output worker can feel sure he has not left anything out provided he works systematically through the list. The main difficulties encountered are, first, the danger of confusing non-factor with factor payments (e.g. patent rights) and, secondly, identifying separately each user in the case of imports of services (e.g. commissions for representing foreign firms). In the end, however, the input–output table should provide a record of all debits and credits on production account with the rest of the world, which in net terms represents the balance in goods and non-factor services. This balance should include non-monetary gold, but it will exclude smuggled goods whose absence is likely to be felt at the balancing stage (see Chapter 8).

All the problems associated with imports have now been discussed except that of their presentation in input–output tables. The simplest presentation corresponds to the case where the only information available on imports is a vector of supply and it is shown as Variant *A* in Table 7.1. It corresponds to the case where all imports in the trade statistics have been grouped according to the classification scheme for home producers without any attempt to identify users separately.

In Variant *A* it is assumed that imports are valued c.i.f. plus protective duties. The net trade balance will therefore be in error when all entries are aggregated, unless the protective duties are separately identified. This is done in Variant *A* by entering them as a positive entry in the import column (whose other entries are all negative) against the row for indirect taxes. The valuation basis for the rest of the table can be assumed to be basic or standard prices, so that the other net indirect tax entries would include revenue duties where appropriate. The difference between commodities and industries is ignored in order to simplify the presentation.

Imports appear in Variant *A* with a negative sign because they represent that part of demand which does not accrue to home producers; the balance equation for the system can therefore be written:

$$x = Ax + h + e - m \tag{7.6}$$

where h is the vector of home final demand, e is the vector of exports and m of imports. If h, e and m are exogenous variables, the model has a simple solution for output as:

$$x = [I - A]^{-1}[h + e - m] \tag{7.7}$$

but this is patently absurd, since one component of m is intermediate import demand and we cannot know how large this is, until we have solved for x. It follows that we have to treat m as an endogenous variable, but with the information at our disposal in Variant *A* the only way we can do this is to assume that each user of the jth commodity divides his absorptions between domestic

Table 7.1 Alternative treatments of imports in the input–output table

Variant A All imports competitive

	Industries 1	2	3	Home final demand	Exports	Less imports	Total
Commodities							
1	30	20	30	30	20	−30	100
2	20	80	60	20	70	−50	200
3	10	20	5	120	15	−20	150
Value added	30	50	35	–	–	–	115
Net indirect taxes	10	30	20	–	–	+10	70
Total	100	200	150	170	105	−90	

Variant B All imports complementary

	Industries 1	2	3	Home final demand	Exports	Total
Commodities						
Home produced						
1	20	15	25	20	20	100
2	15	65	50	–	70	200
3	10	10	5	110	15	150
Imported						
1	10	5	5	10	–	30
2	5	15	10	20	–	50
3	–	10	–	10	–	20
Value added	30	50	35	–	–	115
Net indirect taxes	10	30	20	–	10	70
Total	100	200	150	170	115	

production and imports in the same proportions. It can easily be shown (see, for example, United Nations, 1973, pp. 109–16), that this assumption may involve serious errors.

An alternative treatment of imports is therefore described in Variant *B* of Table 7.1. In this presentation, the import content of each transaction has been separately identified and allocated to an import matrix; industry 1, for example, which previously purchased 20 units from commodity 2 is now shown to divide its absorptions between domestic production and imports as 15 and 5 units respectively. Exports, value added and net indirect taxes are unaffected, since they are assumed to exclude imports,[11] but the export column must now carry a small entry (10 units) representing the element of protective duties in the import price.

This has the effect of inflating both the export and import totals leaving the net balance unaffected and consistent with the balance of payments statement. In Variant B, there are now two sets of balance equations. The set for domestic supply and demand is:

(7.8)
$$x = A_D x + h_d + e$$

where A_D is a matrix of *domestic* input–output coefficients and h_d is home final demand for locally produced goods and services with the solution:

(7.9)
$$x = [I - A_D]^{-1}[h_d + e]$$

while the set for imports is:

(7.10)
$$m = A_m x + h_m$$

where A_m is a matrix of import requirements per unit of output and h_m is a vector of final demand imports. It should be clear from this equation that there is no restriction on the number of rows in the import matrix; although in Variant B there are as many imported commodity groups as home-produced commodities, this is an unnecessary restriction. Indeed, the cases of inequality are of some interest in their own right, as we shall now see.

First, we should consider the case where the import matrix is aggregated row-wise to give only one row for imports. In discussions of imports in input–output tables, this is often treated as a separate variant, but it is most unlikely that it can be adopted unless the information necessary for Variant B is available, in which case there is little point in a single row for imports since a great deal of useful information is lost in the aggregation.

Another possibility is where there are more import rows than home commodity rows. One reason why this can arise is because some imports have been identified for which no domestic counterpart exists. These imports are called 'complementary' because they do not substitute for domestic production (as happens with competitive imports) but are needed in order to sustain a certain level of output. It follows that the demand for complementary imports is determined by the country's output vector; now in equation (7.10) we saw that imports consist of a part assumed exogenous (h_m) and a part assumed determined by home output, so that the matrix presentation of imports in Variant B is equivalent to treating all intermediate imports as complementary.

Such a treatment ignores relative prices as a determinant of import levels and is therefore somewhat extreme. A more flexible approach is obtained by treating some imports as competitive and others as complementary. However, if Variant B is the fundamental form of presentation, this can easily be done; the precise treatment of imports in an input–output model requires a much more sophisticated treatment than is possible here (see Chapter 15) but Variant B gives the greatest flexibility in model-building and it is therefore appropriate to conclude this chapter by considering the kind of difficulties encountered in constructing import matrices.

7.4 THE MATRIX PRESENTATION OF IMPORTS

The preparation of complete import matrices is one of the hardest problems facing the input–output worker. As with other matrices in the social accounts, each entry can be viewed either as a sale or a purchase; on the purchase or demand side, there are two major divisions: final demand and intermediate demand. The main sources for final demand (e.g. household budget surveys) do not usually ask for the origin of goods bought, so a sample survey of retailers and wholesalers is necessary in order to gain some idea of the area of origin of traded commodities. The estimate of intermediate absorption of imports usually comes from a census of production or sample survey, where questions on origin are in general asked, but if the commodities in question have come through a wholesaler, the respondent will not normally know the answer.

Import matrices, therefore, built up entirely from the demand or purchase side are unlikely to be satisfactory; if there are no 'sales' data (as in estimating regional imports), it may be possible to use the purchases data to identify the main complementary imports which can enter as a row in the absorption matrix, while all other imports are treated as competitive and enter as a negative column in final demand.[12] A further difficulty associated with relying exclusively on demand-side data is that the imports estimate will need to be put through a large number of adjustments if the basis of valuation is anything other than standard prices, since they contain protective and revenue duties as well as trade and transport margins involved in getting the goods from port to user.

In the case of a country, 'sales' or supply-side data obtained from trade statistics will normally provide at least a vector of total supplies (valued c.i.f. plus protective duties). This vector has to be balanced against the demand-side estimate obtained by summing all elements of the import matrix column-wise. The two estimates are likely to be very different, not only because of valuation conventions, but also because of the weakness of the purchases data. Simply deflating or inflating the demand-side data (after suitable valuation adjustments) so that they match the supply-side vector estimate is unlikely to remove this weakness.

The best way to improve the quality of the purchases estimate is to prepare a parallel sales estimate. It must always be remembered that trade statistics are tabulated at a very high degree of disaggregation. At this level of detail, it is often quite simple to identify the user or users by simply reading the product description; if this procedure is carried out for each listed import, it should be possible to prepare a 'supply-side' import matrix, in which most supply is allocated to a particular user, while a certain amount remains unallocated. Distribution of the unallocated amount will then rely on the information in the purchases-side matrix and informed guess-work; since this process is inevitably a little crude, there is no point writing out the procedure formally in terms of mathematics.

In some cases, the input–output worker may be lucky enough to find that the allocation by use of the supply vector has already been done for him. In Costa

Rica, for example, the author had access to a two-digit user classification of each import at the nine-digit level which was sufficient to prepare two import matrices (one for imports from Central American Common Market (CACM), the other from the rest of the world (ROW) without the need for a purchase estimate at all. By definition, the column-wise sum of each import matrix was consistent with the vector of competing supplies and the only accounting constraint was provided by the fact that total intermediate demand less imports and home final demand less imports must be positive, i.e.

(7.11) $$A-[A_{M1}+A_{M2}]\geqslant 0$$

(7.12) $$h-[h_{m1}+h_{m2}]\geqslant o$$

where 1 refers to CACM, 2 refers to ROW, 0 is a null matrix and o is a null vector.

Where supply-side data are used, it is usually possible to provide a parallel record of protective duties in each cell of the matrix. If the import matrix from the rest of the world is called M, this means that we can write:

(7.13) $$M^* = M + D$$

where D is a matrix of duties paid in each cell of the import matrix. Knowledge of the D matrix is invaluable in certain input–output applications, such as calculating the Effective Rate of Protection (see Bulmer-Thomas, 1976).

NOTES

1 Many countries use the term 'balance of goods and services' to include factor services (e.g. the return on direct foreign investment). It should be clear that this is not the use of the phrase intended here.

2 It is unusual for firms to include the cost of international transport and insurance, but there are commodities (e.g. primary exports), where wholesalers intervene actively between producers and shippers and this function will not be reflected in the firm's price, although it will appear in the f.o.b. value.

3 If the data are valued in foreign currency, they will need to be converted to home currency at the exchange rate appropriate to the producer of the commodity, so that the home currency value reflects actual receipts. In countries with multiple exchange rates, determination of the appropriate exchange rate can be a laborious task (see Bulmer-Thomas, 1977a, p. 105).

4 In the Notes to its *Balance of Payments Yearbook* (IMF, 1979, p. xi), the International Monetary Fund lists a number of possible bases for recording exports, 'such as the time of contract or commitment, shipment of goods, delivery of goods, customs clearance, performance of services, accrual of income, and payment'. In its *Balance of Payments Manual* (IMF, 1977), the Fund recommends change of ownership as the most suitable basis for recording exports, but it should be clear that this could still result in an imbalance for input–output purposes.

5 In Costa Rica, trade with the Central American Common Market (CACM) was distinguished from trade with the rest of the world other than CACM (ROW), while in Scotland trade with the rest of the United Kingdom (RUK) was distinguished from trade with the rest of the world (ROW).

6 In the application of input–output analysis to inter-regional models, it is sometimes desirable to construct export matrices, where the columns represent the using sectors in

foreign countries (cf. Isard, 1960). The problem of input–output tables for regions, however, is discussed in Chapter 11.

7 Revenue duties are those which 'aim . . . at raising revenue or discouraging consumption and, in the case of competitive commodities, are usually matched by a corresponding excise duty on the domestically produced commodity' (United Nations, 1968, pp. 40–41).

8 Unless, of course, there is only one exchange rate and each user pays the same rate of tariff for the same commodity.

9 In its earlier publication (United Nations, 1968, p. 41), the UN suggested that imports be valued exclusive of protective duties because they are 'often small and present difficulties of definition'. Protective duties in LDCs, however, are usually enormous and very important in determining the competitiveness of home production and the UN is right to recognize this in its later publication.

10 Where standard prices have been adopted, the same basis for imports can be used provided that they are also adjusted for transport and distribution costs up to the first point of use. Only in this way would the valuation of imports be comparable with home production valued at standard prices.

11 In order that this may be so, exports should be net of re-exports. For a realistic discussion of re-exports, see United Nations, 1973, p. 64.

12 In the Scottish input–output tables (Fraser, 1978), two import matrices were prepared almost entirely from demand-side data; one showed imports from the rest of the United Kingdom, while the other showed trade with the rest of the world. In general, however, the input–output team regarded these matrices as the least reliable part of their work.

CHAPTER 8

Balancing, Reconciliation and the Computer's Role

8.1 INTRODUCTION

When all the entries in the make matrix have been filled in, the row sums will give an estimate of industry output and the column sums of commodity supply; when the absorption matrix, supplemented by columns for final demand and rows for value added, has been completed and adjusted to a common price basis (see Chapter 6), the row sums will refer to the demand for commodities and the column sums to industry output. It follows that there are two estimates of both industry and commodity output, although the two industry estimates are normally the same, since industry output in the absorption matrix is measured as the sum of industry inputs with one of the 'inputs' (gross trading profits) usually being treated as a residual.

This equality is most unlikely to be the case, however, with the two commodity estimates. Even after adjusting for differences in valuation, the two will differ for a variety of reasons, the most fundamental being that they are derived from independent sources; the demand for commodities is not constrained to equal the supply and so we are forced to write the balance equation for each commodity group as:[1]

$$q_i + (m_i + d_i) + (t_i - s_i) + dr_i = \sum_j w_{ij} + c_i + gx_i + j_i + \Delta s_i + e_i \pm u_i \qquad (8.1)$$

where

q_i = the output of the ith commodity as given by the ith column of the make matrix summed row-wise.
m_i = the c.i.f. value of imports of the ith commodity group.
d_i = import duties (protective) payable on ith imports.
t_i = indirect taxes levied on ith commodity (including revenue duties).
s_i = subsidies paid on consumption of ith commodity.
dr_i = distributive margins (transport and trade) on ith commodity.
$\sum_j w_{ij}$ = intermediate absorptions of ith commodity.
c_i = household consumption of ith commodity.

gx_i = government current expenditure on ith commodity.
j_i = fixed capital formation involving expenditure on ith commodity.
Δs_i = inventory change involving ith commodity.
e_i = exports of ith commodity.
u_i = a slack variable (positive or negative) to take up the difference between commodity supply and commodity demand.

The above accounting identity is very basic in that it only seeks to identify the main sources of supply and demand; for example, intermediate consumption can be broken down by using sector. Furthermore, equation (8.1) assumes that the data of the absorption matrix are still denominated in purchasers' prices. If the data have already been adjusted for the reasons set out in Chapter 6, alternative formulations are necessary such as:

(8.2) $$q_i + (m_i + d_i) = \sum_j w'_{ij} + c'_i + gx'_i + j'_i + \Delta s'_i + e'_i \pm u_i$$

where a prime (′) notes the use of adjusted data (in this case at basic prices), but u_i is unchanged since the effect of adding valuation adjustments to supply (equation (8.1)) is the same as deducting them from demand (equation (8.2)).

If u_i is divided by estimated supply $\{q_i + (m_i + d_i)\}$ or demand $(\Sigma_j w'_{ij} + c'_i + gx'_i + j'_i + \Delta s'_i + e'_i)$, it becomes a measure of relative error. Percentage errors in excess of $\pm 25\%$ are quite frequent at this stage of input–output work and their elimination can be the single, most time-consuming task of the whole process of constructing tables. Potentially good tables can be ruined by crude and hasty attempts at reconciliation, but unfortunately it is often at this stage in construction that time, money and patience are all at their lowest ebb. It is vital, therefore, that appropriate resources be devoted to this stage, although the purpose of the rest of this chapter is to keep to a minimum the need for such resources by employing them efficiently.

Balancing or reconciliation techniques can be either 'manual' or 'mechanical'; the latter, however, are inappropriate where the relative error is large and so balancing usually begins with a 'manual' stage. Since no component of supply or demand is guaranteed free of error, it seems appropriate therefore to start with a few words on the main sources of error in each variable of equation (8.1).

8.2 MAIN SOURCES OF ERROR IN BALANCE EQUATIONS

Commodity output (q_i) will represent the activities of large, small and artisanal-type establishments (the so-called informal sector). The precision of each component of commodity output is likely to be very different and it may therefore be worthwhile to record output as:

(8.3) $$q_i = {}_bq_i + {}_sq_i + {}_aq_i$$

where ${}_bq_i$, ${}_sq_i$ and ${}_aq_i$ are the commodity outputs produced by big, small and artisan establishments respectively. There are two reasons for this separation; first, the sales pattern of each component may be quite different, so that revisions to demand may require revisions to ${}_bq_i$ but not ${}_aq_i$, for example, and secondly revisions to output will typically alter estimates of intermediate absorptions $(\Sigma_i w_{ij})$ and inventory change (Δs_i), and the change may well depend on what kind of establishment is being considered. The input pattern of 'traditional' firms in the informal sector will be quite different from that of large firms, although they may both market a relatively homogeneous product.[2]

The estimate of imports $(m_i + d_i)$ is likely to be very reliable and, indeed, if one component of the import vector changes, another is likely to change in the opposite direction. Misclassification of trade codes is the most frequent source of error with imports, although a difference in timing can also bring about an inconsistency between supply and demand (see Chapter 7).

The demand for imports is not separately identified on the right-hand side of equations (8.1) and (8.2). If an import absorption matrix is available, it is of course possible to rewrite the balance equations as two sets: one for domestic flows and one for imports. This is an unwise procedure at this stage, however, as the division of demand by origin is never as reliable as the total demand estimate. Once equation (8.1), for example, has been adjusted so that $u_i = 0$, a separate balance equation for imports can then be constructed as:

$$m_i + d_i = \sum_j w_{ij}^m + h_i^m + gx_i^m + j_i^m + \Delta s_i^m \pm u_i^m \tag{8.4}$$

where the superscript m denotes imports and all adjustments will be confined to the right-hand side. When $u_i^m = 0$, the deduction of equation (8.4) from (8.1)—with $u_i = 0$—will automatically give the resource-use equation for domestic flows. The results, however,must still be checked, since it is conceivable that some of the estimates of domestic demand will come out as negative; in this case, an iterative process is needed with equation (8.4) being rebalanced to prevent the occurrence of the negative (or absurd) estimates of domestic demand.

Net indirect taxes $(t_i - s_i)$ usually offer little scope for adjustment, because official statistics must be used and these are often very detailed. Sometimes, they are so detailed that individual commodities within a commodity group will be taxed differently, and the input–output worker is forced to use a crude averaging procedure; in national tables, however, the sum of net indirect taxes—$\Sigma_i(t_i - s_i)$—is a very precise figure and changes in one element of the vector may require compensating changes elsewhere.

We now turn to the estimate of distributive margins (dr_i) in equation (8.1). Because of the difficulties associated with the estimates of trade and transport margins, it is not uncommon to find most of the difference between commodity supply and demand attributed to errors in the estimate of dr_i. This is a natural response, but it should be resisted since it draws attention away from the inevitable errors in the other elements of the supply/demand balance.

If the distributive margins are changed in balancing, it will affect the gross output of the distributive activities and this will in turn affect intermediate absorptions by these activities and conceivably their output of secondary products. On the other hand, changes in intermediate consumption will in turn affect distributive margins, so it can take many iterations to achieve a balance when distributive margins change.

Intermediate consumption ($\Sigma_j w_{ij}$) represents absorptions by many different users, so that errors of estimation are always possible. Sometimes, absorption matrices reach the balancing stage without all purchases allocated to a supplier; these unallocated expenditures arise, for example, because firms (when surveyed) feel unable to offer a breakdown of all their miscellaneous expenses. For the aggregate of all firms, these expenditures can be important, particularly as they tend to be concentrated in certain sectors such as textiles (e.g. cleaning rags) or chemicals (ink, hand-soap, etc.). It is preferable, therefore, to remove all non-classified outlays before balancing, because otherwise there is no guarantee that, when the nth row has been balanced, all unallocated expenditures will disappear. If some remain, the whole balancing exercise may have to start again. Ways of dealing with unallocated expenditures are discussed in Chapter 11.

The remaining entries in equations (8.1) and (8.2) all concern final demand. Household consumption (c_i) is often the dominant entry and one of the easiest to adjust; inventory change, however, is also a frequent candidate for adjustment, since its method of estimation is so unreliable. Government expenditure, on the other hand, fixed capital formation and exports are usually much better estimates, but even in these cases there is always the possibility of some revision.

8.3 MANUAL BALANCING

Although there are a number of computer algorithms available, which can eliminate the error term (u_i) in equation (8.1), this 'mechanical' form of balancing is usually only appropriate at a late stage in the reconciliation process. Mechanical balancing, for example, cannot turn a zero into a positive number[3] and some more flexible means is needed initially to reduce the size of the relative error.[4]

The usual method adopted is a series of 'manual' balancing operations, in which those responsible for the table's construction examine row by row possible sources of error. Since each row corresponds to a group of commodities with certain features in common, it is helpful to seek the participation of sectoral experts who have not been involved in the table's construction; for example, when discussing the commodity groups making up a country's textile industry, there is a host of people—engineers, trade unionists, civil servants, businessmen, etc.—who are in a position to provide the kind of qualitative insights which the more quantitative-orientated input–output worker might have missed.

In the manual balancing stage, it is often helpful to use information obtained from outside the input–output survey; examples are the reports of trades councils, market research data and international comparisons. Occasionally it is possible to carry out the balancing of rows using data on physical quantities, which reduces the source of error to the use of inappropriate prices.

In the manual phase, it is not necessary to reduce all u_i to zero, so that there is no need at this stage to achieve precise reconciliation with any 'hard' statistics, such as the national accounts. Nonetheless, it is essential that at each 'round' of manual balancing, the main macro-economic aggregates—e.g. total consumption, investment, value added—are calculated, since major errors should be removed before mechanical balancing.

In the author's experience, the number of errors—some very basic—revealed at the manual balancing stage is enormous and this can create a sense of despondency in the input–output team. Much of this feeling is misplaced, since input–output tables are very robust and can perform well in model-building despite various imperfections, but the fact remains that the more time the input–output team can devote to the exhausting task of manual balancing the better. Manual balancing is usually carried on until the size of the relative error is reduced to about $\pm 5\%$. More than this is unwise, since it may represent huge errors in a small number of transactions, while less is unrealistic, since at each 'round' it becomes harder and harder to reduce the mean size of relative error. Consequently, the input–output team is left with a small relative error, which needs to be removed by mechanical means.

8.4 MECHANICAL BALANCING

In Figure 8.1, a simplified unbalanced social accounting matrix ($A\tilde{B}S$) is shown. It consists of four parts: intermediate absorptions ($\tilde{W}$), final demands ($\tilde{F}$), value added ($\tilde{V}$) and interactions between the non-production accounts ($\tilde{Z}$) with a ($\tilde{\ }$) denoting estimated values. It can therefore be written in partitioned form as:

$$[A\tilde{B}S] = \left[\begin{array}{c|c} \tilde{W} & \tilde{F} \\ \hline \tilde{V} & \tilde{Z} \end{array}\right] \tag{8.5}$$

The row sums of the matrix yield provisional totals for commodity demands ($\tilde{q} = \tilde{W}i + \tilde{F}i$) and for value added ($\tilde{v} = \tilde{V}i + \tilde{Z}i$). The known totals, however, denoted by q and v, are given by the last column of Figure 8.1. The column sums of the matrix yield totals for industry output ($\tilde{g} = i\tilde{W} + i\tilde{V}$) which are the same as the known totals (g), and for final demands ($\tilde{fd} = i\tilde{F} + i\tilde{Z}$) which may differ from the known totals (fd).[5]

The problem now is to adjust the elements of the partitioned social accounting matrix, so that the known row and column sum totals are satisfied. This will result in a new matrix ($A\tilde{B}S^*$) such that:

$$[A\tilde{B}S^*] = \left[\begin{array}{c|c} \tilde{W}^* & \tilde{F}^* \\ \hline \tilde{V}^* & \tilde{Z}^* \end{array}\right] \tag{8.6}$$

and

$$\begin{aligned} \tilde{W}^*i + \tilde{F}^*i &= q \\ \tilde{V}^*i + \tilde{Z}^*i &= v \\ i\tilde{W}^* + i\tilde{V}^* &= g \\ i\tilde{F}^* + i\tilde{Z}^* &= fd \end{aligned} \tag{8.7}$$

	Production			Consumption		Accumulation		Trade		Totals	
	1	2	3	Private	Public	Gross fixed capital formation	Inventory change	Exports	—Imports	Estimated	'True'
Production 1	10	20	30	20	10	—	10	40	−35	105 $\tilde{q}_1$	100 q_1
2	10	50	40	40	20	40	20	50	−80	190 $\tilde{q}_2$	200 q_2
3	20	50	30	30	10	—	—	—	—	140 $\tilde{q}_3$	150 q_3
Value added	60	80	50	—	—	—	—	—	—	190 $\tilde{v}$	200 v
Estimated Totals	100 $\tilde{g}_1$	200 $\tilde{g}_2$	150 $\tilde{g}_3$	90 $\tilde{fd}_1$	40 $\tilde{fd}_2$	40 $\tilde{fd}_3$	30 $\tilde{fd}_4$	90 $\tilde{fd}_5$	−115 $\tilde{fd}_6$		
True Totals	100 g_1	200 g_2	150 g_3	100 fd_1	40 fd_2	45 fd_3	40 fd_4	90 fd_5	−115 fd_6		

Note: In this simplified unbalanced social accounting matrix, it has been assumed that 'true' commodity output (q) and 'true' industry output (g) are the same.

Figure 8.1 Unbalanced social accounting matrix ($A\tilde{B}S$)

A common solution to this problem is found by assuming that the final matrix $(A\tilde{B}S^*)$ is 'biproportional' to the first (Bacharach, 1970), so that:

$$A\tilde{B}S^* = \hat{r}A\tilde{B}S\hat{s} \tag{8.8}$$

where $(\hat{r})$ and $(\hat{s})$ are two diagonal matrices, whose elements represent the two effects to which the 'base' matrix is subject to arrive at $(A\tilde{B}S^*)$. If this assumption holds, we have:

$$\hat{r}A\tilde{B}Ss = \begin{bmatrix} q \\ \hdashline v \end{bmatrix} \tag{8.9}$$

$$r'A\tilde{B}S\hat{s} = [g_i \,\vdots\, fd] \tag{8.10}$$

i.e. $2n$ equations in the $2n$ unknowns r and s. As has been shown elsewhere (Bacharach, 1970), a convergent iterative procedure exists for solving equations (8.9) and (8.10) to obtain the r and s multipliers. (For details of the method, see the Appendix.) The biproportional method is more usually associated with updating input–output tables (see Chapter 10), but the method is in fact appropriate for many constrained matrix problems, i.e. where a matrix has to be adjusted for given marginal control totals. This is precisely the problem faced in this chapter, but even so the biproportional method cannot be applied indiscriminately.

First, it should be clear from equation (8.8) that every entry in $(A\tilde{B}S)$ is capable of being changed through pre- and post-multiplication by the $(\hat{r})$ and $(\hat{s})$ multipliers respectively. It may be, however, that the input–output team enters the balancing stage knowing that a number of entries in $(A\tilde{B}S)$ are already correct. It is most undesirable that these figures should alter in the balancing process, so that the biproportional method needs to be applied to the absorption matrix net of known values. In Figure 8.2, for example, all known values have been entered (ABS'), so that by subtraction from Figure 8.1 $(A\tilde{B}S)$, we obtain all those flows $(A\tilde{B}S'')$ whose values can legitimately be altered in the balancing process. Equations (8.9) and (8.10) still apply, except of course that the marginal totals also need adjusting; the final matrix $(A\tilde{B}S^{**})$ is then obtained as:

$$A\tilde{B}S^{**} = ABS' + \hat{r}A\tilde{B}S''\hat{s} \tag{8.11}$$

A second problem is that the biproportional method preserves zeros in the solution: if $\tilde{w}_{ij} = 0$, for example, $\tilde{w}^*_{ij} = 0$ as well. Thus, a phase of manual balancing must precede the mechanical stage in order to correct for cells which appear empty, but are known to be positive. This applies particularly to those cells affected by unallocated expenditure and one solution is to enter a small 'trace' element at the manual stage in these cells, so that they will be preserved as positive in the mechanical stage (see also Chapter 11).

A third problem is that the biproportional method works best if the initial matrix $(A\tilde{B}S)$ is non-negative (see Appendix). A good description of the iterative solution to the r and s multipliers is given elsewhere (United Nations, 1973), but it will help to expalin the non-negative restrictions if it is outlined here. First, each

	Production			Consumption		Accumulation		Trade		Totals	
	1	2	3	Private	Public	Gross fixed capital formation	Inventory change	Exports—	Imports	Estimated	'True'
Production											
1	—	5	10	15	10	—	—	40	−35	45	45
2	5	10	10	20	20	—	—	50	−80	35	35
3	—	—	—	—	10	—	—	—	—	10	10
Value added	40	20	10	—	—	—	—	—	—	70	70
Estimated totals	45	35	30	35	40	—	—	90	−115		
True totals	45	35	30	35	40	—	—	90	−115		

Figure 8.2 Known values in the social accounting matrix (*ABS'*)

row (column) is multiplied by a scalar which ensures that the row (column) marginal totals are satisfied; the same thing is then done for the columns (rows), but this will throw out the equality in the rows (columns) so that they must again be given a scalar adjustment. Fortunately, the process is convergent and a solution is usually reached after only a small number of iterations.

Now let us assume the first iteration is carried out on the rows. Let us also suppose that $\tilde{q}_i/q_i = 1.05$, so that the purpose is to reduce all entries by 5%. If all entries are positive, there is no problem, but if one of the entries is negative its reduction by 5% will, *ceteris paribus*, make the row's imbalance worse and will move the negative element in what is likely to be the wrong direction. In other words, the reduction in the positive entries is partly to cure the original imbalance and partly to offset the reduction in the negative entry. The presence of negative entries therefore introduces an unnecessary element of instability into the convergency process.

If the mechanical balance is carried out on a social accounting matrix representing not just intermediate transactions (as suggested above), then negative elements cannot be avoided, since imports will appear in final demand with a minus sign (see Figure 8.1). Furthermore, there *may* be negative entries in all the quadrants of the absorption matrix; if subsidies received exceed indirect taxes in any industry, then value added will contain negative entries, and this will also be the case if sectors make losses (cf. the treatment of financial institutions in Chapter 2). The matrix of intermediate transactions itself may contain negative entries if there are joint- or by-products (see Chapter 9) and the fourth quadrant (Z) is just as likely to contain positive as negative entries (e.g. sales by final buyers).

If the biproportional method is applied to an initial matrix containing negative entries, a solution may result, but convergence can no longer be guaranteed (Henry, 1973a) and another desirable property of the method will also be lost; the choice of the biproportional method is not merely to obtain a balanced matrix, it is also designed to secure a solution which is in some sense 'close' to the initial matrix. It has been shown (Bacharach, 1970) that the biproportional method achieves 'closeness' by minimizing the function $\Sigma_{ij}(\tilde{ABS}^*_{ij} \log \tilde{ABS}^*_{ij}/\tilde{ABS}_{ij})$ where $\tilde{ABS}^*_{ij}$, $\tilde{ABS}_{ij}$ are the i, jth elements of the final and initial absorption matrices respectively. Since the minimand is defined in terms of logarithms and since we cannot take logarithms of negative numbers, the biproportional method applied to an initial absorption matrix with minus signs does not guarantee closeness of fit. Thus, the solution—if one exists—may be very 'distant' from the initial matrix.[6]

The biproportional method may still give satisfactory results if the relative errors are small ($< \pm 5\%$). However, no great confidence can be expressed in the solution and it seems safer to apply the method only where negative entries have been removed from the initial matrix. This can be done in a number of ways; for example, if the negative entries are known with certainty (as is a reasonable assumption in the case of imports and net indirect taxes) they can appear in (ABS') as in Figure 8.2, so that (ABS'') is a non-negative matrix.[7] Another possibility is to aggregate pairs of rows or columns so that the negative entries disappear, disaggregation becoming a separate exercise after the application of the biproportional method.

If none of these devices are possible, the biproportional method can be abandoned in favour of an alternative method of solving a constrained matrix problem (see Appendix). The Friedlander method, for example (Friedlander, 1961), assumes the following relationship between the final absorption matrix $(A\tilde{B}S^*)$ and the initial estimate $(A\tilde{B}S)$:

(8.12) $$A\tilde{B}S^* = A\tilde{B}S + \hat{r}A\tilde{B}S + A\tilde{B}S\hat{s}$$

The final matrix is no longer biproportional to the initial one, but the r and s multipliers have a similar interpretation and can be found either by iterative solution (as in the case of the biproportional method) or by directly solving a set of simultaneous equations (Henry, 1973b), which many might regard as a considerable bonus. The Friedlander method minimizes:

$$\sum_{ij} \frac{(A\tilde{B}S^*_{ij} - A\tilde{B}S_{ij})^2}{A\tilde{B}S_{ij}}$$

so that the minimand will be a misleading measure of closeness of fit if there are positive and negative entries in $(A\tilde{B}S)$. However, by replacing the denominator in the minimand by the modulus $|A\tilde{B}S_{ij}|$, the minimum distance property of the Friedlander method is preserved and the method can therefore be used with reasonable confidence, even where the initial matrix has negative entries.

The Friedlander method has one major drawback in that it does not preserve sign in the final matrix, i.e. positive entries in the initial matrix can turn negative in the final one (and, presumably, vice versa). This problem has prompted two modifications to the method; first, the addition of non-negativity restrictions $(A\tilde{B}S^*_{ij} \geqslant 0)$, which means that 'the simple iterative adjustment is no longer available and $[A\tilde{B}S^*]$ must be found by quadratic programming. However, the resultant problem makes heavy demands on computer time and programming ingenuity', (Lecomber, 1975); secondly, a post-balancing stage of 'tidying up' the final matrix to remove elements where change of sign is inconsistent with *a priori* restrictions.

The first method is unlikely to be attractive to those responsible for input–output tables in LDCs. The second is an acceptable compromise, given that the few tests of the Friedlander method (e.g. Bacharach, 1970, Chapter 11) suggest that the changes of sign are few and relatively trivial. We therefore find ourselves with the following options for mechanical balancing:

1 If there are no negative entries in the absorption matrix $(A\tilde{B}S)$, use of the biproportional method is most appropriate as it preserves sign and satisfies minimal distance criteria.

2 If there are negative entries in the absorption matrix $(A\tilde{B}S)$, which can all be included in $(A\tilde{B}S')$ so that the adjusted absorption matrix $(A\tilde{B}S'')$ excludes negative entries, the biproportional method is still most appropriate.

3 If $(A\tilde{B}S'')$ cannot be written net of negative entries, the Friedlander method

for solving a constrained matrix problem is most appropriate, but the method does not guarantee preservation of sign and may necessitate some slight alteration to the 'final' matrix after balancing.

We may now see how these ideas work out in practice in the case of the simple unbalanced matrix illustrated in Figures 8.1 and 8.2. Since the only negative entries in $(A\tilde{B}S)$ all appear in (ABS'), there will be no negative entries in $(A\tilde{B}S'')$. This suggests that the biproportional method is the most appropriate one for finding a solution; the 'true' row sums of $(A\tilde{B}S'')$ are given by $(u - ABS'i)$, where $u = \begin{bmatrix} q \\ \hdashline v \end{bmatrix}$, while the true column sums are given by $(w - i'ABS')$, where $w = [g:fd]$. Applying the r and s multipliers to $(A\tilde{B}S'')$ subject to these control totals enables us to obtain a new balanced matrix, which must be added to the exogenous entries in (ABS') to give the final balanced social accounting matrix $(A\tilde{B}S^{**})$.

This final matrix is reproduced as Figure 8.3. By comparing it with Figure 8.1 we can identify the main changes; all intermediate transactions entries have changed slightly, while the elements in the value added row have increased quite sharply; the main changes in final demand concern the accumulation columns. We may also note that zero entries in Figure 8.1 have been preserved in Figure 8.3.

So far, it has been assumed that the marginal totals are known with certainty. This is most unlikely to be the case as far as commodity (q) and industry outputs (g) are concerned and may well not be true in the case of final demands (fd) and value added (v).[8] Fortunately, both the biproportional and Friedlander methods can be modified to take account of uncertainty.[9]

When the control totals are not known with certainty, it becomes necessary to partition them into a part which *is* known with certainty and a part which is not; it is then assumed (Allen, 1975) that the part which is *not* known with certainty can change in the balancing process; this means we can write the control totals as:

$$(8.13) \qquad \begin{aligned} u &= [u - e_u + \hat{r}e_u] \\ w &= [w - e_w + e_w\hat{s}] \end{aligned}$$

where e_u is a column vector which records that part of the row sums of the social accounting matrix not known with certainty (both commodity outputs and value added), while e_w is a row vector which records that part of the column sums of the social accounting matrix not known with certainty (both industry outputs and final demands).

If we now apply the biproportional method, say, to the unbalanced absorption matrix $(A\tilde{B}S)$, we obtain the following:

$$(8.14) \qquad \begin{aligned} \hat{r}(A\tilde{B}S)s &= [u - e_u + \hat{r}e_u] \\ r'(A\tilde{B}S)\hat{s} &= [w - e_w + e_w\hat{s}] \end{aligned}$$

so that on rearrangement we get:

$$(8.15) \qquad \begin{aligned} \hat{r}[(A\tilde{B}S)s - e_u] &= [u - e_u] \\ [r'(A\tilde{B}S) - e_w]\hat{s} &= [w - e_w] \end{aligned}$$

	Production			Consumption		Accumulation		Trade		Totals
	1	2	3	Private	Public	Gross fixed capital formation	Inventory change	Exports	—Imports	
Production										
1	8.4	17.4	26.7	20.1	10	—	12.4	40	−35	100
2	9.3	47.3	38.2	42.6	20	45	27.6	50	−80	200
3	20.6	50.9	31.2	37.3	10	—	—	—	—	150
Value added	61.7	84.4	53.9	—	—	—	—	—	—	200
Totals	100	200	150	100	40	45	40	90	−115	

Figure 8.3 Final balanced social accounting matrix ($A\tilde{B}S^{**}$)

which is a system of $2n$ equations from which a solution for the r and s multipliers can be obtained by simple iteration. This time, however, the control totals themselves (see equation 8.13) can be expected to change, so that some of the burden of adjustment is shifted to the row and column sums.

Assuming, as before, that some of the absorption matrix is known with certainty (ABS'), a new balanced absorption matrix is presented in Figure 8.4 on the assumption that the control totals are not known with certainty.[10] The result is quite similar to that obtained in Figure 8.3, although it is noticeable that the control totals have changed slightly in all those cases where they were assumed to be estimated with error; it is also interesting to note that commodity and industry outputs are no longer the same.

We now assume that a final matrix has been obtained, whose row sums equal commodity output and whose column sums equal industry output as given by the appropriate rows and columns of the make matrix. This fixes import supply, but if an import matrix has been prepared, then import demand—as given by the row sums of the import matrix—may not be the same.[11] The column sums of the import matrix are unlikely to be known with certainty and so, again, we have a constrained matrix problem.

We may write the unadjusted import matrix as $\tilde{M}$. The problem is to find a new matrix ($\tilde{M}^*$) such that:

$$\tilde{M}^* i = m$$

where m is the (known) vector of import supply subject to $\tilde{M}^*_{ij} \leqslant ABS^*_{ij}$.

The n^2 constraints are needed, because we cannot allow the elements of the import matrix to exceed the equivalent values in the absorption matrix. However, as in the Friedlander method where strict non-negativity is required, these side conditions involve the use of quadratic programming techniques. Simpler methods are likely to be desirable and the most obvious one is to treat the problem as a degenerate biproportional constrained matrix problem with only one set of marginal (row) totals. Thus, we need a set of row multipliers (r), such that:

$$\begin{aligned} \hat{r}\tilde{M} &= \tilde{M}^* \\ \tilde{M}^* i &= m \end{aligned} \tag{8.16}$$

and this has a very simple solution, since the ith element of $\hat{r}$ is found as:

$$r_i = \frac{m_i}{\sum_j \tilde{M}_{ij}} \tag{8.17}$$

The new matrix ($\tilde{M}^*$) must now be deducted from ($\tilde{ABS}^*$) to check for negative flows. Where these are found, a number of small alterations will need to be made in ($\tilde{M}^*$) to remove them; the process is untidy, but less time-consuming and expensive than quadratic programming.

One problem with equations (8.16) and (8.17) is that all errors in the import matrix are supposed to be removed by the effects of the row multipliers. This is a

	Production			Consumption		Accumulation		Trade		
	1	2	3	Private	Public	Gross fixed capital formation	Inventory change	Exports	—Imports	Totals
Production										
1	8.0	17.1	26.5	20.0	10	—	12.8	40	−35	99.4
2	9.7	47.0	38.2	42.5	20	45.0	27.8	50	−80	200.2
3	20.3	50.9	30.7	37.2	10	—	—	—	—	149.1
Value added	61.7	84.5	54.1	—	—	—	—	—	—	200.3
Totals	99.7	199.5	149.3	99.7	40	45.0	40.6	90	−115	

Figure 8.4 Final balanced social accounting matrix ($A\tilde{B}S^{**}$) when control totals are subject to uncertainty

most heroic assumption and it seems wiser, therefore, to recognize the role played by the column multipliers. This can be done by dividing the column total into a part known with certainty and an uncertain part. We therefore obtain:

$$\tilde{M}^* = \hat{r}\tilde{M}\hat{s} \tag{8.18}$$

such that:

$$\tilde{M}^* i = m \tag{8.19}$$

and

$$i\tilde{M}^* = \mu \tag{8.20}$$

where μ is a row vector consisting of a part known with certainty and an uncertain part (e_μ). As before, we suggest the relationship:

$$\mu = [\mu - e_\mu] + e_\mu \hat{s} \tag{8.21}$$

so that we obtain the $2n$ equations in the $2n$ multipliers as:

$$\begin{aligned} \hat{r}\tilde{M}s &= m \\ r'\tilde{M}\hat{s} &= [\mu - e_\mu] + e_\mu \hat{s} \end{aligned} \tag{8.22}$$

which is sufficient to obtain a solution by a process of iterative convergence. Application of the row and column multipliers so obtained to $\tilde{M}$ will then provide an estimate ($\tilde{M}^*$) of the true, but unknown, import matrix (M).

8.5 THE ROLE OF THE COMPUTER

Mechanical balancing on anything but the smallest matrices cannot be handled without the aid of a computer. However, it may well be desirable to introduce computers at an earlier stage in processing the data; many adjustment operations do not vary from one establishment to another and even with several thousand establishments the computer can carry out the tasks very quickly.

There is a more pressing reason, however, for introducing computers at an early stage. Individual questionnaires, despite the best efforts of survey designers, contain answers in response to the same questions which are not homogeneous in a number of respects; for example, wages and salaries may be recorded inclusive or exclusive of national insurance contributions, income in kind, wage subsidies and so on. All these data have to be standardized before establishments can be aggregated into sectors and this is the kind of task for which computers, with their quick scanning abilities, are well suited. Similarly, valuation adjustments need to be carried out on individual establishments, since not all can be expected to route the same proportion of purchases through wholesalers, for example, nor is it always possible to secure a standard treatment of indirect taxes in the questionnaire.

In what follows, therefore, it is assumed that the computer is used at the earliest stage, i.e. questionnaire data are transferred direct without any preliminary adjustments. Of course, this treatment is inappropriate for many sectors, such as public utilities where a few firms produce virtually all the output and where manual processing and adjustment is likely to be most efficient, but if at least some branches of the table are being estimated by survey techniques, then it is reasonable to assume that the computer will be needed at an early stage.

The flow diagrams in Figures 8.5 and 8.6 show the main phases, based on the Scottish input–output table, in processing data by computer. We begin with the translation of questionnaire returns into coded data (1); the worst anomalies in the survey response are then 'ironed out' (2) (4) to give the first data base (5). The data are then processed and refined on to a completely homogeneous basis (7) (8) (11) (12), giving the second and third data bases (9) (13). At this point (see Figure 8.6), sectors processed manually are entered (15) (assuming that they are on a homogeneous basis with those processed by machine) and the data are then aggregated according to the classification schemes (18) and 'grossed up' to population estimates (20). These 'grossed up' data represent the make and absorption matrices, but they may also provide estimates of imports, stock change, investment, export and employment matrices. Finally, the rows and columns of the make and absorption matrices are reconciled, as outlined in the main body of this chapter, so that commodity-by-commodity and industry-by-industry input–output tables can be formed (Chapter 9).

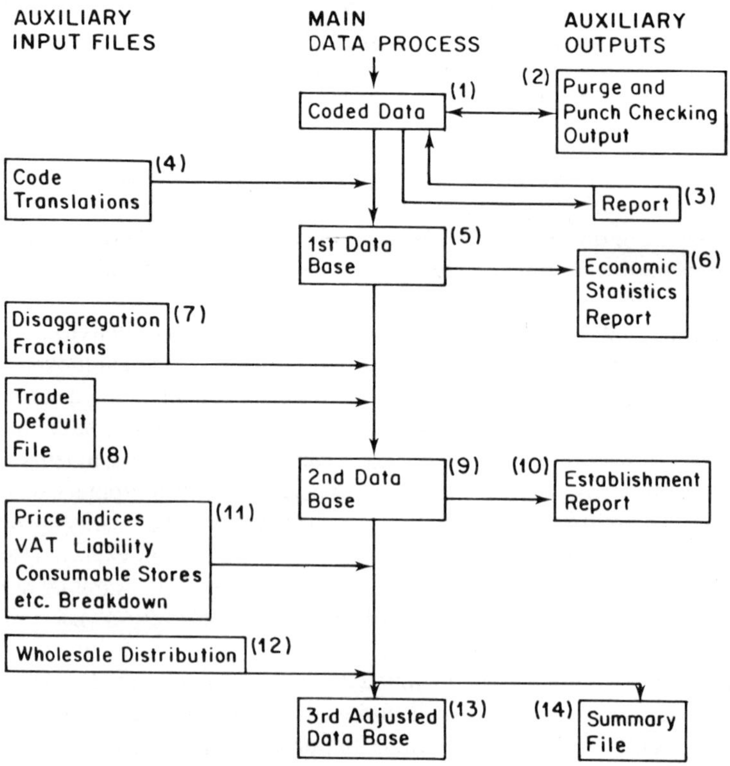

Figure 8.5 Data sequence 1. *Source*: Burdekin (1978a)

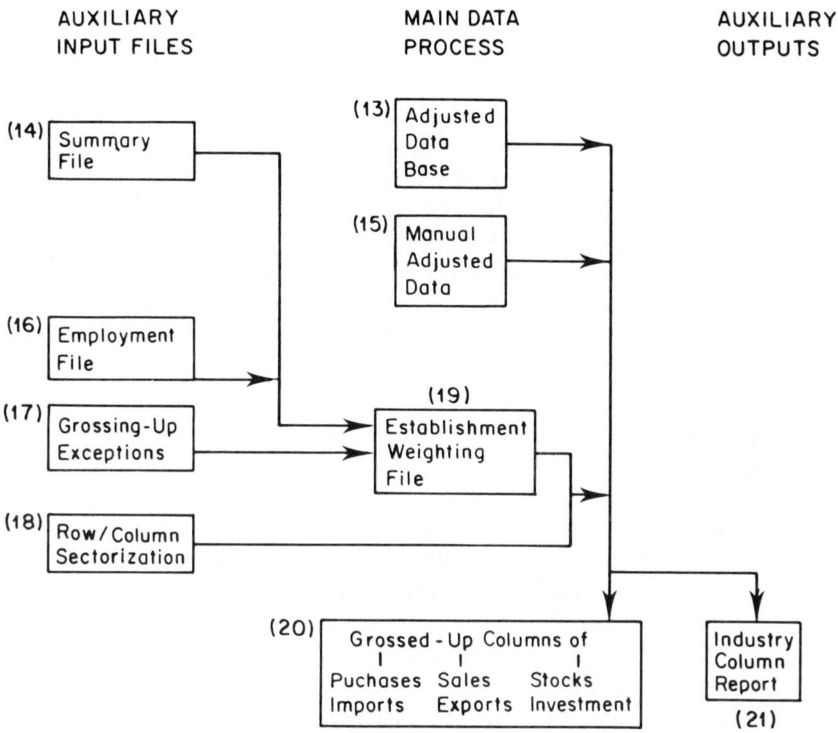

Figure 8.6 Data sequence II = Grossing-up. *Source*: Burdekin (1978a)

Coding the questionnaire data for machine use is the first and, in many ways, the most arduous task. If widely different activities are being processed at this stage, the coding format may be quite different for each; this and the sheer volume of data to be processed—4000 variables per questionnaire in the case of the Scottish input–output table—create the possibility of coding errors and a great deal of thought needs to go into preventing these mistakes.

The number of coding errors in the construction of the Scottish table was generally considered excessive and, in designing the coding stage for the Moroccan table, a scheme was worked out which proved much more satisfactory. First, each questionnaire was given a preliminary examination to make sure that all questions had been answered; where a questionnaire satisfied this condition, the information contained in it was transferred to a precoding sheet; this was so designed as to make it relatively easy to detect logical errors, such as percentages not rounding to 100; finally, the data were transferred to a coding sheet in a form which made as simple as possible the task of punching the necessary computer cards.

The precoding sheet avoided a large number of errors being transferred directly from questionnaire to punched cards; on the other hand, at the precoding stage one meets for the first time the problem of establishment and product codes; the former are needed to protect the anonymity of sampled establishments, while the latter are needed as a bridge to the classification scheme.

If the classification scheme has not been settled in advance, the temptation is to use a coding scheme far more detailed than is really needed; this wastes computer time, uses more cards, increases the probability of error and leads to problems of disaggregation, when it is found that questionnaire responses cannot be coded at the necessary level of detail. It is therefore essential to have at least a preliminary classification scheme, which determines the maximum size of the table.

A preliminary classification scheme, however, cannot eliminate entirely ambiguity in coding; all surveys find a need for general codes, referring to unallocated expenditures or sales, but it can be kept to a minimum by precise wording of headings in questionnaires and by disaggregation of all but the most intractable at the precoding stage. There is a very understandable temptation to 'pass the buck' by using a general code for all difficult items, but this poses grave problems later on; the degrees of freedom is balancing and reconciliation, for example, become too great if a large proportion of expenditure is unallocated.

In principle, the transfer of establishment data from precoding to coding sheets and then to punched cards is a simple matter. In practice, it is exceedingly complicated since each establishment requires from 20 to 30 cards (35,000 cards in all were used in preparing the Scottish input–output table). The possibility of error cannot be ignored, but must be guarded against; double punching is a reliable method, but very expensive; other methods rely on checking the questionnaire's internal consistency. Another method is to compute for each establishment a series of ratios (e.g. gross and net productivity, average wage rates); when the mean and standard deviation of these ratios are worked out for each industry or sector, those with a very low probability—more than two standard deviations, say, from the mean—can be singled out for special examination. Sometimes, external data can be used to check the computed means as well; net or gross productivity, for example, is often available for a whole industry from alternative sources. These kind of checks proved useful in the construction of both the Scottish and Moroccan tables and helped to weed out errors in the precoding and coding sheets, as well as punched card errors.

As Figure 8.5 shows, the coded data are used to form the first data base; this is simply a matter of storing the coded data in appropriate arrays; the main problems are to anticipate correctly the maximum array size likely to be needed and to find an efficient way of suppressing unnecessary information. Of the 4000 variables which could be obtained from the questionnaire used for Scottish manufacturing, some 80 to 95 % could be expected to be zero and their inclusion in each data base would have wasted time and money.

The next stage in data processing is to 'purify' the coded information so that it becomes of a uniform quality as far as valuation, classification, and area of origin are concerned; these operations form the province of Chapters 6, 7 and 11, but can be summarized as follows:

1 Elimination of all aggregations, whether of purchases, sales, stocks or sources by area of origin.

2 Breakdown of unallocated expenditures, such as 'salesmen's subsistence' or 'consumable stores', wherever possible.

3 Reconciling conceptual differences between firms (e.g., 'income from employment' should be treated in the same way by all establishments).

4 Converting all transactions to prices of the calendar year in question (establishments prefer to report for their financial year, which may differ from one firm to another and may not coincide with the calendar year).

5 Converting all transactions to the chosen basis of valuation, whether purchasers', producers', basic or standard prices.

When the second data base has been formed from the purified data, the establishments can be grouped together in sectors according to the classification scheme; at this point, the manually processed sectors must be added to the data base and the data are ready to be 'grossed up'; this stage gives rise to a number of arrays, of which the most important are the make and absorption matrices. Finally, the rows and columns of the make and absorption matrices must be reconciled, as shown in this chapter, and converted to symmetric input–output tables (see next chapter).

Use of computers at an early stage in the data processing involves a great deal of programming work, storage space and central processing unit (CPU) time. In the case of the Scottish table, for example, the programmes and data occupied 5–6 megabytes of storage and three hours of CPU time were required to process the data from punched cards to an input–output table (see Burdekin, 1978(b), p. 8). If all sectors had been entered at a stage and in form corresponding to that for the manual sectors in Figure 8.6, these requirements could have been cut dramatically, but the data purification would have required a very intensive use of comparatively skilled labour. There is, therefore, a capital- and labour-intensive way of processing the data for an input–output table and it might seem that the optimal choice between them should depend on the relative prices of the two major inputs involved.

Such a solution, however, assumes that the final product does not vary in quality, but—as Frances Stewart has taught us (Stewart, 1977)—the quality of the finished article is not independent of the choice of technique for producing it. The great advantage of using a computer at an early stage is flexibility, since assumptions or conventions can be changed and the table re-estimated on the basis of new ones in a matter of hours. A good example of this concerns the problem of updating input–output tables (see Chapter 10), since the updated table can be obtained from the coded data simply by incorporating new prices and control totals into the programmes. As has been said by those who developed the programmes for constructing the Scottish input–output table (Burdekin, 1978b):

> 'It can be seen that a computer does not merely reproduce a manual process but gives a new dimension to the choice of methodologies available . . . It is almost certain that such a thorough series of

adjustments [as was used in Scotland] on a firm by firm basis would have been out of the question without the power and speed of a computer. Neither would it have been possible to compare individual establishments for consistency. Without a computer it would have been necessary to gross up the data in the raw state and carry out modifications later hoping that local biases and errors would largely cancel out.'

APPENDIX CONSTRAINED MATRIX BALANCING TECHNIQUES

In this chapter, as well as Chapter 10, we are faced with a problem of balancing a matrix, subject to known marginal (control) totals. In other words, although we do not know the value of any particular cell in the matrix, we do know the value of the sum of the elements in any given row or column. In this chapter it is a social accounting matrix which needs to be balanced and the marginal totals are given by commodity output and value added (in the rows) and industry output and final demands (in the columns); in Chapter 10, it is the absorption matrix which needs balancing subject to row and column totals for intermediate purchases. Both problems therefore exhibit a common logical structure and it is appropriate to discuss methods of dealing with them in this appendix.

Let us call the true (but unknown) balanced matrix X; we can assume that we start with some estimate ($\tilde{X}$) of this matrix and the problem is therefore one of adjusting or balancing $\tilde{X}$ subject to the known marginal row and column totals. Ideally, we want our adjusted matrix ($\tilde{X}^*$) to be as 'close' as possible to our first estimate ($\tilde{X}$). 'Closeness', however, can be defined in a number of ways and so several methods exist for solving the problem.

'Closeness' can be achieved through minimizing the distance between the comparable cells in $\tilde{X}$ and $\tilde{X}^*$. The formal problem therefore can be stated as minimizing a function subject to the row and column constraints; the row constraints (u) are given by:

(8.1a) $$\tilde{X}^* i = u$$

and the column constraints (v) by

(8.2a) $$i' \tilde{X}^* = v$$

and both u and v are assumed to be known in advance.

In Table 8.1a four ways of solving this matrix balancing problem have been listed and each can be described formally as minimizing a function subject to known row and column constraints. For example, in the case of the Friedlander method, we minimize the χ^2-type function:

$$\sum_{ij} \frac{(\tilde{x}^*_{ij} - \tilde{x}_{ij})^2}{\tilde{x}_{ij}}$$

Table 8.1a Constrained matrix balancing techniques

No.	Minimand	Constraints	Solution	Discussion	Functional relationship	Notes
1	$\sum_{ij} (\tilde{X}^*_{ij} - \tilde{X}_{ij})^2$	$\tilde{X}i^* = u$ $i'\tilde{X}^* = v$	Direct	Geary (1973) Henry (1973b)	$\tilde{X}^*_{ij} = \tilde{X}_{ij}(1 + r_i + s_j)$	This is the least squares (LS) method. It does not guarantee preservation of signs in $(\tilde{X})$ and small elements can change more than proportionately, but the multipliers emerge directly from the solution
2	$\sum_{ij} \frac{(\tilde{X}^*_{ij} - \tilde{X}_{ij})^2}{\tilde{X}_{ij}}$	$\tilde{X}^*i = u$ $i'\tilde{X}^* = v$	Indirect or iterative in original form, but now modified to give direct solution.	Friedlander (1961) Bacharach (1970) Henry (1973b)	$\tilde{X}^*_{ij} = r_i\tilde{X}_{ij} + \tilde{X}_{ij} + s_j\tilde{X}_{ij}$	This method minimizes a χ^2-type function, but does not guarantee preservation of signs in $(\tilde{X})$
3	$\sum_{ij} \frac{\lvert\tilde{X}^*_{ij} - \tilde{X}_{ij}\rvert}{\tilde{X}_{ij}}$	$\tilde{X}^*i = u$ $i'\tilde{X}^* = v$ $\tilde{X}^*_{ij} \geqslant 0$	Quadratic programming	Matuszewski (1964) Bacharach (1970)	None	Signs in $(\tilde{X})$ are preserved, but computational demands too great for the size of most computers
4	$\sum_{ij} \left(\tilde{X}^*_{ij} \log \frac{\tilde{X}^*_{ij}}{\tilde{X}_{ij}} \right)$	$\tilde{X}^*i = u$ $i'\tilde{X}^* = v$	Indirect or iterative	Stone et al. (1963) Bacharach (1970) Lecomber (1975)	$\tilde{X}^*_{ij} = r_i\tilde{X}_{ij}s_j$	The RAS or biproportional method. Signs of $(\tilde{X})$ preserved

Note: Table based on Table 1.1 in Lecomber (1975).

subject to

$$\sum_j \tilde{x}^*_{ij} = u_i \qquad i = 1, \ldots, n$$

$$\sum_i \tilde{x}^*_{ij} = v_j \qquad j = 1, \ldots, n$$

i.e.

$$\text{Min}\,(\Phi) = \frac{\sum_{ij} (\tilde{x}^*_{ij} - \tilde{x}_{ij})^2}{\tilde{x}_{ij}} + \Sigma\lambda_i\left(\sum_j \tilde{x}^*_{ij} - u_i\right) + \Sigma\mu_j\left(\sum_i \tilde{x}^*_{ij} - v_j\right)$$

where λ_i, μ_j $(i, j = 1, \ldots, n)$ are Lagrange multipliers. Differentiating with respect to x^*_{ij} and rearranging (Friedlander, 1961), we obtain:

(8.3a) $$\tilde{x}^*_{ij} = \lambda_i \tilde{x}_{ij} + \tilde{x}_{ij} + \mu_j \tilde{x}_{ij}$$

so that the adjusted matrix $(\tilde{X}^*)$ can be obtained from the initial estimate $(\tilde{X})$ once the Lagrange multipliers are known.[12]

Of the four methods listed in Table 8.1a, the most commonly used in input–output work is the RAS or biproportional method. This is due above all to its mathematical simplicity, although it does have other desirable properties as well; the RAS method is also computationally simple and its theoretical properties (Bacharach, 1970) have been examined in great detail. In practical work it has been used much more frequently than other methods (e.g. CSO, 1976) and this has provided opportunities for testing its efficiency (Paelinck and Waelbroeck, 1963; Allen, 1974; Allen, 1975; Barker, 1975). For these reasons it is sufficient to isolate it for further discussion.

The RAS or biproportional method starts by assuming that each element in the adjusted matrix $(\tilde{X}^*)$ is biproportional to the initial estimate $(\tilde{X})$, i.e.

(8.4a) $$\tilde{x}^*_{ij} = r_i \tilde{x}_{ij} s_j$$

This relationship was first suggested by Leontief (Leontief, 1951) but was independently suggested by Stone (Stone, 1962). The constraints of the model tell us that the row and column sums of the new matrix must equal the known marginal totals, i.e.

(8.5a) $$\sum_j r_i \tilde{x}_{ij} s_j = u_i \qquad (i = 1, \ldots, n)$$

(8.6a) $$\sum_i r_i \tilde{x}_{ij} s_j = v_j \qquad (j = 1, \ldots, n)$$

This is a system of $2n$ equations in the $2n$ unknown row and column multipliers. Unfortunately, only $2n$–1 equations are independent—the last being derivable from the others—so that we can only solve for the multipliers in relative terms, selecting arbitrarily a value for one multiplier.[13]

There is no direct solution to the r and s multipliers in equations (8.5a) and (8.6a). Instead, an iterative procedure is applied which has been shown (Bacharach, 1970) to be convergent. We may begin, for example, by choosing a set of r multipliers which ensures that the n constraints (equation (8.5a)) are met. Next, we choose a set of s multipliers so that the n constraints (equation (8.6a)) are met; but this will upset the row constraints, necessitating a new set of r multipliers and so on. An excellent example of an RAS iterative process for a three-sector matrix can be found elsewhere (United Nations, 1973).

Once a solution for the r and s multipliers has been obtained, they can be applied in equation (8.4a) to give the final matrix. The RAS method guarantees that positive entries in $(\tilde{X})$ will remain positive in $(\tilde{X}^*)$, but it should be clear from equation (8.4a) that zeros will remain zeros. The RAS method also works best if there are no negative numbers in $(\tilde{X})$ since the minimand refers to logarithms (see Table 8.1a); this point is taken up in section 8.4.

NOTES

1 Throughout this and the next chapter, it is important to distinguish very clearly between commodity and industry output. We must therefore introduce the variable q to refer to commodity output and g to refer to industry output, although we shall revert to the variable x later in the book, when it is no longer necessary to distinguish between the two types of output.

2 In Chapter 11, we argue the case for a separate treatment of artisan-type activities; here, however, we follow convention in assuming that establishments are grouped according to their product-use, so that it is possible to find in the same industry establishments from both the modern and traditional/informal sectors.

3 In practice, one can avoid this problem, by distinguishing between those empty cells which are zero in principle and those which could turn positive (see section 8.4).

4 In a private communication with the author, Richard Lecomber has suggested that the crucial distinction is not between manual and mechanical balancing methods, but between those which can be made by previously formulated rule and those which cannot. In terms of this latter distinction, some 'manual' adjustments might, in fact, be 'mechanical', since they could be programmed and handled by computer. In the author's experience, however, the main cause of a large imbalance in any row is usually some very specific error (e.g. exclusion of smuggled goods) for which no programmable rule can usefully be formulated; consequently, the large imbalances should in general be dealt with manually before relying on computer algorithms to balance supply and demand.

5 Note that fd and $\tilde{g}$ appear as *row* vectors in Figure 8.1; we therefore continue to treat them as row vectors in the subsequent analysis. The vector fd refers to the sum of the different components of final demand, e.g. investment, household consumption, for which national accounting control totals usually exist.

6 A method has been proposed (Lecomber, 1975) for using the biproportional method on an initial matrix containing negative elements and subject to error in both the marginal totals and the initial cell estimates, but the method does not guarantee 'closeness' of fit and requires non-negativity restrictions on the error estimates and the marginal totals.

7 Many input–output tables are in fact balanced on intermediate absorptions only, since it is assumed (wrongly, in the author's opinion) that all final demand and value added entries are known with certainty. This will usually guarantee the absence of negative elements.

8 It is at this stage that the input–output team will have to resolve the important question of reconciling the results of the input–output table with the official national accounts. The latter will give, at the very least, totals for the components of final demand (fd) and value added (v) and the input–output team may well decide to accept these as being known with certainty. This is not necessarily a good idea, however, because the

input–output tables' estimates of v and fd may be independent of those used by the National Accounts Office and may have revealed errors in the official figures.

The existence of two competing estimates of the national accounts is not, of course, at all desirable. Part of the difference will be due to methodology and can be resolved fairly easily, but part will be due to the different sources used; it is unlikely that the National Accounts Office will revise their estimates just because different sources are used, but they might be more willing to do so if the input–output team recognizes the possibility of error in their own estimates and modifies the balancing technique to take account of uncertainty. The new control totals which emerge from this exercise, which will obviously be consistent with the input–output table, could then provide a basis for revision of the official national accounts.

9 The modification is due to Richard Lecomber and an outline of the method can be seen in his joint paper with R. I. G. Allen (Allen, 1975).

10 The solution was obtained by assuming

$$e_u = \begin{bmatrix} 10 \\ 10 \\ 20 \\ \hdashline 10 \end{bmatrix} \text{ and } e_w = [5, 10, 10 \,\vdots\, 5, 0, 0, 10, 0, 0]$$

11 This problem will not arise if the import matrix is developed from 'supply-side' data according to the method outlined in the previous chapter.

12 According to Friedlander in his 1961 paper, a solution for λ and μ can be found, although it is not unique. Elsewhere, however (see Geary, 1973; Henry, 1973b), it has been shown that a simpler direct solution is available.

13 It should be clear from equation (8.4a) that $r_i \tilde{x}_{ij} s_j = (\lambda r_i) \tilde{x}_{ij} (\lambda^{-1} s_j)$. Since λ is an arbitrary scalar, we can only interpret r and s multipliers in a relative sense, unless some normalization procedure has been applied (see Bacharach, 1970, p. 22).

CHAPTER 9

Non-principal Production and the Formation of Symmetric Input–Output Tables

9.1 INTRODUCTION

The balanced commodity × industry input–output table of Chapter 8 can be thought of as a statement concerning the supply of and demand for commodity resources over a given period, i.e.

$$q = Wi + f \tag{9.1}$$

where q is a vector of home commodity supply, W is a matrix of commodity absorptions by industries and f is a vector of commodity final demands. Input–output theory assumes a unique relationship between the elements of W and the using industry; in the simplest possible case of linear proportional production functions (see Chapter 4) we assume the following relationship:

$$W = B\hat{g} \tag{9.2}$$

where B is a coefficient matrix whose i, jth element represents the requirements of commodity i per unit of output in industry j, while $\hat{g}$ is a diagonal matrix of industry outputs.

Substitution of equation (9.2) into (9.1) gives:

$$q = B\hat{g}i + f \tag{9.3}$$

which is a system of n equations; if the f vector is given exogenously and B is known by assumption, equation (9.3) still leaves us with $2n$ unknowns (q and g), so it cannot be solved. Only by making some additional assumptions, which enable us to establish a link between commodity and industry output so that equation (9.3) can be written in terms of q or g alone, can we hope to make the system determinate.[1]

The link, of course, is provided by the make matrix; this matrix (see Chapter 2) is a record of commodity outputs by industry and of industry contribution to commodity supply. If we assumed either that industries produce principal and secondary products in fixed proportions (the 'product-mix' hypothesis) or that commodity supply comes in fixed proportions from the different contributing industries (the 'market-share' hypothesis), we could build a bridge between commodity and industry output and resolve the problem of indeterminacy in equation (9.3). Indeed, as we shall now see, either of these hypotheses is sufficient to produce a symmetric input–output table[2] either by adjusting the columns of the commodity × industry input–output table to a commodity reference (commodity × commodity input–output tables) or by adjusting the rows to an industry reference (industry × industry input–output tables).

There are many input–output tables, therefore, which can be produced and this raises a problem of choice between them. The purpose of this chapter is to show how such tables can be produced and what are the various merits of the different tables. Both of these questions, however, can be more easily resolved when we have a clearer understanding of what is meant by secondary production.

9.2 TYPES OF SECONDARY PRODUCTS

There are at least five types of secondary products between which it is worth distinguishing and each will now be discussed in turn. The first refers to products, whose level of output is independent of the scale of principal production in an establishment and for which the technology of production reflects the practice of the industry producing that commodity as principal product (the 'commodity technology' assumption). An example will make this clearer; in Figure 9.1, we observe an industry producing two products, one of which (commodity 2) is secondary to its main activity (production of commodity 1); the credit or incomings side of the account is taken from a make matrix (see Figure 9.2). On the outgoings side, we observe the appropriate column of an absorption matrix (see Figure 9.3) with the inputs needed for both principal and secondary production aggregated together. Assuming that the ten units of secondary production in industry 1 are produced with the technology used for commodity 2, we obtain Figure 9.4, where the first column describes the inputs needed for commodity 1 alone, while the second column describes the inputs needed for commodity 2 regardless of where it is made. (We shall return to the commodity technology assumption in the next section.)

The second type of secondary product occurs where, again, the level of output is independent of the scale of principal production, but where the technique of production reflects the practice of the *producing* industry rather than the industry

Outgoings			Incomings
Commodity 1	20	100	Commodity 1
Commodity 2	30	10	Commodity 2
Commodity 3	10		
Value added	50		
Total	110	110	Total

Figure 9.1 Production account: industry 1

	Industries			
	1	2	3	Total
Commodities				
1	100	—	—	100
2	10	100	—	110
3	—	—	50	50
Total	110	100	50	260

Figure 9.2 Make matrix

	Industries				
	1	2	3	Final demand	Total
Commodities					
1	20	30	—	50	100
2	30	20	20	40	110
3	10	20	10	10	50
Value added	50	30	20	—	100
Total	110	100	50	100	

Figure 9.3 Commodity × industry input–output table

	Commodities				
	1	2	3	Final demand	Total
Commodities					
1	17	33	—	50	100
2	28	22	20	40	110
3	8	22	10	10	50
Value added	47	33	20	—	100
Total	100	110	50	100	

Figure 9.4 Input–Output table (commodity × commodity: commodity technology assumption)

which produces it as principal product (the 'industry technology' assumption). In other words, under the industry technology assumption, all products of an industry are assumed to be produced with the same technology. Using this assumption, we obtain the input–output table in Figure 9.5, where the first and second columns differ quite noticeably from their counterparts in Figure 9.4, because the amount transferred 'in' and 'out' depends crucially on which assumption is made. (We shall return to the industry technology assumption in section 9.4.)

As stated above, either assumption can be used to produce either commodity × commodity tables or industry × industry tables. An example of the latter on the industry technology assumption is given in Figure 9.6: in passing from Figure 9.3 to Figure 9.6, the problem is to decide which of the users of commodity 2 is purchasing the product of industry 1 and in what proportions. In Figure 9.6, we have assumed that industry 1 has a fixed share of commodity 2 output regardless of the user, so that final demand needs adjustment as well; this is an additional

	Commodities				
	1	2	3	Final demand	Total
Commodities					
1	18.1	31.9	—	50	100
2	27.3	22.7	20	40	110
3	9.1	20.9	10	10	50
Value added	45.5	34.5	20	—	100
Total	100	110	50	100	

Figure 9.5 Input–output table (Commodity x commodity: industry technology assumption)

	Industry				
	1	2	3	Final demand	Total
Industry					
1	22.8	31.8	1.8	53.6	110
2	27.2	18.2	18.2	36.4	100
3	10	20	10	10	50
Value added	50	30	20	—	100
Total	110	100	50	100	

Figure 9.6 Input–output table (industry × industry: industry technology assumption)

problem, not present with commodity × commodity tables, and it becomes more acute when it is remembered that imports may enter final demand as a negative entry; it does not make sense to adjust imports to an industry basis and any attempt to do so requires rebalancing of the import matrix. If industry × industry tables are required, therefore, they must be derived from the commodity × industry input–output table net of trade flows (see also section 9.7).

Let us now consider the implications of transferring secondary products. If we convert the inter-commodity flows of Figure 9.4, for example, into coefficient form, we obtain the input–output model:

(9.4) $$q = {}_cA_c q + f$$

where ${}_cA_c$ is a coefficient matrix formed from a commodity × commodity table on the commodity technology assumption. In incremental form, the solution can be written:

(9.5) $$\Delta q = [I - {}_cA_c]^{-1} \Delta f = R \Delta f$$

where $R = \{r_{ij}\} = [I - {}_cA_c]^{-1}$. With all final demands unchanged except commodity 2, we find that the change in the output vector can be written:

(9.6) $$\begin{aligned} \Delta q_1 &= r_{12} \Delta f_2 \\ \Delta q_2 &= r_{22} \Delta f_2 \\ \Delta q_3 &= r_{32} \Delta f_2 \end{aligned}$$

so that the only 'feedback' on the output of commodity 1 provided by a unit change in the final demand for commodity 2 is r_{12}, i.e the direct and indirect requirements of commodity 1 needed for a unit change in demand for commodity 2.

This is clearly an acceptable approximation to the determination of the scale of output of commodity 1 provided that decisions on production of commodity 2 and 1 are independent. If, however, commodity 2 was a *by-product* of commodity 1, such that production levels could not be determined independently, then equation (9.6) would be a very biased measure of the change in output of commodity 1. It is therefore necessary to distinguish two further types of secondary products: *by-products* and *joint products*.

If we return to Figure 9.1, we can now imagine that the secondary production of commodity 2 is a by-product of commodity 1; a frequent example of this is animal feedstuffs produced as a by-product of alcohol distillation. Animal feedstuffs, in fact, are also the principal product of the animal foods industry, but in the case of alcohol producers it is impossible to extract more animal foods from them without producing more alcohol. Because production of the by-product is not independent of the principal product, it makes no sense to distinguish the inputs associated with this by-product, so that neither the commodity nor industry technology is appropriate.

If it is not possible to break down the outgoings column, it is necessary to treat the sale of a by-product as a negative input; the position is shown in Figure 9.7, where the original purchase of 30 units of commodity 2 has been reduced to 20 to

Outgoings		Incomings	
Commodity 1	20	100	Commodity 1
Commodity 2	20		
Commodity 3	10		
Value added	50		
Total	100		

Figure 9.7 Production account: industry 1

	Commodities				
	1	2	3	Final demand	Total
Commodities					
1	20	30	—	50	100
2	20	20	20	40	100
3	10	20	10	10	50
Value added	50	30	20	—	100
Total	100	100	50	100	

Figure 9.8 Commodity × commodity input–output table (with by-products)

allow for the negative input of the by-product. Production is now 100 units, but this refers to principal products only, so that the matrix in Figure 9.3 can be adjusted very simply (as in Figure 9.8) to give a commodity × commodity input–output table.

Now imagine that final demand for commodity 2 rises by 10 units; as before, this will give rise to additional output from the second sector (round 1), which requires additional inputs (3 units) from the first sector (round 2); to produce these 3 units, however, the first sector will generate 0.3 units of the by-product (which will reduce the demand for commodity 2 from other sources) as well as purchasing inputs from the other three sectors. The final result, therefore, will depend not only on the direct and indirect requirements of commodity 1 per unit change in the final demand for commodity 2, but also on the technical relations of production between the principal product and by-product in industry 1.[3]

Our third type of secondary production (by-products) assumed that there existed an industry producing the by-product as principal product. Sometimes, however, the 'by-product' is unique to the industry producing it; in this case it is impossible to follow the treatment outlined above. This kind of secondary product is often called a *joint product* and examples are hides produced by the cattle-raising industry and wool from the sheep-raising industry; as with by-products, the level of production of the joint product is not independent of the level of production of the principal product, so that neither the commodity nor technology assumptions are appropriate.

Let us therefore return to Figure 9.2 and assume that this time the secondary product is a joint product. As with by-products, it does not make sense to try to isolate the inputs associated with the joint product from those associated with the principal product. The only sensible solution is to treat it as a negative 'input' purchased from a dummy industry. This dummy industry has no inputs and a zero level of output, so that a corresponding positive entry representing purchases is required to balance the negative entry in the row representing sales; in Figure 9.9, this purchase is assumed to be made by industry 3, which reduces its purchases from commodity 2 by 10 units to accommodate its purchase of 10 units from the dummy sector.[4]

	Commodities				
	1	2	3	Final demand	Total
Commodities					
1	20	30	—	50	100
2	30	20	10	40	100
3	10	20	10	10	50
Dummy sector	−10	—	10	—	0
Value added	50	30	20	—	100
Total	100	100	50	100	

Figure 9.9 Commodity × Commodity input–output table (with joint products)

The volume of purchases from the dummy sector in Figure 9.9 depends on the volume of output in the third activity; the 'make' of the dummy industry depends on the principal production of industry 1. Consequently, the dummy sector does not enter into the solution to the input–output model, so that in equation (9.5), for example, the Leontief inverse is calculated net of the row for the dummy sector.

The final type of secondary product worth distinguishing is not mentioned in textbooks. If we examine the make matrix for any country, we will note a clustering of entries around the diagonal and a similar clustering around the non-traded commodities (transport and distribution, particularly), which represent an important part of the activity of many manufacturing firms. The secondary products clustered around the diagonal can usually be treated as discussed above; secondary production of non-traded commodities, however, is more awkward, because the activity is often 'sold' at cost so that it is not expected to show a normal commercial return; examples of these activities are canteen operations, factoring and own transport undertakings. Furthermore, if we divide an establishment's costs into direct and indirect (according to the speed with which they adjust to changes in output), then it will generally be true that an expansion of these secondary non-traded activities has no effect on indirect costs. We therefore need to identify a fifth type of secondary product, only semi-independent of principal production, to which we return in section 9.5.[5]

9.3 THE COMMODITY TECHNOLOGY ASSUMPTION

In an ideal world, the input–output team would have knowledge of all inputs into secondary production and the adjustment of a commodity × industry table to a symmetric input–output table could then be carried out without introducing errors. Such knowledge, however, is very rare and in what follows we assume that there is no other information than that contained in the make matrix and the balanced commodity × industry input–output table.

If the treatment proposed above for by- and joint products is followed, then no further adjustments will be needed; the by- or joint product is considered as a negative input, so that there is no longer a difference between principal and total output. The first problem, therefore, is to adjust the absorption matrix for secondary products of the first type, i.e. those for which the commodity technology assumption is appropriate. With this assumption, a commodity requires the same technology regardless of the industry in which it is produced; thus, each coefficient in the absorption matrix (b_{ij}) is a weighted average of the coefficients in the (unknown) commodity × commodity input–output table (a_{ij}), i.e.

(9.7) $$b_{ij} = a_{i1} \cdot w_{1j} + a_{i2} \cdot w_{2j} + \; \ldots \; + a_{in} \cdot w_{nj}$$

where the weights are provided by the proportion of industry output accounted for by each commodity.

The weights in equation (9.7) are those conforming to the product-mix assumption and they can be obtained from the make matrix by forming the relationship:

(9.8) $$C = M\hat{g}^{-1}$$

where C is a matrix of weights obtained by the product-mix assumption, M is the make matrix[6] and g is the vector of industry output. We can, therefore, replace equation (9.7) by:

(9.9) $$b_{ij} = a_{i1} \cdot c_{1j} + a_{i2} \cdot c_{2j} + \; \ldots \; + a_{in} \cdot c_{nj}$$

or in matrix form:

(9.10) $$B = {}_cA_cC$$

and

(9.11) $${}_cA_c = BC^{-1}$$

Equation (9.11) is the solution for the (unknown) commodity × commodity[7] input–output table formed on the commodity technology assumption; it is equivalent to Figure 9.4 in coefficient form, and provided C is a square matrix, it will always have a solution. Unfortunately, however, it involves two problems; first, there is the possibility of negative entries in the A matrix solution and, secondly, the product-mix hypothesis is not necessarily appropriate for all secondary products for which a commodity technology is a reasonable assumption.

The problem of negative elements in the solution arises as follows: suppose, for example, that in Figure 9.1 secondary production of commodity 2 by industry 1 had been 60 units rather than ten. Applying the commodity technology assumption would require the transfer in Figure 9.3 of $(20/100) \times 60 = 12$ units of purchase of commodity 3 from column 1 to column 2. Industry 1, however, only purchased ten units of commodity 3 altogether so that the transfer would leave a negative number. Various methods have been proposed for removing negative numbers (Armstrong, 1975; Stone et al., 1963; Almon, 1970); these methods, however, are quite complicated and it may be simpler to make a number of adjustments to the A matrix manually rather than use a computer routine, if the negative elements are few and small.

The C matrix assumes that the product-mix of industries does not change; this is clearly an appropriate assumption for by- or joint products, but these types of secondary products no longer concern us. For many products, however, it may be an inappropriate assumption; for example, if the secondary product in Figure 9.1 is chemicals, while the principal product is textiles, a sudden increase in final demand for chemicals could alter the industry's product mix so that the C matrix is no longer constant. It might seem, therefore, that some other assumption, such as the market-share hypothesis, might prove acceptable. Unfortunately, this is not possible; the only weights which make sense in equation (9.7) are those embodying the product-mix assumption. The commodity technology assumption therefore *requires* the product-mix hypothesis, although the assumption of a constant C matrix may at times be hard to accept.

The commodity × commodity input–output model can be written:

(9.12) $$q = {}_cA_cq + f$$

and we have shown how a solution for ${}_cA_c$ can be found where a commodity technology for secondary products is assumed. The balance equation for an industry × industry model can be written:

(9.13) $$g = {}_cA_Ig + {}_ce$$

where ${}_cA_I$ is the input–output coefficient matrix for industry × industry tables on the commodity technology assumption and ${}_ce$ is the vector of final demands classified by industries and we have yet to show how ${}_cA_I$ or ${}_ce$ can be estimated. However, the balance equations for the commodity × industry table can be written:

(9.14) $$q = Bg + f$$

and equation (9.8) can be rewritten as:

$$M = C\hat{g} \tag{9.15}$$

Multiplying both sides by the identity vector (i), and noting that $Mi = q$, we find:

$$q = Cg \tag{9.16}$$

so that

$$Cg = Bg + f \tag{9.17}$$

therefore

$$g = C^{-1}Bg + C^{-1}f \tag{9.18}$$

By simple comparison of equation (9.18) with (9.13), we therefore observe:

$${}_cA_I = C^{-1}B \tag{9.19}$$

and

$$C^{-1}f = {}_ce \tag{9.20}$$

Thus, we can form industry × industry tables from the commodity technology and product-mix assumptions as easily as commodity × commodity tables.

9.4 THE INDUSTRY TECHNOLOGY ASSUMPTION

The next type of secondary product to be considered is the one for which the industry technology assumption is most appropriate. This time it is assumed that an industry uses the same technology to produce all its products—including secondary products. Each i,jth coefficient of a commodity × commodity table will therefore be a weighted average of the coefficients in the ith row of the absorption matrix with the weights given by the market-share hypothesis, i.e.

$$a_{ij} = b_{i1} . w_{1j} + b_{i2} . w_{2j} + \ . \ . \ . \ + b_{in} . w_{nj} \tag{9.21}$$

In the case of Figure 9.3, for example, we find for the first row and second column:

$$a_{1,2} = \left(\frac{20}{110}\right) w_{1,2} + \left(\frac{30}{100}\right) w_{2,2} + \left(\frac{0}{50}\right) w_{3,2} \tag{9.22}$$

The (unknown) a_{ij} will depend on the choice of weights; since commodity 2 is made by two industries, it is natural to assume that the weights be determined by the proportions in which each industry contributes to total commodity 2 output. This market-share hypothesis gives:

$$a_{1,2} = \left(\frac{20}{110}\right)\left(\frac{10}{110}\right) + \left(\frac{30}{100}\right)\left(\frac{100}{110}\right) + \left(\frac{0}{50}\right)\left(\frac{0}{110}\right) = 0.29 \tag{9.23}$$

which is the value of the input–output coefficient obtainable from Figure 9.5.

The market-share hypothesis can be given formal expression in matrix terms as:

(9.24) $$D = M'\hat{q}^{-1}$$

where D is a matrix of coefficients formed on the market-share hypothesis and M' is the transpose of the make matrix, so that the solution to the (unknown) input–output coefficient matrix is:

(9.25) $${}_{I}A_{C} = BD$$

where ${}_{I}A_{C}$ indicates a commodity × commodity table produced on an industry technology assumption. As before, however, it may be desirable to produce industry × industry tables; in that case, the balance equations become:

(9.26) $$g = {}_{I}A_{I}g + {}_{I}e$$

where the unknown ${}_{I}A_{I}$ and ${}_{I}e$ are the input–output coefficient matrix and final demand respectively for an industry × industry table on the industry technology and market-share hypothesis. In order to find a solution for these two unknowns, we must proceed as follows: the balance equations for a commodity × industry table are given by equation (9.14) and from equation (9.24) we may note that:

(9.27) $$M' = D\hat{q}$$

so that

(9.28) $$M'i = g = Dq$$

and substituting equation (9.28) in equation (9.14) yields:

(9.29) $$D^{-1}g = Bg + f$$

Therefore

(9.30) $$g = (DB)g + Df$$

so that by looking at equation (9.26) we see that $DB = {}_{I}A_{I}$ and Df is final demand on an industry basis.

So far, nothing has been said about value added which appears in the commodity × industry table on an industry basis. So long as industry × industry tables are produced (whether on the commodity or industry technology assumptions), value added will not change, but this will no longer be the case where commodity × commodity tables are required.

Let V represent the $(m \times n)$ matrix of m value added requirements per unit of industry output (e.g. wages and salaries, depreciation, indirect taxes, subsidies, profits) into the n industries. According to the commodity technology assumption, the wage and salary bill, for example, in the jth industry will be a weighted average of the (unknown) wage bill per unit of each commodity output with the weights given by the product-mix assumption, i.e.

(9.31) $$V = {}_{c}V_{c}C$$

where ${}_{c}V_{c}$ is the $m \times n$ matrix of value added requirements per unit of commodity output on the commodity technology assumption, so that:

(9.32) $${}_{c}V_{c} = VC^{-1}$$

If an industry technology assumption is used, value added per unit of jth commodity output will be a weighted average of value added requirements in all the industries producing the jth commodity with the weights being given by the market-share hypothesis, i.e.

(9.33) $${}_{C}V_{I} = VD$$

where ${}_{C}V_{I}$ is the $m \times n$ matrix of value added requirements per unit of commodity output on the industry technology assumption.

9.5 MIXED TECHNOLOGY ASSUMPTION

It can be seen from the above that the market-share hypothesis goes with the industry technology assumption, while the product-mix hypothesis goes with the commodity technology assumption. Many commentators have expressed dissatisfaction with this combination; for example, if by-products are not treated as negative inputs, they must clearly be treated according to an industry technology assumption, but in the case of by-products or joint products the market share hypothesis is inappropriate, since what is fixed is the proportion of *industry* output contributed by this type of secondary product, i.e. the product-mix assumption. Furthermore, it may well be that for the 'typical' secondary product—produced according to a commodity technology assumption—the market-share hypothesis makes more sense, because its level of production is independent of the output of principal product and therefore determined by market forces for the commodity in question.

It is, however, not possible to pair the assumptions of commodity and industry technology, product-mix and market shares at random. The industry technology assumption requires the market-share hypothesis so that it is far better to dispose of by-products and joint products as negative inputs rather than trying to form them into a mould which does not fit. On the other hand, it is unlikely that all secondary products will conform to *either* the industry *or* commodity technology assumption and it is desirable therefore to combine both assumptions in preparing input–output tables.

Let the make matrix be subdivided into two parts; one records all those products produced under a commodity technology assumption (M_1), while the other records all those produced under an industry technology assumption (M_2). Thus, we find:

(9.34) $$M = M_1 + M_2$$

The column sums of M refer to industry output, so we have $g_1 = M'_1 i$ and $g_2 = M'_2 i$, while the row sums refer to commodity output, so $q_1 = M_1 i$ and $q_2 = M_2 i$.

Under the commodity technology assumption, a coefficient matrix is formed on the product-mix hypothesis, i.e.

$$C_1 = M_1 \hat{g}_1^{-1} \tag{9.35}$$

so that

$$\hat{g}_1 = C_1^{-1} M_1 \tag{9.36}$$

or

$$g_1 = C_1^{-1} q_1 \tag{9.37}$$

Similarly, under the industry technology assumption, a coefficient matrix is formed on the market-share hypothesis, i.e.

$$D_2 = M'_2 \hat{q}^{-1} \tag{9.38}$$

so that

$$D_2 q = M'_2 i = g_2 \tag{9.39}$$

Since $g = g_1 + g_2$, we now have:

$$g = C_1^{-1} q_1 + D_2 q = C_1^{-1}\{q - q_2\} + D_2 q \tag{9.40}$$

Now $q_2 = M_2 i = \{\widehat{D'_2 i}\} q$ so

$$g = \{C_1^{-1}(I - \widehat{D'_2 i}) + D_2\} q \tag{9.41}$$

and since $q = Bg + f$

$$q = BRq + f \tag{9.42}$$

where $R = \{C_1^{-1}(I - \widehat{D'_2 i}) + D_2\}$ so that the matrix product BR is the commodity × commodity input–output table on a mixed technology assumption. We can switch to an industry reference very easily, however, by putting the solution for q in equation (9.42) into equation (9.41), which gives:

$$g = R[I - BR]^{-1} f = [I - RB]^{-1} Rf \tag{9.43}$$

No mention has yet been made of the fifth type of secondary product, where the commodity technology assumption applies only to the direct costs. Suppose, for example, it is possible to partition the absorption matrix as follows:

$$B = \begin{bmatrix} B_1 \\ \hline B_2 \end{bmatrix} \tag{9.44}$$

where B_1 represents direct costs and B_2 indirect costs of production.

As before, if we make the commodity technology assumption, we have:

$$B_1 = A_1 C \tag{9.45}$$

where A_1 is the partition of the (unknown) A matrix corresponding to B_1.

With the elements of B_2, we assume that each is a weighted average of the unknown input–output coefficients corresponding to the commodities included in industry output. This time, however, secondary production receives a zero weight because it is assumed that indirect costs are zero, i.e.

(9.46) $$B_2 = A_2\hat{C}$$

where $\hat{C}$ is the matrix formed by taking only the diagonal entries in the C matrix.

For the i, jth element of B_2 we get:

(9.47) $$B_{ij}^{(2)} = a_{i1}^{(2)}.0 + a_{i2}^{(2)}.0 + \ldots + a_{ij}^{(2)}.C_{jj} \ldots + a_{in}^{(2)}.0 = a_{ij}^{(2)}C_{jj}$$

and each indirect cost coefficient in the absorption matrix is seen to be equal to the underlying input–output coefficient corresponding to principal production weighted by the share of principal production in total output. The solution to the (unknown) A is therefore:

(9.48) $$A = \begin{bmatrix} A_1 \\ \hline A_2 \end{bmatrix} = \begin{bmatrix} B_1 C^{-1} \\ \hline B_2 \hat{C}^{-1} \end{bmatrix}$$

and this model can be combined with the more conventional industry and commodity technology assumptions, if the make matrix is partitioned according to the three types of products.

9.6 SOME POSSIBLE SHORT-CUTS

The preparation of symmetric input–output tables from a balanced commodity × industry table can be a very tedious task. With highly aggregated tables (see, for example, the make matrix for Brazil—Table 2.1), secondary production is very modest and even with large tables it is unusual for commodity and industry output in each sector to differ by more than 5%; in order to save scarce resources being unduly wasted on the problem of secondary production, it is therefore worth looking at possible short-cuts.

Let us rewrite the balance equations for the absorption matrix as:

(9.49) $$q = Bg + f$$

The problem of symmetric tables arises because we have two sets of unknowns (q and g) and a solution depends on finding the relationship between them. In the commodity technology model, the relationship is:

(9.50) $$g = C^{-1}q$$

while with an industry technology assumption it becomes:

(9.51) $$g = Dq$$

and in the case of the hybrid model:

(9.52) $$g = Rq$$

Now the simplest possible link between g and q is to assume that there are always fixed proportions between the jth commodity and jth industry output, i.e.

(9.53) $$q = \hat{\lambda}g$$

where the elements of λ show this fixed relationship. We then observe:

$$q = B\hat{\lambda}q + f \tag{9.54}$$

so that $B\hat{\lambda}$ defines the (unknown) input–output coefficient matrix.

Clearly $B\hat{\lambda}$ will be the same as BD (industry technology) or BC^{-1} (commodity technology) only under exceptional circumstances (i.e. $g = q$), but if industry and commodity outputs are very close it may give an acceptable approximation. For example, the i, jth element of A can be written on this simple assumption as:

$$a_{ij} = b_{ij}\lambda_j \tag{9.55}$$

while on the industry technology assumption (see equation (9.25)) it becomes:

$$a_{ij} = b_{i1}d_{1j} + b_{i2}d_{2j} + \ldots + b_{ij}d_{jj} + \ldots + b_{in}d_{nj} \tag{9.56}$$

Most of the d_{ij} will be close to zero, but d_{jj} will be close to unity. It may be the case, therefore, that crude projections or forecasts from an input–output model can be adopted using equation (9.56) if the details of the input–output matrix are not of interest.

For many purposes, however, the details of the input–output table are important and this particular short-cut cannot be adopted, so it is worth showing one other way in which symmetric tables can be produced quickly. In Figure 9.6, an industry × industry table is shown in which purchases have been put on an industry basis on the assumption of an industry technology. It can be seen that the adjustment falls both on final demand and intermediate purchases; examination of the make matrix, however, may well reveal that the secondary products are all sold to final demand. This is quite likely to be the case in many LDCs, where final sales still dominate industrial output.

If secondary products *can* be defined in this way, all that is needed is a simple redrawing of the final demand vector consistent with an industry classification, i.e. we must convert f into e subject to $i'f = i'e$. In that case, the balance equations become:

$$g = Bg + e \tag{9.57}$$

so that B is already an industry × industry input–output coefficient matrix. This procedure was adopted for the Moroccan input–output table and it saved a great deal of work, although its greatest drawback is that it cannot be used to produce commodity × commodity tables.

9.7 CONCLUSIONS

There is no simple answer to the question of which kind of table or which kind of assumption is most appropriate. Ideally, both industry × industry and commodity × commodity tables should be produced, since the former are needed in studies of employment, income distribution and sectoral planning, while the latter are most appropriate for studies of international trade, price movements or linkage analysis. If only one table is possible, a commodity × commodity one may be best because it avoids the need for reclassification of final demand, which can always be assumed to be initially on a commodity basis (see United Nations, 1973, p. 36).

It is not at all easy to divide the make matrix precisely into the five types of secondary products; the most important joint and by-products can usually be identified with some care, but it needs the help of sectoral experts to sort out those commodities where an industry technology assumption is appropriate from those to which the commodity technology assumption applies and some thought must always be given to those products for which neither assumption is appropriate. In the absence of any information, the commodity technology assumption is likely to be the best, provided by-products and joint products can be treated as negative inputs.

Finally, mention must be made of the adjustments needed to the import matrix, if one has been prepared. The initial matrix, like the absorption matrix, will show industries in the columns and commodities in the rows; however, in the case of imports there is no difference between imports of commodities and imports of industries, since whether a particular import is the principal or secondary product of an industry in the rest of the world is of no concern.

The import matrix, therefore, can be thought of as commodity × industry or industry × industry. In that case, no adjustments need to be made if the final input–output table is of type industry × industry. Consequently, if industry tables are being produced it is important that adjustments be carried out on the domestic absorption matrix only, i.e. the total absorption table net of imports. The addition of the import matrix to the adjusted industry × industry domestic flows table will then give the total flows industry × industry table.

In the case of commodity × commodity tables, the columns of the import matrix need to be adjusted, but in the absence of additional information it is necessary to assume that the adjustment will be the same as for domestic transactions. Thus the adjustments can be carried out initially on the total absorption matrix and subsequently on the domestic absorption matrix, so that subtraction of the commodity × commodity domestic flows input–output table from the commodity × commodity total flows input–output table will give the import matrix on a commodity × commodity basis.

NOTES

1 Unless we are exceptionally fortunate and observe no secondary production, in which case $q = g$ and equation (9.3) can be solved directly.

2 A 'symmetric' input–output table is one in which both the rows and columns have the same output dimension, i.e. symmetric tables are either commodity × commodity or industry × industry. In Chapter 8, balancing and reconciliation was done on a commodity × industry input–output table, which was therefore not symmetric.

3 An excellent example of the solution to an input–output model with by-products treated as negative inputs can be found in Richard Stone's monograph (Stone, 1961, pp. 39–40).

4 This treatment is not the only possible one; in order to preserve references to the value of joint production, some input–output workers prefer to leave it in the make matrix and

add it to the diagonal entry in the absorption matrix; nothing of substance is changed by this procedure, which can also be used for by-products, but the author prefers the method outlined in the main text, because it is difficult to give an economic justification to the 'purchase' of the joint or by-product by the producing industry on the diagonal of the absorption matrix. (See, for example, O'Connor, 1975, Chapter 5.)

5 It may be remembered that in Chapter 6, the author proposed for certain LDCs the valuation of input–output tables at standard prices; under standard prices, flows are valued inclusive of transport and distribution (wholesale) costs, so that it is no longer necessary to treat the transport and wholesaling of their own goods by manufacturing firms as secondary production. Instead, these activities 'disappear' into principal production, so that standard prices have the additional advantage of making much easier the preparation of symmetric input–output tables since our fifth kind of secondary product will in general no longer exist.

6 In Figure 9.2, the make matrix is written with commodities in the rows and industries in the columns. The product-mix assumption requires that we divide each column by industry output, which is what is achieved by equation (9.8).

7 In equation (9.11), the solution ${}_cA_c = BC^{-1}$ yields, on a commodity technology assumption, a *commodity* × *commodity* table. This is so because if in equation (9.3) we substitute ${}_cA_cC$ for B, we get $q = {}_cA_cCg + f$; now $Cg = Mi$ (see equation (9.8)) and $Mi = q$, so we have $q = Aq + f$, which is a system of balance equations for commodities not industries.

CHAPTER 10

Updating and Projecting Input–Output Tables

10.1 INTRODUCTION

The transfer of secondary products according to the procedures outlined in Chapter 9 produces an input–output table of commodity × commodity or industry × industry type. If this table is in flow form, i.e. referring to transactions in current prices, it can easily be converted to coefficient form; for example, we can form the relationship (see Chapter 4):

$$A = W\hat{x}^{-1} \qquad (10.1)$$

where A is an input–output coefficient matrix, W is a matrix of intermediate transactions either on a commodity × commodity or industry × industry basis and x is a vector either of commodity or industry outputs. (In subsequent analysis, we shall usually make use of x rather than q or g, because the analysis will apply to input–output tables whether of the industry or commodity type.)

The A matrix in equation (10.1) refers to the base year; as input–output tables can take many years to complete, use of an A matrix referring to the base year for anything other than historical analysis may produce biased results. In the case of Brazil, for example, the 1970 table was not published until 1979, by which time so many changes in technology, relative prices, product-mix, etc. had taken place that it could not be used unadjusted in forecasting work or for current policy decision-making.

The delay in publication in Brazil is longer than most, but even in developed countries delays of five to seven years are common. This is far longer than the gestation period for most statistics, so that in the current year much information is available, such as the national accounts, of more recent vintage than the input–output tables. There are, therefore, two problems faced by input–output workers; first, to reconcile the input–output table with more recent statistics, and secondly to produce an input–output table which is relevant in the current or future years. We shall call these the problems of updating and projecting respectively.

10.2 UPDATING INPUT–OUTPUT TABLES—PRICE CHANGES

In both updating and projecting a common set of problems is faced. The methods used have to take account of the many ways in which an input–output table can be rendered obsolete, while at the same time paying heed to the requirements of input–output theory. This theory, in its original form (Leontief, 1951), deals with the constancy of input–output coefficients in *physical* form, e.g. so many tons of iron per ton of steel. Since data on physical quantities are rarely available in such detail, this amounts to stating the key assumption of input–output theory as the fixed relationship between inputs and outputs in constant prices. Thus, in the base year (subscript 0) we observe the relationship:

$$ {}_0a_{ij} = \frac{{}_0w_{ij}}{{}_0x_j} \tag{10.2} $$

where units of i and j have been chosen so that their price is equal to one. In the current year (subscript 1) we would observe (if we had the data):

$$ {}_1a_{ij} = \frac{{}_1w_{ij}}{{}_1x_j} \tag{10.3} $$

and, in general, ${}_1a_{ij} \neq {}_0a_{ij}$, because of changes in relative prices.[1]

The numerator and the denominator on the right-hand side of equation (10.3) differ from those in equation (10.2) through a quantity change and a price change, so we can write:

$$ {}_1a_{ij} = \left(\frac{{}_0w_{ij} + \Delta w_{ij}}{{}_0x_j + \Delta x_j}\right)\left(\frac{p_i}{p_j}\right) \tag{10.4} $$

where p_i, p_j are the price relatives for the two goods respectively. According to input–output theory, however, the relationship between inputs and outputs in constant prices is fixed, so that equation (10.4) can be written:

$$ {}_1\tilde{a}_{ij} = {}_0a_{ij}\left(\frac{p_i}{p_j}\right) \tag{10.5} $$

or in matrix terms:

$$ {}_1\tilde{A} = \hat{P}\,{}_0A\,\hat{P}^{-1} \tag{10.6} $$

where $(\hat{P})$ is a diagonal matrix whose jth element is p_j, so that we can approximate the input–output coefficient matrix of the current year $({}_1\hat{A})$ by combining the vector of price relatives with the base year matrix $({}_0A)$.

As we shall see below, this is only a first step. However, it is by no means as simple as it looks. First, we have assumed that the price change for commodity group i is the same for all users, i.e. $p_{i,j} = p_{i,k}$ for all $j \neq k$. This is most unlikely to be the case for various reasons; each row of an input–output table, however detailed, usually refers to a bundle of commodities which are sold in different proportions and each of which is subject to different price changes; furthermore, the ith row of a table may refer to an aggregate of imported and domestically produced goods, whereas the ith output refers to domestic output only, so that the price index for the ith commodity will be different for the row and column if domestic goods and imports are imperfect substitutes.

Recognition of this problem requires that we rewrite equation (10.5) as:

$$(10.7) \qquad {}_1\tilde{a}_{ij} = {}_0a_{ij}\left(\frac{p_{ij}}{\bar{p}_j}\right)$$

where $p_{i,j}$ is the price index for the ith commodity (domestic and imported) sold to the jth user, while $\bar{p}_j$ is a weighted average of price indices for those commodities included in the output of the jth sector. However, few countries have price statistics at this level of detail, and so equation (10.7) is not really operational. It is possible, however, to improve on equation (10.5) by allowing for different price indices for imported and domestic goods. The author used this approach in updating input–output tables for Costa Rica (Bulmer–Thomas, 1977a) using the matrix formula:

$$(10.8) \qquad {}_1\tilde{A} = [\hat{P}(T)]_0A[\hat{P}(H)^{-1}]$$

where $\hat{P}(T)$ is a diagonal matrix whose elements are a weighted average of the price movement in home and imported goods, while the elements of $\hat{P}(H)$ refer to home-produced goods only.

The second problem refers to the price indices themselves, even when the simplest formula (equation (10.6)) is being applied. For the manufacturing sectors, it is usually possible to find an appropriate price index among official statistics, but for the primary sectors it is often necessary to resort to the use of unit values, while for the service sectors, input–output workers are reduced to 'rough and ready measures' (see Tilanus, 1966, p. 32). When marginal changes in prices are being considered, this might not matter too much, but the gap between ${}_0A$ and ${}_1A$ is frequently five years or more. Even with modest rates of inflation, this implies substantial changes in prices.

Large changes in price raise two difficulties; first, the spread or range between the minimum and maximum price change may be very great, and equation (10.5) will produce poor results, if the underlying price indexes are unreliable; secondly, large price changes reduce the credibility of the assumption of input–output theory that the relationship between inputs and outputs is fixed in physical terms, since this assumption implies a price elasticity of substitution between inputs of zero. This problem will be returned to below.

10.3 UPDATING INPUT–OUTPUT TABLES—OTHER CHANGES

Despite the difficulties involved in applying price indices to a base year coefficient matrix, we shall assume for the time being that ${}_1\tilde{A}$ represents our best estimate so far of the coefficient matrix in the year to which the table is being updated. The flow or transactions table for the update year is by definition not known, but is estimated by:

(10.9) $$_1\tilde{W} = {_1\tilde{A}}\, {_1\hat{x}}$$

where $_1x$ is the (known) output vector for the update year.

Now consider the simple SAM shown in Figure 10.1, where only the production account has been filled in. If the update year is one for which national accounts are available, then all the entries (except W) will normally be known. Net national income at factor cost is $(y'i)$, net national income at market prices is $\{(y'+t')i\}$, gross national product is $\{(y'+t'+d')i\}$, while gross national expenditure is $\{i'(c+gx+j+\Delta s+e-m)\}$. Although W is unknown, the given information imposes certain restrictions on the estimated transactions matrix; in particular, it fixes the row and column sums of the W matrix, since

(10.10) $$Wi = x - (c + gx + j + \Delta s + e - m) = u$$

and

(10.11) $$i'W = x' - (y' + t' + d') = v$$

where u is a column vector whose ith element refers to the marginal total of the ith row of the transactions matrix, while v is a row vector whose jth element refers to the marginal total of the jth column of the transactions matrix.

If the input–output assumption of fixed coefficients in physical terms held strictly both over scale and over time, then we would find $_1\tilde{W}i = u$ and $i'_1\tilde{W} = v$. However, this in practice never happens for various reasons; these include a price elasticity of substitution between inputs greater than zero, changes in product-mix and technological change. The problem is therefore to adjust $(_1\tilde{W})$ or $(_1\tilde{A})$ in such a way that the row and column constraints are satisfied.

A number of methods have been proposed for adjusting $(_1\tilde{W})$ or $(_1\tilde{A})$; these divide into those which can be applied with a single base year matrix (see appendix to Chapter 8) and those which can only be applied if there are at least two input–output tables available for different years. With two or more tables, a whole class of stochastic models is available for estimating current input–output coefficients; an example is the use of a linear trend derived from previous tables to predict current input–output coefficients, but experiments with this model on both Dutch data (Tilanus, 1966) and UK data (Barker, 1975) have proved very disappointing.

In view of these poor results and since only a few LDCs have two or more comparable input–output tables, it will be sufficient to concentrate on the models which assume the availability of only a single input–output table.[2] These all have one thing in common; since $_1\tilde{W}$ is our only estimate of the unknown $_1W$, the final matrix $_1\tilde{W}^*$ should be as 'close' as possible to $_1\tilde{W}$. 'Closeness', however, can be defined in a number of ways and so the main differences in the methods refer to the nature of the minimands. (In the appendix to Chapter 8 on matrix balancing techniques, for example, four minimands were listed, all of which are very similar.)

The formal problem can be stated as minimizing a function subject to row and column constraints. This gives rise to a set of row and column multipliers which

	Production	Consumption		Accumulation		Trade	Total
	$1, \ldots, n$	Private	Public	Gross fixed capital formation	Stock change	Exports – imports	
Production							
$1, \ldots, n$	W	c	gx	j	Δs	e $-m$	x
Consumption							
Private	y'						
Public	t'						
Accumulation	d'						
Total	x'						

Notes: The distinction between commodities and activities has been ignored. Upper case letters denote matrices, lower case column vectors, and a prime (′) a transposed vector.

Figure 10.1 SAM for updating

can be applied to the initial estimate $({}_1\tilde{W})$ to give the final matrix $({}_1\tilde{W}^*)$. In the case of the RAS or biproportional method, for example (see appendix to Chapter 8), the row multipliers $(r_i, i = 1, \ldots, n)$ and the column multipliers $(s_j, j = 1, \ldots, n)$ have to capture all the deviations from the assumption of fixed coefficients (other than relative price changes) between the base and update year. The row multipliers may be considered an acceptable approximation for capturing the effects of price substitution and the column multipliers for the effects of technological progress (provided both these effects are transmitted fairly rapidly to all branches of the economy), but the assumption of biproportionality clearly cannot capture the consequences of introducing new products or new industries, since any zero element in $({}_1\tilde{A})$ must remain zero in $({}_1\tilde{A}^*)$.

Although it would be too much to expect the *r* and *s* multipliers to capture the full effect of all changes in the coefficient matrix over time, the crucial question is how well the method performs in practice. For this, we need an actual (firmly-based) matrix $({}_1A)$ with which we can compare the RAS update $({}_1\tilde{A}^*)$. A great deal of work has been done on these lines, particularly in the United Kingdom; when the first tests on the RAS method were carried out (Paelinck and Waelbroeck, 1963), the conclusion was one of cautious optimism, but as time goes by, the results appear less and less satisfactory (Allen, 1974; Barker, 1975; Allen, 1975). The most recent work is indeed extremely pessimistic; for example, in an unpublished study (Lynch, 1979) an RAS update for 1968 from a firmly based table for 1963 was compared with an actual table for 1968 for the United Kingdom. Comparing only those coefficients corresponding to a flow greater than £10 million (85% of the total by value), over 50% were in error[3] by more than 25% and 25% were in error by more than 50%.

These are distinctly disappointing results and the blame cannot be laid at the door of the RAS method as such, since the other comparable methods show a similar performance. The response to the problem has been two-fold; first to modify the methods to take account of exogenous or *ex ante* information and secondly to re-examine the key assumption of input–output theory. It is the second approach which we will consider first.

10.4 UPDATING INPUT–OUTPUT TABLES—FURTHER MODIFICATIONS

Stating the fixed relationship between inputs and outputs in physical terms implies a zero price elasticity of substitution between inputs. This is not very realistic and over time the assumption has not stood up well to tests; if the price elasticity is not zero, however, it is tempting to assume that it is unity, because in this case a given percentage change in price will be matched by a change in quantity in the opposite direction. With unit price elasticities, *ceteris paribus*, input–output coefficients in value terms will be unchanged, so that ${}_0A$ would be our initial best estimate of ${}_1A$. Indeed, experiments on input–output tables for the

Netherlands (Tilanus, 1966) suggest that forecasts using value coefficients are much more reliable than those in constant prices.

Of course, an assumption of elasticities of demand for all inputs of either zero or unity is rather extreme. A less heroic assumption is to assume that all own-price elasticities are some value $(-\partial)$, which implies that the input–output coefficients are weighted averages of volume and value coefficients, the weights being $(1-\partial)$ and (∂) respectively. It can be shown (Barker, 1975) that in this case the estimating equation for the matrix of intermediate transactions is now

$$(10.12) \qquad {}_1\tilde{W} = {}_1\tilde{A}^{(1-\partial)}\hat{p}_w^{-\partial}\,{}_0A^{\partial}\hat{p}_x^{\partial}\,{}_1\hat{x}$$

where ${}_1\tilde{A}$ is to be interpreted as a matrix of volume coefficients, ${}_0A$ as a matrix of value coefficients and $\hat{P}_w$, $\hat{P}_x$ are (diagonalized) vectors of price indexes relating to intermediate demand and gross output respectively.[4]

Parametric variation of ∂ in equation (10.12) will yield different forecasts of, say, intermediate demand. By comparing these with actual results, a ∂ can be selected which minimizes prediction error. In the Dutch experiments (Tilanus, 1966), the best results were achieved with a value of ∂ between 0.75 and 0.5. This is a far cry from a price elasticity of substitution of zero and invites the use of value coefficients in updating; however, Barker's experiments on the UK suggested the optimal value of ∂ lay between 0 and 0.1.

One possible explanation of the difference in the optimal value of ∂ in the two tests lies in the exclusion of competitive imports from intermediate flows in the Dutch case, so that Holland's high ∂ may reflect the relative ease of substitution of domestic for imported goods and vice versa. Thus, for LDCs with imports separately articulated in the base year and with poor price statistics, it seems preferable to base the initial estimate of the coefficient matrix in the update year on the firmly-based coefficient matrix of the base year $({}_0A)$, since this implies coefficients fixed in value terms.

Of course, the use of $({}_0A)$ rather than $({}_1\tilde{A})$ in the initial estimate does not eliminate the need for some constrained matrix technique, but it does ease the computational and statistical problem and it may reduce the size of the initial errors. The smaller the size of initial errors, the more likely it is that constrained matrix techniques will give acceptable results. Nevertheless, none of these techniques in practice appear sufficiently reliable in themselves and we must therefore turn to the other suggestion for improvement: the use of exogenous information.

If the update year is the most recent one for which national accounts statistics are available, it is improbable that nothing is known about the elements of the transactions or coefficient matrix other than the row and column sums. For example, reports of state controlled industries will usually provide details of their intermediate inputs, while a complete matrix of imports by source and use may be available from supply-side data. As part of the national accounts exercise, several rows of the table may be obtainable from a 'commodity-balance' exercise, while the sources and uses of energy may be published or estimated on an annual basis.

All this exogenous information will be in flow form, so it is convenient to focus upon the transactions matrix (${}_0W$), its initial update estimate (${}_1\tilde{W}$) and the final update estimate (${}_1\tilde{W}^*$). The exogenous information may be contained in a matrix (${}_1W'$) for the update year, so that what is uncertain is $[{}_1\tilde{W} - {}_1W'] = {}_1\tilde{W}''$. Adoption of the biproportionality assumption, for example, suggests the relationship (see appendix to Chapter 8):

$$(10.13) \qquad {}_1\tilde{W}^* = {}_1W' + \hat{r}\,{}_1\tilde{W}''\hat{s}$$

As before, the constraints can be written ${}_1\tilde{W}^*i = u$ and $i'\,{}_1\tilde{W}^* = v$, so that again sufficient information is available to estimate the $2n$ row and column multipliers.

A number of tests have been carried out on the effects of incorporating exogenous information[5] and the results are in general quite satisfactory (see, for example, Allen, 1974). In the study for the UK referred to above (Lynch, 1979), an effort was made to relate the mean absolute percentage error to the size of the table and the extent of exogenous information (see Figure 10.2). With the largest table (69 sectors), the average percentage error falls dramatically with the incorporation of additional exogenous information, while percentage error can also be reduced by judicious aggregation.

If a mean percentage error of 20% is regarded as the maximum permissible,

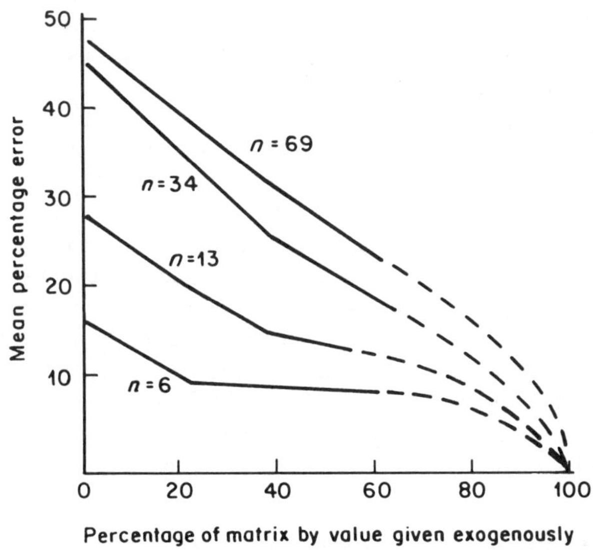

Figure 10.2 Relationship of mean percentage error in UK input–output table for 1968 to exogenous information. The figure relates mean absolute percentage error in estimates of 1968 symmetric absorption matrix to levels of exogenous information by value for given levels of aggregation, n being the number of industries separately identified. *Source*: Taken from Lynch (1979)

then some 70% of the value of the transactions matrix must be given exogenously for the larger tables (69 and 34 sectors). This sounds a formidable requirement, but it is well known that inter-industry relationships are dominated by a handful of key coefficients.[6] If these are known in advance, then it should be possible to update the transactions matrix with an acceptable level of accuracy.

The key coefficients, however, may not be provided exogenously. Given their importance, it seems worthwhile, therefore, to budget for sufficient sampling resources to estimate them *ex ante*. This could be done as part of the initial survey work, if it is already known which are likely to be the key coefficients. Failing that, the exercise needs to be carried out at a later date and a number of procedures have been suggested (see, for example, Fisher, 1975a).

It has been assumed above that the row and column totals of the transactions matrix are known with certainty. This is clearly not the case with projections and may well not be true for updated matrices. Furthermore, we have also assumed that matrix balancing is carried out on symmetric tables. This implies that in the case of commodity × commodity tables, the commodity rather than industrial composition of value added is known, while in the case of industry × industry tables it implies that the industrial composition of final demand is known. Thus, the efforts to present row and column totals for symmetric tables are likely to introduce further errors into either the u or v vectors, since value added is normally given on an industry basis and final demand on a commodity basis.

Of course, the biproportional and other constrained matrix techniques can be applied to the commodity × industry absorption matrix just as easily as to a symmetric transactions table (see Chapter 8), although derivation of the symmetric input–output table then assumes knowledge of the make matrix in the update or projection year.[7] Nevertheless, use of an absorption matrix cannot wholly remove the probability of error in the control totals and so the problem remains.

The problem of error in the control totals can be solved by appropriate modification of one of the constrained matrix balancing techniques described in the appendix to Chapter 8. The adaptation of the RAS and Friedlander methods, for example, has been pioneered by Lecomber (Lecomber, 1964; 1975) and the case of the RAS method has already been illustrated (see section 4 of Chapter 8). This method has been tested on UK data (Allen, 1975) and found to perform satisfactorily; in particular, it improves estimates of the row and column totals themselves, which could prove useful in national accounts work in LDCs.

10.5 PROJECTIONS OF INPUT–OUTPUT TABLES

Frequently, an updated table is nothing more than a first step towards projecting an input–output table to some future year, since many applications are concerned with predictions or forecasts as part of a general planning exercise. If we denote the estimates of transactions and coefficient matrices in the projection year as $({}_2\tilde{W}, {}_2\tilde{A})$ respectively, then the problem of projection becomes one of estimating these matrices given input–output tables for years 0 and 1.

By definition, constrained matrix techniques are inappropriate since marginal totals for future years are not known. On the other hand, if coefficients have changed between years 0 and 1, it is tempting to assume that any discernible trends will continue up to year 2. In the case of the biproportional model, for example, this suggests as the estimating equation:

$$(10.14) \qquad {}_2\tilde{A} = (\hat{r}^t)\,{}_1\tilde{A}^*\,(\hat{s}^t)$$

where r and s are obtained from the updating exercise, and the form of equation (10.14) implies that individual elements of the coefficient matrix follow an exponential time-trend. Thus, if the number of years between 0 and 1 is the same as between 1 and 2, we can set $t = 2$, while if it is half as much, $t = 3$ and so on.

Various modifications to equation (10.18) have been suggested (e.g. Bacharach, 1970) since it was first introduced by Stone (Stone et al., 1963), but all are subject to the same problem that over all but very short periods—in which case $({}_2\tilde{A})$ can be approximated by $({}_1\tilde{A}^*)$—exponential trends are rather explosive and produce absurd results. Even linear trends (as suggested by the Friedlander method—see Table 8.1a), do not perform well in projecting input–output coefficients, as Tilanus (1966) and Barker (1975) have shown. It is therefore necessary to look for alternatives.

One possibility arises if there are time-series for row and column totals.[8] In this case, we have $(2n \times t)$ constraints, where t is the number of years for which marginal totals are available, and this gives a time-series for the row and column multipliers. The trick is now to find some variable on which the multipliers themselves are dependent. Many suggestions have been made (of which time itself is the most obvious), but the most theoretically attractive is relative prices,[9] i.e.

$$(10.15) \qquad r^* = \hat{\pi}^*\lambda + e$$

$$(10.16) \qquad s^* = \hat{\pi}^*\mu + \varepsilon$$

where an asterisk denotes logarithms, e, ε are vectors of stochastic disturbances and the jth element of $\hat{\pi}$ is the relative price of the jth commodity. Estimates of λ and μ can be derived by regression analysis, and incorporated in a model (see Parikh, 1979) which reflects the impact of relative price changes on technological coefficients, i.e.

$$(10.17) \qquad a_{ij}(t) = {}_1\tilde{a}_{ij}\,[\pi_i(t)^{\lambda_i}]\,[\pi_j(t)^{\mu_i}]\,u_{ij}(t)$$

where u_{ij} (t) is again a disturbance term.

Although this model may be considered an improvement on the application of a simple time trend to row and column multipliers, it still requires forecasts of relative price changes and assumes that only relative prices affect the elements of the technology matrix over time. The latter assumption is surely not true and the accurate forecast of relative prices will be beyond the capabilities of most LDCs.

In projections, the input–output table, rather than an end in itself, is usually a means to forecast output, incomes, employment, etc. If we are prepared to lose information on the coefficient matrix in the year for which predictions are required, Tilanus (1966) has shown that a theoretically satisfactory model is available, which can predict output, incomes and so on and compares favourably with an RAS procedure. This model or Statistical Correction Method (SCM) is very simple; first, we may note that in the update year the prediction of any vector (intermediate output, for example) will differ from the observed vector. If the difference between these two is expressed as a ratio for each sector, the model for predicting output becomes:

$$ {}_2\tilde{x} = {}_1\hat{C}[I - {}_1\tilde{A}^*]^{-1}\,{}_2f \tag{10.18}$$

where the ith element of ${}_1\hat{C}$ is the ratio of the observed to predicted value of, say, ith sector intermediate sales in year 1. This model must surely hold considerable advantages for LDCs, since it is simple in terms of required statistics, and works at least as well as the RAS method, while the information lost is unlikely to be of great importance.

10.6 CONCLUSIONS

In desperation at the limitations of mechanical methods, several input–output workers have resorted to survey techniques for projecting input–output tables. These methods either rely on extrapolating 'best practice' techniques in base years (Miernyk et al., 1970) or require the forecast by firms themselves of input requirements in future years (Fisher, 1975(b)).[10] While recognizing the potential involved in these methods, particularly with regard to their flexibility, it must be admitted that few LDCs are likely to be able to take advantage of them. Projection of input–output tables for LDCs, therefore, are likely to be most effective if carried out on the trends-in-multipliers approach or the SCM. No method, however, can be expected to give satisfactory results if input–output tables are constructed at infrequent intervals and a period of seven or eight years between the base (0) and projection (2) year must be considered the maximum permissible. This implies the construction of tables much more rapidly than historically has been the case, but a major purpose of this book is to provide directions for reducing what has hitherto been an unacceptable gestation lag.

NOTES

1 There is a well-known theorem in the input–output literature, called the Samuelson no-substitution theorem, which states that relative prices *cannot* change in an input–output world, but this is only true where there is a single primary input (see Dorfman, 1958, pp. 224–7).

2 Work on stochastic models requiring two or more input–output tables is still very much in its infancy; for a good review of the whole subject, see Lecomber (1975) and Parikh (1979).

3 'Error' is here defined as $({}_1\tilde{a}^*_{ij} - {}_1a_{ij})/{}_1a_{ij} \times 100$.

4 Note that taking logarithms and differentiating equation (10.12) yields:

$$\mathrm{d}\log({}_1\tilde{W}_1\hat{x}^{-1}) = -\partial\,\mathrm{d}\log(p_w i'\hat{p}_x^{-1})$$

which is consistent with the assumption that all own-price elasticities are $(-\partial)$. See Barker (1975).

5 Sometimes, the exogenous information does not refer to specific cells but to blocks of cells (i.e. the aggregate value of a set of (unknown) cells within the transactions matrix). This information cannot be incorporated in the RAS method, but can be fitted into one of the more general optimizing techniques using Lagrangian multipliers (see Morrison and Thumann, 1979).

6 Allen (1974) has shown the crucial dependence of forecasts of intermediate output for the UK on a relatively small number of key coefficients and has suggested a criterion for selection which measures the sensitivity of intermediate demand projections to changes in particular coefficients. A similar exercise for other countries could provide a guide as to which coefficients should be estimated *ex ante*.

7 The make matrix itself can be updated by the biproportional method quite easily, because *its* row and column totals are commodity and industry outputs respectively (see Bacharach, 1970, pp. 34 and 124).

8 The projection would then have to be carried out on the absorption matrix, since it is most improbable that a time-series of marginal totals is available for symmetric tables, but this is not a very serious problem.

9 Another possibility is industry outputs.

10 For a powerful critique of this method, see Miernyk (1977).

CHAPTER 11

Methodology and Construction of Input–Output Tables—Some Special Problems

11.1 REGIONAL INPUT–OUTPUT TABLES

In the previous chapters, it has been assumed that the objective is construction of a national input–output table; when converted into coefficient form, this table provides a basis for predicting output, incomes, employment, etc. at the *national* level. For some countries, however, the spatial distribution of economic activity is of great importance and the regional or even urban implications of any solution need to be established.

In some cases it will be possible to derive regional results even from a national input–output table; this will be so whenever the regions in question are specialized in products which correspond to the sectors of the input–output table. In many LDCs, industry is heavily concentrated in one region or urban complex, while other regions are concentrated in specific primary products so that the interactions between primary and secondary activities in a national input–output model would compare roughly to the national division of economic activity.

In other cases, however, these rough and ready measures are inappropriate, while some LDCs are so large (e.g. India, Pakistan) that industrial concentrations occur in most regions. For these countries, it may be desirable to prepare input–output tables at the subnational level so that the regional impact of, say, federal expenditure can be measured directly.

If the input–output table to be prepared is for a single region in which interactions with other regions are treated very much like trade with the rest of the world in a national input–output table, then most of what has been said in the previous chapters about construction of national tables still applies. A single region input–output model, however, ignores the multiplier effects on regional activity induced by the inter-regional trade flows and the inter-regional feed-back mechanism, while if the exercise involves construction of a multi-regional model based on input–output tables for different regions then special problems arise from the difficulty of obtaining reliable estimates of inter-regional trade flows.

The major difference between a national and a single region input–output table is that the latter has additional rows and columns to allow for extra-regional imports and exports. The simplest case is where one extra column in final demand is provided for exports to other regions and one extra column for (competitive) imports from other regions so that the matrix of intersectoral transactions, when translated into coefficient form, represents the technical structure of the region. Exports to other regions are then treated as exogenous and the solution for imports can be linked to the solution for regional outputs along the lines suggested in Chapter 7.

Any subdivision of a nation, however, is more open to trade than the nation itself; if the regional economy is very open, the above treatment of imports will prove unreliable since what is required is a matrix of extra-regional imports by using sectors which can be used to give more accurate multiplier results. Such a matrix means that the region's intersectoral coefficient matrix can no longer be interpreted as technical, since it is calculated net of extra-regional imports; if imports from the rest of the world are also excluded, the intersectoral matrix will refer to intra-regional transactions only, which can be thought of as a 'domestic' transactions matrix.

In the construction of a regional input–output table, many sources will be used which are similar to those for national tables (see Chapter 2). Household consumption can be obtained from regional budget survey data, regional gross output and primary inputs from the regional census of production and regional investment from the same source; typically, however, there will be no details on intra-regional transactions and on extra-regional trade flows including those to and from the rest of the world.

In order to avoid estimating these flows by survey methods, which are costly and time-consuming, some input–output workers have started from the assumption that the technical coefficients at the regional level (a^r_{ij}) are the same as those at the national level (a^n_{ij}). If this were true, then the matrix of intra-regional flows could be calculated as a residual if the matrix of extra-regional flows were known or viceversa.

Unfortunately, there is no evidence that this is the case. In a recent study (Harrigan, 1980) comparing the national technical structure of the United Kingdom with a single region (Scotland), it was found that the two technical coefficient matrices differed substantially and that use of the UK matrix served as a poor predictor of regional gross output; some of the differences between the two matrices arise from problems associated with aggregation to a common classification scheme and from problems of product-mix within each sector which could in principle be allowed for in adapting the national table for regional purposes (see Czamanski, 1969), but this would not eliminate the problem entirely.

Even if the national input–output table is used as a starting point, there is still the problem of estimating either the matrix of intra-regional transactions or the matrix of extra-regional imports as well as extra-regional exports. Non-survey methods have been proposed for this too (see below), but these are generally unreliable; if survey methods are used, however, the extra effort required to obtain estimates of regional technical coefficients is not very great and is to be recommended (*pace* Su, 1970).

In a regional survey, additional questions are needed on extra-regional imports and exports from those that are required in a national survey. The problems associated with the design of such a questionnaire have been discussed elsewhere (Burdekin, 1978a); in the author's experience few firms are unable to provide some indication of the regional breakdown of sales and purchases, although the experience of others has not been so fortunate (Isard, 1971). Sometimes, firms are unable to identify the source of supply or destination of sales beyond the wholesale stage in which case a supplementary survey of wholesalers is required in order to break down purchases and sales by region.

The greatest problems in regional surveys arise in the context of valuation and grossing-up. Imports and exports for a nation can be derived from trade sources which not only provide a control total, but also use a valuation convention which is similar to that which will be needed in the input–output table; in the case of regional imports, however, the survey will report these in purchaser's prices which it may be difficult to adjust because the 'border price' in such cases is artificial. More serious is the problem posed by lack of control totals; 'grossing-up' sales, as will be argued below, is not a reliable method and so the vector of extra-regional exports cannot be held in much confidence if the sample is small, although the problem may not be so serious in the case of extra-regional imports. The only effective answer to this problem is a survey comprehensive enough to cover the bulk of outputs, exports and imports.

We now turn to consider the problem posed by multi-regional input–output tables. It can be assumed that one of the purposes of such tables is to show the links between the different regions of the economy; in the spirit of traditional input–output analysis it is therefore necessary to know the origin of imports and the destination of exports by sector as well as by region; a very thorough survey for a single region might reveal the sectoral origin of imports, but it could not be expected to reveal the sectoral destination of sales. It is therefore clear that a fully-articulated multi-regional model requires surveys to be carried out simultaneously in all the regions.

The resource-intensive nature of this 'ideal' system of multi-regional input–output analysis is so great that frequent use is made of non-survey techniques. These come in two forms; those that spread the vectors of extra-regional exports and imports across using and supplying sectors according to some simple proportionality assuming, and those which are used to generate the vectors of exports and imports themselves, as well as the intra-regional coefficients in some cases.

The first type of non-survey technique is necessary if a set of mutually consistent input–output tables is to be turned into a multi-regional model in which the regions are locked together through their productive structures. It is discussed elsewhere (Chapter 14.2) and a good summary of the techniques can be found in Richardson (1972); the second type of technique is often necessary for the construction of a regional input–output table, and is therefore discussed here.

Regional exports and imports have sometimes been estimated as a residual from the regional balance equations; given a vector or regional outputs and a vector of home demands (including intermediate demand), it is possible to construct a vector of net trade flows as the residual. The method, however, has two very serious drawbacks; first, it implies that a sector either produces an exportable surplus or requires imports to satisfy demand but not both, ruling out intra-industry trade which in practice is very important; secondly, the net trade vector—if treated as a residual—reflects all the errors in supply and demand estimates which are not necessarily self-cancelling. This type of non-survey technique is therefore advisable in only the most pressing situations.

The more popular form of non-survey technique involves generating intra-regional trade coefficients from knowledge of the national coefficients; the techniques are well surveyed in Schaffer (1969), but they all suffer from the fact that intra-industry trade is ruled out by implication and from the fact that national coefficients are used as a starting point for the construction of regional technical coefficients.

The position, as far as LDCs are concerned, is not a happy one; the construction of regional tables by survey methods is extremely costly, while the use of non-survey techniques cannot yet be regarded as reliable. Progress in this field depends on finding sectors or blocks of coefficients within an input-out table for the estimation of which non-survey techniques could be used with confidence; although this goal has been frequently stated, it has not yet been realized.

The only consolation for LDCs is that most of them do not in fact require regional input–output analysis; a well-designed national input–output table can in fact yield reliable regional forecasts or predictions if the division of economic activity between the chosen regions is complementary rather than competitive. Even where it is competitive, there are relatively simple ways of recognizing the interdependence of regions (see Chapter 14.2) which do not depend on the construction of extra-regional export and import matrices.

11.2 SALES AND PURCHASES DATA

It has so far been assumed that the elements of the commodity × industry input–output table are built up from primary sources denominated in purchasers' prices. As a result of this, a problem of valuation adjustment occurs (see Chapter 6) in order to effect a reconciliation between demand and supply; this reconciliation is awkward and runs the danger of introducing errors into otherwise reliable data.

The problem will occur whenever the primary source indicates the origin of purchases rather than the destination of sales. Where survey techniques are used, however, it is possible to expand the questionnaire to include not only information on purchases (absorptions), but also on the distribution of sales by sector; if the absorption table is built up on the basis of the latter data alone, there can be no valuation problem since supply and demand will be denominated in the same prices.

For this reason, among others, use of sales data has attracted the interest of input–output workers. Furthermore, there are some sectors in LDCs (e.g. public utilities) for which the sectoral breakdown of sales is regularly published providing an immediate translation into the elements of an absorption matrix without the need for further adjustments. The simplicity of the method, however, is somewhat illusory as it suffers from a number of defects.

First, data on the distribution of sales exclude imports; in order to estimate a matrix of technical coefficients—the core of an input–output model—a matrix of imports must also be constructed; if this is constructed from purchases data, the valuation problem remains, although if it is constructed from trade sources (i.e. 'supply' side data), it may be possible to leave the elements of the matrix unadjusted at c.i.f. prices. Summation of the column sums of the two matrices, however, would then yield an initial estimate of total intermediate purchases which—when deducted from gross output—would leave value added as the residual; this estimate is likely to be different from the figure for value added from other sources leaving a problem of reconciliation.

Secondly, sales data refer to the *purchases* of sector i by sector j, not the *absorptions*. It is quite impossible to extract the stock change element in purchases from sales data alone, although the fundamental assumption of input–output theory refers to the stability of the relationship between absorptions (not purchases) and gross output.

Thirdly, if sample survey techniques are used to derive sales data, there is the problem of extrapolation to the population. While input–output theory provides the necessary underpinning for grossing-up purchases data by column, the same cannot be said for sales data by row. If $x\%$ of sales in the sample of sector i go to sector j, there is no reason for believing that $x\%$ of sales in the population of sector i will go to the same destination; indeed, there are strong grounds for believing the opposite since sector j may have received all its requirements from the sampled firms.

The most serious difficulty, however, facing the sales data technique is provided by the unreliability of the estimated distribution. In the author's experience, firms have comparatively little knowledge of the sectoral distribution of sales; in carrying out a survey of manufacturing firms in Scotland, for example, the input–output team was forced to abandon questions on the distribution of sales, although questions on purchases were answered satisfactorily.

Other input–output teams (e.g. Miernyk, 1970) have achieved better results from questions on sales. At best, however, these can be used to provide a second estimate of any cell entry in the absorption matrix; the two estimates—one based on purchases data, one on sales data—will not normally be the same, so that a reconciliation is required. After appropriate valuation adjustment, so that they adopt the same valuation convention, the two entries can be reconciled by attaching subjective probability weights to each estimate; the single entry table derived from the dual estimates can then be reconciled with known row and column totals using one of the matrix balancing techniques described in the appendix to Chapter 8 (see Jensen, 1976).

11.3 MODELS OF INVESTMENT BEHAVIOUR AND CAPITAL STOCK MATRICES

The balance equations for the input–output system can be written as:

$$x = A_D x + f_d$$
(11.1)
$$m = A_m x + f_m$$

where x is the vector of gross outputs, m of imports, A_D is the matrix of domestic coefficients, A_m of trade coefficients and f_d, f_m are final demand vectors for home output and imports respectively.

Models derived from equation (11.1) assume that the final demand vectors are exogenous; the latter, however, include investment expenditures which are very difficult to forecast exogenously, if only because their level is often thought to depend on the increase in the level of output itself. Investment expenditures consist of replacement expenditures and new investment so that the balance equations can now be written:

$$x = A_D x + J_D i + R_D i + h_d$$
(11.2)
$$m = A_m x + J_m i + R_m i + h_m$$

where h refers to final demand exclusive of investment expenditures, J is a matrix of new investment requirements whose i, jth element (j_{ij}) records the purchases of the ith capital good by the jth sector for capacity expansion, while R is a matrix of replacement expenditures similarly defined.

The matrix of new investment requirements is the same as the difference between the nation's capital stock matrix at the end (S_1) and start (S_0) of the period calculated on a gross basis, i.e.

$$J_D = S_D(1) - S_D(0)$$
(11.3)
$$J_m = S_m(1) - S_m(0)$$

The stock of any capital good i held by sector j is often thought to bear a fixed relationship to the level of capacity output in sector j, i.e.

$$S(1)_i = B_i \hat{x}^*(1)$$
(11.4) $$i = d, m$$
$$S(0)_i = B_i \hat{x}^*(0)$$

so that the matrix of new investment expenditures can be written:

(11.5) $$J_i = B_i \Delta \hat{x}^* \qquad i = d, m$$

where $\hat{x}^*$ is a diagonalized vector of capacity outputs.

Ignoring the difference between actual (x) and capacity output levels (x^*), the balance equation now becomes:

$$x = A_D x + B_D \Delta x + R_D i + h_d$$
(11.6)
$$m = A_m x + B_m \Delta x + R_m i + h_m$$

This system of equations can become the basis of a dynamic model of an economy (see Chapter 14.3); it can also be used in static models to predict output levels in a particular year provided the vector Δx can be made more tractable. The latter is equal to $[x(1)-x(0)]$, i.e.

(11.7)
$$\Delta x = \{A_D x(1) + B_D \Delta x' + R_D(1)i + h_d(1)\} - \{A_D x(0) + B_D \Delta x + R_D(0) + h_d(0)\}$$

or

(11.8)
$$\Delta x = A_D \Delta x + B_D\{\Delta x' - \Delta x\} + \Delta R_D i + \Delta h_d$$

where $\Delta x'$ is the change in output from the first to the second period;with linear rather than exponential growth in output, $\Delta x' = \Delta x$ and we can write equation (11.8) as:[1]

(11.9)
$$\Delta x = \{I - A_D\}^{-1} \Delta h_d^*$$

where h^* now includes replacement expenditures, so that the balance equations become:

(11.10)
$$x = A_D x + B_D\{I - A_D\}^{-1} \Delta h_d^* + h_d^*$$
$$m = A_m x + B_m\{I - A_D\}^{-1} \Delta h_d^* + h_d^*$$

and the solution for the output vector is now:

(11.11)
$$x = (I - A_D)^{-1}\{B_D(I - A_D)^{-1} \Delta h_d^* + h_d^*\}$$

The interpretation of equation (11.11) is well discussed in United Nations (1973); by making new investment endogenous, allowance is made for the additional increase in output created directly and indirectly by investment expenditures. Purchases of capital goods from domestic industry require expansions to capacity in the supplying industry which generate further demands for capital goods and so on.

The above solution to an input–output model with investment endogenous was made possible by assuming $\Delta x' = \Delta x$; this will only be realistic if a relatively short period (a year, for example) is chosen. Input–output models (see Chapter 17) are, however, often used for forecasting output levels five or even ten years ahead, in which case it is quite unrealistic to assume $\Delta x' = \Delta x$.

An alternative approach can be taken by writing the balance equations with time subscripts, i.e.

(11.12)
$$x(t) = A_D x(t) + h_d^*(t) + J_D(t)i$$
$$x(0) = A_D x(0) + h_d^*(0) + J_D(0)i$$

where $t > 1$ by assumption. By subtraction this yields:

(11.13)
$$\Delta x = A_D \Delta x + \Delta h_d^* + J_D(t)i - J_D(0)i$$

Now according to the accelerator-type relationship used to explain new investment expenditure above, the investment throughout the plan period will be given by the product of the matrix of capital–output ratios and the vector of changes in output, i.e.

(11.14)
$$\sum_{t=0}^{T} J_D(t) = B_D \Delta \hat{x}$$

This, however, is investment throughout the plan period; in order to work out investment in the terminal year (t)— so that equation (11.13) can be solved—we need to know the ratio of investment in the terminal year to total investment over the plan period; this ratio is known in the literature as a stock-flow conversion factor[2] and can be derived very easily if investment is assumed to grow at a constant geometric rate throughout the plan period (Manne, 1963) or a constant arithmetic rate (Sandee, 1960). Once this ratio for each sector (∂_i) is known, terminal year investment can be estimated as:

(11.15)
$$J_D(t)_i = \hat{\partial} B_D \Delta x$$

and the solution for the change in output vector (Δx) can now be written:

(11.16)
$$\Delta x = \{I - A_D - \hat{\partial} B_D\}^{-1} \{\Delta h_d^* - J_D(0)i\}$$

where $\{J_D(0)i\}$ is assumed to be known since it refers to investment in the base year.

It would seem, therefore, that it is possible to work with input–output models which make new investment endogenous provided that the matrices of capital–output ratios (B_D, B_m) can be obtained; furthermore, replacement expenditure can be built into the model by assuming that capital goods wear out at some predictable rate given by the product of the capital stock and the 'rate of depreciation', i.e.

(11.17)
$$R_D = \delta_D S_D = \delta_D B_D \hat{x}$$
$$R_m = \delta_m S_m = \delta_m B_m \hat{x}$$

where δ is a matrix of depreciation rates whose i,jth element records the proportion of the value of capital good i held by sector j wearing out each year. If replacement expenditure is made endogenous in the model, equation (11.11) becomes:

(11.18)
$$x = \{I - A_D - \delta_D B_D\}^{-1} \{B_D \{I - A_D - \delta_D B_D\}^{-1} \Delta h_d + h_d\}$$

and (11.16) becomes:

(11.19)
$$\Delta x = \{I - A_D - (\delta_D + \hat{\partial}) B_D\}^{-1} \{\Delta h_d - J_D(0)i\}$$

Models based on equations similar to (11.18) and (11.19) have been attempted for a number of the larger developing countries, in particular India (Bergsman, 1966) and Mexico (Manne, 1966). The age of these models should not blind the reader to the difficulty of implementation, since this is an area where neither technique nor statistical sophistication has moved very fast.

Before discussing the problems encountered in constructing the matrices of capital–output ratios, it would be as well to clear away a few methodological issues. If the matrix of domestic capital–output ratios (B_D) is null, the equations (11.18) and (11.19) collapse to the traditional static input–output form with investment expenditure treated exogenously. In other words, there is no point in going to a lot of trouble to construct these matrices if there is no domestic capital goods industry and all capital requirements are imported. In reality, there will always be some positive entries in B_D because the (non-traded) distribution sectors earn margins on imported capital goods, while one important part of capital outlays involves expenditure on construction—another non-traded sector. It may well be, however, that these entries do not justify treating investment endogenously, especially when the other methodological problems discussed below are taken into account.

If the country in question does have a significant capital goods industry, it is not necessarily the case that accelerator-type relationships are the best way of explaining the demand for capital goods; the price elasticity of substitution for capital goods is generally thought to be high, while the establishment of a capital goods industry will take place through import substitution, thereby disturbing the assumed stable relationship implied by a fixed capital coefficients matrix. Furthermore, in most LDCs it is unrealistic to assume either that actual output equals capacity output (as is implied by equations (11.18) and (11.19)) or that it bears a fixed relationship to capacity output. Additional demand will frequently be met by making better use of installed capacity rather than by additions to capacity.

Another serious methodological problem occurs because of the lags which arise in practice between installation of capital goods and increases in capacity output; in the above analysis, we have implicitly assumed that investment in year (t) is linked to the increase in output between years (t) and ($t+1$), i.e.

$$j_{ij}(t) = b_{ij}\{x_j(t+1) - x_j(t)\} \tag{11.20}$$

so that

$$x_j(t+1) = \left(\frac{j_{ij}(t)}{b_{ij}}\right) + x_j(t) \tag{11.21}$$

i.e. next year's output can be explained by this year's output and this year's investment. In reality, it may be some years before this year's investment bears fruit. If this gestation lag (g) is included, the correct formulation becomes:

$$j_{ij}(t) = b_{ij}\{x_j(t+g) - x_j(t+g-1)\} \tag{11.22}$$

so that

$$x_j(t+g) = x_j(t+g-1) + \left(\frac{j_{ij}(t)}{b_{ij}}\right) \tag{11.23}$$

The inclusion of gestation lags complicates the mathematics of the above models, although not too seriously;[3] more disturbing is the problem of estimating the lags correctly, since virtually no countries – let alone LDCs – have access to the necessary information. It has been attempted, however, for some countries and the interested reader may find the details elsewhere (e.g. Eckaus, 1968).

One final methodological problem concerns the estimation of the matrix of 'depreciation rates' (δ). In practice, it is usually necessary to use information on depreciation allowances, although these are usually very arbitrary measures of physical life in view of their use as a weapon of tax policy; furthermore, in a growing economy, depreciation and replacement expenditures tend to diverge more and more (see Domar, 1957) so that use of depreciation information to estimate the elements of δ can give a misleading impression of replacement expenditure.

In the above analysis, the reader has been spared one additional thorny issue – the determination of inventory changes. Some models have gone so far as to explain this change on lines similar to the explanation of new fixed investment, i.e. as the product of an inventory coefficients matrix and a vector of changes in gross output. Much inventory change, however, is unintended, and it therefore seems unreasonable to use observed stock levels to generate 'equilibrium' relationships between the levels of stocks and the level of output. In LDCs, furthermore, information on stock change is always inadequate, so it seems best to continue to treat it as exogenous and include it in the final bill of goods.

We now turn to the problems involved in constructing the capital coefficient matrices B_D and B_m. With gestation lags up to g years, there will be g matrices for each, i.e. $2g$ matrices in all; however, as equations (11.22) and (11.4) make clear, each of the coefficient matrices is derived from a matrix of investment flows (11.22) or capital stocks (11.4) so that the problem boils down to constructing the two flow or stock matrices, from which the desired coefficient matrices can be obtained by dividing through by the output change corresponding to the required gestation lag.

The balance equations show that the capital–output coefficients should be of the incremental rather than average sort, since what is involved is the relationship of the *increase* in the capital stock of the ith good held by the jth sector to the *increase* in capacity in the jth sector; if incremental coefficients are needed, the implication is that a matrix of investment flows is preferable to one of capital stocks in order to derive the capital–output ratios, since the ratio of capital stock to output will only yield *average* capital–output coefficients.

The purchase of capital goods as investment flows by sector j, however, is likely to be highly cyclical; it is therefore unwise to base the coefficient matrices on investment flow data for one year alone. With several investment flow matrices for different years, it is possible to construct 'average' incremental capital–output coefficients using regression or other types of analysis.

Investment flow matrices are difficult enough to produce for one year (Green, 1975) let alone a series of years. For that reason, it may be best to ignore the difference between average and incremental capital–output coefficients and construct a single year capital stock matrix; the information required for this can usually only be obtained from a census and suffers from being estimated at historic rather than replacement costs. Nonetheless, capital stock matrices have been constructed for some LDCs—e.g. Nigeria (see Kuyvenhoven, 1978).

The primary source for investment flow and capital stock matrices usually breaks down sectoral purchases into four main divisions: (1) machinery and equipment; (2) transport equipment; (3) buildings; and (4) land; the last category, except in so far as it gives rise to current income through being bought or sold, is of no concern for the balance equations and the third category can be allocated directly to the sector construction. If the input–output table is highly aggregated, there will be only one sector corresponding to 'transport equipment', but otherwise fairly arbitrary divisions are needed for this and the first category in order to allocate stocks/flows to supplying sector; the division between domestic and imported goods can usually be made by reference to trade sources.

Once the stocks/flows have been allocated to the sector of origin, it is necessary to adjust them for distributive margins to achieve a consistent basis of valuation with the rest of the input–output table; this will create entries in the rows corresponding to transport, commerce and net indirect taxes. There may also be entries in the service sectors corresponding to the transfer cost of land and buildings.

For some sectors (e.g. agriculture, services) it is very difficult in LDCs to obtain any estimates of capital stock; it is, however, possible to construct a hybrid capital–output coefficients matrix based on capital stock *and* investment flow matrices and this in fact is quite often done. Where investment flow data are used, LDCs are paradoxically at an advantage over DCs; their capital goods industries are so embryonic that it is sometimes quite easy to allocate the output of the capital goods sector directly to the using industry and the same can be done for imports of capital goods.[4] If this procedure is adopted, no valuation adjustments will be needed, but the margin earned on sales (if any) by the distributive sectors must be credited to the appropriate rows.[5]

11.4 UNALLOCATED INPUTS AND OUTPUTS

The construction of an input–output table requires that all purchases of new goods and services be allocated to sector of origin and that all sales be allocated to sector of destination. In practice, whatever method of construction is used, there are always cases of unallocated inputs, which produce imbalances between supply and demand; if a proportion of purchases are unallocated, then sectoral supply will exceed demand while if sales in the make matrix are unallocated, then commodity output will fall short of industry output.

It must be said straightaway that many of the problems of unallocated inputs and outputs are caused by badly designed questionnaires; insufficient space is given for detailed answers, firms are encouraged to make use of general rubrics (e.g. 'other purchases') or are not aware of the purpose of the questionnaire so that they do not understand the need for detail. Furthermore, input–output workers often have to make use of questionnaires designed for other purposes than input–output tables where commodity detail is not important.

If the input–output team has responsibility for design of the questionnaires, one possibility is to prejudge the firm's purchases and sales. This can be done using a structured questionnaire with the firm's expected pattern of commodity inputs and outputs written into the form; the expected pattern can be derived from the previous input–output table for the country (if one exists) or the input–output tables for other countries. The danger with this approach is that any omissions in other tables will be carried over to the current table and that new purchases, reflecting technological change, will not be included, but this danger can be averted by allowing sufficient space for any 'unexpected' purchases or sales.

Even with a well designed questionnaire, however, the problem will not disappear. A fairly typical solution is to use one of the matrix balancing techniques described in the appendix to Chapter 8. With known row and column totals for the absorption and make matrices, the unallocated absorptions and sales are spread across the non-zero entries in the two matrices. Although commonly adopted, this approach is quite wrong; there is no reason to believe that the unallocated entries will consist of commodities already articulated in the questionnaire and, indeed, there are good reasons for believing the opposite—a firm may include in the residual entry all purchases and sales of commodities which it has *not* entered elsewhere.

Another favoured possibility is to create a dummy account; in the case of the absorption matrix, the row for this account consists of unallocated purchases; a column is then created in which entries consist of the difference between commodity supply and demand. (In the case of the make matrix, the dummy account consists of a row only corresponding to unallocated sales.) Construction of symmetric industry by industry or commodity by commodity tables then proceeds without reference to the dummy accounts, which are also ignored in the Leontief inverse.

This procedure has the merit of simplicity, but little else; the most serious problem is that all errors in the matrices tend to be absorbed by the dummy column in the absorption matrix; thus, if distributive margins have been miscalculated or purchases coded incorrectly, these errors will be reflected in the dummy column's entries. Multiplier analysis, based on the Leontief inverse, will not be too seriously affected if the unallocated entries are small and if their (unknown) commodity composition corresponds to the entries given in the tables, but this—as was argued above—cannot be assumed.

The other possibility is to distribute the unallocated entries in some rough and ready way; if a survey is taken, this is best done questionnaire by questionnaire telephoning the firm where possible. It may also be possible to conduct a small postal survey for the unallocated entries on their own, since these tend to have fairly standard rubrics (e.g. 'salesmen's subsistence', 'other services n.e.c.'). Judgement is also essential at this stage; a large firm, for example, must purchase minor items like soap, towels, inks, pens, etc., but very rarely will it feel obliged to list them all. Although such purchases are very trivial for one firm, when taken across the population of all firms, they may constitute a significant proportion of commodity supply.

Even if the input–output worker can do no more than enter a 'trace' element corresponding to the appropriate row of the absorption and make matrices, this is helpful. A trace element, however small, means that the entry is non-zero so that it will be a candidate for change if matrix balancing techniques are used at any stage. In practice, as we saw in Chapter 8, it is virtually impossible to avoid the use of such techniques so that the exercise of qualitative judgement by input–output workers to provide trace elements plays an important part in the construction of input–output tables.

11.5 THE INFORMAL SECTOR

A large body of literature has been devoted in the last decade to the traditional or informal sector in LDCs. Because activities in this sector are generally very labour-intensive making use of local raw materials (which are often recycled), it has been argued (ILO, 1972) that the informal sector can make a major contribution to the employment problem; in order to exploit this potential, however, government policies would need to be changed so as to remove discrimination against the sector and develop the linkages between the formal or modern sector and the informal or traditional sector.

In conventional input–output studies, no distinction is made between formal and informal sector activities. Yet if the above description is correct, the technological conditions governing production in an 'informal' establishment are sufficiently different from those in a formal establishment to suggest a case for disaggregation of the two activities within the same sector. However, it is not only the input structure of the two activities within the same 'sector' which differs; the output also is non-homogeneous and often performs different functions. There is therefore a theoretical case as well for treating the two activities differently.

This does not mean that there should be $2n$ sectors in each input–output table where there were previously only n. In practice, informal sector activities are restricted to a few (k) branches of production such as textiles, furniture and footwear, giving rise to at most $(n+k)$ sectors where $k < n$. Furthermore, for many purposes aggregation of all informal sector activities into one sector would be legitimate.

If the decision is made to include k informal sector activities in the input–output tables, k rows and columns must be added to both the absorption and make matrices. The problem is that very little information is ever available about the purchases and sales patterns of these small establishments, which are frequently ignored in a census or survey. (Most censuses in LDCs ignore establishments with less than a certain number of employees—e.g. five—although these establishments account for virtually all informal sector activity; the production of the informal sector, however, is included in the control totals so that, when 'grossing-up', it is implicitly assumed that the input structure is the same for formal and informal activities.)

Since an elaborate census or survey of informal sector activity is unrealistic, various simplifying procedures must be adopted. In the first place, it is reasonable to assume that for each of the k sectors, commodity and industry output coincide; this means that the only entries in the make matrix corresponding to the informal sector will be diagonal ones. In the second place, we may, to start with, ignore overhead costs and other indirect expenditures in estimating the input structure of informal sector establishments.

As far as direct purchases are concerned, it is also reasonable to assume that these correspond more closely to the pattern exhibited by 'small' rather than 'large' establishments in the survey/census. As a first approximation, therefore, the direct input structure of the former may be used, although this will need to be modified in the light of whatever additional information may be obtained. This was the procedure adopted in the construction of the Moroccan input–output table for 1975 (see Dar Al-Handasah, 1979) which resulted in a series of columns for informal sector activities in the absorption matrix.

In constructing the Moroccan tables, the informal sector absorption matrix was superimposed on the absorption matrix derived from larger establishments; no separate rows for informal sector activities were created and the main purpose in dividing establishments in this way was to avoid distortions in the 'grossing-up' stage and to help in reconciliation and balancing. (Since informal sector output figures were considered rather unreliable, they were in many cases changed at the balancing stage.)

In order to use the input–output table to analyse the relationship between the formal and informal sectors, it is not sufficient to produce a set of columns for informal sector activities in the absorption matrix; k rows must also be included, which means that the purchases of the formal sector from the k informal sectors and the k informal sectors from each other, as well as final demand purchases from the k informal sectors, must all be recorded.

The position is as set out in Figure 11.1. W_{jk} refers to formal sector sales to informal sectors and vice versa with W_{kj}. Intra-informal sector absorptions are W_{kk}, while W_{jj} is intra-formal sector transactions. The subscripts for v (value added) and f (final demand) are self-explanatory.

The problem faced when constructing input–output tables along the lines of Figure 11.1 is that no survey or census ever distinguishes purchases by size of supplying establishment; there is, therefore, no obvious way in which W_{kj} can be distinguished from W_{jj}, W_{jk} from W_{kk} and f_k from f_j. The position, however, may not be as bad as it looks. It is in the nature of informal sector activity that most of it is sold to final demand; indeed, one of the purposes of the International Labour Organizations's concentration on the informal sector is to draw attention to the absence of links between the formal and informal sectors; this means that W_{kj} will be a very sparse matrix with most of its elements equal to zero.

If W_{kj} is a null matrix, the output of the informal sector must go either to itself (W_{kk}) or to final demand (f_k). This division corresponds to that between intermediate and final goods; examination of the output of the k informal sectors should provide a rough guess as to this division which can be used to apportion informal sector output along the rows.

If the rows for the informal sectors are built up in this way, corresponding

		Formal sectors $1, \ldots, n$	Informal sectors $(n+1), \ldots, (n+k)$	Final demand
Formal sectors	1 $\ldots$ n	W_{jj}	W_{jk}	f_j
Informal sectors	$(n+1)$ $\ldots$ $(n+k)$	W_{kj}	W_{kk}	f_k
Primary inputs		v_j	v_k	

Figure 11.1 Schematic representation of relationship between formal and informal sectors in an absorption matrix

adjustments will need to be made in the formal sector rows. For example, if households are estimated to purchase 1000 pesos worth of furniture of which 300 pesos are assumed to come from the informal sector, then households purchase from the formal furniture sector must be reduced to 700 pesos.

It may be argued that if W_{kj} as a null matrix, or very sparse, there is little point in creating separate rows and columns for the informal sectors; the answer is first that even if W_{kj} is null, W_{jk} is certainly not so that the two sectors are interrelated; secondly, by presenting the table in this fashion it becomes easy to work out the employment and income distribution implications of changes in policy which increase the sales of the informal to the formal sectors; this can be done by simulating changes in the W_{kj} matrix to reflect the new purchasing pattern.

NOTES

1 Even with exponential growth, the expression involving $\Delta x'$ in equation (11.8) can easily be simplified (see Brown, 1962).

2 The *stock* of capital built up over the plan is converted to the *flow* of new investment goods in the terminal year.

3 On the other hand, it complicates the mathematics of the fully dynamic model very considerably (Johansen, 1978), because the difference equations are now of the gth order. See also Chapter 14.3.

4 This is how gross fixed capital formation is estimated in the national accounts in several LDCs (e.g. Costa Rica).

5 The most thorough attempt to develop capital stock matrices so far has been carried out in the United States; methodology and data can be found in Bureau of Labour Statistics (1979).

CHAPTER 12

Multiplier and Linkage Analysis

12.1 INTRODUCTION

In the remaining chapters of this book, we concentrate on the most appropriate uses to which LDCs might put input–output tables. Despite the heavy resource requirements imposed on LDCs by the construction of input–output tables, it is not uncommon to find them still-born, collecting dust on the shelves of government offices. The reasons for this are complex, but in the author's opinion stem principally from the fact that the traditional uses for input–output tables have been developed with advanced countries in mind and these uses are often inappropriate for LDCs.

The most obvious application for input–output tables—to act as a check on the reliability of the national accounts—has already been considered in Chapters 1 and 2. In this chapter, the focus of attention is on multiplier and linkage analysis; the mathematics of this type of analysis was sketched out in Chapter 4, which means that more concentration can be given here to its economic applications.

12.2 OUTPUT AND INCOME MULTIPLIERS

In Chapter 4, it was shown that the solution to the input–output model can be written:

$$x = [I - A]^{-1} f \tag{12.1}$$

where f is a vector of final demands, x of gross output and $[I - A]^{-1}$ is the Leontief inverse. In that chapter, however, no mention was made of imports and, although these will be discussed in more detail in Chapter 15, we have to distinguish between the case where imports are included in intermediate absorptions and final demand (as a negative column) and the case where they are excluded, entering instead as a row of primary inputs (see Chapter 7). In the latter case, we must write the solution to the input–output model as:

$$x = [I - A_D]^{-1} f_d \tag{12.2}$$

where f_d is a vector of 'domestic' final demand and $[I - A_D]^{-1}$ is the Leontief inverse net of intermediate imports.

When written out in full, equation (12.2) becomes:

$$
\begin{aligned}
x_1 &= r^d_{11} f^d_1 + r^d_{12} f^d_2 + \cdots + r^d_{1n} f^d_n \\
x_2 &= r^d_{21} f^d_1 + r^d_{22} f^d_2 + \cdots + r^d_{2n} f^d_n \\
&\vdots \\
x_n &= r^d_{n1} f^d_1 + r^d_{n2} f^d_2 + \cdots + r^d_{nn} f^d_n
\end{aligned} \tag{12.3}
$$

where r^d_{ij} is the i, jth element of $(I - A_D)^{-1}$ so that $\Sigma_i r^d_{ij}$ measures the total (direct and indirect) impact on gross output when final demand for the jth sector changes by unity and all other final demands are set at zero. The term $\Sigma_i r^d_{ij}$ is therefore known as an output multiplier and they are reproduced for the 41 sectors of the Costa Rican input–output table in column 1 of Table 12.1 with rankings in brackets.

Each r^d_{ij}, measures the total stimulus to the ith gross output when the jth final demand only changes by one unit; it can therefore be broken down into its intermediate and primary input components. The intermediate input component can in turn be broken down into *its* intermediate and primary input components until eventually we arrive at the cumulative primary inputs associated with any change in final demand.

Assuming that the relationship between each primary input and gross output in the same sector is constant with respect to scale, we can write the primary input requirement as:

$$Vx = V[I - A_D]^{-1} f_d = B f_d \tag{12.4}$$

where V is a $(k \times n)$ matrix of the k primary input requirements per unit of output. The matrix B is therefore of type $(k \times n)$ and each element b_{ij} gives the direct and indirect requirement for the ith primary input when the jth final demand only changes by one unit; the elements of this matrix for Costa Rica are shown in Table 12.1 (columns 2 to 5) for the same sectors as before; this time, however, the rankings have changed so that the final demand change which achieves the highest total increase in the economy's gross output is not necessarily the one which achieves the highest increase in any given primary input.

The primary input multipliers in Table 12.1 tell us the total increase in each type of primary input, which the economy will experience when final demand for the relevant sector rises by one unit. What happens, however to the total of primary inputs? To answer this, we need first to remember that the sum of primary inputs in each sector is simply output less intermediate inputs. It follows that, using our previous notation,

$$V'i = [I - A'_D]i \tag{12.5}$$

and therefore

$$i'V = i'[I - A_D] \tag{12.6}$$

From equation (12.4) we can get the following formula for the scalar value of all

Table 12.1 Output and factor income multipliers for Costa Rica, 1968

Sector	(1) Output multipliers	(2) Labour income	(3) Non-labour income	(4) Net indirect taxes	(5) Imports
1 Bananas	1.2105 (30)	0.3566 (17)	0.4844 (9)	0.0246 (29)	0.1344 (23)
2 Coffee	1.2525 (27)	0.6034 (2)	0.2485 (34)	0.0315 (20)	0.1166 (26)
3 Sugar-cane	1.1802 (36)	0.5055 (5)	0.3979 (18)	0.0230 (30)	0.0736 (37)
4 Cocoa	1.1945 (32)	0.6991 (1)	0.2166 (36)	0.0251 (28)	0.0592 (40)
5 Basic grains	1.1906 (34)	0.3146 (22)	0.5654 (6)	0.0138 (38)	0.1062 (28)
6 Cotton	1.2105 (31)	0.2451 (30)	0.6570 (2)	0.0140 (37)	0.0839 (35)
7 Tobacco	1.1834 (35)	0.3928 (12)	0.5060 (8)	0.0151 (35)	0.0861 (34)
8 Livestock	1.3788 (18)	0.2198 (35)	0.6569 (3)	0.0252 (27)	0.0981 (31)
9 Forestry and fishing	1.2627 (26)	0.2647 (28)	0.5362 (7)	0.0296 (21)	0.1695 (20)
10 Other agricultural products	1.3408 (21)	0.3896 (13)	0.4513 (12)	0.0195 (32)	0.1396 (22)
11 Meat and milk products	2.0862 (3)	0.2618 (29)	0.6103 (4)	0.0292 (23)	0.0987 (30)
12 Fish tinning	1.9096 (5)	0.3753 (14)	0.4227 (13)	0.0514 (14)	0.1506 (21)
13 Edible oils	1.6634 (9)	0.2255 (34)	0.3988 (17)	0.0146 (36)	0.3611 (7)
14 Coffee processing	2.1461 (1)	0.5686 (3)	0.2611 (32)	0.0586 (13)	0.1117 (27)
15 Grain milling	1.6713 (8)	0.1971 (36)	0.4101 (15)	0.0958 (4)	0.2970 (10)
16 Bakeries	2.1418 (2)	0.3374 (19)	0.3580 (24)	0.0703 (8)	0.2343 (15)
17 Sugar	1.8737 (6)	0.4377 (10)	0.3857 (20)	0.0762 (7)	0.1004 (29)
18 Other food manufacturers	1.9151 (4)	0.3668 (16)	0.3845 (21)	0.0436 (19)	0.2051 (18)
19 Drinks	1.3978 (17)	0.1566 (38)	0.3670 (23)	0.3853 (2)	0.0911 (33)
20 Tobacco products	1.3147 (23)	0.1505 (39)	0.2296 (35)	0.4864 (1)	0.1335 (24)
21 Textiles and clothing	1.5711 (11)	0.3208 (21)	0.3351 (26)	0.0474 (16)	0.2967 (11)
22 Leather and shoes	1.6389 (10)	0.3550 (18)	0.3643 (25)	0.0481 (15)	0.2326 (16)
23 Wood and furniture	1.8307 (7)	0.4829 (7)	0.2993 (28)	0.0857 (5)	0.1321 (25)
24 Paper and printing	1.1918 (33)	0.2353 (32)	0.2079 (38)	0.0471 (17)	0.5097 (5)
25 Chemicals	1.4469 (14)	0.2388 (31)	0.2743 (31)	0.0682 (10)	0.4187 (6)
26 Oil refining	1.0661 (41)	0.0852 (40)	0.1550 (40)	0.0041 (39)	0.7557 (1)
27 Tyres	1.3298 (22)	0.2732 (26)	0.4159 (14)	0.0176 (33)	0.2933 (13)
28 Plastic and rubber NEC	1.4618 (13)	0.2735 (25)	0.4024 (16)	0.0256 (26)	0.2985 (9)
29 Ceramics and Glass	1.5604 (12)	0.3357 (20)	0.2991 (29)	0.0698 (9)	0.2954 (12)
30 Construction materials	1.3518 (20)	0.2673 (27)	0.4757 (10)	0.0833 (6)	0.1737 (19)
31 Metal goods	1.1690 (37)	0.1944 (37)	0.2088 (37)	0.0610 (12)	0.5358 (3)
32 Electrical goods	1.3549 (19)	0.2274 (33)	0.1884 (39)	0.0664 (11)	0.5178 (4)
33 Transport equipment	1.1049 (39)	0.2828 (24)	0.1015 (41)	0.0221 (31)	0.5936 (2)
34 Other manufacturing	1.4375 (15)	0.3054 (23)	0.2534 (33)	0.0969 (3)	0.3443 (8)
35 Construction	1.4235 (16)	0.4505 (8)	0.2881 (30)	0.0328 (19)	0.2286 (17)
36 Banking, finance, insurance	1.2360 (28)	0.5375 (4)	0.3952 (19)	0.0035 (40)	0.0638 (39)
37 Commerce	1.3085 (24)	0.4384 (9)	0.4654 (11)	0.0264 (25)	0.0698 (38)
38 Transport	1.3003 (25)	0.4306 (11)	0.3106 (27)	0.0164 (34)	0.2424 (14)
39 Services	1.2241 (29)	0.4987 (6)	0.3766 (22)	0.0292 (22)	0.0955 (32)
40 Electricity	1.1489 (38)	0.3695 (15)	0.5678 (5)	− 0.0154 (41)	0.0781 (36)
41 Ownership of dwellings	1.0836 (40)	0.0307 (41)	0.9332 (1)	0.0288 (24)	0.0073 (41)

Source: Bulmer-Thomas (1977a.)

primary inputs:

$$i'Vx = i'V[I - A_D]^{-1}f_d \tag{12.7}$$

and substitution from equation (12.6) gives:

$$i'Vx = i'[I - A_D]^{-1}f_d = i'f_d \tag{12.8}$$

Equation (12.8) is the fundamental national accounting identity that final expenditure ($i'f_d$) and primary inputs ($i'Vx$) are always the same; it follows that a unit change in final demand must lead eventually to a unit change in primary inputs in the economy; thus in Table 12.1 we find that the sum of the primary input multipliers for each sector (columns 2 to 5) is indeed unity.

Although interesting, calculations such as those reported in Table 12.1 are not necessarily of much relevance to policy-makers, because it is difficult to adjust final demand for one sector in isolation; a more realistic situation is where a government wants to compare the impact of a given expansion in aggregate private consumption, say, with a similar increase in public consumption; because the composition of aggregate expenditure is different in the two domains, the final impact is unlikely to be the same; for example, if we assume the composition of each category of final expenditure is unchanged, we can evaluate the impact on primary inputs applying the formula:

$$Vx = V[I - A_D]^{-1}f_d^k \tag{12.9}$$

where f_d^k is the kth vector of final demand for domestic output, normalized so that

Table 12.2 Primary input composition of final expenditures (%) Brazil, 1970

	Final expenditures				
	(1) Households (%)	(2) Government (%)	(3) Investment (%)	(4) Exports (%)	(5) All final demands (%)
Primary inputs					
(1) Imports	4.2	5.0	12.9	4.2	6.7
(2) Net indirect Taxes	17.9	9.2	13.4	1.0	14.0
(3) Wages and Salaries	21.8	34.9	32.1	24.7	25.0
(4) Self-employed income	3.7	5.9	1.6	4.2	3.1
(5) Gross trading profits	52.4	45.0	40.0	65.9	50.3
(6) Total	100.0	100.0	100.0	100.0	100.0

Source: Derived by the author from tables in IBGE (1979).

each vector sum is unity (i.e. the jth component of f_d^k measures the relative importance of the demand for the jth sector in total demand by the kth activity). Since the final demand change is unity, the total primary input change must also be unity, i.e. $i'Vx = 1$.

In Table 12.2, the results of this experiment are given for Brazil. It can be seen that the primary composition of different final expenditures is quite different; investment is the most import-intensive, while government expenditure is the most favourable to labour income (both wages and salaries and self-employed income). It is worth noting that exports are not particularly labour-intensive, while investment—perhaps surprisingly—is; indeed, an expansion of exports is more conducive to increases in capital income (gross trading profits) than any other branch of final expenditure.

12.3 EXTENDED MULTIPLIER ANALYSIS

The reason why multiplier analysis can be applied to input–output economics is that at each 'round' of the multiplier process leakages occur, so that the impact of each round is diminished and the system is not explosive. These leakages consist of payments for primary inputs, but the recipients cannot be assumed to make no use of the receipts and if they should choose to spend even a small part on new goods and services, there will be further multiplier repercussions.

Input–output economists have been aware of these further effects for some time and efforts have been made to incorporate the impact of payments to households by means of extended (Type II) multipliers;[1] this amounts to treating households as an endogenous activity with any change in income matched by changes in consumption and savings so that the consumption change leads to additional multiplier effects.[2]

Type II multipliers have been shown (see, for example, Burdekin, 1978c) to increase considerably the measured impact of any exogenous change and so the question arises whether any other primary inputs besides payments to households should be treated as endogenous; payments of non-labour income or taxes may also have further repercussions on the system, while payments for imports could stimulate exports if foreign trade multipliers are important. Furthermore, with the efforts currently being made to model the distribution of income (see Chapter 13), it seems sensible to disaggregate the household sector into a number of divisions.

A more extended treatment of multipliers is therefore called for and so we must return to Chapter 4, where a social accounting matrix was presented in schematic form which distinguished between accounts for producers, factors of production and institutions and showed how the ramifications of any exogenous change on one of these accounts was felt by all other accounts. The crucial equation is provided by (4.36) in Chapter 4, i.e.

$$q = M_3 M_2 M_1 e = Me \qquad (4.36)$$

where the M matrix measures the total impact on the endogenous vector (q) of any change in the exogenous vector (e) and the total impact is given by an intra-group effect (M_1), an inter-group effect (M_3) and an extra-group effect (M_2).

It would be desirable for illustrative purposes to build up the total impact from these three effects by simple addition, but as can be seen from equation (4.36) they combine multiplicatively. Fortunately, we can easily derive an additive equivalent (Stone, 1978) as:

$$M = I + [M_1 - I] + [M_2 - I]M_1 + [M_3 - I]M_2M_1 \tag{12.10}$$

The first term on the right-hand side of equation (12.10) is the unit matrix which therefore measures the initial injection; the second term measures the intra-group effects net of this initial injection, i.e. the net contribution of transfer[3] multiplier effects; the third term measures the additional impact of the extra-group effects, i.e. the net contribution of 'open-loop' or cross-multiplier effects, while the final term measures the additional impact of the inter-group effects, i.e. the net contribution of circular or 'closed-loop' multiplier effects.

It was said in Chapter 4 that one of the major weaknesses of extended multiplier analysis is the assumption of fixed coefficients; the main problem of fixed coefficients derived from one SAM is that average and marginal propensities must necessarily be the same. While this may be a reasonable approximation to the production function for producers, it is clearly inadequate when describing the consumption function of households, since the equality of average and marginal propensities to consume requires the income elasticity of each class of consumption to be unity.

It follows that we must at least replace submatrix B_{13} in equation (4.26) with a matrix of *marginal* propensities to consume for each type of household. This new matrix will affect M_2 and M_3, and therefore some of the components of equation (12.10), so that any results obtained using 'accounting-price' multipliers (Pyatt, 1979) as in equation (12.10) can be compared with the 'fixed-price' multipliers one obtains when marginal and average propensities are allowed to diverge and consumers' behaviour reflects differences in income elasticities for particular goods when prices are asumed fixed.

An experiment on these lines is shown for Sri Lanka in Table 12.3. Because the M matrix is very large even for a small system, it has been found necessary to restrict the table to measuring the impact (broken down as in equation (12.10)) of exogenous changes for (1) tea and rubber, (2) other agriculture, (3) services and (4) urban households, i.e. three producer accounts and one institutional account. It is also necessary to restrict details of the accounts affected by the injection as shown in the table.

The first point to notice about Table 12.3 is that the total impact of accounting and fixed price multipliers is not the same. For example, when final demand for 'other agriculture' increases by 100 units, the total impact is smaller with fixed-price as compared to accounting-price multipliers. The difference is accounted for by the 'closed-loop' or inter-group effects which means that, after factors have paid households, less is being spent on other agricultural products when marginal rather than average propensities to consume are used; this is so, because the

Table 12.3 Extended multiplier analysis: selective decomposition of changes in the exogenous vector (*e*). Fixed price multipliers in brackets

Account in which injection originates	Account affected by the injection	Initial injection	Net intra-group effect	Net extra-group effect	Net inter-group effect	Totals: Accounting-price multipliers	Totals: Fixed-price multipliers
(1) Tea and rubber	Tea and rubber	100 (100)	—	—	2 (1)	102	101
	Other agriculture	—	2 (2)	—	59 (60)	61	62
	Food processing	—	1 (1)	—	32 (37)	33	38
	Urban households	—	—	8 (8)	31 (37)	39	45
	Rural households	—	—	25 (25)	78 (88)	103	113
	Estate households	—	—	50 (50)	3 (3)	53	53
(2) Other agriculture	Other agriculture	100 (100)	5 (5)	—	57 (48)	162	153
	Food processing	—	1 (1)	—	31 (30)	32	31
	Other manufactures	—	4 (4)	—	36 (50)	40	54
	Urban households	—	—	17 (17)	31 (34)	48	51
	Rural households	—	—	68 (68)	77 (78)	145	146
	Estate households	—	—	2 (2)	2 (2)	4	4
(3) Services	Other agriculture	—	2 (2)	—	52 (43)	54	45
	Food processing	—	1 (1)	—	29 (27)	30	28
	Other manufactures	—	5 (5)	—	34 (45)	39	50
	Urban households	—	—	31 (31)	29 (31)	60	62
	Rural households	—	—	52 (52)	71 (71)	123	123
	Estate households	—	—	1 (1)	3 (3)	4	4
(4) Urban households	Tea and rubber	—	—	* (*)	1 (*)	1	1
	Other agriculture	—	—	22 (14)	31 (24)	53	38
	Food processing	—	—	11 (7)	17 (15)	28	22
	Other manufactures	—	—	16 (17)	22 (25)	37	42
	Services	—	—	33 (35)	36 (37)	69	72
	Urban labour	100 (100)	—	9 (9)	10 (10)	19	19
	Rural labour	—	—	17 (15)	21 (19)	38	34
	Estate labour	—	—	1 (1)	1 (*)	2	1
	Urban households	—	—	—	32 (31)	132	131
	Rural households	—	—	—	77 (68)	77	68
	Estate households	—	—	—	3 (2)	3	2

* = absolute value less than one.
Source: Taken from Pyatt and Round (1979), Table 5.

income elasticity of demand for this group of products is less than unity. 'Other manufactures', on the other hand, have an income elasticity greater than one, so it is no surprise to find that when demand for 'other agriculture' increases, the impact on other manufactures—primarily *via* inter-group effects—is greater for fixed price than accounting multipliers.

The second point to notice is that extra-group or open-loop effects only influence the results for those accounts outside the subsystem where the initial injection occurred. 'Other agriculture', for example, belongs to the subsystem of production accounts, so none of the producer sectors are affected by extra-group effects when final demand for 'other agriculture' increases; on the other hand, some of the impact of the injection ends up in the accounts for factors and institutions (e.g. urban households) and this is captured by inter-group effects and by extra-group effects.

12.4 BACKWARD AND FORWARD LINKAGES

Let us now consider what use can be made of multiplier analysis in either its simple form (the Leontief inverse) or its extended form (the M matrix). One of the objectives all LDCs have set themselves is rapid growth in income per head and rising incomes are associated in both time-series and cross-section studies with a rising share of industry in GDP; the industrialization process can be carried out in a number of ways, but each new industrial investment will offer opportunities for other suppliers (backward linkages) and provide inputs for utilization by other users (forward linkages). Furthermore, these backward and forward linkages are not reflected in market prices and therefore represent an externality, which could cause the social benefits of an investment to diverge from the private benefits.

It might appear, therefore, that by concentrating on those sectors with high backward or forward linkages, the industrialization process could be speeded up. If, furthermore, we were prepared to assume (Hirschman, 1958) a common technology across countries for each sector, a common set of relative prices and a distribution of income consistent with the eventual emergence in each LDC of the structure of demand to be found in developed countries (DCs), then we could select our key industrial sectors for promotion by reference to the backward and forward linkages found in DCs.

We shall argue below that these assumptions are too strong and that the ranking of sectors or investments in terms of linkages in this way is not a very satisfactory guide to industrial planning, but first we must show how we might measure such linkages using input–output tables, for it should be clear that the latter offer an excellent opportunity to measure a concept which would otherwise remain empirically intractable.

Consider backward linkages first; the aim is to measure the potential stimulus to other activities from investment in any sector j. One possibility (Chenery, 1958) is:

$$U_j = \frac{\sum_i W_{ij}}{x_j} = \sum_i a_{ij} \qquad (12.11)$$

but this only measures direct backward linkages and takes no account of the indirect stimuli given to the economy if the investment goes ahead. To measure both effects, we need the Leontief inverse; to make comparisons between sectors, however, a normalization procedure is often carried out (Rasmussen, 1957) by comparing the 'average' stimulus created by sector j with the overall average; the direct and indirect backward linkage index then becomes:

$$Y_j = \left(\frac{1/n \sum_i r_{ij}}{1/n^2 \sum_i \sum_j r_{ij}} \right) \tag{12.12}$$

where r_{ij} denotes the i, jth element of the Leontief inverse, n is thenumber of sectors, the numerator denotes the average stimulus imparted to other sectors by a unit's worth of demand for sector j and the denominator denotes the average stimulus for the whole economy when all final demands increase by unity. It follows that $Y_j > 1$ implies a jth sector where investments yield above average backward linkages, while the opposite is true where $Y_j < 1$.

Reference to the ranking of Y_j alone would not be sufficient to determine industrial planning for a number of reasons; first, a high index could have been achieved although only one or two sectors stand to gain from the backward linkages created by the investment; this can be taken into account by considering the dispersion of the stimuli according to the formula for the coefficient of variation:

$$V_j = \sqrt{\frac{1/(n-1) \sum_i (r_{ij} - 1/n \sum_i r_{ij})^2}{1/n \sum_i r_{ij}}} \tag{12.13}$$

so that a low V_j means that the investment in sector j would stimulate other sectors in an even manner, while a high V_j means that the benefits of the stimuli provided by backward linkages would be unevenly shared.

So far, we have attempted to measure direct and indirect backward linkages using the Leontief inverse; from what was said above, it should by now be clear that the latter measures only intra-group effects, i.e. those stimuli or inducements to increase output which result from tracing the initial exogenous 'shock' through the subsystem of producers' accounts where it originated. Intra-group effects, however, are not the whole story and it is worth including the inter-group effects as well since these also offer inducements to increase output (extra-group effects are not relevant in this context, since by definition they will be zero for producers where the exogenous shock for factors and institutions is zero). This can easily be done by replacing r_{ij} in equations (12.12) and (12.13) by m_{ij} where m_{ij} is the i, jth element of the extended multiplier M matrix. The summation $\sum_i r_{ij}$, however, must now be replaced by $\sum_i m_{ij}$, where i runs only over the production accounts.

In terms of selecting 'key' sectors, backward linkages are useful, but measures such as Y_j and V_j need to be supplemented by indices of forward linkages. As has been pointed out elsewhere (Jones, 1976), the index of backward linkages can tell us nothing about forward linkages, because a high backward linkage for, say, textiles is consistent with high or low forward linkages, since the textile output could be either all used in clothing industry or all exported.

High forward linkages occur when a sector's output is or could be used by many other sectors as an input; by expanding capacity in such a sector, 'inducements' are provided to using industries which now have an incentive to expand output to take advantage of the increased availability of inputs. Given our interpretation of the i, jth element of the Leontief inverse, a suitable measure of forward linkages might therefore be the row sum of this inverse, which (when normalized as for backward linkages) becomes:

$$Z_i = \left(\frac{1/n \sum_j r_{ij}}{1/n^2 \sum_i \sum_j r_{ij}} \right) \tag{12.14}$$

so that $Z_i > 1$ implies a sector with high forward linkages, while the opposite is true where $Z_i < 1$.

The numerator in equation (12.14) refers to the ith row sum of the Leontief inverse which in turn measures the total impact on sector i when final demand for *all* sectors increases by unity. If this impact is large, it suggests that increased investment in sector i would induce output increases in all using sectors, as users take advantage of the increased availability of inputs. It might seem, therefore, that Z_i is a good measure of forward linkages.

Unfortunately, it is not; the assumption that final demand for all sectors increases by unity is misleading since not all sectors are of equal importance in the structure of demand. With a large input–output table, a small sector (j) which relies heavily on sector i for inputs will lead to a biased index of forward linkages for sector i. Capacity expansion in sector i based on 'high' forward linkages might therefore have a disappointing impact on the overall rate of growth of the economy, because of the small size of (using) sector j.

Various proposals have been made for overcoming this problem (McGilvray, 1977) including the weighting of elements in the Leontief inverse by the importance of each sector in the structure of final demand (Laumas, 1976). None of these proposals are entirely satisfactory and it is therefore wiser to approach forward linkages from a different angle.

The basic idea of forward linkages is to trace the output increases which occur or might occur in *using* industries when there is a change in the sector supplying inputs, just as with backward linkages we trace the output increases which occur in *supplying* sectors when there is a change in the sector using their outputs as inputs. Indices of backward linkages such as Y_j measure the impact to some extent, but indices of forward linkages such as Z_i seem to miss the point.

Let us now consider[4] an n sector input–output table; we can write the balance equations by summing down the columns as:

$$x' = i'W + v' \tag{12.15}$$

where a prime (′) denotes a row vector and (v) is a vector whose elements represent value added in each sector. Now when examining forward linkages, the crucial relationship is that between output of sector i and its uses by other sectors. If this relationship is fixed so that each sector distributes a fixed proportion of its output to other sectors, we get the output coefficient matrix:

$$B = \hat{x}^{-1}W \tag{12.16}$$

so that

$$x' = x'B + v' \tag{12.17}$$

and this gives the solution:

$$x' = v'[I - B]^{-1} = v'B^* \quad \text{(say)} \tag{12.18}$$

which when written out in full becomes:

$$\begin{aligned} x_1 &= b^*_{11}v_1 + b^*_{21}v_2 + \cdots + b^*_{n1}v_n \\ x_2 &= b^*_{12}v_1 + b^*_{22}v_2 + \cdots + b^*_{n2}v_n \\ &\vdots \\ x_n &= b^*_{1n}v_1 + b^*_{2n}v_2 + \cdots + b^*_{nn}v_n \end{aligned} \tag{12.19}$$

Suppose now that value added in the ith sector increases by unity; because of the assumption of fixed output proportions this will induce (forward) linkages throughout the economy as using sectors respond to the stimulus; the total increase in output for the whole system is given by $\Sigma_j b^*_{ij}$—i.e. the *row* sum of the B^* matrix—and this is a measure of forward linkages for sector i. When normalized as above, the index becomes:

$$Z^*_i = \frac{1/n \sum_j b^*_{ij}}{1/n^2 \sum_i \sum_j b^*_{ij}} \tag{12.20}$$

and the coefficient of variation becomes:

$$V^*_i = \sqrt{\frac{1/(n-1) \sum_j \left(b_{ij} - 1/n \sum_j b^*_{ij} \right)^2}{1/n \sum_j b^*_{ij}}} \tag{12.21}$$

This new measure of forward linkages (Z^*_i) is quite different from the previous one (Z_i), because it measures the forward linkage as the increase in output of *all* using industries rather than as the increase in output of the (one) supplying industry. It therefore seems to be more in the spirit of the original conception of forward linkages (Hirschman, 1958) as well as capturing the causality of the process by building up the cumulative impact through a *forward* iteration ($I + B + B^2 + B^3 + \cdots$). As this iteration shows, output expands first in sector i to meet the unit increase in the value added product for sector i; this output is then distributed to using sectors ($\sum_j b_{ij}$), whose increase in output is then made available to other sectors (B^2), and so on; this is surely the essence of forward linkages.

12.5 THE INTERPRETATION OF LINKAGES

This long digression on the most appropriate way of measuring linkages is merely a prelude—although a necessary one—to show how linkage analysis may be used. The original intention (Hirschman, 1958) was to rank sectors in terms of their potential stimuli to growth *via* the inducement mechanism and to select 'key' sectors for promotion corresponding to those with the highest backward and forward linkages. This corresponds to what we shall call *ex ante* linkage analysis and should be based on technology coefficients (a_{ij}).

Since by definition the sectors in which the investments are contemplated do not yet exist in the country under study, it is necessary to obtain linkage measures by indirect means. Hirschman proposed using the ranking of sectors found in developed countries, since it had been found (Chenery, 1958) that there was a considerable similarity in the pattern of sectoral inter-dependence for advanced industrial countries suggesting that there is indeed a 'fundamental structure of production' (Simpson, 1965).

This approach is only valid, however, if the pattern of interdependence found in LDCs can be expected to approximate eventually that found in DCs today. A number of assumptions are required in order that this may be so and these include (a) that 'the commodity composition of the underdeveloped country's output . . . bear eventually some resemblance to that of the country on whose input–output tables we perform the statistics' (Hirschman, 1958, p. 105, note 5) and (b) the absence of any real choice of techniques. It has been shown (Raj, 1975) that neither of these assumptions are realistic and that even with rising incomes consumer demand in LDCs could fail to approximate that in DCs due to differences in tastes, the distribution of income, relative prices, historical traditions, etc. so that sectoral interdependence and the path to industrialization of LDCs need not necessarily mirror that in DCs.

If we cannot select key sectors by reference to input–output tables of advanced countries, it is necessary to use the table of the country in question supplemented by rows and columns for those activities where investments are contemplated. There is not much difficulty about the column which can be calculated from the kind of information obtained in feasibility studies, but the rows are more problematic because some assumption has to be made about the allocation of sales. Even if this can be done, all the difficulties involved in linkage analysis are far from being resolved.

First, as Hirschman himself realized, there is no guarantee that the *potential* stimulus measured by backward and forward linkages will be translated into actual growth; the stimulus may simply be absorbed as increased imports, higher prices or under-utilized capacity unless certain conditions are met; these conditions include the existence of a minimum market size consistent with capacity expansion, availability of complementary inputs (credit, skilled labour, etc.) and government policies consistent with the ranking of sectors. The last point is most important, since the government may be operating a structure of protection which discourages firms from responding to any stimulus.

It must not be thought that these are merely theoretical curiosa; in a major study of linkages for several Asian countries (Panchamukhi, 1975) it was found that the simple correlation coefficient between the size of linkages and capacity under-utilization in India was significant and positive, suggesting that expansion of sectors with high input dependence may simply produce spare capacity rather than growth stimuli; in another study for Central America (Bulmer-Thomas, 1979) it was found that the difference between potential and actual linkages over a five-year period had not narrowed, indicating that government policy and the structure of protection were not conducive to the expansion of supplying industries at the expense of imports.

Secondly, however, one needs to consider a more fundamental set of objections to linkage analysis based on economic theory. Industrialization is not usually considered as an objective in itself, but as a proxy for the rise in real incomes which is supposed to accompany it. If, however, we consider real income growth per head as our objective, then each investment needs to be evaluated in terms of its direct and indirect income (not output) impact, which can be done by reference to the income multipliers introduced at the start of this chapter. In the Asian study referred to above (Panchamukhi, 1975), an inverse relationship was found between a sector's output and income multiplier effects which suggests that selection of key sectors by reference to their linkage indices may not satisfy the income-generation objective.

Furthermore, sectors with high backward linkages have a high dependence on intermediate goods which are typically capital-intensive. In the context of LDCs, we are therefore asking countries to give priority to sectors which directly or indirectly are capital-intensive; although the argument over choice of techniques is complex, this is not a position to which most LDCs would want to be committed.

Finally, there is no consideration of efficiency or comparative costs in the selection of 'key' sectors by reference to linkage indices. Although it is not a simple matter to determine where a country's comparative advantage lies, international trade theory can be used to suggest that LDCs have a comparative advantage relative to DCs in labour-intensive manufactured exports. If we define 'labour-intensive' to mean the direct and indirect labour requirements per unit of output, such an activity will substitute labour for capital not only directly, but also indirectly by making little use of intermediate inputs or importing rather than purchasing them locally; such a sector will therefore have low backward linkages and yet *ex hypothesi* it is a suitable candidate for promotion (Riedel, 1975; 1976).

The absence of considerations of efficiency is particularly serious when we consider that much of the potential stimulus provided by expansion of a 'key' sector is translated into growth through import substitution. Linkage analysis does not permit one to distinguish between the cases where (a) the stimulus is big enough to justify establishing a supplying or using industry which is efficient,

(b) the stimulus is big enough to justify establishing a supplying or using industry which is not efficient and (c) the stimulus is not big enough to justify establishing a supplying or using industry. In the first case, government policy should ensure that the stimulus is translated into growth, while in the second it should only do so if the protection/subsidy needed to make the activity competitive is justified in terms of some other criteria (e.g. infant industry arguments).

The fact that not all potential linkages can be translated into actual linkages suggests the need for a modified form of linkage analysis, in which technological coefficients are adjusted for those growth stimuli which are not feasible for the country in question; such non-feasibility will be determined by considerations of market-size, efficiency, comparative costs, natural resources, etc. and would vary from country to country. The inducement which remains, as measured by the backward or forward linkage analysis, would then be a better guide to the selection of 'key' sectors.

Although there are major theoretical and methodological obstacles posed by *ex ante* linkage analysis, the same is not true of *ex post* analysis in which actual, currently prevailing linkages are measured. *Ex post* linkage analysis requires the use of domestic coefficients (a_{ij}^D) rather than technological coefficients and it is by now well established that the ranking of sectors in terms of *ex post* and *ex ante* measures can differ markedly (Bulmer-Thomas, 1978c).

Ex post linkage analysis measures the inducement which is offered to a sector or a group of sectors if final demand changes at the margin; it can therefore be used for a country at a point in time to see if government policy is consistent with the ranking of sectors; it can also be used to isolate 'enclave' sectors and to help promote policies for the integration of the enclave with the national economy; it can be used for a country over time (Weisskopf, 1971) to establish the change in sectoral interdependence and it can be used for a series of countries at a moment in time to make international comparisons.[5]

12.6 CONCLUSIONS

Linkage analysis for LDCs is probably the most common use to which their input–output tables have been put. Much of this chapter has been concerned with showing how these applications are often invalid. It would be wrong, however, to conclude on a pessimistic note and it is therefore appropriate to summarize the appropriate uses for linkage analysis.

The most important point to remember is that the stimulus provided to other sectors by an investment in one sector is an externality which is ignored by both market and accounting price cost–benefit analysis (cf. Stewart, 1972). Since the externality may well be important, investment decisions which do not take it into account could lead to a misallocation of resources; it behoves us, therefore, to measure it somehow or other even though current linkage indices are deficient in a number of respects.

Although the externality argument is important,[6] it does not follow that linkage analysis should be used to select 'key' sectors; this is a misuse based on a confusion of the objective of rising incomes with industrialization; *ex ante* linkage analysis is akin to a second-order argument, which is appropriate when two mutually inconsistent, but socially desirable, investments are under consideration.

Ex post linkage analysis will always remain appropriate, although its ambitions are much more limited than the *ex ante* kind. Indeed, to use an old-fashioned distinction, *ex post* linkage analysis belongs to the world of positive economics, while *ex ante* analysis has normative ambitions. As so often in economics, techniques with normative ambitions tend to be more controversial and *ex ante* linkage analysis is no exception.

NOTES

1 As compared with Type I multipliers which arise from treating all payments to households as a leakage (see Richardson, 1972).

2 This treatment of the household sector is, of course, consistent with Leontief's original closed input–output system (Leontief, 1951) in which all payments to primary inputs return into the system.

3 'Transfer multiplier effects' is the phrase preferred by Pyatt (1979) to describe the containment of the impact within the subsystem where it originates.

4 This section owes much to Jones (1976), but a similar argument can be found in Hoover (1971).

5 It has also been suggested (Yotopoulos, 1973) that it can be used to shed light on the balanced *v.* unbalanced growth hypothesis. The null hypothesis proposed is that countries which have 'unbalanced' their economies in favour of sectors with high backward linkages would experience a faster overall rate of growth than countries which have pursued a balanced growth strategy. Unfortunately, this test is invalid because in an unbalanced growth strategy à la Hirschman, it is not the high linkage sectors which necessarily grow at an above-proportionate rate, but the sectors tied to the high linkage ones through the inducement mechanism (see McGilvray, 1977).

6 Little and Mirrlees (1974) give a spirited defence of the exclusion of this externality from their proposed method of cost–benefit analysis of investment decisions, but it is not wholly convincing.

CHAPTER 13

Employment and the Distribution of Income

13.1 INTRODUCTION

The first two development decades (1950–70) centred on the rate of growth of real income per head in LDCs as the target variable. Despite a few cases of zero or negative rates of growth, the performance of LDCs in terms of this objective was in general satisfactory; paradoxically, however, there has been a deep disillusionment in recent years with real income growth as the appropriate standard for measuring performance.

This disillusionment is primarily due to the fact that the extra resources created by real income growth appear to have been distributed very unevenly; if, furthermore, growth is accompanied by the absolute impoverishment of the poorest groups in the population, then with a declining marginal utility of income, it may well be that total welfare is lower than before growth.

The failure of real income growth in many cases to bring about a relative improvement of the poorest groups means that little reliance can be put on 'trickle down' effects; the evaluation of public policy therefore requires a framework in which, first, the causal link between growth and income distribution can be examined and, secondly, the welfare of the target groups can be analysed. In this way, we can hope to find out more about why certain groups do not appear to benefit even from rapid growth and which policies might be most effective in redistributing benefits.

Input–output techniques are a useful starting point for examining both these questions. By suitable modification of the initial soial accounting matrix, we can observe the impact of different policies on the target groups; in particular, we can use input–output techniques to study employment and income distribution and these themes will provide the focus of this chapter.

It should be recognized from the start that there are limitations in the applicability of input–output techniques in this field. Inequalities in the size distribution of income appear highly correlated with variables such as education and land distribution which do not figure in the input–output model; input–output analysis therefore works on only a small subset of the variables thought to influence the size distribution of income significantly. Nevertheless, it is essential that LDCs have some framework for evaluating the impact of public policy in this area and the models outlined in this chapter offer a good starting point.

13.2 EMPLOYMENT CREATION

We saw in the previous chapter how the i, jth element of the Leontief inverse can be interpreted as the total effect (direct and indirect) on the gross output of the ith sector when the jth final demand changes by one unit. With each output change there will be associated a change in employment (as we saw in Chapter 4), and the simplest assumption is that of a fixed proportional relationship between employment and output. This assumption can be formalized for each sector as:

$$n_j = \frac{l_j}{x_j} \qquad j = 1, \ldots, n \tag{13.1}$$

where l_j is employment in the jth sector in any period and n_j the labour requirement per unit of gross output (x_j). We can therefore write:

$$l = \hat{n}x \tag{13.2}$$

where l is a vector of employment requirements and $\hat{n}$ is a diagonalized matrix formed from the vector n whose elements are defined by equation (13.1). Substituting for x the solution to the input–output model, we get:

$$l = \hat{n}[I - A]^{-1} f = Kf \tag{13.3}$$

so that k_{ij}, the i,jth element of K, measures the employment created directly and indirectly in the ith sector when the jth final demand changes by one unit, and $\Sigma_i k_{ij}$ measures the total employment created throughout the economy, when final demand for the jth sector increases by one unit.

Equations (13.1) to (13.3) imply that labour is homogeneous. In practice this is not so, since one kind of skill or occupation is often a very poor substitute for another; if the country in question can provide the data on employment by sector in terms of different skills or occupations, then we can form a matrix of labour coefficients (N) with as many rows as there are different types of labour and re-estimate labour creation using the modified formula:

$$l^* = N[I - A]^{-1} f = K^* f \tag{13.4}$$

where l^* is a vector of requirements for each type of labour, while the i, jth element of K^* tells us the total requirements for the ith type of labour when final demand for the jth sector increases by one unit.[1]

The sum of the elements in each column of the K matrix ($\Sigma_i k_{ij} = k_j$) denotes the total employment created when final demand for the jth sector increases by one unit. It does not necessarily follow, however, that we can use this information to select the 'key' sectors for generation of employment; first the crude sum total (k_j) ignores the difference between direct and indirect employment effects; secondly, it ignores the degree to which the employment effects are spread evenly across the other sectors and, thirdly, a ranking of sectors according to (k_j) treats final demand changes in each sector as if they were equally probable.

Some of these criticisms can be overcome using variants of the linkage indices discussed in the previous chapter. The index of employment backward linkages (Y_j') becomes:

$$Y_j' = \frac{\left[\left(\frac{1}{n}\right)k_j\right]}{\left(1/n^2 \sum_{j=1}^{n} k_j\right)} \qquad j = 1, \ldots, n \tag{13.5}$$

while the index of employment forward linkages[2] is now:

$$Z_i' = \frac{\left[\left(\frac{1}{n}\right)k_i\right]}{\left(1/n^2 \sum_{i=1}^{n} k_i\right)} \qquad i = 1, \ldots, n \tag{13.6}$$

The degrees of dispersion for backward and forward linkages respectively are given by:

$$V_j' = \sqrt{\frac{\{1/(n-1) \sum_{i=1}^{n} (k_{ij} - 1/n \sum_{i=1}^{n} k_{ij})^2\}}{1/n \sum_{i=1}^{n} k_{ij}}} \qquad j = 1, \ldots, n \tag{13.7}$$

and

$$V_i' = \sqrt{\frac{\{1/(n-1) \sum_{j=1}^{n} (k_{ij} - 1/n \sum_{j=1}^{n} k_{ij})^2\}}{1/n \sum_{j=1}^{n} k_{ij}}} \qquad i = 1, \ldots, n \tag{13.8}$$

Indirect employment effects (l') can be isolated from the total effects very easily since:

$$l' = [K - \hat{n}]f = K'f \tag{13.9}$$

so that new rankings and degrees of dispersion can be obtained for each sector by replacing each k_{ij} by the corresponding element of (K') in equations (13.5) to (13.8).

According to the above approach (cf. Diamond, 1975), a 'key' employment sector is one with a high Y_j' and Z_i' and a low V'_j and V_i'. Such a sector will create above average employment in other sectors when final demand increases by unity $(Y'_j > 1)$, while employment within the sector will respond above proportionately when final demand for all sectors increases by unity $(Z_i' > 1)$. At the same time, the employment effects will be spread widely with a low V'_j and V'_i.[3]

In the previous chapter we had occasion to criticize linkage analysis and much of what was said still applies in the case of these linkage employment indices. Nonetheless, it is interesting to see which sectors might be selected as 'key' employment generators using either these indices or the cruder indicator k_j. In Table 13.1, therefore, various measures are given for the 36-sector input–output table for Turkey.

Table 13.1 Employment linkage indices for Turkey (1967)

Sector	Forward linkages			Backward linkages		
	Z'_i	Rank	V'_i	Y'_j	Rank	V'_j
1 Agriculture	7.857	1	2.482	3.037	2	5.496
2 Forestry	1.788	4	3.684	1.294	6	4.870
3 Animal husbandry, fishing	3.893	3	3.654	3.609	1	4.300
4 Coal mining	1.148	9	3.900	0.953	13	4.710
5 Iron-ore mining	0.804	12	5.697	0.997	12	4.586
6 Other mining and quarrying	1.177	8	3.988	0.948	14	4.968
7 Sugar	0.201	32	5.411	1.297	5	4.155
8 Tobacco	0.241	31	5.999	0.928	17	3.561
9 Alcoholic beverages	0.149	34	5.955	0.692	26	2.709
10 Other food products	0.282	29	4.340	2.157	3	3.640
11 Textiles, apparels	0.612	20	4.972	1.121	9	3.217
12 Wood products	0.669	16	4.606	1.138	8	3.310
13 Paper and printing	0.523	23	4.439	0.605	29	3.933
14 Leather	0.283	28	5.786	0.935	16	2.952
15 Rubber, plastics	0.268	30	4.710	0.397	34	3.297
16 Chemicals, pharmaceuticals	0.508	24	3.352	0.580	30	2.924
17 Fertilizers	0.530	22	5.473	0.788	20	3.707
18 Petroleum refinery	0.057	36	2.399	0.207	36	1.877
19 Non-metallic products	0.648	19	4.602	0.743	24	4.025
20 Cement	0.439	25	5.091	0.663	28	3.387
21 Iron and steel	1.128	10	3.107	0.894	19	3.889
22 Non-ferrous metals	0.738	13	4.281	0.694	25	4.525
23 Metal products	0.192	33	4.059	0.509	32	2.143
24 Non-electrical machinery	0.390	26	3.985	0.495	33	3.250
25 Electrical machinery	0.348	27	4.940	0.524	31	3.374
26 Transport equipment	0.566	21	4.481	0.753	22	3.394
27 Electricity	0.106	35	3.138	0.310	35	2.072
28 Railway transportation	1.482	6	4.108	1.336	4	4.566
29 Other transportation	1.236	7	2.539	0.788	21	4.025
30 Trade	2.280	2	2.144	0.914	18	5.523
31 Communications	1.128	11	5.175	1.097	10	5.324
32 Banking, insurance, co-ops	1.585	5	2.408	0.753	23	5.207
33 Professions, personal services	0.728	14	4.528	1.062	11	3.324
34 Non-building construction	0.651	18	5.999	1.139	7	3.444
35 Building construction	0.652	17	5.999	0.936	15	4.147
36 Public Services	0.711	15	5.420	0.688	27	5.604

Source: Derived from Diamond (1975), Appendix II.

Examination of this table reveals some disturbing results; the 'key' employment sectors—as measured by those whose rankings in terms of backward and forward linkages are in the top third—are all non-industrial; four are primary sectors (agriculture, forestry, animal husbandry and iron-ore mining), while the other two are non-traded sectors (railway transportation and communications). A similar result (Hazari, 1970) was found for India, where only three of the 30 most important sectors (as measured by the ranking of k_j) were non-agricultural in a table with 77 activities. Furthermore, as Diamond (1975) has shown, those sectors in Table 13.1 which perform worst in terms of employment generation (i.e. in the bottom third of both backward and forward linkage index rankings) are precisely the 'modern' sectors which have been promoted in Turkey's development plans.[4]

The implication of Table 13.1 is a clear trade-off between employment and growth; sectors with high linkages as calculated in the previous chapter tend to be those with low employment generation effects and vice versa, while a policy of import-substituting industrialization seems destined to confine employment to a slow rate of growth. In what follows, we shall see why both these pessimistic implications need to be qualified.

13.3 EXTENDED MULTIPLIER ANALYSIS—EMPLOYMENT EFFECTS

The employment multipliers discussed so far are all of the 'intra-group' type (see Chapter 12). They do not take into account the repercussions on employment brought about by factors of production spending their incomes; these additional employment effects can be captured by making the household sector 'endogenous', as in Type II multipliers (Richardson, 1972), or by adaptation of the extended multiplier system.

In the previous chapter, the extended multiplier system was introduced and it was shown how intra-, inter- and extra-group effects combine to give the solution:

$$q = M_3 M_2 M_1 e = Me \tag{13.10}$$

where e is a vector of exogenous and q of endogenous variables. We can partition this as:

$$\begin{bmatrix} q_1 \\ \hline q_2 \end{bmatrix} = \left[\begin{array}{c|c} M_{11} & M_{12} \\ \hline M_{21} & M_{22} \end{array}\right] \begin{bmatrix} e_1 \\ \hline e_2 \end{bmatrix} \tag{13.11}$$

where the subscript 1 refers to the accounts for producers and the subscript 2 refers to all other accounts. It follows that the solution for the vector of gross output can be written:

$$q_1 = x = M_{11} e_1 + M_{12} e_2 \tag{13.12}$$

As before, we wish to study the impact of changes in the exogenous vector on employment. Using our simple employment coefficients (see equation (13.1)), we can write the vector of employment requirements as:

$$l = \hat{n}x = \hat{n}M_{11}e_1 + \hat{n}M_{12}e_2 \tag{13.13}$$

We now wish to compare the employment created when using this extended multiplier system with the employment created when using the simple multiplier system. This means we have to assume $e_2 = 0$ and we then compare the matrix product $\hat{n}(I-A)^{-1}$ with the matrix product $\hat{n}M_{11}$.

Such an exercise has been carried out for the United Kingdom in Table 13.2. The table shows what happens to employment when final demand for the sector recorded in the row changes by £1 million; thus, on the simple multiplier system, employment generated throughout the UK when final demand for agriculture rises by £1 million is 501 whereas on the extended multiplier system it becomes 1524.

The table also shows how employment generation in the extended system is built up. Recalling equation (12.10), which gives a formula for M involving inter-, intra- and extra-group effects in an additive form, we can write the solution for q as:

$$q = [I + \{M_1 - I\} + \{M_2 - I\}M_1 + \{M_3 - I\}M_2M_1]e \tag{13.14}$$

or

$$q = [I + B + C + D]e \tag{13.15}$$

where B, C, D correspond to the second, third and fourth terms respectively in the bracketed expression of equation (13.14), so that in partitioned form this becomes:

$$\begin{bmatrix} q_1 \\ \hline q_2 \end{bmatrix} = \left\{ \begin{bmatrix} I & \\ \hline & I \end{bmatrix} + \begin{bmatrix} B_{11} & B_{12} \\ \hline B_{21} & B_{22} \end{bmatrix} + \begin{bmatrix} C_{11} & C_{12} \\ \hline C_{21} & C_{22} \end{bmatrix} + \begin{bmatrix} D_{11} & D_{12} \\ \hline D_{21} & D_{22} \end{bmatrix} \right\} \begin{bmatrix} e_1 \\ \hline e_2 \end{bmatrix} \tag{13.16}$$

and the solution for the gross output vector is:

$$q_1 = x = e_1 + B_{11}e_1 + B_{12}e_2 + C_{11}e_1 + C_{12}e_2 + D_{11}e_1 + D_{12}e_2 \tag{13.17}$$

The employment requirements vector (l) can now be written:

$$l = \hat{n}x = \hat{n}e_1 + \hat{n}B_{11}e_1 + \hat{n}B_{12}e_2 + \hat{n}C_{11}e_1 + \hat{n}C_{12}e_2 + \hat{n}D_{11}e_1 + \hat{n}D_{12}e_2 \tag{13.18}$$

which, with $e_2 = 0$, collapses to:

$$l = \hat{n}e_1 + \hat{n}B_{11}e_1 + \hat{n}C_{11}e_1 + \hat{n}D_{11}e_1 \tag{13.19}$$

The first term in equation (13.19) describes the direct employment effects; the second term (see previous chapter) records the intra-group effect net of the direct effect, so it follows that the first two terms when added together give the employment generated by the intra-group effect, i.e. the simple input–output system. The third term measures the additional impact of the extra-group effects, but by definition these are zero in our example because we are only interested in

Table 13.2 Employment multipliers for the United Kingdom (1968). Jobs created per £ million of exogenous change in final demand

	Sector	Simple employment multiplier	Extended employment multiplier	Direct effect	Net contribution of intra-group effect	Net contribution of inter-group effect
1	Agriculture and extraction	510	1524	302	208	1014
2	Metal manufacture and metal using industries	566	1582	433	133	1016
3	Other manufacturing	476	1361	310	166	885
4	Construction	537	1608	323	214	1071
5	Gas, electricity and water	382	1445	182	200	1063
6	Services	528	1642	478	50	1114

Source: Derived by the author from tables in CSO (1973) and Stone (1978).

intra- and inter-group effects; the final term therefore measures the net contribution of circular or 'closed-loop' effects, so that the difference between the simple and extended systems can be interpreted as the additional employment attributable to inter-group effects.

As the table shows, there is a considerable difference between the simple and extended systems and the additional employment creation can be entirely attributed to the net contribution of the inter-group effects, i.e. the employment created as the result of factors of production 'paying' the institutional accounts (e.g. households), which distribute their receipts over producers (e.g. as consumption expenditure) thereby creating more employment and so on; with low marginal propensities to save and import and with low taxation rates, this 'closed loop' system can have very powerful effects. Marginal propensities, however, may differ from average propensities and if they are higher—as is usually assumed in the case of savings, taxation and imports—then the extended system will give an exaggerated impression of the employment change associated with any perturbation to the exogenous vector. It should, therefore, be used with caution, although the results are likely to be more realistic than the simple system which in effect treats all factor payments as a leakage.

13.4 THE PROBLEM OF SURPLUS LABOUR

The previous equations used to measure employment generation assume a fixed proportional relationship between the number of workers and the level of output; this is an oversimplification for many reasons, as was shown in Chapter 4, where suitable modifications were made to the employment equation to deal with non-proportionality in the relationship between employment and output.

Each of these modifications still assumes that the distinction between number of hours worked (labour time) and the number of workers (labourers) can be ignored. In an industrial society with a fully employed labour force this is a reasonable assumption, but in a developing country with a large traditional sector it is not appropriate if the average number of hours worked in any sector (h_j) is below the legal, physiological or cultural maximum (h_j^*). If $h_j < h_j^*$, the demand for increased employment may simply be met by the existing labour force working longer hours rather than by creating new jobs.

This is made clearer if we define n_j and l_j in equation (13.1) as referring to labour time. This means that n_j now denotes the labour time in hours required per unit of output, so that dividing through by h_j will give the number of labourers; in an industrial society, h_j is more or less constant, but in the traditional sector of a developing country, h_j can be made to vary.

This distinction has been applied to Bangladesh (often thought of as a 'labour surplus' country) and the results are given in Table 13.3. In the column labelled 'unadjusted' are the assumed increases in employment when h_j is fixed, while in the 'adjusted' column are the increases in employment when h_j increases towards h_j^*. The difference in the case of the agricultural sector is very marked, since its ranking as a 'key' employment generator changes from first to last.

Table 13.3 Employment multipliers for Bangladesh (1964/5). Jobs created per 10 million taka of exogenous change in final demand

Sector	Total number of jobs created			
	Adjusted	Rank	Unadjusted	Rank
Agriculture	1127	7	12886	1
Industry	7382	2	9809	2
Construction	5329	3	7198	4
Electricity and Gas	1701	6	2200	7
Transport	4556	5	4785	6
Trade	7972	1	7992	3
Government and services	5178	4	5416	5

Source: Krishnamurthy (1975).

Although the choice of h_j in Table 13.3 is somewhat arbitrary, it serves as a healthy reminder that in LDCs employment generation is not necessarily job creation; furthermore, if reasonable assumptions are made about increases in hours worked in the traditional sector, then the employment generated by the industrial sector in relative terms no longer looks quite so poor.[5]

13.5 EMPLOYMENT AND INDUSTRIALIZATION

In this section we examine in further detail the argument that the growth of employment in industry in LDCs has been disappointing. Various versions of this argument exist, which can best be summarized in one of three headings:

1 The numbers employed in the industrial sector have grown very slowly.

2 The proportion of the labour force employed in industry in many LDCs has remained virtually constant.

3 The growth of employment in industry has been disappointing relative to the growth of industrial value added.

The first proposition will be of most concern to us here; under the commonly made assumptions of a fixed supply of land, surplus labour in agriculture, rural–urban migration, rapid population growth and a small urban economy, it is easy to show that the growth of employment in industry would have to be very rapid in order to maintain existing rates of unemployment, let alone decrease them. Furthermore, although final demand for industry output has often grown rapidly, the elasticity of industrial employment with respect to industrial output has been so low (Edwards, 1974) that employment has failed to keep up with expectations.

However, with industrial final demand growing rapidly, industry will be generating employment directly and indirectly not only in the industrial sectors, but also in the primary and tertiary sectors. At the same time, *measured* industrial employment consists not only of employment created by industry in industry, but also of employment created in industry by non-industrial sectors. It is therefore possible that the poor measured performance of employment is due to the poor performance of the non-industrial sectors in creating employment for industry.

We can make this clearer by returning to equation (13.3) and writing it out in full for the case of a three-sector economy (agriculture, industry, services being sectors one, two and three respectively):

$$\begin{aligned} l_1 &= k_{11} f_1 + k_{12} f_2 + k_{13} f_3 \\ l_2 &= k_{21} f_1 + k_{22} f_2 + k_{23} f_3 \\ l_3 &= k_{31} f_1 + k_{32} f_2 + k_{33} f_3 \end{aligned} \tag{13.20}$$

From the second line of equation (13.20) we can see that the change in measured industrial employment (Δl_2) is given by:

$$\Delta l_2 = k_{21} \Delta f_1 + k_{22} \Delta f_2 + k_{23} \Delta f_3 \tag{13.21}$$

while, when industrial final demand increases by (Δf_2), total employment *created* by industry (Δl_2^*) is:

$$\Delta l_2^* = (k_{12} + k_{22} + k_{32}) \Delta f_2 \tag{13.22}$$

so that:

$$\Delta l_2^* = \Delta l_2 + (k_{12} + k_{32}) \Delta f_2 - (k_{21} \Delta f_1 + k_{23} \Delta f_3) \tag{13.23}$$

We can think of Δl as measuring employment by sector of *destination* and Δl^* as measuring employment by sector of *origin*. The two will be equal for any given sector only when the second and third terms in equation (13.23) cancel out; this is most unlikely, if only because even an equal increase in final demand for industry and agriculture ($\Delta f_2 = \Delta f_1$) will lead to different employment effects in each other's sector ($k_{21} \neq k_{12}$).

In Table 13.4, the K matrix for Brazil showing total employment effects (see equation (13.3)) has been written out in full for a nine-sector model. When all final demands increase by unity, it can be seen that measured employment in the industrial sectors (the row sum of K) rises by much less than employment *created* by industry (the column sum of K). For example, while the agro-industrial sectors generate an extra 282 jobs (245 of which 'accrue' to agriculture) measured employment only rises by 38 jobs.

By multiplying the elements of the K matrix by the *observed* vector of final demand for 1970 and summing down the columns, we can convert employment from a destination to an origin basis; the results are shown in Table 13.5 and the differences are astonishing; it appears that most agricultural employment owes its origin to non-agricultural sectors, while all the industrial sectors 'create' much more employment than they 'receive'.

If an exercise similar to the above were carried out for other LDCs, where employment on a destination basis is also dominated by primary activity, it would almost certainly produce similar results. The point to be made is that much

Table 13.4 Employment generation matrix for Brazil ($K = \hat{n}\,[I - A]^{-1}$), 1970

Sectors	(1)	(2)	(3)	(4)	(5)	(6)	(7)	(8)	(9)	Total
1 Agriculture	714.89	5.177	13.66	57.618	245.357	56.18	32.04	7.385	12.62	1144.94
2 Mining and quarrying	0.124	34.73	0.361	1.311	0.186	0.591	0.479	0.063	0.039	37.88
3 Metal mechanical industries	0.204	1.606	31.246	0.966	1.068	1.776	4.834	0.822	0.532	43.05
4 Chemicals	0.93	0.574	1.073	13.819	1.287	1.209	1.144	0.517	0.270	20.82
5 Agro-industries	0.791	1.196	0.490	1.323	27.362	4.573	2.038	0.535	0.913	38.22
6 Other industry	0.073	0.283	0.732	0.612	0.338	38.331	4.86	0.209	0.597	46.03
7 Construction	0.011	0.0198	0.042	0.035	0.043	0.043	63.057	0.499	0.016	63.77
8 Transport and distribution	1.313	2.443	5.175	4.363	5.328	5.314	8.314	61.396	1.961	95.6
9 Services	0.310	1.72	1.373	1.04	1.187	1.310	0.99	1.918	68.36	78.21
Total	718.66	46.75	54.15	81.08	282.16	109.32	117.76	73.34	85.31	1568.53

Note: Employment coefficients (n) obtained by dividing total employment in each sector by the value of production in millions of cruzeiros.
Source: Derived by the author from tables in IBGE (1979).

Table 13.5 Structure of employment in Brazil (1970)

Sector	Measured employment	Structure of employment (%)	
		By destination	By origin
1 Agriculture	17496000	65.6	26.5
2 Mining and quarrying	65339	0.2	0.1
3 Metal mechanical industries	761010	2.9	3.7
4 Chemicals	246760	0.9	2.2
5 Agro-industries	1052788	3.9	34.1
6 Other industry	574360	2.2	3.4
7 Construction	1729249	6.5	14.6
8 Transport and distribution	2831600	10.6	11.0
9 Services	1914500	7.2	4.4
Total	26671000	100.0	100.0

Source: Derived by the author from tables in IBGE (1979).

employment in the primary sectors is underpinned by activity in the non-primary sectors, so that the true impact of industrialization, for example, on employment creation is not captured by conventional measures on a destination basis. This does not mean that the employment effects of industrialization can be ignored—it simply means that they must be measured differently and equation (13.23) shows how.

13.6 THE DISTRIBUTION OF INCOME

The simple open static Leontief input–output model has proved its worth in a number of fields. With respect to income formation, however, it is somewhat unsatisfactory; consumption expenditure is assumed to be exogenous and this prevents changes in the composition of consumption expenditure from bringing about changes in the level of total income.

In the real world, changes in the commodity composition of consumers' expenditure (total expenditure unchanged) are generally thought to have an impact on total income *and* its distribution (cf. Miyazawa, 1976, Chapter 2). This impact comes about because different income groups have different marginal propensities to consume the products of each sector; changes in income distribution will therefore bring about changes in sectoral rates of output, but this will imply different demands for factors of production, which will again alter the distribution of income and so on.

It should be clear that this 'real world' impact can only be captured by the input–output model if consumers' expenditure is made endogenous and broken down between different income groups. This, as we saw in Chapter 12 and shall see again below, is not difficult to do; it enables us to study the impact of exogenous changes for the output of sectors on income formation and—perhaps more importantly—the size distribution of income.[6] Furthermore, we can use this extended system and 'impose' on it various income distributions, from which the output, income, import and employment implications can be derived.

All of this assumes that the size distribution of income is a target for which it is appropriate to design public policies. There is no doubt that governments, including those in LDCs, do set great store by the distribution of income and would like to be able to influence it; most of them have become dissatisfied with growth in real income per head as the sole objective of social policy, since it has been found that rapid growth in mean incomes is consistent with a worsening of the size distribution of income, so that we can no longer state unambiguously that welfare has improved.

The idea that income distribution can be changed at will, however, runs counter to the hypothesis that there is a U-shaped relationship between real income and income distribution such that the size distribution at first becomes more unequal as incomes rise from very low levels, and then improves as incomes increase still further. This hypothesis, associated primarily with the name of Kuznets (1955; 1963), has been tested in some detail and is generally confirmed by the cross-section evidence (e.g. Ahluwahlia, 1974). However, the conclusions reached from time-series analysis of individual countries have tended to be much more agnostic and, in particular, have pointed to the distinct possibility that, although countries may experience increasing inequality in the size distribution of income with rising incomes, they may fail to advance beyond it to a point where equality improves (Weisskopf, 1976). Thus, according to this line of argument, the only scope for improving the distribution of income is by the introduction of appropriate policies.

Whether input–output analysis is suitable for this kind of study depends on whether the policies thought to influence the distribution of income can be introduced within the framework of the input–output model. In a study of the determinants of income distribution, Adelman and Morris (1973) found that the level of real income per head as an explanatory variable was less important than the degree of socio-economic and technical dualism, the abundance of natural resources, the degree of development of human resources, the degree of social mobility, the degree of cultural and ethnic homogeneity, the methods of agricultural organization and the extent of government participation in the economy. Of these determinants, all but the last two (and of course real income) must be regarded as given in input–output studies, so that the opportunities for experimenting with policies to change the distribution of income are of necessity somewhat limited in the present context of input–output techniques; this may help to explain why experiments using input–output models have not reached very optimistic conclusions about the possibilities for changing income distribution (cf. Taylor, 1979a).

All of this applies to models which study the impact of changes in the exogenous vector on income distribution; one way round the problem, however, is to assume that the required income distribution has been introduced in some unexplained fashion; in other words, the changed distribution is assumed to have been imposed and we then work out the implications for sectoral output, GDP, imports, employment, savings, etc. Recalling the schematic social accounting matrix introduced in Chapter 4 (Table 4.1), we may write the balance equation for producers in accordance with equation (4.26) as:

$$q_1 = B_{11}q_1 + B_{13}q_3 + e_1 \tag{13.24}$$

where q_1 is a vector of sectoral gross outputs, B_{11} is the technology matrix (A), B_{13} is a matrix of consumption coefficients[7] and e_1 is an exogenous vector of demand for sectoral outputs. The crucial vector, from the point of view of studying income distribution, is q_3 which records the income from all sources received by the institutional accounts; if the latter are broken down by income group, variations in q_3 imply variations in the size distribution of income. If q_3 is set outside the model, it becomes exogenous and so the solution for the output vector becomes:

$$q_1 = [I - B_{11}]^{-1}B_{13}q_3 + [I - B_{11}]^{-1}e_1 \tag{13.25}$$

and when the size distribution of income varies from its observed value (q_3^0) to some new value (q_3^1), the change in the output vector can be written:

$$\Delta q_1 = [I - B_{11}]^{-1}B_{13}[q_3^1 - q_3^0] \tag{13.26}$$

The above equation has been applied to a number of countries (e.g. Maton, 1978; Paukert, 1974). Unfortunately, it suffers from a major inconsistency; if we return to equation (4.26), we can see that the solution for institutional account incomes (q_3) depends on factor incomes (q_2) and the solution for factor incomes depends on sectoral gross output (q_1). Thus, the above equation implies a certain solution for the income vector (q_3) which may differ from that introduced at the start; the way round this problem is to proceed by iteration, use the income vector implied by equation (13.25) in equation (13.24), work out a new solution for q_1 and q_3 and continue until the implied income distribution is equal to the one assumed exogenously.

This iterative method, which has the merit of internal consistency, has been applied to the Philippines and South Korea in a recent study (Paukert, 1979) and some results are shown in Table 13.6. These are given on the assumption that the Australian distribution of income in 1965–7 has been introduced into the countries in question; the Gini coefficient[8] for Australia in those years was 0.312, compared with an observed coefficient of 0.493 for the Philippines and 0.398 for Korea. The experiment therefore implies a fairly radical shift in the distribution of income towards greater equality; in particular, we may note that the experiment implies a shrinking in the income share of the top 10% to 23.76% from 40.6% in the Philippines and from 34.88% in the case of Korea.

The results are very mixed; they show that in the Philippines a redistribution of income towards greater equality would increase employment, GDP and personal income substantially while leading to a sharp fall in the overall savings rate;

Table 13.6 Consequences of a simulated change in income distribution (percentage change from initial levels). Change involves introduction of Australian size distribution

	Philippines (%)	South Korea (%)
Employment	+10	+1
GDP	+ 7	+1
Personal income	+ 7	0
Private savings	−24	−4
Imports	+ 5	0

Source: Paukert (1979).

contrary to popular belief, imports would also rise. In South Korea, on the other hand, the redistribution would have almost no effect on the economy at the aggregate level; the reconciliation of these apparently paradoxical results has to do with the sources of output change; when income is redistributed towards the poor, income accrues to those with low marginal propensities to save and is taken from those with high ones. The reduction in savings is matched by a rise in consumption, which stimulates output, employment, etc. provided that the marginal propensity to import of the poor does not exceed that of the rich; in the case of South Korea, the poor appear to have the higher marginal propensity to import (Paukert, 1979), while at the same time the rich do not have the highest propensity to save. Hence, in South Korea the savings-consumption effect of income redistribution is rather modest and is cancelled out by the greater import leakages associated with redistributing income to the poor.

The main weakness of this approach should be readily apparent and has been well summarized by Morawetz (1974):

> '. . . little attention is paid to the way in which the initial income redistribution is to be achieved; it must surely be significant for final factor use patterns whether it is by capital or income transfers or by indirect taxation.'

to which we may add that the simulated change with which the models experiment are rather arbitrary; in an effort to circumvent this last problem, Ghosh (1979a) and others have proposed a programming approach in which the objective function is a weighted average of the incomes of various groups and the model's constraints are the input–output balance equations; this proposal has the merit of avoiding the arbitrary imposition of a given income distribution, but suffers from the fact that artificial limits must be set on the permissible range for changes in the output vector in order to avoid absurd solutions and there is still no explanation of how the income distribution implied by the solution might be introduced in practice.[9]

13.7 INCOME DISTRIBUTION—SOME EXTENSIONS

If the imposition of arbitrary changes in income distribution is considered unrealistic, then it is necessary to recognize the interdependence between the systems of production and distribution and use the extended input–output system defined by equation (4.28). In this model, we explicitly recognize that exogenous changes (in exports, for example) imply changes in production, which imply changes in the distribution of income, which imply changes in consumption, which imply further changes in production and so on; thus, income redistribution is a consequence rather than a cause of exogenous 'shocks' to the system and this is surely more consistent with reality.

All this can be seen very clearly in Table 13.7 where an attempt has been made to work out for Sri Lanka the implications of a number of exogenous changes on income distribution when the inter-dependence between production and distribution is allowed for. In the first two columns of the table, the initial incomes and their distribution are recorded for six factors of production and three income groups. The impact of an exogenous change of 100 Rs. million in the demand for tea, textiles and domestic services respectively is then worked out; in the case of tea, it can be seen that the existing income distribution would be moved in favour of the estates (both the factors and households); in the case of textiles the existing distribution is re-enforced (except that the share of estates would decline still further), while in the case of domestic services expansion, the distribution would move in favour of urban labour and urban households.

These experiments are very useful. Nonetheless they suffer from a number of drawbacks; first, the relationship between factor inputs and outputs is assumed to be governed by fixed coefficients without the possibility of factor substitution or productivity change and secondly, income distribution is often described in terms of some scalar parameter, such as the log variance or the Gini coefficient which cannot be derived directly from the solution to the extended input–output system.

The first drawback can be dealt with through modification of the factor demand equations,[10] but the second requires further comment. Let us assume that there are m institutional accounts or groups; the solution to the input–output model will, on summation, give us the total income in each group. If a labour or skill matrix has been developed in parallel with the institutional accounts, it should be possible to determine the number of individuals among whom this income is distributed; even without such a matrix, some assumptions about wage rates can be made to derive the mean income for each group ($\bar{Y}_i$, $i = 1, \ldots, m$).

Now within each of the m groups assume that income is distributed according to some functional form. Although it does not matter what form is adopted, the assumption of a log-normal distribution (Aitchison, 1957) has often been made for income groups and has repeatedly been supported by evidence, so we shall assume it here in preference to, say, a Pareto distribution. According to the log-normal distribution, with the variable $x_i = \log Y_i$, x_i is normally distributed with mean μ_i and variance σ_i^2, i.e. $x_i \sim N(\mu_i, \sigma_i^2)$. The within-group mean income ($\bar{Y}_i$) is related to the parameters of the log-normal distribution(μ_i,σ_i^2) by the

Table 13.7 Impact of exogenous increase of 100 Rs. million for various activities on income distribution in Sri Lanka (1970)

	Initial income	(%)	Sector in which injection originates					
			Tea		Textiles		Domestic services	
			Income change	Distribution (%)	Income change	Distribution (%)	Income change	Distribution (%)
(A) Factors of production								
1 Urban labour	1673	14.7	20	9.1	16	13.2	57	21.9
2 Rural labour	3184	28.0	42	19.1	31	25.6	93	35.8
3 Estate labour	711	6.3	57	25.9	2	1.7	9	3.5
4 Housing	633	5.6	11	5.0	7	5.8	15	5.8
5 Other private capital	4985	43.9	88	40.0	62	51.2	84	32.3
6 Public capital	175	1.5	2	0.9	3	2.5	2	0.7
Total	11361	100.0	220	100.0	121	100.0	260	100.0
(B) Institutions								
1 Urban households	3004	28.1	42	20.5	31	28.4	84	34.1
2 Rural households	6902	64.5	105	51.2	75	68.8	157	63.8
3 Estate households	791	7.4	58	28.3	3	2.8	5	2.1
Total	10697	100.0	205	100.0	109	100.0	246	100.0

Source: Derived from Pyatt (1977).

expression:

(13.27) $$\overline{Y}_i = e^{(\mu_i + \frac{1}{2}\sigma_i^2)}$$

so that μ_i can be derived from the above given the known group-mean income ($\overline{Y}_i$) and assuming an exogenous value for the group log variance (σ_i^2).

So far, we have found a way of calculating the log-mean group income, given log-mean group variance and group mean income, but we have not yet found any useful scalar measure for the *overall* distribution of income. One such measure is the log variance (σ^2) which can be decomposed into between-group and within-group log variance (cf. Szal, 1977) as:

(13.28) $$\sigma^2 = \sum_i w_i \sigma_i^2 + \sum_i w_i (\mu_i - \mu)^2$$

where w_i is the population share of the ith group and $\mu = \Sigma_i w_i \mu_i$ is the overall log-mean income.

It follows that we now have all the information we need to compute the overall log variance and can therefore compare each 'run' of the input–output model in terms of its impact on income inequality via the log variance. The latter, however, is not above criticism as a measure of inequality (Sen, 1973) and is not as widely used as other measures of income inequality and poverty against which it would be desirable to test different runs of the model.

The main problem is that, although each within-group distribution may be log-normal, it does not follow that the overall distribution can be so characterized.[11] Fortunately, an algorithm has been developed (Robinson, 1976) for computing the overall distribution given the log-normality of the within-group income distributions.[12] This means that it is possible to compute quantiles for the overall size distribution,[13] and thereby determine the proportion of income accruing to, say, the bottom and top 10% of the population; these quantile measures are very popular for describing income distribution (Ahluwahlia, 1974) and, in particular, with the quantiles of the overall size distribution known, it is a very simple matter to compute the Gini coefficient. Thus, each run of the input–output model can be used to test its implications for the size distribution of income using a series of measures (see Adelman, 1977; and de Melo, 1979).

NOTES

1 Unfortunately, few LDCs can supply information on different types of labour input by sector so that equation (13.3) is more commonly applied than (13.4). However, in the case of Scotland, the author's former colleagues are working on labour matrices which break down labour requirements by sector into 90 occupations. Such a detailed matrix is indispensable for manpower planning and for matching educational requirements with employment needs. See also Pyatt (1977), where a labour skill matrix is developed for Sri Lanka.

2 As was pointed out in Chapter 12, however, the index of forward linkages makes most sense when based on the row sums of the output inverse and this is equally true of the employment forward linkage index.

3 A low V'_i, for example, means that employment increases in the sector are not over-dependent on final demand increases in a few sectors.

4 The industrial sectors affected are rubber and plastic products, chemicals and pharmaceuticals, petroleum refineries, cement, metal products, electrical appliances and non-electrical machinery.

5 In the text, it was assumed that the input of labour time in man-hours was known for each sector. In many cases, this is not so; what is known is labour costs per unit of output (c_j). The total impact on labour costs per unit increase in the final demand for the jth sector is:

$$\sum_{i=1}^{n} c_i r_{ij}$$

when r_{ij} is the i, jth element of the Leontief inverse; it follows that the total impact on man-hours is given by:

$$\sum_i \frac{c_i r_{ij}}{w_i}$$

where w_i is the hourly wage rate paid in the ith sector and the total impact on jobs is therefore given by:

$$\sum_i \frac{c_i r_{ij}}{w_i h_i}$$

where h_i is the average number of hours worked in the ith sector. The experiment in Table 13.3 was therefore carried out by varying h_i in the above expression.

6 The size distribution of income records the proportion of total income accruing to different proportions of the population. If these proportions are defined as deciles, the size distribution shows first the income share of the poorest 10%, then the income share of the next 10% and so on; it differs from the functional distribution of income which records the proportion of income accruing to different factors of production.

7 The matrix B_{13} therefore records the consumption requirements, expressed in coefficient form, of different classes of income recipients. The basic source for this matrix is budget survey data and a detailed example for Sri Lanka is given in the appendix to Pyatt (1977).

8 The Gini coefficient is a measure of inequality in the size distribution of income varying from 1.0 in the case of complete inequality (one individual with all income) to zero in the case of complete equality. LDCs are typically in the range 0.4 to 0.6.

9 The paper by Ghosh (1979a) introduces one important modification which is worth mentioning; models experimenting with income redistribution are often applied over a number of years or at least require updating the basic tables. In the case of B_{13} —the consumption coefficient matrix—it is unreasonable to expect constancy of coefficients over time. On the other hand, time-series evidence for consumption is often available which permits estimation of the Engel-type relationship $C_{ik}(t) = \alpha_i Y_k(t)^{\eta_{ik}}$, where $C_{ik}(t)$ is consumption of the ith commodity at time (t) by the kth income group, η_{ik} is the corresponding income elasticity of demand and $Y_k(t)$ is the income of the kth group at time t. In the base year (0), we observe $C_{ik}(0) = b_{ik}(0)\, Y_k(0)$, where b_{ik} is the i, kth element of B_{13}, so that $b_{ik}(0) = \alpha_i Y_k(0)^{(\eta_{ik}-1)}$, $b_{ik}(1) = \alpha_i Y_k(1)^{(\eta_{ik}-1)}$ and so on. Consequently, a satisfactory means has been found for updating the consumption coefficient matrix.

10 In section 5 of chapter 4, some of the rigidity in labour demand equations was removed by allowing for non-constant returns to scale. This approach can be extended in a number of directions through production function analysis; in the latter, net output is produced with variable factor proportions, the optimal combination of factor inputs varying with factor prices. This is consistent with input–output analysis, since the latter in its traditional form only determines *value added* in each sector (i.e. net output) according to the assumption of fixed coefficients of production and the breakdown of net output among

primary inputs can thus be done by reference to production function analysis. An example of this type of model (for South Korea) can be found in Chapter 2 of Adelman (1977).

11 Unless σ_i is the same for all groups and the distribution of μ_i itself is log-normal (see Aitchison and Brown, p. 110, 1957).

12 In fact, as Robinson (1976) points out, any functional form will do, but the assumption of log-normality is the one usually made.

13 The technique is mathematically quite complicated, involving as it does the solution to a non-linear differential equation, but Robinson (1976) has produced a complete statement of the computer algorithm so that the input–output worker only has to furnish the necessary exogenous data.

CHAPTER 14

Some Extensions of the Basic Input–Output Model

14.1 INTRODUCTION

Although rich in interpretation, the basic input–output model described so far suffers from a number of weaknesses; some of these, such as the assumption of fixed coefficients of production, cannot be resolved very easily, while others can be dealt with through various extensions of the basic model.

In this chapter, we consider four such extensions; this is by no means an exhaustive list of possibilities and the choice has been made by reference to its relevance to LDCs. Not all the extensions discussed here hold out immediate prospects for many LDCs (e.g. the dynamic model), but they have all been widely discussed in the development literature and therefore deserve critical treatment.

Of the four extensions, the inter-regional and dynamic models will not be mentioned again in this book, but the price and optimization models will be referred to at various points; the price model is in many ways the most useful of the four for LDCs and is still comparatively neglected.

14.2 THE INTER-REGIONAL INPUT–OUTPUT MODEL

In Chapter 11, some thought was given to the additional problems incurred when preparing input–output tables for a single region. These tables, when converted to coefficient form, can be used in any number of single region input–output models which parallel models developed for a national economy; thus regional output, income and employment multipliers can be estimated and forecasts of regional gross output can be made on the basis of regional final demand (see, for example, Burdekin, 1978c).

Regional economists, however, have for years been pointing out the errors in regional studies when inter-regional feedback mechanisms are ignored (Metzler, 1950). Regional final demand is met in part by supplies from outside the region; this increases output and incomes in other regions which stimulates demand for the products of the first region and so on. The absence of this feedback in the single region model has led to persistent efforts to develop inter-regional input–output models which do not suffer from this defect.

Incorporation of the feedback mechanism is bought at a high price, however; it is necessary not only to have a record of inter-regional trade flows, but also to introduce some assumptions about the stability of trade patterns; the first problem has proved insuperable for all but a few developed countries (for the case of France, see Courbis, 1979), while the second has received little empirical support (see, for example, Jarvin Emerson, 1976). As has been said elsewhere: 'The major problem in the development of inter-regional input–output models arises from the fact that input–output analysis itself has no mechanism for explaining trade patterns, yet the derivation of inter-regional trade flows is the key distinctive feature of the inter-regional model' (Richardson, 1972, p. 56).

Basically, inter-regional input–output models are of three kinds:

(a) Those which require a complete matrix statement of inter-regional trade flows, so that the flow from sector *i* in region *m* to sector *j* in region *n* is separately recorded (e.g. the 'ideal' inter-regional model—Isard, 1951);

(b) Those which assume a certain stability in trade patterns within a region such that region *m* purchases from region *n* of commodity *i* will be proportionately the same for all sectors (e.g. the 'column coefficients' model—Moses, 1955);

(c) Those which derive regional totals essentially from the solution to a national input–output model (e.g. the Leontief intra-national model—Leontief, 1953).

The first of these three kinds of models has never been fully implemented and has been partially implemented only for DCs (e.g. for the California and Washington regions of the USA—Riefler, 1970); it is therefore inappropriate for even the largest LDCs given their present state of statistical sophistication; the second type of model could be implemented in some LDCs in principle, while the third is only appropriate where regions are so defined that a significant number of industries do not have extra-regional sales; this is unlikely to be the case in LDCs where the productive power of industry usually exceeds the limitations of the home market.[1]

The costs of implementing inter-regional models are clear enough; the benefits arise from incorporation of the feedback mechanism. If this benefit is small (in the sense that little is lost by ignoring the feedback), then LDCs are best advised to use single region input–output models to work out regional impacts; if it is large, there is a case for using one of the second type of inter-regional models described above. It is therefore of some importance to establish the size of the 'benefit'.

Let us imagine a country with two regions which also trades with the rest of the world; the balance equations for such a system can be written:

$$\begin{bmatrix} x_1 \\ x_2 \\ x_r \end{bmatrix} = \begin{bmatrix} A^D_{11} & M_{12} & M_{1R} \\ M_{21} & A^D_{22} & M_{2R} \\ M_{R1} & M_{R2} & A^D_{RR} \end{bmatrix} \begin{bmatrix} x_1 \\ x_2 \\ x_r \end{bmatrix} + \begin{bmatrix} f_1 \\ f_2 \\ f_r \end{bmatrix} \qquad (14.1)$$

where x_1, x_2 are the output vectors in regions 1 and 2, while x_r is the output vector in the rest of the world, A_{jj}^D is the intra-regional domestic coefficients matrix for the jth region, while M_{ij} is the import coefficient matrix for region j from region i and f_j is final demand for the output of region j.

When final demand for a region increases, its output rises stimulating imports from other regions and the rest of the world; the rise in their output stimulates imports from the first region, which again increases imports from other regions and the rest of the world. Assuming that final demand for region 1 *only* changes and ignoring all but first- and second-order terms in the power-series approximation to the Leontief inverse, we find in our simple two-region model that the increase in the output of the first region can be written:

$$\Delta x_1 = [I + A_{11}^D + (A_{11}^D)^2 + (M_{12}M_{21}) + (M_{1R}M_{R1}) \ldots]\Delta f_1 \tag{14.2}$$

Equation (14.2) contains both the international feedback mechanism—$(M_{1R}M_{R1})$—and the inter-regional feedback mechanism—$(M_{12}M_{21})$. If the former is ignored,[2] the balance equations become:

$$\begin{bmatrix} x_1 \\ x_2 \end{bmatrix} = \begin{bmatrix} A_{11}^D & M_{12} \\ M_{21} & A_{22}^D \end{bmatrix} \begin{bmatrix} x_1 \\ x_2 \end{bmatrix} + \begin{bmatrix} f_1^* \\ f_2^* \end{bmatrix} \tag{14.3}$$

where f_j^* now includes exports of intermediate goods to the rest of the world, and the increase in output becomes:

$$\Delta x_1 = [I + A_{11}^D + (A_{11}^D)^2 + (M_{12}M_{21}) \ldots]\Delta f_1^* \tag{14.4}$$

while if inter-regional feedback is ignored it becomes:

$$\Delta x_1 = [I + A_{11}^D + (A_{11}^D)^2 + \cdots]\Delta f_1^{**} \tag{14.5}$$

where f_1^{**} also includes exports of intermediate goods to region 2.

The 'benefits' of inter-regional models therefore depend on the size of the matrix products $M_{12}M_{21}$ and $M_{1R}M_{R1}$; in practice, the latter are always ignored and, in the case of most LDCs, this is reasonable because very few are sufficiently large importers to affect substantially the income of their trading partners, while their exports do not usually constitute an important element in the cost structure of importing countries (with the exception of oil).

The inter-regional feedback—$(M_{12}M_{21})$ in this example—will be large when industries in region 1 sell intermediate goods to region 2 and buy them from region 2; in many LDCs, industry is heavily concentrated in one region and produces mainly consumer goods; even if it then imports intermediate goods from the other region, the feedback mechanism will be slight because the stimulus to output in region 2 will not result in increased demand for intermediate goods from region 1.

In most LDCs, the impact of economic activity in one region on another is felt through the purchase and sale of consumer goods; when the income of an agricultural region, for example, increases as a result of a rise in primary exports to the rest of the world, part of this increase will be spent on consumer goods produced by the more industrial regions; the latter's rise in income will be partly spent on agricultural consumer goods from the first region; these 'consumer goods' multiplier effects are likely to be more important for many LDCs than the more conventional 'intermediate goods' multiplier effects and inter-regional input–output models for LDCs need to be adapted to take them into account.

Let us assume, as before, that there are two regions within a country (one primarily agricultural, the other industrial). The balance equations can now be written:

$$\begin{bmatrix} x_1 \\ x_2 \end{bmatrix} = \begin{bmatrix} A_{11}^D & - \\ - & A_{22}^D \end{bmatrix} \begin{bmatrix} x_1 \\ x_2 \end{bmatrix} + \begin{bmatrix} C_{11} & C_{12} \\ C_{21} & C_{22} \end{bmatrix} \begin{bmatrix} Y_1 \\ Y_2 \end{bmatrix} + \begin{bmatrix} f_1 \\ f_2 \end{bmatrix} \tag{14.6}$$

where x_1, x_2 are the output vectors for the two regions, A_{11}^D, A_{22}^D are the domestic input–output coefficient matrices for the two regions, Y_1, Y_2 are income in the two regions, C_{ij} is a matrix whose elements represent the proportion of income in region j spent on the final products of region i and f_1, f_2 are the exogenous demands for the output of the two regions including exports to the rest of the world and exports of capital goods and intermediate goods (but not consumer goods) to the other region. Income is given by:

$$\begin{bmatrix} Y_1 \\ Y_2 \end{bmatrix} = \begin{bmatrix} V_1' & - \\ - & V_2' \end{bmatrix} \begin{bmatrix} x_1 \\ x_2 \end{bmatrix} + \begin{bmatrix} e_1 \\ e_2 \end{bmatrix} \tag{14.7}$$

where V_1', V_2' are row vectors of value added coefficients in the two regions and e_1, e_2 are receipts of net transfer payments. The output matrices can therefore be written:

$$\begin{bmatrix} x_1 \\ x_2 \end{bmatrix} = \left\{ \begin{bmatrix} I & - \\ - & I \end{bmatrix} - \begin{bmatrix} A_{11}^D & - \\ - & A_{22}^D \end{bmatrix} - \begin{bmatrix} C_{11}V_1' & C_{12}V_2' \\ C_{21}V_1' & C_{22}V_2' \end{bmatrix} \right\}^{-1} \begin{bmatrix} f_1^* \\ f_2^* \end{bmatrix} \tag{14.8}$$

or

$$\begin{bmatrix} x_1 \\ x_2 \end{bmatrix} = \begin{bmatrix} I - A_{11}^D - C_{11}V_1' & -C_{12}V_2' \\ -C_{21}V_1' & I - A_{22}^D - C_{22}V_2' \end{bmatrix}^{-1} \begin{bmatrix} f_1^* \\ f_2^* \end{bmatrix} \tag{14.9}$$

where $f_1^* = (C_{11}e_1 + C_{12}e_2 + f_1)$ and $f_2^* = (C_{21}e_1 + C_{22}e_2 + f_2)$.

Equation (14.9) can be used to measure inter-regional feedbacks when the links provided by consumer goods, but not intermediate goods, are taken into account. Unlike conventional inter-regional trade models, there is no need to assume stability in inter-regional trade between industries; the only data requirements, additional to those provided by a single region model, are the consumption coefficients where stability is quite plausible if the model's regions are specialized in different types of consumer goods.

For some of the larger, more industrialized LDCs such as India, it may well be necessary to allow for the inter-regional feedback caused by the purchase and sale of intermediate goods between different regions of the same country; in that case, use must be made of one of the second type of models mentioned above which are very adequately summarized elsewhere (Richardson, 1972). Even in the case of these larger LDCs, however, the consumer goods effect is likely to be quite important and needs to be incorporated in the model if a closer approximation to the reality of inter-regional relationships is to be realized.

Regional and inter-regional input–output models will not be mentioned again in this book, so a few concluding remarks are in order. Regional input–output analysis is extremely demanding in terms of statistical and human resources and planners need to feel confident that this extra investment (i.e. over and above what is required by national input–output analysis) will justify itself; for this to be the case, there have to be industrial centres in at least two regions—a condition which probably does not apply to the majority of LDCs. For the remaining LDCs, the priority remains preparation of *national* input–output tables at regular intervals with much shorter delays in publication and this task is likely to absorb the energies of all those who can be allocated to input–output work. Only when the quality of national tables has been considerably improved is regional input–output analysis likely to come into its own.

14.3 DYNAMIC INPUT–OUTPUT MODELS

In Chapter 11, section 3, a method was suggested for making investment endogenous so that the feedback from demand for capital goods to increases in sectoral output can be incorporated into the input–output model. This technique requires the construction of a capital matrix (B) whose i,jth element shows the requirement of the ith capital good per unit output in the jth sector.

Only new investment (net fixed capital formation) is made endogenous by the adoption of this technique, so that replacement expenditures and inventory change still have to be specified exogenously.[3] Furthermore, the technique is only appropriate where there is a relatively advanced capital goods industry (which is true of only a few of the larger LDCs), because where capital goods are imported one can ignore the interaction between output increases and the capital goods industries.

In the input–output models discussed so far, no attempt is made to predict the time-path of output, incomes and employment, etc.; instead, solutions are found for a particular year. There is an understandable interest, therefore, in formulating a dynamic version of the input–output model which sets out time profiles for the endogenous variables; as we shall see, the model suffers from a number of difficulties, but we shall reserve criticism until after the model has been presented.

We may begin by writing the balance equations in the form:

$$x(t) = A(t)x(t) + j(t) + f(t) \tag{14.10}$$

where all variables are given a time dimension and j is the vector of investment by origin; assuming that the latter is explained by the accelerator-type relationship (see section 11.3):

$$j(t) = B(x_{(t+1)} - x(t)) \tag{14.11}$$

where B is the capital matrix, and assuming that the two technology matrices (A, B) are invariant with respect to time, we get the following form for the balance equations:

(14.12) $$x(t) = Ax(t) + Bx(t+1) - Bx(t) + f(t)$$

In year 1, we may presume that the output vector of the previous year—$x(0)$—is known. The solution for $x(1)$ is therefore:

(14.13) $$x(1) = [I + B^{-1}(I - A)]x(0) - B^{-1}f(0)$$

so that the solution for $x(2)$ becomes:

(14.14) $$x(2) = [I + B^{-1}(I - A)]x(1) - B^{-1}f(1)$$

where $x(1)$ is now known and so on. The general solution (Taylor, 1975) becomes:

(14.15) $$x(t) = [I + B^{-1}(I - A)]^t x(0) + x^*(t)$$

where the first term on the right-hand side is the 'homogeneous' equation and the second is the 'particular' solution.

Once appropriate assumptions have been made about the particular solution $x^*(t)$, the dynamic input–output model can be solved to give the time profile of output. Unfortunately, there are strong theoretical grounds (Chakravarty, 1969) for having little confidence in the results; solutions involving absurd rates of sectoral growth can only be avoided with certainty if very arbitrary restrictions are placed upon the model.

The instability of the dynamic model arises because the matrix involved in the solution—$[I + B^{-1}(I - A)]$—will not necessarily be 'well behaved'; the literature on this question is very technical, but we may note at once that the inverse of the capital matrix (B) is involved in the solution. If the capital goods industry is very undeveloped, this matrix will consist mainly of zeros so that it will be singular and cannot be inverted; solutions to this problem have, however, been suggested (Livesey, 1976).

A further problem with the dynamic model arises because the solution for the output vector in each period requires that the lag between capital installation and output increases be estimated correctly; if interpreted strictly, this means the balance equations would need to be written as:

(14.16) $$\begin{aligned} x(t) = {} & Ax(t) + B_1[x(t+1) - x(t)] + B_2[x(t+2) - x(t)] \\ & + \ldots + B_k[x(t+k) - x(t)] + f(t) \end{aligned}$$

where B_k refers to the capital matrix involving a gestation lag of k years and $\Sigma B_k = B$. This formulation vastly complicates the mathematics of the model and makes it even more uncertain that the implied sectoral growth rates will be plausible; if gestation lags are long, however, while the plan period is quite short, it means that the impact of investment on output increases can be ignored so that endogenous formulation of investment is not in any case needed.

The dynamic input–output model, unlike the inter-regional input–output model, is not particularly demanding in terms of additional data requirements.

The main problem is the construction of a capital stock or investment flow table from which the *B* matrix can be derived, but this is the same problem faced in 'static' models of investment behaviour within an input–output framework.

For LDCs to justify the use of 'static' or 'dynamic' models of investment behaviour, there must be in existence a capital goods industry of some description. Although only a handful of LDCs produce the bulk of their own plant and machinery requirements, it is quite possible that the number will grow in the next decade. For such countries, the dynamic input–output holds out considerable interest and they should not be put off unduly by the model's theoretical difficulties. Practical work with the model (e.g. Almon, 1974) has shown that it is in general stable and many of the mathematical problems can be solved with ingenuity. No more, however, will be said about the dynamic model in this book.

14.4 PRICE MODELS

In the simple input–output model (and even in most of its refinements), prices play the most marginal of parts; quantities are chosen (Leontief units) such that their price is unity and everything is cast in real terms; all price elasticities of substitution are assumed zero and money plays no more than an accommodating role.

It may therefore come as some surprise to readers unfamiliar with input–output techniques to find that price models can be computed from input–output tables which are useful in two very different contexts: (i) the study of efficiency; and (ii) the study of price determination. 'Efficiency price' models[4] have been developed primarily by East European economists in order to provide a rational basis for reforming the price systems of their countries; price determination models, on the other hand, have been developed mainly in the context of Western economies in an effort to understand better such things as the process of intersectoral price transmission and the wage-price spiral; both systems, with suitable modifications, can be useful to LDCs.

The reason why the input–output table can be used to compute price models is because the basic assumption of the input–output model concerns fixed coefficients of production and constant returns to scale; it follows that the long-run (supply) price of any commodity (sector) is not determined by the scale of output but by the invariant *unit* cost of production; thus, quantities do not appear in the price model (as we shall see) and it is possible to compute a set of prices without simultaneously determining a set of quantities.[5]

In the above paragraph, the phrase 'long-run (supply) price' is used advisedly because short-run (demand) considerations do not enter into the formation of prices in a simple input–output model; in practice, observed prices for commodities are affected by demand considerations and so the supply prices computed from input–output models have to be interpreted with care; following on Hicks' famous distinction between flex-price and fix-price systems (Hicks, 1965), some input–output economists have tried to partition the input–output matrix so as to conform to the division of commodities between those where demand considerations affect prices ('flex-price') and those where prices are determined by supply price alone ('fix-price') and have then used the input–output model to reflect this division; we shall mention below some examples of this work.

The efficiency and price determination models are rather different animals and it is best to describe them separately; we may begin with price determination models and note that the value of output is by definition equal to the value of inputs and can be written for the jth sector as:

$$x'_j p_j = x'_{1j} p_1 + x'_{2j} p_2 + \ldots + x'_{nj} p_n + l_j w_j + \Pi_j \tag{14.17}$$

where a prime (′) denotes physical quantities, each p_j is the price per unit of quantity, l_j is the direct physical labour input, w_j is the wage rate and Π_j is a residual equivalent to gross operating surplus.

If we now make the fundamental input–output assumption of fixed (physical) coefficients of production, we may divide equation (14.17) through by (x'_j) to obtain:

$$p_j = \sum_i \alpha_{ij} p_i + n_j w_j + \pi_j \tag{14.18}$$

where α_{ij} is the *physical* requirement from sector i per unit physical output of sector j, n_j is the labour requirement per unit of output and π_j is equivalent to profit per unit of output. Quantities have therefore been written out of the system and the price of one commodity is seen to depend on the price of all other goods.

With a few notable exceptions (e.g. China), input–output tables are not prepared in physical terms so that the α_{ij} are unobservable; instead, input–output tables are prepared in value terms, but by choosing quantities such that their price is unity, value coefficients (a_{ij}) and physical coefficients (α_{ij}) will coincide in the base year.[6] We may therefore write equation (14.18) as:

$$1 = \sum_i a_{ij} + n_j w_j + \pi_j \tag{14.19}$$

or in matrix form for all sectors:

$$i = [I - A']^{-1} [\hat{n} w + \pi] \tag{14.20}$$

where A' is the transpose of A—the input–output coefficients matrix—and $(\hat{n})$ is a diagonal matrix of labour coefficients, while w and π are vectors of wage rates and profits per unit respectively.

There are several interesting things to note about equation (14.20); the 'price' of any sector's output always equals unity and can be decomposed into accumulated labour and non-labour costs.[7] If factor costs should change, however, from those ruling in the base year, there will be a departure from this system of unit prices. This means that the price equations can be used to model price changes on the assumption of changing factor costs and can be written for any future period (t) as:

$$\tilde{p}(t) = [I - A']^{-1} [\hat{n}(t) w(t) + \pi(t)] \tag{14.21}$$

where $\tilde{p}(t)$ is a vector of price indices for period (t) with $\tilde{p}(0)$ equal to unity.[8]

Equation (14.21) is the fundamental equation for modelling price changes. It can be used, for example, to show the effect on prices of changes in the 'price' of any primary input; it can also be used to model inflation by allowing for observed changes in normal wage rates over time. It can be adapted in many ways, however, and indeed must be in the case of LDCs; most of the latter can be described as small, open economies for whom the principal source of cost-push inflation is not the rise in unit labour costs, but the influence on domestic costs of the steady rise in dollar prices for imports and of their conversion to domestic currency *via* depreciating exchange rates. These influences are not explicitly considered in equation (14.21) and need to be taken into account.

A model of inflation along these lines for Central America has been presented elsewhere by the author (Bulmer-Thomas, 1977b). The countries of Central America are joined in the Central American Common Market (CACM) so that free trade takes place within the region effectively in a common currency, while trade with the rest of the world (ROW) is subject to trade taxes and valued at world prices converted to home currency *via* the exchange rate plus protective duties. The cost of production per unit of output is therefore a function of domestic material (intermediate) costs per unit of output, foreign costs per unit of output and primary input costs other than foreign exchange but including tariffs. The system of equations can therefore be written for each of the countries in question as:

$$(14.22) \qquad \tilde{p}_D(t) = A'_D\tilde{p}_D(t) + A'_{cm}\tilde{p}_{cm}(t) + A'_{rw}(t)\tilde{p}_{rw}(t) + V'(t)i$$

where $\tilde{p}_D$, $\tilde{p}_{cm}$, $\tilde{p}_{rw}$ are the vectors of home prices, CACM prices and dollar prices from the rest of the world respectively, each with a base of unity; A_D is the domestic coefficients matrix, A_{cm} is the matrix of CACM import requirements per unit of output and $A_{rw}(t)$ is the matrix of ROW import requirements at time (t) per unit of output at c.i.f. prices, which is therefore obtained by multiplying each element of the base year matrix $(A_{rw}(0))$ expressed in dollar prices by index numbers representing the depreciation of the exchange rate. Finally V is a matrix of primary input requirements consisting of labour costs, indirect taxes, subsidies, tariffs and profits per unit of output, while a prime (′)—as before—denotes a transposed matrix.

Under the simplifying assumptions of the model, home and CACM prices are the same; the solution to the model can therefore be written:

$$(14.23) \qquad \tilde{p}_D(t) = [I - A'_D - A'_{cm}]^{-1}[A'_{rw}(t)\tilde{p}_{rw}(t) + V'(t)i]$$

The exogenous forces affecting home prices are therefore world prices, exchange rates and other primary input prices. By varying these, one can work out the contribution to domestic inflation of the change in question; for example, one element in $\tilde{p}_{rw}(t)$ is the c.i.f. price of crude oil in dollar terms; by varying this in line with observed OPEC price increases, one can work out the impact on domestic prices of oil price increases.

The trouble with this approach is that it is somewhat partial; if oil prices rise, thereby driving up home prices, it is unreasonable to expect workers not to attempt to preserve the real value of their wages; similarly, although profits are a residual, this does not mean entrepreneurs do not have some notion about the equilibrium relationship between profits and the value of output which they attempt to secure; by assuming that the price of labour responds like any other price in an input–output world to changes in its cost of production and by assuming that entrepreneurs seek a fixed relationship between profits and the value of output, we can increase the realism of the model and write:

$$(14.24) \qquad \tilde{p}_D(t) = [I - A'_D - A'_{cm} - \hat{\pi}^*]^{-1}[A'_{RW}(t)\tilde{p}_{rw}(t) + V'(t)i]$$

which is a system of $(n+1)$ equations with the extra equation being accounted for by the price of labour (so that A_D, A_{CM} and A_{RW} each have one extra row and column), where $\hat{\pi}^*$ is a diagonal matrix whose elements denote the ratio between profits and the value of output sought by entrepreneurs, and V is now written exclusive of labour costs and profits.

Three simulations in Central America were carried out using equation (14.24) in order to compare the observed rise in prices with the simulated ones;[9] the results are given in Table 14.1 which shows that actual price changes (see column 1) are usually underestimated when entrepreneurs do *not* respond to squeezed profits by raising prices to protect margins (see columns 2 and 3), while they are in general overestimated when it is assumed that they *do* succeed in securing the desired ratio between profits and the value of output (see column 4). This emphasizes the importance of short-run demand considerations in determining actual, observed prices and so we now turn to ways of incorporating these effects into input–output analysis.

In a fixed-price world, demand–supply adjustments are carried out through output changes; with constant returns to scale (as in the simple input–output model), increases in supply can occur without a change in price. As the demand curve shifts out, equilibrium occurs at the same price at different points on the supply schedule.

In many sectors, output changes are not a realistic response to short-run demand changes; in the extreme case, output can be produced at constant cost up to a certain limit, but cannot be increased at all beyond it; the supply curve is now vertical and equilibrium is achieved by price rather than quantity variations; this price, however, will depend on the shift of the demand curve and so the simple input–output model in which prices are set by unit costs of production no longer holds.

The adaptation of the input–output model to deal with this problem requires a simple partition of the price vector and coefficient matrices according to whether prices are set by costs of production alone (p_1) or whether demand considerations are also relevant (p_2). The latter have to be assumed exogenous, so the solution for the former is:

$$(14.25) \qquad \tilde{p}_1 = A'_{11}\tilde{p}_1 + A'_{21}\tilde{p}_2 + V_1 = [I - A'_{11}]^{-1}A'_{12}\tilde{p}_2 + [I - A'_{11}]^{-1}V_1$$

where A_{ij} is the i, jth partition of the A matrix corresponding to the partition of

Table 14.1 A simulated wholesale price index for Costa Rica, 1974 (1968 = 1.00)

		(1)	(2)	(3)	(4)
1	Basic grains	1.910	1.4407	1.692	2.465
2	Other agricultural products	3.433	1.384	1.510	2.716
3	Meat and milk products	1.828	1.284	1.428	2.767
4	Grain milling	2.441	1.509	1.773	2.684
5	Bakeries	2.441	1.477	1.719	2.804
6	Sugar refining	2.441	1.344	1.517	2.777
7	Other manufactured foods	1.499	1.543	1.819	2.680
8	Drink	1.376	1.348	1.527	2.701
9	Tobacco products	1.596	1.203	1.306	2.698
10	Textiles and clothing	2.132	1.705	2.071	2.519
11	Leather products and shoes	2.132	1.568	1.845	2.720
12	Wood products and furniture	2.310	1.426	1.632	2.774
13	Paper and printing	1.729	1.770	2.243	2.021
14	Chemical products	1.838	1.800	2.263	2.253
15	Oil refining	2.860	3.179	3.449	3.665
16	Glass and ceramics	1.874	1.817	2.279	2.280
17	Construction materials	2.196	1.595	1.939	2.398
18	Metal products	2.569	1.832	2.353	2.032
19	Electrical goods	2.350	1.840	2.345	2.114
20	Other manufactured goods	2.244	1.920	2.443	2.265
21	Electricity	1.720	1.294	1.429	2.801
	Wholesale price index	2.0833	1.5916	1.9135	2.4314

(1) Actual price relative.
(2) Derived assuming a 10% annual average rate of increase of dollar prices, and profits fixed in absolute money terms per unit of output.
(3) As for (2), but assuming 15% annual average rate of increase of dollar prices.
(4) As for (2), but assuming profits to bear a fixed relation to the value of output.
Source: Bulmer-Thomas (1977b), Table 7.

the price vector and V_1 is the (column) vector of value added coefficients for the fix-price commodities.

The distinction between fix- and flex-price commodities was first introduced into the input–output literature by Mathur (1977), and an empirical study on these lines has been attempted for India (Radhakrishna, 1979) with particular reference to the edible oil industries; in that study, it was found that cost-based prices alone underestimated observed price changes, but by superimposing demand considerations on the former, much greater accuracy was introduced into the model.

We now turn to the second main use of input–output price models, the calculation of efficiency prices; if we return to equation (14.18), we may see that the price of commodity j depends, among other things, on π_j—the profit per unit of output. The latter, however, is a residual which in the base year reflects short-run demand considerations, monopoly profits, the effects of price control, etc.; an 'efficient' system of prices should not depend on anything so arbitrary. Furthermore, the profit per unit of output should bear some relationship to the cost of capital; we may therefore re-estimate profit per unit of output (π_j^*) in the most general case (Brown, 1977) by making it a function of material, labour and capital costs; if this relationship is assumed to be proportional it can be written:

$$\pi_j^* = \beta_1 \sum_i \alpha_{ij} p_i + \beta_2 n_j w_j + \beta_3 \sum_i b_{ij} p_i \tag{14.26}$$

where (β_1, β_2, β_3) are the factors of proportionality for material costs ($\Sigma_i \alpha_{ij} p_i$), labour costs ($n_j w_j$) and capital costs ($\Sigma_i b_{ij} p_i$) respectively, and b_{ij} is the physical stock of capital good i per unit of output in sector j.

If we now rewrite the price equations making use of the new definition of profits per unit of output (π_j^*), they become in matrix form:

$$p^* = (1+\beta_1)\alpha' p^* + (1+\beta_2)\hat{n} w + \beta_3 B' p^* \tag{14.27}$$

where p^* is the new (unobserved) vector of efficiency prices consistent with rational determination of the residual profits per unit of output, B is the matrix with b_{ij} as its i, jth element and α is the matrix of physical input–output coefficients. The physical input–output coefficients are not in general known; it is therefore necessary to rewrite the formulae in terms of the observed value coefficients (a_{ij}). We may do this by defining at the start an index number p_j^{**} equal to the ratio of the efficiency price (p_j^*) to the absolute price (p_j), i.e. $p_j^{**} = p_j^*/p_j$. We can therefore replace all (p_j^*) by ($p_j p_j^{**}$) and equation (14.27) becomes:

$$\hat{p} p^{**} = (1+\beta_1)\alpha' \hat{p} p^{**} + (1+\beta_2)\hat{n} w + \beta_3 B' \hat{p} p^{**} \tag{14.28}$$

In the base year, however, by choosing quantities to correspond to Leontief units all elements of the p vector are unity, so we may replace ($\alpha'\hat{p}$) with (A') and ($B'\hat{p}$) with ($B^{*\prime}$)—the matrix of capital output ratios in value terms. Thus, we get:

$$p^{**} = (1+\beta_1)A' p^{**} + (1+\beta_2)\hat{n} w + \beta_3 B^{*\prime} p^{**} \tag{14.29}$$

which differs from the price determination equation (14.21) because profit per unit is now estimated on the basis of its equilibrium relationship to material, labour and capital costs. If the jth element of p^{**} is less than unity, the efficiency price is less than the actual price so that the latter may be said to exceed the opportunity cost of the factors employed directly and indirectly.

In equation (14.29), efficiency prices are shown to depend on material, labour and capital costs; for that reason, they are sometimes called 'three-channel prices' (Sekerka, 1970). Equation (14.29), however, cannot yet be solved because it contains $(n+3)$ unknowns (p^{**}, β_1, β_2, β_3) and only n equations. In applications to socialist economies (e.g. Bródy, 1970), it is customary to add an additional constraint[10] and set two of the proportionality constants exogenously; an alternative is to set $\beta_1, \beta_2 = 0$, and to assume a certain rate of return on capital ($= \beta_3$), so that the system of efficiency prices is then equivalent to the price that would rule if the rate of profit was equalized in all branches of the economy. A comparison of these prices with actual prices would then show up those sectors which were uncompetitive and so making 'monopoly' profits. For example, with an assumed 10 % rate of return on capital, the solution for the vector of efficiency prices becomes:

(14.30) $$p^{**} = [I - A' - 0.1B^{*\prime}]^{-1}\hat{n}w$$

so that $p_j^{**} < 1$ implies that the jth sector is making monopoly profits.

The author knows of no studies for LDCs which make use of these efficiency prices, but there is no reason why such studies could not be carried out; there are a large number of price sets which can be computed according to the assumptions made about the proportionality factors and some of these are more appropriate than others for LDCs; there is one way, however, in which LDCs could make use of efficiency prices, and that is to provide a basis for international comparisons of input–output tables. By revaluing the input–output coefficient matrices of two countries in terms of one set of efficiency prices, international comparisons can be carried out which are not disturbed by differences in relative prices; in this way, underlying differences in technology are more likely to be revealed without the distortions imposed by a comparison of value coefficients (cf. Drábek, 1980).

14.5 OPTIMIZATION MODELS

In simple input–output models, there is nothing to optimize; in the quantity model, a given bill of final goods yields one and only one feasible set of outputs while in the price model a given set of primary input coefficients provides only one possible vector of prices; with only one consistent and feasible solution, there is no room for choice and therefore nothing to optimize.

Choice can, of course, be introduced into the input–output model; because of its thorough-going linearity, a common method adopted for doing this is linear programming (LP); we may begin, therefore, by setting up the input–output model as if it were an LP problem, although we already know that the one feasible solution will be the optimal one. By setting it up this way, however, we can see more clearly how to introduce choice into the model.

In terms of LP semantics, the input–output quantity circuit is known as the primal and the price circuit as the dual; let us suppose, therefore, we are concerned with maximizing aggregate value added; this maximization problem involves the output vector (x) and a set of unknown value added coefficients (v) and the functional constraints are provided by the input–output balance equations; the formal statement of the primal is therefore:

$$\text{Max. } u = \sum_{i=1}^{n} v_i x_i$$

subject to:

(14.31)
$$\begin{aligned} (1-a_{11})x_1 - a_{12}x_2 - \cdots - a_{1n}x_n &\geqslant f_1 \\ -a_{21}x_1 + (1-a_{22})x_2 - \cdots - a_{2n}x_n &\geqslant f_2 \\ \vdots \qquad\qquad \vdots \qquad\qquad\qquad \vdots \quad &\quad \vdots \\ -a_{n1}x_1 - a_{n2}x_2 - \cdots + (1-a_{nn})x_n &\geqslant f_n \end{aligned}$$

and $x_i \geqslant 0 \qquad i = 1, \ldots, n.$

As with all LP models, there is a dual associated with this problem which can be written:

$$\text{Min. } z = \sum_{i=1}^{n} p_i f_i$$

subject to:

$$\begin{aligned} (1-a_{11})p_1 - a_{21}p_2 - \cdots - a_{n1}p_n &\leqslant v_1 \\ -a_{12}p_1 + (1-a_{22})p_2 - \cdots - a_{n2}p_n &\leqslant v_2 \\ \vdots \qquad\qquad \vdots \qquad\qquad\qquad \vdots \quad &\quad \vdots \\ -a_{1n}p_1 - a_{2n}p_2 - \cdots + (1-a_{nn})p_n &\leqslant v_n \end{aligned} \tag{14.32}$$

and $p_i \geqslant 0 \qquad i = 1, \ldots, n.$

The reason why there is no choice in input–output models is now easy to see; in equation (14.31), the balance relationships have been written as inequalities, but any excess of production over demand will simply go into inventories (a component of f). The relationships can therefore be written as equalities; the number of activities is now n (x_i; $i = 1, \ldots, n$), but there are the same number of functional constraints. There are therefore no degrees of freedom and the one feasible solution to equation (14.31) is therefore the one which solves the maximization problem; as for the dual, we know from LP theory that the shadow price of any resource in the optimal solution (p_i) should be exactly equal to the opportunity cost of its inputs; this means that the functional constraints of the dual (14.32) must also be written as equalities giving one feasible price set which is also the one which solves the minimization problem. The latter is equivalent to minimizing national expenditure ($\Sigma p_i f_i$), while the maximization problem is equivalent to maximizing national income ($\Sigma v_i x_i$); just as required by LP theory, therefore, the maximum value of u is also the minimum value of z.

The solution to the quantity model will certainly be consistent, but it may not necessarily be economically feasible; it may, for example, put undue strain on primary inputs, some of which are in fixed supply; furthermore, its balance of payments implications may be unacceptable. This suggests that we can add additional constraints to equation (14.31) which can be written as inequalities since not all of the scarce resource will necessarily be used up. Furthermore, the elements of f in equation (14.31) include exports and competitive imports; it is therefore unreasonable to write each f_i as a constant, since we want the choice between the two to be based on considerations of comparative cost. We can therefore expand the functional constraints of equation (14.31) by including exports and imports as (unknown) variables and add additional resource constraints written as inequalities; this will give us more activities than there are functional constraints and so a choice of variables becomes necessary. By using the Simplex criterion (see Dorfman, 1958) only those variables which make the greatest contribution to the maximand will be included in the optimal solution, and their shadow price will be exactly equal to their opportunity cost of production, which in turn will measure the marginal contribution of the resource to the maximand.

There are other ways of introducing choice into the input–output model,[11] but the above is in barest outline the form most commonly adopted for LDCs (e.g. Bruno, 1966; 1971). The advantages of this approach are to be found not so much in its point optimal solution, but in its ability through parametric programming to trace out efficiency frontiers for an economy; furthermore, as individual constraints are relaxed (e.g. the availability of foreign aid), it is possible to rank sectors in terms of comparative advantage according to the point at which they leave the optimal solution. This has obvious implications for development planning, and we shall return to this point in Chapter 17.

Optimization models based on input–output techniques enjoyed an enormous popularity for about fifteen years from 1960 and became very sophisticated, including their extension to a dynamic framework (e.g. Bruno, 1972a). As our understanding of the way these models work has increased, there has been something of a reaction; the major difficulties appear to arise because of the linear character of the models. This gives rise to all or nothing solutions, which are reflected in the primal by unrealistic output levels and in the dual by zero shadow prices for resources which are not fully utilized; the economics of LP models are therefore rather crude and, although practitioners have attempted to circumvent the problem by putting upper and lower bounds on variables, this always looks somewhat arbitrary and runs the danger of imposing a solution on the model before it is run.[12] We shall, however, return to the optimization model in Chapter 15, section 6.

NOTES

1 Even in Scotland, a large region of a developed country, it is not possible to find more than a handful of industries whose output is confined to intra-regional sales.

2 On the grounds that what we are trying to measure is the inter-regional feedback not the international feedback.

3 Replacement expenditures can be related to sectoral output levels and made endogenous (see Taylor, 1975, p. 53) and inventory change can also be made endogenous (see Shishido, 1976), but the underlying data in LDCs on these two types of capital expenditure almost never justify this kind of investment in technique.

4 The prices in these models are called 'efficient', because they are supposed to be based on a full-cost pricing principle with each input evaluated at its shadow price.

5 Some input–output economists at the frontier of this subject have become dissatisfied with the 'duality' between quantity and prices and have started to work with models in which quantities and prices depend on each other (as in the Walrasian general equilibrium scheme) and have to be solved simultaneously (see Dieckheuer, 1979; and Ghosh, 1979b). It is fair to say, however, that these models are still at a very preliminary stage and do not yet offer concrete planning possibilities for LDCs.

6 The definition of a_{ij} is $(x'_{ij}p_i/x'_jp_j) = \alpha_{ij}(p_i/p_j)$. With $p_i = p_j = 1$, we get $a_{ij} = \alpha_{ij}$.

7 Let $[I - A']^{-1} = R' = \{r'_{ij}\}$. Then the unit price of the ith sector is equal to $\Sigma_j r'_{ij} n_j w_j + \Sigma_j r'_{ij} \pi_j$, i.e. direct and indirect labour costs and direct and indirect non-labour costs. We have already seen an example of this in Table 12.1, where accumulated primary inputs in each sector sum to unity.

8 Equation (14.21) has been written on the assumption that the coefficient matrix (A) is invariant with respect to time, although this assumption could easily be relaxed.

9 Equation (14.24) can only be carried out for one country at a time and the country chosen was Costa Rica.

10 An example is that the aggregate value of all commodities consumed should be the same whether efficiency or actual prices are used (see Brown, 1977, p. 193).

11 For example, by allowing alternative techniques of production for each commodity, only one of which can actually be chosen (Chenery, 1959) or by entering as activities industries where demand is currently met by imports, (Clark, 1970).

12 For further criticism of the shadow prices emerging from LP models, see the essays by Bruno and Taylor in Blitzer (1975).

CHAPTER 15

Imports, Exports and Comparative Advantage

15.1 INTRODUCTION

In their efforts to accelerate economic development, many LDCs have experienced acute foreign exchange shortages. As a result, economists have come to view the foreign exchange constraint as a major obstacle to a rapid rate of economic growth and an extensive literature has evolved in support of this claim (see, for example, Landau, 1971). Economic development programmes have often been concerned with saving foreign exchange through import substituting industrialization (ISI); these efforts, however, to save foreign exchange appear in many cases to have exacerbated the foreign exchange shortage and one of the purposes of this chapter will be the resolution of this paradox using input–output techniques (see section 2).

Although ISI policies are often designed primarily to save foreign exchange, it is clear that some ISI programmes can be more efficient than others. What is needed is a ranking of sectors in terms of their comparative efficiency in saving foreign exchange so that import substitution can be carried out rationally. Furthermore, with the renewed interest in exports being shown by LDCs, it becomes important to carry out the same analysis in terms of the ability of sectors to *earn* foreign exchange so that the division between importing and exporting sectors can be determined by reference to comparative advantage.

Input–output analysis can contribute to establishing the ranking of sectors in terms of comparative advantage, as will be shown in this chapter (see section 5). However, a more accurate assessment of comparative advantage requires that domestic and foreign costs be evaluated in terms of shadow prices; this involves a programming extension of the basic input–output model, which will be considered as well in section 6.

We also consider in this chapter two closely related issues, where input–output analysis plays a fundamental role: the measurement of import substitution and the determinants of the pattern of international trade (sections 3 and 4 respectively). In the former case, we consider how indirect imports affect the measurement problem while in the latter, we look at the factor content (direct and indirect) of exports and import replacements.

15.2 THE IMPORT INTENSITY OF IMPORT SUBSTITUTING INDUSTRIALIZATION

When domestic production is substituted for imports of any commodity, there is a gross saving of foreign exchange equivalent to the dollar cost of the import; the net saving, however, will be less than the gross if increased domestic production requires foreign exchange directly (as imported inputs) or indirectly (as imports into domestic inputs).

In Chapter 7, alternative treatments of imports were discussed at some length; it was shown that, although data limitations may compel the use of a single vector for imports as negative final demand, the preferred treatment involves a complete matrix statement of imports. Such a statement, involving the allocation of all imports by source and by use, maximizes the alternatives for modelling imports.

In the case of ISI, there tends to be a complementary relationship between imports and domestic production. Industry tends to obtain its intermediate and capital inputs from abroad until such time as policy changes induce local production and there is a switch from imports. The demand for non-consumer good imports, therefore, is primarily a function of the level of industry output and we can write the equation for imports in accordance with equation (7.10) as:

$$m = A_m x + h^m \tag{15.1}$$

where m is the vector of imports, x of activity levels, h^m is the (exogenous) vector of final demand imports and A_m is a matrix of import coefficients; if we employ the solution for the output vector given by equation (7.9), we obtain for imports:

$$m = A_m[I - A_D]^{-1}\,[h^d + e] + h^m = Mf^d + h^m \tag{15.2}$$

where $M = A_m[I - A_D]^{-1}$ and f_d represents both home final demand (h^d) and exports (e).

If equation (15.2) is written out in full, it becomes:

$$\begin{aligned} m_1 &= m_{11}f_1^d + m_{12}f_2^d + \cdots + m_{1n}f_n^d + h_1^m \\ m_2 &= m_{21}f_1^d + m_{22}f_2^d + \cdots + m_{2n}f_n^d + h_2^m \\ &\vdots \\ m_n &= m_{n1}f_1^d + m_{n2}f_2^d + \cdots + m_{nn}f_n^d + h_n^m \end{aligned} \tag{15.3}$$

which makes it easier to follow the process of ISI. Assume, for example, that a decision is taken to replace one unit of imports in the first sector ($\Delta h_1^m = -1$) by local production for final demand ($\Delta f_1^d = 1$). The direct and indirect requirements of imports from all sources are then given by $\Sigma_i m_{i1}$, so that the net savings of foreign exchange from ISI become $(1 - \Sigma_i m_{i1})$ in terms of domestic currency, which can be converted to foreign currency by application of the appropriate exchange rate.[1]

The column sums of the M matrix denote total import requirements when final demand for the activity listed in the column increases by unity; direct import requirements are given by the column sums of A_m so that indirect import requirements are given by the column sums of $(M - A_m)$. Examples of these calculations are given in Table 15.1 for Costa Rica, where in addition imports from the Central American Common Market (CACM) are distinguished from imports from the rest of the world (ROW).

The results show the importance of including indirect imports in the calculation of import intensity (see last column of Table 15.1); there are several cases where indirect imports are more important than direct (such as wood products) and in all cases except the 'finishing touch' industries (e.g. metal products) they account for a sizeable proportion of total import requirements. The table also shows the unimportance of CACM as a source of intermediate goods, confirming the view that industrialization in Central America has been very largely restricted to consumer goods production.

A complete understanding of how ISI can exacerbate a foreign exchange shortage requires more than input–output analysis, since we need to show the impact of ISI policies on the traditional export sectors (*via* changes in the internal terms of trade) and to introduce the lag between import needs and output increases (see Little, 1970, and Diaz-Alejandro, 1965). However, improvements can be made in input–output analysis by allowing for the effect of capacity expansions in the import-substituting industries.

When domestic production increases as a result of ISI policies, we may assume that new capacity will be laid down; if the new capacity requires imports of capital goods, there is a further direct stimulus to the import bill; if it requires locally made capital goods, there is an indirect stimulus to imports through the demand for intermediate imports needed directly and indirectly to meet the increased output in the capital goods industry. With capital–output matrices available as described in Chapter 11 (section 3), it is possible to capture both these effects.

Making use of equation (11.6) we can write the solution for imports as:

$$m = A_m x + B_m \Delta x + h_m^* \qquad (15.4)$$

where B_m is the imported capital–output coefficient matrix, h_m^* is final demand imports including replacement expenditure, and Δx is a vector of capacity expansions. As was shown in section 3 of Chapter 11, we can replace Δx by the expression $[I - A_D]^{-1} \Delta h_d^*$, so that equation (15.4) now becomes:

$$m = A_m x + B_m [I - A_D]^{-1} \Delta h_d^* + h_m \qquad (15.5)$$

where Δh_d^* is the change in the domestic final demand vector inclusive of replacement expenditure.

When allowance is made for capacity expansion, the solution for x (see Chapter 11.3) becomes:

$$x = [I - A_D]^{-1} \{ B_D [I - A_D]^{-1} \Delta h_d^* + h_d^* \} \qquad (15.6)$$

so that the solution for imports can now be written:

$$\begin{aligned} m &= A_m [I - A_D]^{-1} \{ B_D [I - A_D]^{-1} \Delta h_d^* + h_d^* \} + B_m [I - A_D]^{-1} \Delta h_d^* + h_m^* \\ &= MK \Delta h_d^* + M h_d^* + L \Delta h_d^* + h_m^* \qquad (15.7) \\ &= [MK + L] \Delta h_d^* + M h_d^* + h_m^* \end{aligned}$$

Table 15.1 The import intensity of Costa Rican industry (1968) by area of origin per 1000 unit change in output

Sector		Direct and indirect imports from CACM	Direct and indirect imports from ROW	Total import intensity	Direct import requirements	Indirect import requirements
1	Meat and milk products	27.7	71.1	98.8	13.7	85.1
2	Fish tinning	22.6	128.1	150.7	52.2	98.5
3	Edible oils	255.1	106.6	361.7	263.3	98.4
4	Coffee processing	19.9	91.9	111.8	1.3	110.5
5	Grain milling	54.7	242.4	297.1	223.9	73.2
6	Bakeries	81.1	153.8	234.9	57.3	177.6
7	Sugar refining	11.9	88.6	100.5	17.2	83.3
8	Other manufactured foods	63.7	142.2	205.9	123.5	82.4
9	Drinks	38.0	92.2	130.2	87.3	42.9
10	Tobacco products	4.3	91.6	95.9	55.2	40.7
11	Textiles and clothing	113.7	183.3	297.0	196.1	100.9
12	Leather products and shoes	65.8	167.0	232.8	140.2	92.6
13	Wood products and furniture	19.6	112.6	132.2	25.9	106.3
14	Paper and printing	50.5	492.2	542.7	509.8	32.9
15	Chemical products	51.2	368.2	419.4	351.6	67.8
16	Oil refining	36.1	719.6	755.7	745.5	10.2
17	Tyre production	20.0	273.6	293.6	233.9	59.7
18	Plastic and rubber products	25.1	269.5	294.6	229.1	65.5
19	Glass and ceramics	59.3	253.5	312.8	251.8	61.0
20	Construction materials	36.9	137.0	173.9	112.7	61.2
21	Metal products	57.9	478.2	536.1	506.1	30.0
22	Electrical goods	52.5	466.1	518.6	464.3	54.3
23	Transport equipment	4.6	581.9	586.5	563.8	22.7
24	Other manufacturing	23.8	320.7	344.5	276.2	68.3

Notes: CACM = Central American Common Market.
ROW = Rest of World excluding CACM.
Source: Derived from Bulmer-Thomas (1977a).

where

$$M = A_m[I - A_D]^{-1}$$
$$K = B_D[I - A_D]^{-1}$$
$$L = B_m[I - A_D]^{-1}$$

Equation (15.7) looks formidable, but is really quite straightforward. As before, imports are seen to consist of an exogenous part h_m^* (which is mainly consumer goods imports), as well as intermediate imports required to sustain current output levels—Mh_d^*. This time, however, allowance is made for imports needed to produce extensions to the local capital goods industry—$MK\Delta h_d^*$—as well as capital goods imports themselves—$L\Delta h_d^*$.

Imagine now that a decision is taken to expand local industry by one unit at the expense of imports with no changes elsewhere. The increase in imports will be:

$$\Delta m = [MK + L]\Delta^2 h_d^* + M\Delta h_d^* + \Delta h_m \tag{15.8}$$

where $\Delta^2 h_d^*$ is the change *in the change* in final demand between two periods. For the industry in question, however, this change is unity with no change in the other industries so that the additional imports can be calculated by summing down the appropriate columns of M, MK and L.

Results from these experiments are given for Brazil in Table 15.2.[2] Import substitution in intermediate goods is far advanced in Brazil and this is reflected in the first two columns of the table giving the direct and total import intensity when the import intensity of capacity expansion is excluded. When the latter is included, however (see columns 4 and 5), import intensity increases substantially, reflecting the comparatively underdeveloped nature of the Brazilian capital goods industry.

15.3 THE MEASUREMENT OF IMPORT SUBSTITUTION AND THE IMPACT OF ISI

In the previous section, it was noted how the net savings of foreign exchange from ISI might be less than the gross saving as a result of the import intensity of the industrialization process itself. It follows that a net saving in foreign exchange of unity requires a greater increase in local production than that implied by a gross saving of unity and, furthermore, that these production increases will need to take place in sectors outside the one where (direct) import replacement is occurring.

An example will make this clearer; suppose a decision is taken to replace 1000 units of imported cloth by local production; in order that imports should fall by 1000 units, local production of cotton, yarn, textiles, etc. will have to increase—otherwise the cloth industry's direct and indirect input requirements will either be met from abroad or deprive some existing user.

The increased cloth production is clearly due to import substitution; however, the increase in related industries (cotton, textiles, yarn) is also due to import

Table 15.2 Direct and indirect import intensity of Brazilian production (1970) per 1000 unit change in output

Sector	Direct imports	Indirect imports excluding those due to capacity expansion	Sub-total	Indirect imports due to capacity expansion	Total
Agriculture	5.2	12.1	17.3	89.7	107.0
Mining	0.4	9.9	10.3	84.4	94.7
Metal products	37.5	30.2	67.7	108.3	176.0
Chemicals	125.9	25.5	151.4	101.7	253.1
Agro-industries	18.9	22.6	41.5	112.3	153.8
Other industrial products	18.4	21.4	39.8	139.9	179.7
Construction	20.0	27.0	47.0	121.9	168.9
Transport and distribution	15.8	7.7	23.5	81.2	104.7
Services	1.3	5.5	6.8	82.0	88.8

Source: Derived by the author from tables in IBGE (1979) and elsewhere.

substitution in the cloth industry. It follows that, when measuring the contribution of import substitution to the growth of an industry, we must also take account of any increase in output which was caused by import substitution in other sectors.

In a seminal article some years ago, Chenery (1960) pioneered an approach to industrialization which enables one to isolate the import substitution effect from other effects in the above proportional growth of an industry, i.e. above what would be expected if the industry's growth rate were the same as that of GDP. The Chenery measure can be written:

$$(15.9) \quad x_i(1) - x_i(p) = \Delta x_i = [1 - u_i(0)](\Delta h_i + \Delta e_i) + [u_i(0) - u_i(1)]Z_i(1)$$

where

- $x_i(p)$ = the output of the ith industry in the terminal year on the assumption of proportionality.
- $x_i(1)$ = the actual output of the ith industry in terminal year.
- Δh_i = the non-proportional increase in intermediate and final demand.
- Δe_i = the non-proportional increase in exports.
- $Z_i(1)$ = total supply of ith product in terminal year.
- $u_i(0)$ = the ratio of imports to total supply of ith product in base year.
- $u_i(1)$ = the ratio of imports to total supply of ith product in terminal year.

so that non-proportional increases in output are broken down into non-proportional changes in demand—$[1 - u_i(0)](\Delta h_i + \Delta e_i)$—and import substitution $[u_i(0) - u_i(1)]Z_i(1)$.

The Chenery approach has stimulated a great deal of research on patterns of industrialization and has focused our attention on the crucial role played in industrialization by import substitution. It is an inadequate measure, however, to the extent that the import substitution effect is limited to the direct effect of substitution in an industry and does not take account of the increases in output which may be due to substitution elsewhere (see Morley, 1970).

When a distinction is made between home sales (h_i) and exports (e_i), we may note a further deficiency in the Chenery measure; this arises because the growth of exports in an industry above a factor of proportionality, for example, generates increases in output elsewhere in the economy which are due to the increase in exports in the first industry; with the Chenery measure (even though modified to allow for a separate export effect) these increases would be incorrectly accredited (see Tyler, 1976).

We shall now show how input–output analysis can be used to provide a more adequate measure of the sources of industrial growth.[3] In matrix terms, the balance equations can be written in the terminal year:

$$(15.10) \qquad x(1) + m(1) = Ax(1) + h(1) + e(1)$$

so that

(15.11) $$x(1) = [I-A]^{-1}h(1)+[I-A]^{-1}e(1)-[I-A]^{-1}m(1) = h^*(1)+e^*(1)-m^*(1)$$

The vectors e^*, m^* now represent the redefinition of exports and imports respectively to take account of the indirect impact of export promotion and import substitution on the output of all sectors. For example, if exports in all sectors are to increase by one unit, then the output of all sectors of the economy must increase by $[I-A]^{-1}i$ in order to achieve this without depriving existing users or absorbing additional imports. Similarly, if imports in all sectors are to be reduced by one unit, output will have to rise by the same amount.

Since imports enter into home sales only and not into exports, we can write equation (15.11) as:

(15.12) $$x(1) = [I-\hat{u}(1)^*]h(1)^* + e(1)^*$$

where

$$\hat{u}(1)^* = [\hat{m}(1)^*][\hat{h}(1)^*]^{-1}.$$

which by sleight of hand becomes:

(15.13) $$x(1) = h(1)^* - \hat{u}(1)^*h(1)^* + \hat{u}(0)^*h(1)^* - \hat{u}(0)^*h(1)^* + e(1)^*$$

or

(15.14) $$x(1) = [I-\hat{u}(0)^*]h(1)^* + [\hat{u}(0)^* - \hat{u}(1)^*]h(1)^* + e(1)^*$$

With proportional growth, output can be written as:

(15.15) $$x(p) = [I-\hat{u}(0)^*]h(p)^* + e(p)^*$$

so that

(15.16) $$[x(1)-x(p)] = [I-\hat{u}(0)^*]\Delta h^* + \Delta e^* + [\hat{u}(0)^* - \hat{u}(1)^*]h(1)^*$$

where $[I-\hat{u}(0)^*]\Delta h^*$ is the growth in output due to non-proportional changes in home final demand, (Δe^*) is the growth in output due to non-proportional changes in exports and $[\hat{u}(0)^* - \hat{u}(1)^*]h(1)^*$ is the growth in output due to import substitution.

Equations such as (15.16) have been used to measure the contribution of import substitution and export promotion to industrial growth. By dividing the right-hand side of the equation by the output change on the left-hand side, the contribution of domestic demand, export promotion and import substitution can be expressed in percentage form; in Brazil, for example (see Tyler, 1976, Table III.2), import substitution was important as a source of above proportional growth in industry (23.5 %) from 1949 to 1964, but negligible thereafter. Export expansion, however, increased in importance from 2 % in the earlier period to nearly 6 % in 1967–71. In all periods, domestic demand shows up as a very important source of above proportional growth, although the position varies considerably when individual sectors within industry are examined.

15.4 THE DETERMINANTS OF THE PATTERN OF INTERNATIONAL TRADE

In the pure theory of international trade, there has been no more popular idea to explain the pattern of international trade than that associated with the names of Hecksher and Ohlin; the Hecksher–Ohlin model can be used to demonstrate rigorously that, on the basis of some rather restrictive assumptions,[4] countries will export commodities which are intensive in the use of that country's relatively abundant factor of production and will import commodities which are intensive in the use of the relatively scarce factor.

The model has been extensively criticized (see, for example, Minhas, 1962) for its restrictive assumptions and it works best where the number of factors of production in question is limited to two;[5] nonetheless, it has stood the passage of time remarkably well, having been subject to extensive empirical testing.

The model can be extended to the case of many commodities (but not factors) quite easily (see Jones, 1956–7); it is then possible to test the model's hypothesis against the trade data of a given country. In the case of exports there is no great problem, because what is required is an examination of their factor content as given by the country's existing economic structure and destination of sales; in the case of imports, however, there is a serious difficulty because their factor content may differ according to the country of origin.

The solution is provided by the definition of relative factor abundance; a country can only be described as relatively abundant in a particular factor when compared with another country or group of countries; it follows that the factor content of imports should be determined in relation to that same country or group of countries.

This means that we cannot determine the factor content of imports by reference to import replacing industries, as is done in some studies (Leontief, 1966). Instead, we must examine the factor content of exports in the country or group of countries from which the first country is importing. If the assumptions of the Hecksher–Ohlin model are correct, it would not make any difference which procedure was adopted; when testing the model, however, one is really testing its assumptions and so it is more appropriate to consider the factor content of actual imports.

If the model holds, analysis of the factor content of imports and exports can serve as a useful check on the rationality of the pattern of international trade. Thus, confirmation of the Hecksher–Ohlin hypothesis by the factor content of trade provides *prima facie* evidence that a country has chosen to specialize in products which reflect her comparative advantage, whereas the opposite results would prove either that trade policies need drastic revision or that the assumptions of the model do not hold.

How do we assess the factor content of trade? If we examine the direct factor content of a unit of exports, say, we may obtain a misleading idea of its factor intensity because we have ignored indirect factor use; to produce one unit of exports requires intermediate inputs which in turn have factor requirements. The indirect requirements of any factor may be sufficiently important to reverse the ranking of sectors according to direct requirements and they must therefore be taken into account.

Input–output analysis is ideally suited to determining the total factor content of trade and therefore has a crucial role to play in any test of rationality of trade patterns. We may recall that the sum of the elements of the jth column of the Leontief inverse represents the increase in output in all sectors when final demand for the jth sector increases by unity; thus, $\Sigma_i r_{ij}$ is the increase in output when exports of the jth sector increase by unity.

Each of these output increases will generate extra demand for factors of production. With two factors of production (labour and capital, say) and labour and capital requirements per unit of output in the jth sector given by n_j, b_j respectively, the total labour content of the jth sector's unit of exports is $\Sigma_i n_i r_{ij}$ (cf. Chapter 13.2) and its capital content $\Sigma_i b_i r_{ij}$.

We can imagine the same exercise being carried out for a unit of exports by all sectors; however, not all exports have equal weight in a country's trade structure, so it is appropriate to weight the exports of each sector by their importance in total exports. These weights (w_j) mean that the total labour content of a proportionate increase in exports can be written $\Sigma_j w_j \Sigma_i n_i r_{ij}$ and the capital content as $\Sigma_j w_j \Sigma_i b_i r_{ij}$. The relative factor content of exports (N_e) now becomes:

$$N_e = \frac{\Sigma_j w_j \Sigma_i b_i r_{ij}}{\Sigma_j w_j \Sigma_i n_i r_{ij}} \tag{15.17}$$

which is the direct and indirect capital content of exports divided by the direct and indirect labour content.

In the case of imports, once the country or group of countries from which they originate has been selected, we can perform the same calculations. The input–output coefficients will refer to the other country/group of countries, although the weights will be determined by the import structure of the importing country. The relative factor content of imports can then be denoted by N_m and the so-called 'Leontief statistic':

$$\Omega = \left(\frac{N_m}{N_e}\right) \tag{15.18}$$

then provides us with a test of the rationality of trade; if Ω is consistent with the country's relative factor endowments, we have *prima facie* evidence that the country is pursuing a trade pattern consistent with comparative advantage. If not, we get a 'Leontief paradox'.[6]

If the Leontief statistic Ω is greater than unity, then exports are more labour-intensive than imports; this is the result one expects to find when analysing the trade pattern of a typical LDC with a typical DC. Where imports are not broken down by region, interpretation of the Leontief statistic is made more difficult because LDCs also trade with other LDCs who may be even more 'capital poor' than the country in question. This problem is brought out very clearly by Table 15.3, where the factor content of Japanese trade is considered.

Table 15.3 Factor content of Japanese and United States trade per million currency units of exports and import replacements

	Exports					
	World		Japan		USA	
	Capital	Labour	Capital	Labour	Capital	Labour
Imports						
World			1,330,926[1]	8.233[2]	3,091,339[3]	170.004[2]
			161,657(N_m)		18,184(N_m)	
Japan	1,385,780[1]	5.52[2]			1,026,387[1]	18.8839[2]
	251,047(N_e)				54,352(N_m)	
USA	2,550,780[3]	182.313[2]	2,741,786[3]	141.2169[2]		
	13,992(N_e)		19,415(N_e)			

(1) Yen (1951).
(2) Man-years.
(3) Dollars (1947).
Source: Tatemoto (1959). Reproduced by permission of North-Holland Publishing Company.

When the factor content of Japanese trade is considered irrespective of its geographical division, exports appear more capital intensive than imports and the value of the Leontief statistic ($\Omega = N_m/N_e = 161{,}657/251{,}047$) is less than unity. When Japan's exports to the USA only are considered, however, they appear much more labour-intensive ($N_e = 54{,}352$) than for all exports ($N_e = 251{,}047$). Similarly, when US exports to Japan are considered in isolation, they appear much more capital-intensive ($N_e = 19{,}415$) than when all exports are considered irrespective of destination ($N_e = 13{,}992$).

The pattern of Japanese trade therefore appears rational according to the Hecksher–Ohlin test. The opposite has been found for other countries such as India, however (see Bhagwati, 1964), and a good deal of work still remains to be done in this area. One interesting development has been the inclusion of natural resources as a separate factor of production, so that the pattern of trade can be examined in the context of its natural resource content. The latter is measured using input–output techniques in exactly the same way as the labour or capital content and the interested reader may refer to the study by Naya (1967) for an empirical application.

15.5 COMPARATIVE ADVANTAGE—THE SEMI-INPUT–OUTPUT METHOD

There is no more important question facing LDCs than the problem of determining in which sectors their comparative advantage lies. By following trade policies, which have largely ignored questions of comparative advantage, LDCs have promoted sectors which have frequently been inefficient; they may have saved foreign exchange, but only at a huge cost in terms of (other) scarce resources so that the contribution to growth of these same resources has been smaller than in alternative uses.

This approach to planning is justified if the shadow price of foreign exchange is infinity or if the shadow price of domestic resources is zero. Neither of these assumptions holds in practice and LDCs have come to realize that the early 'export pessimism' is not fully warranted; there are opportunities for rational export promotion and import substitution and the question arises whether input–output analysis can help to determine them.

It must be said straightaway that neither of the measures discussed earlier in this chapter are of much use. Measuring the import intensity of ISI enables us to determine the net saving of foreign exchange implied by unit expansion of a particular sector, but it tells us nothing about the efficiency with which domestic resources are converted into foreign exchange; if a net saving of foreign exchange of one dollar requires 10 pesos worth of domestic resources, while the shadow rate of exchange is eight pesos to the dollar, it is preferable to continue to import the product in question.

We cannot, however, rely on the implications of the Hecksher–Ohlin theorem either to determine comparative advantage. Even if we could state unambiguously that the LDC in question was relatively well endowed with labour in relation to all possible trading partners, it does not follow that we could calculate the relative factor intensity of all traded activities, rank them in terms of labour intensity and promote them accordingly; this is because such an approach would assume the truth of all the assumptions of the model and this is something which in the present state of our knowledge it would be unwise to do. It also assumes that we can estimate relative factor intensities in terms of physical units; in practice, values have to be used (at least for capital) so that the ranking of sectors by factor intensities will be disturbed if market and shadow prices diverge.

In order to establish in which activities a country's comparative advantage lies, it is necessary to compare the opportunity cost of production for each commodity with the price at which the commodity can be imported or exported. In the presence of intermediate goods (which can be imported) this amounts to comparing net foreign exchange earnings (savings) with domestic resource costs.

If all imports are complementary, import requirements per unit of export or import-replacement are clearly defined; yet if comparative advantage is being studied, the pattern of trade cannot be taken as given. It may turn out that some commodities which are currently imported should be replaced and vice versa; this would affect the calculations of comparative advantage, because some foreign costs would become domestic costs and so on.

This problem of interdependency between the calculation of comparative advantage and the pattern of trade can be resolved using programming techniques (see next section). Simpler methods, however, have been proposed, of which one of the most interesting is the so-called semi-input–output method (SIOM), first proposed by Tinbergen (1965) and developed more formally by Kuyvenhoven (1978).

The basis of the SIOM is the division between the international and national sectors, where the output of the former can enter into trade while the latter cannot (e.g. construction). When an investment takes place in an international sector (to promote exports, for example) it may make demands on the output of the other international sectors through the system of inter-industry linkages, although these demands could be satisfied through imports. Demand for the output of the national sectors, however, *must* be met by increased domestic production which requires complementary investments in those sectors; this additional investment must be added to the original investment in the international sector in order to determine the total capital required for export promotion or import substitution.

Because increased demand for the output of the international sectors could be met by imports, the SIOM excludes their investment needs from total capital requirements. Each international sector can then be evaluated in isolation, with complementary investments in the national sectors *only* added to its own capital requirements.

In order to rank the international sectors, the 'yield' on total capital requirements must be compared; this could be done by examining the net foreign exchange saving associated with the total investment in each international sector, but in empirical studies of the method (e.g. Kuyvenhoven, 1976), it is usually taken to be the total increase in value added, i.e. the value added change in the international sector (where the investment is contemplated) plus the value added change in the national sectors (the other international sectors being ignored because the demand for their output could be met from abroad).

The ranking of sectors is therefore carried out in terms of the efficiency for each sector with which scarce capital resources are converted into value added.[7] The sectors with the highest rankings then become *prima facie* candidates for export promotion or import substitution, although this might require modification in the light of current trading possibilities.

We now come to an algebraic statement of the model itself. The balance equations can be written:

$$\left[\begin{array}{c} x_I \\ \hline x_N \end{array}\right] = \left[\begin{array}{c|c} A_{II} & A_{IN} \\ \hline A_{NI} & A_{NN} \end{array}\right] \left[\begin{array}{c} x_I \\ \hline x_N \end{array}\right] + \left[\begin{array}{c} j_I \\ \hline j_N \end{array}\right] + \left[\begin{array}{c} f_I \\ \hline f_N \end{array}\right] \tag{15.19}$$

where the subscripts I and N refer to international and national sectors, j is a vector of investment and f of final demand. Investment in the base period is assumed to be known, whereas in the subsequent period it is given by the accelerator-type relationship:

$$\left[\begin{array}{c} j_I \\ \hline j_N \end{array}\right] = \left[\begin{array}{c|c} B_{II} & B_{IN} \\ \hline B_{NI} & B_{NN} \end{array}\right] \left[\begin{array}{c} \Delta x_I \\ \hline \Delta x_N \end{array}\right] \tag{15.20}$$

where B is a matrix of capital output ratios, the subscripts are self-explanatory and Δ is the first difference operator.[8] The change in output from period 0 to period 1 can then be written:

$$\left[\begin{array}{c} \Delta x_I \\ \hline \Delta x_N \end{array}\right] = \left[\begin{array}{c|c} A_{II}+B_{II} & A_{IN}+B_{IN} \\ \hline A_{NI}+B_{NI} & A_{NN}+B_{NN} \end{array}\right] \left[\begin{array}{c} \Delta x_I \\ \hline \Delta x_N \end{array}\right] + \left[\begin{array}{c} \Delta f_I \\ \hline \Delta f_N \end{array}\right] - \left[\begin{array}{c} j_I^0 \\ \hline j_N^0 \end{array}\right] \tag{15.21}$$

We now suppose that output in the kth international sector changes by unity and we are interested in calculating the resulting change in the economy's value added (ΔV^*) and its associated capital requirements (ΔK^*). From equation (15.20) we may note that the aggregate capital requirements can be written:

$$i' \left[\begin{array}{c} j_I \\ \hline j_N \end{array}\right] = [b'_I \mid b'_N] \left[\begin{array}{c} \Delta x_I \\ \hline \Delta x_N \end{array}\right] \tag{15.22}$$

where b' is a row vector of sectoral capital–output ratios. By assumption, however, the other international sectors do not increase their output when output in the kth sector expands by unity, so the overall change in capital requirements (ΔK^*) can be simplified to:

$$\Delta K^* = (b'_I)_k + b'_N \Delta x_N \tag{15.23}$$

where $(b'_I)_k$ is the kth member of the vector of sectoral capital–output ratios for the international sectors.

Much the same argument applies to the change in value added (ΔV^*), which is the sum of the value added change in the kth international sector plus the change in the national sectors, i.e.

$$\Delta V^* = (V'_I)_k + V'_N \Delta x_N \tag{15.24}$$

where V'_I, V'_N are row vectors of value added coefficients for the international and national sectors respectively and $(V'_I)_k$ is the kth member of the row vector for the international sectors.

The only remaining problem is to solve for Δx_N in equations (15.23) and (15.24). From equation (15.21) we see that this can be written:

$$\Delta x_N = A^*_{NI} \Delta x_I + A^*_{NN} \Delta x_N + \Delta f^*_N \tag{15.25}$$

where $A^*_{ij} = [A_{ij} + B_{ij}]$ and $\Delta f^*_N = [\Delta f_N - j^0_N]$. By assumption, however, all elements of Δx_I are zero except the kth which equals unity and Δf^*_N is a null vector, so that:

$$\Delta x_N = [I - A^*_{NN}]^{-1} (A^*_{NI})_k \tag{15.26}$$

where $(A^*_{NI})_k$ is the kth column of A^*_{NI}, and the criterion by which the kth sector is to be ranked now becomes:

$$r_k = \frac{\Delta V^*}{\Delta K^*} = \frac{(V'_I)_k + V'_N [I - A^*_{NN}]^{-1} (A^*_{NI})_k}{(b'_I)_k + b'_N [I - A^*_{NN}]^{-1} (A^*_{NI})_k} \tag{15.27}$$

Experiments on these lines using the SIOM have been carried out for a number of developing countries. One of the most interesting concerns Nigeria (Kuyvenhoven, 1976; 1978); in this study, the problem of distinguishing between national and international sectors is circumvented to some extent by transferring sectors from one division to the other and recalculating the rankings. The rationale for this is that, although some sectors are in theory international, in practice, there may be severe restrictions on their ability to enter into trade (e.g. downward sloping demand curves for exports which impose restrictions on the volume exported).

The switching of a sector from international to national and vice versa can affect the ranking of all those sectors which remain in the international group; a good example in the case of Nigeria is provided by what happens when agriculture—normally considered an international sector—is added to the national ones. This change has the effect of increasing the attractiveness, in terms of the rankings, of those processing industries using local raw materials which are now assumed to be obtained from agriculture rather than from abroad; it is clear therefore that use of the SIOM requires great skill and sensitivity in drawing the most appropriate division between the two types of sectors.

15.6 COMPARATIVE ADVANTAGE—THE PROGRAMMING APPROACH

The ranking of sectors by the SIOM is sensitive to the division between national and international sectors; yet there is no really satisfactory way of making this division. Furthermore the method, although it takes account of the complementary nature of the investment decision and therefore embraces (some) indirect effects, does not escape from other criticisms which have been levelled against the orthodox theory of comparative advantage (see Chenery, 1961). In particular, it ignores the distinction between market and shadow prices, the possibility of declining marginal revenues from trade activities and it does not resolve the question of the optimal scale of output.[9]

It is worth recalling the objectives of trade policy as stated by the doctrine of comparative costs: 'the optimum pattern of production and trade for a country is determined from a comparison of the opportunity cost of producing a given commodity with the price at which the commodity can be imported or exported. In equilibrium, no commodity is produced which could be imported at lower cost, and exports are expanded until marginal revenue equals marginal cost' (Chenery, 1961).

A private sector enterprise, contemplating an export or import-substituting project, would consider the marginal revenue to be earned from production in foreign exchange, then convert this to domestic currency at the official rate of exchange and compare this with its marginal cost schedule based on the market price of goods and factors. The project would go ahead if marginal revenue should exceed marginal cost and the optimal point of production would be selected by the interaction of the two marginal schedules.

In the absence of full employment and perfect competition, the resulting allocation of resources and in particular the choice of sectors for export promotion or import substitution might be very far from socially optimal. From the planners' point of view, what is needed is a recalculation for each potential traded activity of marginal revenues and costs in terms of shadow prices.

Let us now suppose that marginal revenue per unit of the ith traded activity for a given output level is mr_i in dollar terms. The dollar costs per unit of production are given by the direct and indirect import content (μ_i) which can be derived using input–output techniques as in the first part of this chapter. Other costs of production consist of domestic goods and factors, but the former can be reduced to the latter by means of input–output techniques to give the total physical factor content per unit of production ($\Sigma_j f_{ji}; j = 1, \ldots, k$), when there are k factors of production.

In equilibrium, the value of these dollar and factor costs in domestic currency will just equal the value of foreign exchange earnings converted to domestic currency, i.e.

$$mr_i p_\$ = \mu_i p_\$ + \sum_j f_{ji} p_j \tag{15.28}$$

where $p_\$$ is the shadow price of foreign exchange and p_j is the shadow price of the jth factor of production. mr_i is a datum, μ_i and f_{ji} are obtained by input–output techniques (see above) so that all that remains is the determination of the set of shadow prices. Once these shadow prices are known, a sector will be a candidate for import substitution or export promotion if $mr_i p_\$ \geqslant \mu_i p_\$ + \Sigma_j f_{ji} p_j$, while sectors can be ranked in terms of comparative advantage in accordance with their social profitability (π_i), where:

$$\pi_i = mr_i p_\$ - \left(\mu_i p_\$ + \sum_j f_{ji} p_j \right) \qquad (15.29)$$

The calculation of shadow prices is beyond the scope of this book; it is appropriate, however, to mention the solution for shadow prices obtained from programming models since these are so closely related to input–output models (e.g. Bruno, 1966; 1971). In these models (see Chapter 14.5), the trade activities (exports and competitive imports) are treated as endogenous; there are therefore more variables (activities) than equations (constraints) and the problem is to eliminate some of the activities according to some optimizing criterion or decision rule.

There will be many solutions which satisfy the system of equations (constraints) which are feasible, but some will be more efficient than others (in terms of their contribution to the stated objective function). The procedure for solving this problem is to select any feasible solution and to calculate the set of shadow prices which reduces the social profitability of all those activities in the solution to zero; if at this set of shadow prices, some activity outside the solution yields a positive social profit it should be included; this procedure continues until all activities in the solution yield zero social profit and all activities outside yield negative social profit, at which point an optimal solution has been reached.

The optimal solution will simultaneously determine the structure of production, consumption and trade. It can therefore be used to determine in which activities a country's comparative advantage lies. By varying the parameters of the model, however, or by relaxing the constraints, it is possible to show how comparative advantage might change (e.g. Weisskopf, 1971). Furthermore, by introducing time subscripts and optimizing for each period over the planning horizon, it is possible to trace out the evolution of dynamic comparative advantage (Bruno, 1972a).

These programming models represent the limit of sophistication reached so far in the treatment of comparative advantage. They have been mentioned, because of the key role played by input–output relations in the formulation of the model; as experience in the use of these models has grown, however, there has been an understandable reaction against them. This is partly due to the complexity of these models and the difficulty of finding suitable data to implement them. In the next chapter, therefore, we shall look at some other simpler techniques, also based on input–output analysis, which have been used to shed light on questions of trade policy.

NOTES

1 Assuming that the imports are valued f.o.b. If imports are valued c.i.f. or c.i.f. + duties some modifications are needed. See Chapter 7.

2 The results cannot be interpreted too literally, because the capital matrices were constructed from the data for several countries—not just Brazil. The broad orders of magnitude, however, are probably correct.

3 The Chenery measure has been subject to other criticisms besides those mentioned here; for a good review, see Sutcliffe (1971). An additional criticism concerns the failure to incorporate technological change as a source of output growth; this can be done using the change in input–output coefficients between two periods (see Syrquin, 1976; and Robinson, 1979), provided that at least two comparable input–output tables are available.

4 The assumptions (see, for example, Bhagwati, 1964) are: (a) international identity of production functions; (b) nonreversibility of factor intensities; (c) constant returns to scale; and (d) identity of the consumption pattern between countries at each relevant commodity price ratio.

5 With more than two factors, the meaning of 'relative' abundance is ambiguous.

6 When tests on the Hecksher–Ohlin hypothesis were first carried out for the United States (Leontief, 1966), the results suggested that US exports were relatively labour-intensive and her imports relatively capital-intensive. Given the factor endowments of the United States, this result appeared paradoxical—hence the phrase 'the Leontief paradox'. A great deal of work has subsequently been done to try and resolve the paradox (see Bhagwati, 1964).

7 Readers familiar with the literature on investment criteria in development economics will notice the similarity between the criterion proposed here and the 'minimum capital–output ratio' proposed by Buchanan, Polak and others (see Chenery, 1961). The advantage of the criterion as calculated by the SIOM, however, is that it explicitly takes account of indirect capital use.

8 In Kuyvenhoven's presentation, use is made of a 'stock-flow conversion factor' for converting the increase in the capital stock during the plan period into the investment flow occurring in the terminal year. This refinement is avoided here by assuming that the plan period is one year.

9 In fairness, it should be pointed out that Kuyvenhoven (1978) has attempted to modify the SIOM to deal with many of these criticisms.

CHAPTER 16

Input–Output Analysis in an Imperfect World

16.1 INTRODUCTION

Input–output tables are typically constructed at market prices so that measures obtained from the tables (e.g. output multipliers) reflect the prevailing system of prices. If the latter are distorted, then the measures will be similarly affected and this could throw into doubt the utility of input–output analysis for countries where market prices do not reflect the social costs and benefits of commodities and factors.

It is widely accepted that prices are seriously distorted in LDCs; the conditions for equality of market and shadow or accounting prices include perfect competition in markets, full utilization of factors of production and absence of external effects (Little, 1974) and these conditions are manifestly absent in LDCs. The problem therefore is how to revalue input–output tables to take account of the distortions.

In the last section of the previous chapter, one solution to this problem was presented; the programming model discussed there yields a set of shadow prices for goods and factors which could in principle be used to revalue input–output tables. Because of the thorough-going linearity of the programming model, however, some of the resulting shadow prices appear unrealistic; if a resource is not fully utilized in the optimal solution, its shadow price is automatically set to zero while the set of shadow prices itself appears sensitive to the choice of objective function or specification of constraints. For these reasons, many economists[1] appear sceptical of the wisdom of generating shadow prices from a programming approach alone.

There are three sets of prices involved in input–output tables: those of inernational (traded) goods, those of national (non-traded) goods and those for primary inputs or factors of production. Given the different markets in which these goods/factors are traded, it would be surprising if the method of conversion to accounting prices was the same in all cases. Indeed, this is exactly what we shall find to be the case (see section 2). Consideration of the conversion problem then enables us to tackle several methods which have been proposed in the literature for dealing with input–output analysis in an imperfect world.

The first of these (section 3) makes use of the concept of the Effective Rate of Protection in order to compare each sector's value added under market prices with what it would be in a regime of undistorted (free trade) prices. The second (section 4) explores the related Domestic Resource Cost criterion, which turns out to be very useful in the analysis of comparative advantage. The next section is then concerned with the use of input–output tables in applied cost–benefit analysis of project appraisal, while the final section looks at input–output analysis carried out on tables revalued at accounting prices.

16.2 CONVERSION FACTORS FOR INPUT–OUTPUT PRICES

In principle, input–output tables can be constructed in physical terms; with a given set of accounting prices, the tables could then be valued in a way which would reflect directly social costs and benefits in the economy. In practice, almost all tables are constructed in value terms,[2] so that revaluation to reflect a given system of accounting prices is not so straightforward.

Fortunately, there is a convenient device which enables us to resolve this problem. In a given system of values, we can always select our physical units such that the price of each commodity/factor is unity; it is not even necessary to know the nature of this physical unit (sometimes called 'Leontief' units) provided that in the base year it can be assumed to have a unit price.

Consider, therefore, the case of traded goods; in the case of importables (i.e. goods produced locally for which an imported equivalent is also available), these are sold in LDCs subject to the effects of trade taxes and other distortions; if we make the 'small country' assumption that the economy in question cannot affect the world price of imports by purchasing more or less from abroad, so that the price elasticity of foreign supply can be assumed to be infinite, then domestic prices for importables will be given by:

$$p_j^* = p_j(1 + t_j) \tag{16.1}$$

where p_j^* is the price of the jth commodity in the home market, p_j is the world price converted to domestic currency at the appropriate exchange rate and t_j measures those taxes on imports which raise the home above the world price.[3]

In an input–output table, however, the jth commodity is measured in Leontief units; it follows that $p_j^* = 1$, so that:

$$p_j = \left(\frac{1}{1 + t_j}\right) \tag{16.2}$$

If the world price (p_j) is a good measure of the social opportunity cost of the jth commodity, we can then use the conversion factor $(p_j/p_j^*) = (1/1 + t_j)$ as a means of revaluing importables in the input–output table to accounting prices.

There is considerable controversy as to whether world prices for importables *do* offer LDCs a ready-made set of accounting prices. Suffice it to say that this is now a frequently made assumption in the literature on project appraisal and cost–benefit analysis (Little, 1974) and it has the overriding advantage of simplicity.[4]

It might seem that a similar exercise could be carried out in estimating conversion factors for exportables (i.e. goods produced at home which are also sold abroad). This is possible wherever LDCs face infinitely elastic demand curves for their exports, because in that case:

(16.3) $$p_j^* = p_j(1 + s_j)$$

where s_j is the rate of subsidy applied to exports,[5] and the conversion factor (p_j/p_j^*) is $(1/1 + s_j)$. Many LDCs, however, produce commodities where additional exports can only be sold at lower prices; the conversion factor therefore needs to reflect this market imperfection.

The accounting price of an exportable should reflect the additional resources made available by selling one extra unit; where the resources are measured in terms of the domestic equivalent of foreign exchange, it implies that the accounting price should be taken to be marginal export revenue (mr_j). This is related to the world price (p_j) by the function:

(16.4) $$mr_j = p_j\left(1 + \frac{1}{\eta_j}\right)$$

where η_j is the price elasticity of demand for the jth sector's exports and is therefore negative so that $mr_j < p_j$ unless this elasticity is infinity. The conversion factor is therefore:

(16.5) $$\left(\frac{p_j}{p_j^*}\right) = \left(\frac{mr_j}{p_j^*}\right) = \frac{p_j(1 + 1/\eta_j)}{p_j(1 + s_j)} = \frac{(1 + 1/\eta_j)}{(1 + s_j)}$$

so that the conversion factors for exportables require knowledge of the foreign price elasticities of demand unless these can be assumed to be infinite.[6]

We now come to the conversion factors for non-traded goods. In Chapter 14.4, we saw that prices in an input–output world are given on a cost-plus basis as the sum of intermediate and primary input costs per unit of output, i.e.

(16.6) $$p^* = A^{*\prime}p^* + V^{*\prime}\pi^*$$

where an asterisk denotes the use of market prices, V^* is a matrix of physical factor inputs per unit of output and π^* is now a vector of factor prices. We now need to make use of the distinction between traded (I) and non-traded goods (N) and write equation (16.6) in partitioned form (cf. equation 15.19) as:

(16.7) $$\begin{bmatrix} P_I^* \\ \hline P_N^* \end{bmatrix} = \begin{bmatrix} A_{II}^{*\prime} & A_{IN}^{*\prime} \\ \hline A_{NI}^{*\prime} & A_{NN}^{*\prime} \end{bmatrix} \begin{bmatrix} P_I^* \\ \hline P_N^* \end{bmatrix} + \begin{bmatrix} V_I^{*\prime} \\ \hline V_N^{*\prime} \end{bmatrix} [\pi^*]$$

so that the price equation for non-traded goods becomes:

(16.8) $$P_N^* = A_{NI}^{*\prime}P_I^* + A_{NN}^{*\prime}P_N^* + V_N^{*\prime}\pi^*$$

and its solution is:

(16.9) $$P_N^* = [I - A_{NN}^{*\prime}]^{-1}A_{NI}^{*\prime}P_I^* + [I - A_{NN}^{*\prime}]^{-1}V_N^{*\prime}\pi^*$$

It can be seen from equation (16.9) that the price of non-traded goods is composed of two parts: the cumulative inputs of traded goods valued at their market price (first term) and cumulative factor inputs similarly valued (second term). If, therefore, conversion factors are applied to the price of traded goods and primary inputs, the result will be the accounting price of non-traded goods, i.e.

$$P_N = [I - A^{*\prime}_{NN}]^{-1} A^{*\prime}_{NI} P_I + [I - A^{*\prime}_{NN}]^{-1} V^{*\prime}_N \pi \tag{16.10}$$

where P_N, P_I and π are the accounting prices for non-traded goods, traded goods and primary inputs respectively.

From equation (16.10), we can see that the information necessary to obtain accounting prices for non-traded goods consists of input–output coefficients at market prices and accounting prices for traded goods and factors. Only the latter are unknown, since we have already shown how the accounting prices for traded goods may be obtained; further on in this chapter (section 6) we will show how accounting prices for factors can be determined simultaneously with those for non-traded goods. For the moment, however, we assume that they are known exogenously so that all entries in input–output tables at market prices can be converted to entries at accounting prices.

In the case of the input–output coefficient matrix the conversion is done as follows: at market prices based on Leontief units (so that all prices are unity) this matrix (A^*) is given by:

$$A^* = W^* \hat{x}^{*-1} \tag{16.11}$$

where W^* is the matrix of intermediate transactions and x^* the vector of gross outputs both at market prices. We are interested in deriving the matrix at accounting prices (A), where $A = W\hat{x}^{-1}$ and W, x are also expressed in accounting prices.

When Leontief units are used, there is no difference between conversion factors (p_j/p_j^*) and accounting prices (p_j). By applying the latter to flows at market prices, we obtain the intermediate transactions matrix and gross output vector at accounting prices. It follows that:

$$A = [\hat{p} W^*] [\hat{x}^* \hat{p}]^{-1} \tag{16.12}$$

or

$$A = \hat{p}[W^* \hat{x}^{*-1}]\hat{p}^{-1} = \hat{p} A^* \hat{p}^{-1} \tag{16.13}$$

so that the accounting price coefficient matrix (A) can be obtained directly from the market price matrix (A^*) through application of the accounting price vector (p). The latter consists of conversion factors for traded and non-traded goods and their derivation has been discussed above. In section 6, we shall return to an example of input–output analysis carried out on the input–output coefficient matrix (A) at accounting prices.

16.3 THE EFFECTIVE RATE OF PROTECTION

All LDCs make considerable use of taxes on trade; one of the most important of these taxes is the nominal tariff which is imposed on imports. By raising the price at which imports can be sold in the home market, it is widely recognized that consumption of the goods in question will be reduced; the effect on production, however, cannot be so easily predicted and yet knowledge of this effect is essential if we want to estimate the impact of the tariff on resource allocation.

The reason why the production effect cannot be determined from knowledge of the nominal tariff alone is as follows: tariffs raise the price at which locally produced goods can be sold if they compete with the taxed imports, but they also change the price of intermediate inputs; we cannot therefore determine *a priori* what effect they will have on value added in each sector and so the impact on resource allocation is indeterminate. Factors of production will only be attracted into an activity if their expected reward exceeds what it would have been before the imposition of trade taxes. What we therefore need is a comparison of the return to factors of production pre- and post-trade taxes. This return or 'effective price' is measured by the difference between the value of output and the value of all intermediate inputs; by comparing this effective price pre- and post-trade taxes, we obtain the Effective Rate of Protection (ERP). The ERP therefore measures the proportionate change in the return to all factors of production after taxes are imposed and is a much better measure of resource pull than the *nominal* rate of protection.

The effective price in the post-tax situation can be obtained from input–output tables at market prices; to calculate it in the pre-tax situation, we need to know the prices for output and intermediate inputs which would exist under free trade. This is precisely what the conversion factors of the previous section try to determine and so through application of these factors to input–output tables at market prices, we can obtain the effective price in the pre-trade tax situation.

The effective price for a sector will only be the same as sectoral value added when all commodities are traded. When some commodity inputs are non-traded, great care has to be taken in defining the ERP; non-traded inputs can be assumed to be in less than infinitely elastic supply so that when demand for non-traded inputs rises, they will only be supplied at a higher price; this raises the return to domestic factors of production directly and indirectly employed in the non-traded goods sector. The ERP, however, is meant to measure the net increase available to primary resources as a result of the system of trade taxes in force; the effective price should therefore include that part of the value of non-traded inputs attributable to factors of production directly and indirectly (see Corden, 1966).

We may now see how input–output techniques can be used to solve this problem; let us assume for simplicity one traded input into the jth activity and one non-traded input.[7] Value added at market prices in the jth sector (V_j^*) can be written:

(16.14)
$$V_j^* = x_j^* - W_{ij}^* - W_{hj}^*$$

when W_{ij}^*, W_{hj}^* are the i, jth and h, jth elements of the matrix of intermediate transactions (W^*), and i, h refer to the traded and non-traded inputs respectively. At accounting prices value added in the jth sector (v_j) becomes:

$$v_j = x_j^* p_j - W_{ij}^* p_i - W_{hj}^* p_h \tag{16.15}$$

where p_j, p_i, p_h are conversion factors for the sector's output and two inputs respectively.[8]

Assuming the output of the jth sector is traded, the conversion factors p_j and p_i are determined by the difference between world and domestic prices as in section 2; the conversion factor for the non-traded input is more complicated, but can be derived from equation (16.10) since:

$$p_h = \sum_j \alpha_{hj} p_j + \sum_k \beta_{hk} \pi_k \tag{16.16}$$

where α_{hj}, β_{hk} are the h, jth and h, kth elements of the matrix products $\{[I - A_{NN}^{*\prime}]^{-1} A_{NI}^{*\prime}\}$ and $\{[I - A_{NN}^{*\prime}]^{-1} V_N^{*\prime}\}$ respectively. We can therefore rewrite equation (16.15) as:

$$v_j = x_j^* \left(\frac{1}{1+t_j}\right) - W_{ij}^* \left(\frac{1}{1+t_i}\right) - W_{hj}^* \sum_j \alpha_{hj} p_j - W_{hj}^* \sum_k \beta_{hk} \pi_k \tag{16.17}$$

The last two terms of equation (16.17) break down the value of the non-traded input into its cumulative traded and factor components respectively. The latter, however, is precisely what needs to be added to value added in the jth sector (v_j) to obtain the return to all domestic factors of production (tv_j), i.e.

$$tv_j = \left(v_j + W_{hj}^* \sum_k \beta_{hk} \pi_k\right) = x_j^* \left(\frac{1}{1+t_j}\right) - W_{ij}^* \left(\frac{1}{1+t_i}\right) - W_{hj}^* \sum_j \alpha_{hj} p_j \tag{16.18}$$

and we can perform a similar exercise for value added in the protected situation to get:

$$tv_j^* = \left(V_j^* + W_{hj}^* \sum_k \beta_{hk} \pi_k^*\right) = x_j^* - W_{ij}^* - W_{hj}^* \sum_j \alpha_{hj} \tag{16.19}$$

so that the ERP formula becomes:

$$Z_j = \frac{(tv_j^* - tv_j)}{tv_j} = \frac{x_j^* \left(\frac{t_j}{1+t_j}\right) - W_{ij}^* \left(\frac{t_i}{1+t_i}\right) - W_{hj}^* \sum_j \alpha_{hj} \left(\frac{t_j}{1+t_j}\right)}{x_j^* \left(\frac{1}{1+t_j}\right) - W_{ij}^* \left(\frac{1}{1+t_i}\right) - W_{hj}^* \sum_j \alpha_{hj} \left(\frac{1}{1+t_j}\right)} \tag{16.20}$$

or

$$Z_j = \frac{\left(\frac{t_j}{1+t_j}\right) - a_{ij}^* \left(\frac{t_i}{1+t_i}\right) - a_{hj}^* \sum_j \alpha_{hj} \left(\frac{t_j}{1+t_j}\right)}{\left(\frac{1}{1+t_j}\right) - a_{ij}^* \left(\frac{1}{1+t_i}\right) - a_{hj}^* \sum_j \alpha_{hj} \left(\frac{1}{1+t_j}\right)} \tag{16.21}$$

The formula given in equation (16.21) has been derived according to the so-called Corden method (see Corden, 1971) in which the value of non-traded inputs is broken down into its traded and factor component. Because it requires knowledge of an inverse matrix to calculate all α_{hj}^* in the formula, simpler methods have often been necessary. If, for example, we treated the whole value of the non-traded input as being part of the protected activity, (the so-called crude Corden method—see Corden, 1966) the formula simplifies to:

$$Z_j' = \frac{\left(\frac{t_j}{1+t_j}\right) - a_{ij}^*\left(\frac{t_i}{1+t_i}\right)}{\left(\frac{1}{1+t_j}\right) - a_{ij}^*\left(\frac{1}{1+t_i}\right)} \tag{16.22}$$

On the other hand, we could treat non-traded goods as traded goods subject to a zero tariff (the so-called Balassa method—see Balassa, 1965). In that case the formula simplifies to:

$$Z_j'' = \frac{\left(\frac{t_j}{1+t_j}\right) - a_{ij}^*\left(\frac{t_i}{1+t_i}\right)}{\left(\frac{1}{1+t_j}\right) - a_{ij}^*\left(\frac{1}{1+t_i}\right) - a_{hj}^*} \tag{16.23}$$

An example of the different results obtained from using the alternative definitions of ERP is given in Table 16.1. As the table shows, it can make a big difference as to which method is chosen. The Balassa method, by assuming that additional use of non-traded inputs does not drive up their price, tends to overstate ERP, while the crude Corden method understates it by assuming that the whole of the non-traded input is part of the protected activity. It is much better, therefore, to base estimates of the ERP on (Z_j) as in equation (16.21); as the formula shows, however, (Z_j) cannot be calculated without knowledge of the Leontief inverse so that input–output tables are a pre-condition for correct calculation of the ERP.

Table 16.1 Alternative measures of ERP for manufacturing (%)

Country	Year	Z	Z'	Z''
Argentina	1958	n.a.	162	247
Brazil	1966	118	82	155
Mexico	1960	n.a.	27	28
India	1961	n.a.	313	733
Philippines	1965	n.a.	49	52
Taiwan	1965	n.a.	33	50

Source: Taken from Little (1970), Table A.5.a, p. 431.

16.4 THE DOMESTIC RESOURCE COST CRITERION

The ERP has by now been measured for a large number of LDCs and it has proved very useful as an *ex post* measure of the incentives created by the system of trade taxes. It has also been of service in determining the direction of resource pull (particularly between primary and secondary activity), although there are some theoretical difficulties involved in this interpretation of the ERP (see, for example, Khang, 1973). It is not, however, much use as a measure of inefficiency in resource allocation (*pace* Balassa, 1968), because a sector's contribution to social income is not measured by the size of the ERP (see Bhagwati, 1978).

We may therefore turn to an alternative measure for ranking sectors both in terms of comparative advantage and in terms of inefficiency in resource allocation which makes use of input–output tables at accounting prices. This measure is known as the Domestic Resource Cost (DRC) criterion and is now well established in the trade and development literature (see, for example, Bruno, 1972b).

If we return to equation (16.7), we can see that the price for international goods depends, among other things, on the matrix of primary input requirements; one of these is non-competitive imports which, in the case of accounting prices, need to be evaluated at the shadow price of foreign exchange ($p_\$$). The system of accounting prices can therefore be written:

$$\left[\begin{array}{c} P_I \\ \hline P_N \end{array}\right] = \left[\begin{array}{c|c} I - A_{II}^{*\prime} & -A_{IN}^{*\prime} \\ \hline -A_{NI}^{*\prime} & I - A_{NN}^{*\prime} \end{array}\right]^{-1} \left\{ \left[\begin{array}{c} m_I \\ \hline m_N \end{array}\right] [p_\$] + \left[\begin{array}{c} V_I^{*\prime} \\ \hline V_N^{*\prime} \end{array}\right] [\pi] \right\} \tag{16.24}$$

where m_I, m_N are the vectors of non-competitive imported inputs for the traded and non-traded sectors respectively, V_I^*, V_N^*, are defined exclusive of imports and π now excludes foreign exchange. The solution for the jth international sector now becomes:

$$p_j = \mu_j p_\$ + \sum_i \lambda_{ij} \pi_i \tag{16.25}$$

where μ_j is the direct and indirect import content of unit production in the jth sector and λ_{ij} is the direct and indirect ith factor content.

The accounting price of the jth activity has already been defined as marginal import cost or marginal export revenue which needs to be evaluated at the shadow price of foreign exchange ($p_\$$). In the case of an exportable we therefore have:

$$(mr_j - \mu_j) p_\$ = \sum_i \lambda_{ij} \pi_i \tag{16.26}$$

or

$$p_\$ = \frac{\sum_i \lambda_{ij} \pi_i}{(mr_j - \mu_j)} \tag{16.27}$$

The expression on the right-hand side of equation (16.27) consists of two parts;

in the numerator is found the direct and indirect domestic factor content per unit of production in the jth sector; in the denominator is the net saving of foreign exchange; it follows that $p_\$$ measures the efficiency with which domestic resources are converted into foreign exchange, i.e. the shadow price of foreign exchange.

If optimal policies are pursued, the efficiency with which domestic resources are converted into foreign exchange would be the same for all sectors; the cost of foreign exchange, however, can be estimated for *each* sector using equation (16.27) and a large spread of rates indicates inefficiency in resource use. On the other hand, a sector with a low $p_\$$ is clearly more efficient than one with a high $p_\$$ at earning or saving foreign exchange, so equation (16.27) can be used to rank sectors in terms of their comparative advantage; this is known as the DRC criterion and its superiority over the ERP measure is now well established (see Pearson, 1976; Bhagwati, 1978) as far as inefficiency in resource allocation and ranking by comparative advantage are concerned.

In Table 16.2, some calculations according to the DRC criterion are given for Sudan. In order to evaluate these, some estimate must be made of the equilibrium exchange rate; in the study in question this was assumed to be £0.44 Sudanese = \$1 dollar. A DRC above this (e.g. wheat flour) therefore suggests inefficiency in transforming domestic resources into foreign exchange, while one below (e.g. soaps) suggests efficiency.

The DRC criterion has been applied to many LDCs; its great merit is that it does not require explicit knowledge of the shadow price of foreign exchange. Against that, however, it should be clear from equation (16.27) that the criterion can only be applied correctly when a Leontief inverse matrix exists and where all other factors of production have been evaluated at shadow prices. All too often, case studies of countries to determine DRC are deficient in one or both of these respects.

Table 16.2 Estimates of domestic resource cost criterion for a sample of sectors in Sudan (1968/9)

Sector	DRC[1]
Vegetable oils	0.26
Wheat flour	1.31
Sugar	0.84
Sweets	0.32
Textiles	0.28
Footwear	0.29
Soaps	0.19
Petroleum products	0.21

[1] Expressed as a ratio of Sudanese pounds (£) to foreign exchange costs (\$).
Source: Rabih (1979).

16.5 PROJECT APPRAISAL AND COST–BENEFIT ANALYSIS

At first sight it might seem as if input–output analysis has little to contribute to project appraisal and cost–benefit analysis (CBA) and, indeed, the reader of CBA manuals (e.g. Little, 1974) would be hard pressed to find any significant reference to input–output techniques. Despite this, however, input–output analysis has an important role to play in this field.

We may note at once that there is a close correspondence between the DRC criterion (which *does* depend on input–output techniques) and the decision criterion used in project evaluation. Assuming that the shadow price of foreign exchange ($p_\$$) is known, we may rewrite the DRC criterion in the case of an exportable as:

$$NB_j = (mr_j - \mu_j)p_\$ - \sum_i \lambda_{ij}\pi_i \tag{16.28}$$

where NB_j is now the net benefit associated with unit operation of the jth sector. If $NB_j \geqslant 0$, the sector's 'internal' shadow price of foreign exchange, i.e. its efficiency in earning (saving) an extra dollar, is lower than the accounting rate ($p_\$$) and, *ceteris paribus*, projects in this sector should be encouraged. Now in project appraisal, the output of the project is evaluated at shadow prices and compared with the value of all inputs at shadow prices; the latter, however, can be decomposed into the direct and indirect foreign exchange and other primary input costs so that under certain circumstances (see, for example, Srinivasan, 1975), there is a formal equivalence between the decision criterion in project evaluation and the DRC criterion (see also Bruno, 1975).

Project evaluation is normally carried out in terms of Net Present Values (NPV) obtained by discounting back to the present the net benefits yielded by a project over its lifetime, i.e.

$$NPV = (B_0 - C_0) + \left(\frac{B_1 - C_1}{1+r}\right) + \left(\frac{B_2 - C_2}{(1+r)^2}\right) + \ldots \tag{16.29}$$

where B_t, C_t are social benefits and costs in period t respectively and r is the social rate of discount with the project being approved if NPV $\geqslant 0$. Now social benefits and costs need to be evaluated at accounting prices and where a distinction is made between traded and non-traded goods (as in the Little–Mirrlees method of CBA—see Little, 1974), input–output techniques have an important role to play.

Assume for simplicity that the project's output is a traded good; it must then be evaluated at the world or border price using conversion factors equivalent to equations (16.2) or (16.5). In each period, the project's inputs consist of traded goods, non-traded goods and primary inputs; the traded inputs are again evaluated at world or border price to get their value in accounting prices, but for the non-traded inputs there is no border price by definition; each non-traded input, however, can be decomposed into its cumulative traded and factor input and its shadow price evaluated according to equations such as (16.10); the accounting prices so derived can then be used as conversion factors whenever a non-traded input is found.

In the above analysis, it was assumed that the shadow price of factors was already known; this is indeed the case in some practical applications of project appraisal (e.g. Scott, 1976) where the shadow price of factors is estimated independently; the shadow price of non-traded goods, however, enters into the formula for the shadow price of factors (e.g. unskilled labour), so that an iterative procedure is necessary to ensure consistency between the two sets of accounting prices. There are methods, however, for simultaneously determining the two sets of prices which make iterative procedures unnecessary (cf. Seton, 1973) and these will be explored in the next section.

16.6 INPUT–OUTPUT MEASURES AT ACCOUNTING PRICES

In section 2 of this chapter, it was shown how conversion factors for traded and non-traded goods can be derived which may be used to put input–output tables at market prices on an accounting price basis. In the last three sections, we have demonstrated some uses to which these conversion factors can be put, but we have yet to show how input–output tables at accounting prices can be employed.

In section 2, the derivation of the accounting-price input–output table assumed that the shadow price of factors was known. This is most unlikely, however, because of the inter-dependence between the shadow price of goods and factors (see previous section), so we need to show how the two sets of prices can be determined simultaneously.

As before, let us make the now familiar distinction between traded (international) and non-traded (national) goods with the accounting price for the former given by the difference between domestic and world prices; this time, however, in order to simplify matters, primary inputs will not be disaggregated so that there is only one value added input in each sector; this means that the accounting-price equations can be written:

$$\left[\begin{array}{c} p_I \\ \hline p_N \end{array}\right] = \left[\begin{array}{c|c} A^{*\prime}_{II} & A^{*\prime}_{IN} \\ \hline A^{*\prime}_{NI} & A^{*\prime}_{NN} \end{array}\right] \left[\begin{array}{c} p_I \\ \hline p_N \end{array}\right] + \left[\begin{array}{cc} \hat{V}^*_I & \pi_I \\ \hline \hat{V}^*_N & \pi_N \end{array}\right] \tag{16.30}$$

where $\hat{V}^*_I$, $\hat{V}^*_N$ are diagonal matrices of value added coefficients at market price in the international and national sectors respectively and π_I, π_N are the accounting price ratios for value added. Equation (16.30) is very similar to equation (16.7), the only difference being that with only one primary input in each sector (value added), the vector of shadow factor prices (π) must now be partitioned ($\pi_I \;\vdots\; \pi_N$) to take account of (different) accounting price ratios for value added in each sector.

The above system consists of $(I+N)$ equations in the $(I+2N)$ unknowns—p_N, π_I, π_N. It is therefore underdetermined and additional equations are needed if a solution is to be found; this can be done in several ways (cf. Kuyvenhoven, 1978, pp. 169–171), of which one of the most appealing is to assume that all elements of the π_N vector are the same and that each is equal to the inverse of the excess of the economy's value added at market prices over value added at accounting prices, i.e.

$$\pi_{Nk} = \frac{\sum_j \pi_j v_j^*}{\sum_j v_j^*} \qquad k = 1, \ldots, N \tag{16.31}$$

where v_j^* is value added at market prices in the jth sector and is, of course, known.

Equations (16.30) and (16.31) now represent a system of $(I + 2N)$ equations in the $(I + 2N)$ unknowns (since the accounting price ratios for traded goods (p_I) are assumed to be given exogenously) and the system can therefore be solved. Once the accounting price ratios are known, the structural input–output coefficients at market prices can be converted to a shadow price basis using equation (16.13). This must also be done for the value added coefficients and capital–output coefficients (if any).

We now have input–output tables at accounting prices so that in principle all the applications of input–output analysis described in previous chapters can be carried out free from the distortions of market prices. An example is provided by the application of the semi-input–output method (see Chapter 15.5) to Nigeria (see Kuyvenhoven, 1978).

In the Nigerian study, a semi-input–output method was used to compare the performance of different international sectors; by assuming a unit change in the final demand for each sector, it is possible to compute the total (direct and

Table 16.3 A comparison of the value added to capital criterion for Nigeria at market and accounting prices

Sector	Value added to capital criterion (market prices)[1]	Rank	Social income to capital criterion (accounting prices)	Rank
Watches and clocks	1.172	1	1.028	1
Special machinery	0.841	2	0.606	9
Motor Body and shipbuilding	0.823	3	0.689	5
Basic industrial chemicals	0.793	4	0.553	11[1]
Knitted goods	0.639	5	0.634	8
Wooden furniture and fixtures	0.636	6	0.211	38[1]
Misc. food and animal feed	0.630	7	−0.046	50[1]
Craft weaving and dyeing	0.591	8	0.720	3
Wearing apparel	0.590	9	0.479	14[1]
Miscellaneous manufacturing	0.586	10	0.574	10

Source: Kuyvenhoven (1978), Tables 7.7 and 7.9. Reproduced by permission of Martinus Nijhoff Publishers N.V.

(1) The study from which these figures are taken lists 50 sectors of which only the top ranked ten (at market prices) are given here; at accounting prices several of these sectors fall below the first ten in the ranking.

indirect) increase in value added and compare this with the total (direct and indirect) capital required;[9] at market prices this measure is known as the value added to capital criterion while at accounting prices it becomes the social income to capital criterion. Some comparisons of the two criteria with the variation in rankings are given in Table 16.3.

The table shows quite clearly that measures derived from input–output tables at accounting prices can differ quite sharply from those derived from tables at market prices. The sector 'miscellaneous food and animal feed', for example, drops from seventh in the rankings at market prices to last place at accounting prices; fortunately, six of the top ten sectors in the market-price rankings figure in the top ten at accounting prices, so that policy can still be based on the unadapted measures to some extent. The table serves as a useful reminder, however, of the degree to which market and shadow prices diverge in LDCs and of the importance in input–output analysis of trying to correct for it.

NOTES

1 See, for example, the essays by Bruno and Taylor in Blitzer (1975)

2 For an exception, see the description of the input–output table for China (Si-kang, 1979).

3 The most important of these taxes is the tariff and t_j therefore measures tariffs, etc. as a proportion of the world price. t_j can be estimated either from a country's tariff schedule or from looking at duties collected in the trade statistics.

4 The circumstances under which world prices can be used to reflect social opportunity costs are well discussed in Sen (1972) and Seton (1973).

5 Where exports are subject to *ad valorem* taxes, the domestic price can be assumed to be below the world price so that s_j can be interpreted as a negative subsidy.

6 Where the foreign supply curve of imports is less than infinitely elastic, the accounting price should be interpreted as marginal import cost and the conversion factor becomes $(1+1/\varepsilon_j)/(1+t_j)$, where ε_j is the price elasticity of supply.

7 Extension to the case of many traded and non-traded inputs presents no new issues of principle, but complicates the algebra.

8 Each conversion factor is a ratio with market prices (p^*) in the denominator; the latter, however, are assumed to be unity so that the conversion factors and accounting prices are the same (see section 2).

9 The derivation of this measure is shown in more detail in Chapter 15.5.

CHAPTER 17

Input–Output and Development Planning

17.1 INTRODUCTION

So far in this book, the reader has been led from the most preliminary stages in the design of input–output tables, to their application in various forms of structural economy-wide analysis; all examples of input–output analysis have been chosen by reference to their relevance for LDCs and yet almost nothing has been said about development planning, which is often the principal use to which input–output tables in LDCs are put. It is fitting, therefore, that the final chapter should be on this topic.

All LDCs are concerned with accelerating their rate of economic development; in order to achieve this, most of them indulge in some kind of development planning exercise. These plans can be of very different sorts, but there is often a common ingredient; the aim is to reduce the risk and uncertainty inherent in economic activity by making some prognosis about the future. If the prognosis is believed by enough people, it may actually be self-fulfilling, so the planning exercise needs to be serious and professional.

There is a vast literature on development planning and good surveys (e.g. Taylor, 1975) can be found elsewhere. The aim of this chapter is not to provide a summary of the literature, but to illustrate the role which input–output techniques can play in the planning exercises. Of course, many of the previous chapters have already done this; a development plan based on input–output techniques requires, for example, the projection of input–output coefficients (see Chapter 10.5) and estimates of labour requirements (see Chapter 13) and it may involve the introduction of choice (see Chapter 14.5); what is significant about this chapter, however, is first the macro-economic nature of the exercise and secondly the time scale. We may assume that the plan is concerned with the next five to ten years and that an effort is being made to forecast or predict the change in all economic activity over this period with calculations being made of the implications of this change on primary and other scarce resources.

17.2 AN OVERVIEW OF DEVELOPMENT PLANNING

Since Tinbergen (1967), it has been customary to think of planning in 'stages'; the most important are the macro-economic, sectoral and project stages with interdependency between each stage. In the 'macro' stage, some simple model (e.g. Harrod–Domar or 'two-gap'—see Taylor, 1979b) is used to predict the rate of growth of GDP over the plan period with implied values for the macro-economic variables such as investment, consumption, imports, exports and employment; the results of the macro-model are then fed into the sectoral stage, at which point an input–output model is customarily used.

In the sectoral stage, the given rate of growth of GDP and terminal values for the macro-economic variables enable the planner to work out the sectoral composition of final demand; in this exercise investment can be exogenous or endogenous, but in any case the results must be checked later on for consistency between output growth, capital accumulation and supply of finance (see section 3). The given vector of final demands is then translated into a vector of gross outputs *via* the Leontief inverse.

The solution for gross output will be *consistent* with the predicted pattern of demand if the Leontief inverse is used; the output of each sector will be large enough to support the given level of final demand even after allowance is made for intermediate demands. The solution may not be *feasible*, however, and it may also make demands on scarce resources (such as credit or skilled labour) which are inconsistent with the rate at which these resources are expected to expand; furthermore, some of the results of the sectoral model, when aggregated, may contradict the results of the macro-model, and a non-formal iterative procedure is required in order to achieve consistency between the two stages.

When consistency is achieved and provided the solution to the sectoral stage does not make unreasonable demands on scarce resources and is feasible, the planner may proceed to the project stage. This stage is the province of the vast literature on cost–benefit analysis and project appraisal (e.g. Little, 1974); although it cannot be reviewed here, it is sufficient to note that the aim is to find efficient projects in each sector capable of achieving the sectoral targets without exceeding the country's resource limitations.

This chapter is concerned above all with the problems encountered at the sectoral stage in the planning process because this is the point at which input–output techniques are used (see section 3). Since the model is run over time, its parameters must allow for inter-temporal variations (section 4); final demand must be forecast accurately, which means that variations in imports due to import substitution must be allowed for (see section 5). The feasibility of the solution requires knowledge of historical rates of growth of sectoral output and estimates of the supply of scarce resources as well as the demand for them obtained from the input–output model.

If the resource constraints are known, there are likely to be many feasible solutions consistent with them; the 'best' solution will be the one which, for given resources, achieves maximum growth of output/consumption or which, for a given rate of output, achieves the result at minimum social cost. This 'best' or 'optimal' solution can be analysed using programming techniques and the last part of this chapter (section 6) is devoted to a discussion of these techniques.

17.3 THE SECTOR STAGE MODEL

In the sector stage, the input–output model can be either static or dynamic. If the latter, the solution will include an output vector for each period of the plan, while if the former the solution will involve only one output vector for the terminal year of the plan. The dynamic input–output model was discussed in Chapter 14.3, and will not be mentioned here (it is surveyed very competently in Taylor, 1975); its great merit—the solution of all endogenous variables for each year of the plan—can be incorporated in the static model by running the latter for some of the intra-plan period, so that the resource implications during the plan as well as at the end of the plan can be worked out.

For the tth period of the plan, the balance equations can be written:

$$x(t) = A(t)x(t) + h(t) + e(t) - m_c(t) \tag{17.1}$$

where m_c is competitive imports, h is home final demand, e is exports and a time dimension (t) is attached to the technological coefficients matrix (A) to remind us of the need to allow for inter-temporal variations. The home final demand vector can be expanded into its components:

$$h(t) = c(t) + gx(t) + j(t) + r(t) + \Delta s(t) \tag{17.2}$$

where c, gx, j, r and Δs are vectors of private consumption, government expenditure, new investment, replacement expenditure and inventory change.

Competitive imports (see Chapter 7.5) enter into the balance equations as a separate argument, because the burden of adjustment for import substitution during the plan period will fall upon them; this is made clear if we write their solution as:

$$m_c(t) = [I - \hat{d}(t)]A(t)x(t) + [I - \hat{d}(t)]h(t) \tag{17.3}$$

where the elements of the diagonal matrix $(\hat{d})$ reflect the proportion of total supply in each sector met by home output so that the elements of $[I - \hat{d}(t)]$ denote the proportion of supply provided by competitive imports. Typically, the elements of $(\hat{d})$ will be rising during the plan period since an important source of output growth is provided by import substitution (see Chapter 15.3).

Treating competitive imports in this fashion means that the balance equations can now be written:

$$x(t) = \hat{d}(t)A(t)x(t) + \hat{d}(t)h(t) + e(t) \tag{17.4}$$

so that the solution for the output vector becomes:

$$x(t) = [I - \hat{d}(t)A(t)]^{-1}[\hat{d}(t)h(t) + e(t)] \tag{17.5}$$

or

$$x(t) = R(t)f^*(t) \tag{17.6}$$

where $R(t) = [I - \hat{d}(t)A(t)]^{-1}$ and $f^*(t) = [\hat{d}(t)h(t) + e(t)]$.

The output solution—$x(t)$—will always be consistent, but it must be checked for feasibility. For example, by comparing $x(t)$ with $x(0)$, the implied sectoral rates of growth can be worked out; if any of these are very high by historical standards or if there are major differences between the growth rates of service and commodity sectors, we might as well—as Lewis (1966) so aptly puts it—stop right away. In particular, there is no point 'planning' for a growth rate of agriculture which is well in excess of what has been recorded historically, unless it is known that investments in innovations, new lands or land reform will be paying off during the plan period.

The implied sectoral growth rates should also be shown to sectoral experts (cf. Chapter 8.3). This is useful for two reasons; first, they may have been carrying out a preliminary planning exercise using a quite different rate of growth; secondly, they may well have special knowledge of the sectors which permits them to dismiss as unrealistic the implied rate of growth.

Once the sectoral rates of growth are accepted as being plausible, the next task is to check the solution for its resource implications. We may begin with foreign exchange; exports are given exogenously in equation (17.1). while competitive imports are given by equation (17.3); that leaves non-competitive imports (m_{nc}) and various transfers and net factor payments ($e_f(t)$). Some of the latter (e.g. profit remittances) are linked to the solution for the input–output model, but we may ignore this complication and assume that $e_f(t)$ is known in advance, perhaps being projected from historical trends.

Non-competitive imports can be consumer, capital or intermediate goods; in LDCs, the decision to treat a commodity as a non-competitive import amounts to saying that no attempt will be made at import substitution during the period of the plan. Most non-competitive imports will therefore consist of intermediate and capital goods, but we recognize the possibility of non-competitive consumer goods imports by writing the solution as:

(17.7) $$m_{nc}(t) = A_m(t)x(t) + j_m(t) + f_m(t)$$

where A_m is a matrix of non-competitive import requirements per unit of output (see Chapter 7.5), j_m is a vector of imported capital goods and f_m is a vector of consumer goods non-competitive imports. The time dimension on A_m is important not only because of technological change in the plan period, but also because the decision to set up an import-substituting industry will affect the elements of A_m even without technological change. (In some countries, A_m must be replaced by a diagonalized vector since the commodity composition of non-competitive imports is not known.) The reason for separating j_m from f_m in equation (17.7) is that imports of capital goods can be linked to the solution for output according to the methods outlined in Chapter 11.3 (see, for example, equation (11.5)).

The balance of payments deficit on current account (β) is:

(17.8) $$\beta(t) = e(t) + e_f(t) - [m_c(t) + m_{nc}(t)]$$

which can now be worked out from the above equations. This borrowing requirement can be compared with the results of the 'macro' stage if a 'two-gap' model has been used; in any case, it seems likely that a country will have some idea about the inflow of foreign resources and the maximum balance of payments deficit it can support over the plan period; if $\beta(t)$ is too large, an iterative procedure is required, going back if necessary to the 'macro' stage.

The next resource to consider is labour; the usual aggregated treatment of labour requirements in LDCs is far from adequate, since labour is not homogeneous; in particular, the solution for the output vector is likely to imply excess demand for skilled labour of various types and excess supply of unskilled labour. We may therefore write the labour requirements (see Chapter 13.2) as:

$$l(t) = N(t)x(t) \tag{17.9}$$

where $l(t)$ is a $(k \times 1)$ vector of the different types of labour and $N(t)$ is a $(k \times n)$ matrix whose i, jth element shows the requirement of the ith type of labour per unit of output in the jth sector. This matrix is written with a time dimension to emphasize the need to allow for changes in (gross) labour productivity in each sector (cf. Chapter 4.5).

The vector of labour requirements—$l(t)$—can be compared with the likely supply of labour by type over the plan period; as long as the plan is of less than ten years' duration, this is a relatively easy exercise since those who are going to enter the labour force have already been born. Nonetheless, it still requires careful consideration of the 'inputs' and 'outputs' from the educational system; there are formal models (cf. Blitzer, 1975) which can be used to link educational requirements to the solution to the input–output model, but informal methods are usually sufficient to tell whether a particular labour skill is likely to be a constraint on the implied plan solution. These informal methods can also direct the planner's attention to areas of the educational system which need strengthening; if this requires revision in educational expenditures, an iterative procedure is involved, going back again (if necessary) to the 'macro' stage.

Whether investment is estimated exogenously or endogenously, its financing could prove sufficiently difficult to undermine the feasibility of the plan. The sources of investment finance can be derived from a social accounting matrix (Table 1.3 in Chapter 1) as (a) household saving; (b) business saving; (c) public saving; and (d) foreign lending (i.e. borrowing from abroad). The solution to the input–output model serves as a starting point for the estimation of all these forms of finance and so it can be used to check on the feasibility of the investment programme.

Foreign borrowing, since it is by definition equal to the current account balance of payments deficit, need not detain us further since it has already been discussed above. Household saving is the difference between disposable income and consumption; the latter is given exogenously, while the former can be derived from estimated national income by knowledge of the appropriate tax rates. Business saving is closely related to gross trading profits, which emerge from the solution to the input–output model as the residual after calculation of labour income, and public saving is the difference between government current expenditure (given exogenously) and government current revenues. The latter consists of all the direct and indirect taxes, whose levels can be worked out from the input–output model's solutions for production, exports, imports and factor incomes.

If investment is estimated exogenously, a further check on the feasibility of the plan is provided by estimating the change in the capital stock over the plan period; this can be done by premultiplying the vector of the change in output by a diagonalized vector of incremental capital–ouput ratios ($\hat{b}$), i.e.

$$\Delta k = \hat{b}[x(t) - x(0)] \tag{17.10}$$

where Δk is a vector whose jth element measures the change in the jth sector's capital stock over the plan period. The build-up in capital throughout the life of the plan implied by equation (17.10) may be quite inconsistent with the amount of investment estimated exogenously for the terminal year, suggesting revisions to the latter.

We have now looked at the most obvious obstacles to the successful operation of the plan. Many other possible obstacles, such as shortages of administrative personnel and lack of entrepreneurship, have not been considered because they defy formal analysis, although that must clearly occupy the attention of planners in practice. There is one additional potential threat, however, to the successful operation of the plan which is worth discussing—the flow of funds or supply of finance.

Although the investment-savings balance may look acceptable to the planners, it is still possible that the plan may fail through lack of adequate finance. Much agricultural and industrial output in LDCs is dependent on short-term credit for working capital from the banking system; this credit will not be forthcoming unless the economy's money supply is expanding at a rate consistent with output, price and velocity changes. The money supply 'rests' on the monetary base, movements in which are linked primarily to movements in foreign exchange reserves and government debt held by the Central Bank.

In their estimation of the feasible level of imports and exports, the planners may already have made allowances for changes in net foreign exchange reserves; furthermore, in many LDCs no real market for government bonds exists so that the public sector borrowing requirement is equivalent to the increase in Central Bank holdings of government debt. In such a case, it might seem relatively simple to work out the implied change in monetary base, money supply and credit and to compare this with the productive system's need for short-term finance (see, for example, Taylor, 1979b, Chapters 2 and 3).

Unfortunately, unless the gap between demand for and supply of credit is enormous, the exercise is unlikely to be very fruitful. Over all but the very short-run, large errors are likely to be made in 'financial programming', because of the difficulty in forecasting changes in the monetary base; many LDC governments, despite received wisdom, do succeed in marketing public debt to the private sector and changes in net foreign exchange reserves are notoriously difficult to predict. If bank credit is unavailable, alternative sources of funds can often be found (albeit at higher interest costs) and it seems unwise to abandon an otherwise feasible plan because of anticipated credit bottlenecks several years ahead.

In our brief summary of the planning process, the need for a 'dialogue' between the macro and the sectoral stage was frequently stressed; this iterative procedure, however, is costly and time consuming and it is tempting to consider whether the macro stage can be eliminated altogether. The main source of inconsistency between the two stages is most likely to be the choice of a rate of growth for GDP at the macro stage which cannot be supported by the economy when translated to the sectoral stage. If, therefore, the growth rate were to emerge from the solution to the sectoral model rather than being imposed on it, a way out of the *impasse* might have been found.

The main component of GDP is consumer's expenditure; if this becomes endogenous, GDP and therefore the implied growth rate can be made endogenous as well. Consumers' expenditure depends above all on households' disposable income, which in turn depends on factor incomes; the latter depend on production levels which in turn depend, among other things, on consumers' expenditure. We are therefore in a highly interdependent system which can be solved relatively easily if we restrict ourselves to relationships capable of linear algebraic formulation.

Such a system was outlined in Chapter 4.5 and was illustrated in Chapter 12.3. The basic equation is provided by equation (4.26) in which the vectors for output, factor incomes and institutional incomes are seen to depend on each other in a strictly linear fashion. In this model, a solution can be found once the exogenous demand for each set of accounts has been estimated; in the case of producers, for example, exogenous demand is limited to exports, government expenditure and (if necessary) investment, but consumption is determined by the model.

Equation (4.26) looks like a neat answer to our problem. However, as was pointed out in Chapter 4.5, the model makes very heavy use of the assumption of fixed coefficients and absence of price effects; although this may be acceptable for structural analysis at a moment in time (as in Chapter 12.3), it is pushing credibility to assumed fixed coefficients for all relationships in equation (4.26) for the life of the plan. We shall see below how—with great difficulty—allowance can be made for changes in the input–output technology (A) matrix, but as yet we have few ideas about changes in the other matrices referred to in equation (4.26).

It would seem, therefore, that a macro stage in the planning process is unavoidable. This means that consumers' expenditure in the sectoral model must first be forecast and we shall consider how this can be done shortly; in addition, other elements in final demand need to be forecast and allowance needs to be made for changes in the coefficient matrices. We shall discuss each of these in turn.

17.4 FORECASTING COEFFICIENTS

Forecasts of final demand and the coefficient matrices can be carried out in constant or current prices and the choice between these alternatives first has to be resolved. Since the fundamental assumption of input–output theory (see Chapter 4.2) refers to the constancy of physical inputs per unit of physical output, it might seem sensible to work in constant prices; this would have the considerable advantage of making unnecessary any forecasts or predictions of price changes in each sector while keeping within the spirit of input–output theory.

This advantage is likely to prove spurious, however; with the passage of time, the evidence that some input–output coefficients are price sensitive (de Boer, 1979) is becoming overwhelming (see Chapter 10.4); even if LDCs can still afford to ignore this evidence for various reasons (see below), there can be no doubt that elements of final demand—above all consumers' expenditure—are sensitive to price changes so that a good final demand forecast can only be made if the movement in relative prices over the plan period is first estimated.

If relative price changes are forecast, it is still possible to work in constant prices—once the effect on volumes of the price changes have been taken into account. However, many of the planning exercises (e.g. estimating balance of payments deficits) are more normally carried out in current prices, while only if the future technology matrix is estimated at current prices can one be sure that the column sum of coefficients (including value added) will sum to unity (see Miernyk, 1977). It would seem, therefore, more sensible to forecast final demand and the coefficient matrices in current prices with the ability to deflate value changes to volume changes through knowledge of the appropriate price indices.

The estimation of future price levels is not an easy matter. One possibility is to extrapolate from past trends; this can be dangerous and, in any case, assumes that available price statistics are compatible with the sectorization of the input–output table (which is unlikely to be the case). Another possibility is to estimate future prices using the input–output model (see Chapter 14.4); all that is needed is an estimate of primary input prices in the terminal year from which a set of price relatives for all sectors in the input–output table can be derived.

It has to be admitted that many LDCs will continue to plan in constant prices, because no estimates of relative price changes have been made; such plans may still have something to offer and the remarks below on forecasting coefficients and final demand should prove helpful even in such cases. In most of what follows, however, we shall assume that the price change in each sector over the plan period *has* been estimated.

The coefficient matrices with which we are concerned are $A(t)$, $A_m(t)$, $\hat{d}(t)$, $N(t)$ and $\hat{b}$, as described in equations (17.1) to (17.10). In addition, mention must also be made of the capital coefficient matrices B_D and B_M used to estimate investment endogenously (see Chapters 11.3 and 14.3). The most important of these is the matrix of technical coefficients $A(t)$. At current prices, on the assumption of a zero price elasticity of substitution, a first estimate of this matrix (see Chapter 10.2) is given by $\hat{P}A(0)\hat{P}^{-1}$, where $(\hat{P})$ is a diagonalized vector of price relatives for each sector over the plan period; with a price elasticity of substitution of unity, the first estimate is just $A(0)$. The truth, however, is likely to lie between these two extremes.

When input demand functions are derived from cost minimizing first principles (see Diewert, 1971), prices enter explicitly into the function as arguments; tests on these functions (e.g. P. Taylor, 1979) suggest that the influence of relative price change on input demands is not negligible. These functions, however, require a time-series of input–output tables for their estimation, which is something unavailable to LDCs, but in view of the tests mentioned it is reasonable for LDCs to start by assuming a price elasticity closer to unity and use $A(0)$ as the first estimate of the unknown $A(t)$, as suggested in Chapter 10.4.

The preferred method in the past of projecting the technology matrix on the basis of this first estimate has been one of the matrix balancing techniques described in the appendix to Chapter 8. It was shown in Chapter 10.4 that these methods cannot be considered very satisfactory for updating, let alone projecting, coefficients if none of the elements of $A(t)$ are estimated exogenously. The problem becomes even more acute when it is remembered that the row and column matrix sums used as marginal totals in a projection will be very uncertain; if past trends in coefficients are simply extrapolated, however, the method is inherently unstable (see Chapter 10.5).

An alternative to mechanical matrix balancing techniques is the so-called *ex ante* method (Fisher, 1975b). Basically, the method consists of finding sectoral experts whose knowledge of each sector in the input–output table can be used to forecast the change in technological coefficients over the plan period; this technique relies heavily on the existence of a set of competent experts whose judgements will need to embrace not only technological change, but also price changes and product mix changes (see Miernyk, 1977). It is doubtful if such experts can forecast accurately all changes in the matrix of technical coefficients, but fortunately this is not necessary; as was shown in Chapter 10.4, knowledge of the major coefficients in the matrix *ex ante* can make a substantial difference to the success of matrix balancing techniques. It follows that every effort should be made, either by survey[1] or by consultation with experts, to prepare exogenous estimates of the change in at least the main technical coefficients.

The next matrix to be considered is $(\hat{d})$, whose elements represent the proportion of total home demand accounted for by domestic producers in each sector. Changes in this matrix reflect changes in import substitution; given the importance of the latter as a source of economic growth (see Chapter 15.3), great care must be taken in estimating the parameters of the $(\hat{d})$ matrix.

An increase in the value of any element in the $(\hat{d})$ matrix means that planners expect producers to increase their output at the (relative) expense of imports. Such a decision should be based on considerations of comparative costs; by calculating the Domestic Resource Cost (DRC) criterion (see Chapter 16.4) for each sector, planners can get a first idea of where the country's comparative advantage lies. This will at least help to determine which elements of $(\hat{d})$ should be increased, which decreased and which left unchanged.

The *extent* of the change, however, is another matter. If all relationships in the economy were strictly linear (in particular, production should be subject to constant returns to scale while the supply of imports should be infinitely elastic), then those elements of $(\hat{d})$ to be increased would move to unity and those to be decreased would move to zero. In practice, production is subject to important non-linearities which the planner must try to allow for despite the fact that they are not reflected formally in the input–output model. In particular, the planner should probably err on the side of caution; increases and decreases in the elements of $(\hat{d})$ should be small because of the difficulties likely to be incurred if capacity is forecast to double or shrink by half, for example.

There are some cases, however, where it is legitimate to assume large changes in the elements of $(\hat{d})$. At the start of the plan period, it may already be known that large extensions to capacity will be coming on stream before the terminal year; in some sectors, furthermore, the minimum viable plant size constitutes a substantial chunk of the market so that import substitution, if it is to occur at all, requires relatively large changes in some elements of $(\hat{d})$.

Assuming that competitive imports are perfect substitutes for home output, the $(\hat{d})$ matrix need not be corrected for price changes, since the same price change enters into both the numerator and denominator. We may therefore leave the $(\hat{d})$ matrix and turn to (A_m), the matrix of non-competitive imports. Some import substitution will, in fact, occur in sectors where there was previously no home output; imports in those sectors would initially be classified as non-competitive, but as soon as home output begins, imports become 'competitive' so that changes in the $(\hat{d})$ matrix may frequently require compensating changes in (A_m). (A good example is provided by imports of refined oil, which leave the A_m matrix, once local refinery capacity is installed, to be replaced by crude oil imports.) Apart from these obvious changes, it will also be necessary to forecast changes in the (A_m) matrix due to technological progress or changes in relative prices and here, again, the advice of sectoral experts could prove invaluable.

The matrix of labour requirements—$N(t)$—is liable to change quite substantially over the plan period; some of these changes (e.g. those due to the change in the price of output in the denominator) are obvious enough; others are likely to be very difficult to incorporate (e.g. those due to a non-zero elasticity of substitution between labour and capital). If we ignore the change in $N(t)$ due to changes in the relative price of factors of production, then the most important influence on the elements of $N(t)$ is likely to be the scale of output. As was shown in Chapter 4.5, the relationship between labour use and output is likely to be non-linear; it should be possible, however, to develop simple labour demand equations for each sector along the lines of equation (4.22) and these can be used to project the absorption of labour, in which case the matrix of fixed coefficients—$N(t)$—becomes redundant (see also Chapter 13.4). If $N(t)$ must be used, it should at least be adjusted for the change in (gross) productivity extrapolated from time trends.

The remaining coefficient matrices—$\hat{b}$, B_D and B_M—all refer to capital requirements and forecasting them to the terminal year can be difficult. Changes in B_D—the matrix of domestic capital requirements per unit of output—due to import substitution will of course produce compensating changes in B_M—the matrix of imported capital requirements—and again for the more advanced LDCs, i.e. those thinking of establishing or expanding their capital goods industries, the DRC criterion can be used to change many of the elements of the two matrices by establishing which capital goods producing sectors are most suitable for promotion.

Other changes in B_D, B_M and $\hat{b}$ (the diagonal matrix of sectoral capital–output ratios) are likely to be due mainly to technological progress. Furthermore, as equation (17.10) shows, these matrices have to be interpreted as *incremental* capital–output ratios so that consultation with sectoral experts is indispensable. In practice, particularly in LDCs, major technical innovations are often confined to a limited number of sectors, and even on occasions a small number of establishments within sectors, so that the possibility of a supplementary survey of such sectors or establishments, with a view to establishing expected changes in capital coefficients, should not be ruled out.[1]

The relationship between the three capital coefficient matrices in any year is given by:

$$i'\hat{b} = i'[B_D + B_M] \tag{17.11}$$

so that it is not necessary to estimate all three independently. The minimum requirement in development planning is some estimate of $(\hat{b})$ in order to prepare estimates of the build-up in each sector's capital stock over the plan period (see previous section), but B_D and B_M are needed if the planning model is to estimate investment endogenously.

17.5 FORECASTING FINAL DEMAND

We now turn to the elements of final demand, of which the most important is consumers' expenditure. As has been shown elsewhere (Taylor, 1975), the most usual method of forecasting sectoral consumption is by the Engel curve relationship:

$$\frac{c_i(t)}{POP(t)} = \Phi_i \left[\frac{C(t)}{POP(t)} \right]^{\varepsilon_i} \qquad i = 1, \ldots, n \tag{17.12}$$

where $POP(t)$ is population at time (t), C is the total of consumers' expenditure (as given, for example, by the macro-model), c_i is consumption of ith commodity and ε_i is the Engel elasticity. The latter is always derived from cross-section studies (usually households budget surveys) although equation (17.12) is applied to time-series forecasts; the most serious weakness, however, of this equation is the absence of price effects.

Since we are assuming that price changes have been forecast, there is no reason why sectoral consumption could not be estimated using a functional form which incorporates price effects. A very popular model for this is the Linear Expenditure System (LES) which can be derived from first principles to give demand functions of the form:

$$c_i = p_i \gamma_i + \beta_i (C - \Sigma p_j \gamma_j) \tag{17.13}$$

where β_i, γ_i are parameters of the model which need to be estimated. The LES suffers from a number of theoretical weaknesses (see Deaton, 1974), but has the great merit of being easy to apply. It has been widely used in the context of LDCs (see Lluch, 1977) and represents a distinct advance on models such as equation (17.12) which ignore price substitution effects in measuring consumption.

If the vectors of new investment—$j(t)$—and replacement expenditure—$r(t)$—are estimated exogenously, a few general points need to be kept in mind. Once non-competitive imports have been excluded from these vectors, most of what remains will consist of expenditure on construction; the output of the civil engineering side of the construction industry can usually be predicted quite accurately in view of the long gestation period of the projects involved, while the housebuilding programme is often subject to considerable government influence and can also be forecast. The building of offices, warehouses, factories, etc. is not so easy to predict, but here too knowledge of new projects to be started in the plan period will help.

There is little that can be said in a chapter of this nature on the other elements of final demand. In the case of exports, their planned rate of growth should be affected by the results of applying the DRC criterion, but will also depend on expected world market conditions. Elaborate models now exist (e.g. Behrman, 1978) for forecasting the supply of and demand for primary commodities and these models should prove of some assistance to LDCs in forecasting their primary exports.

17.6 PLANNING AND OPTIMIZATION

We have now outlined an input–output model, with its associated data problems, which can be used to provide a consistent and feasible development plan. There could be many such plans, however, each corresponding to a given set of model parameters and given final demands; since one of the purposes of planning is to accelerate the rate of economic growth, it is worth asking whether there is one among all these feasible plans which is in some sense optimal (see Chapter 14.5). In other words, given the constraints under which the economy works, can we find that pattern of final demand which makes the greatest contribution to society's welfare?

If the constraints are presented as a set of linear inequalities and if the objective function (e.g. the maximization of consumption) is also linear, then the appropriate technique for solving this problem is linear programming. This technique, reviewed briefly in Chapter 14.5, has proved very popular with economists, perhaps primarily because a by-product of the technique is the calculation of shadow prices which measure the marginal social cost of all commodities and factors in the model.

In the context of development planning, the principal advantage of linear programming techniques is the introduction of some degree of choice or flexibility; for example, the model can be asked to choose between home output or imports in each sector (the so-called 'make or buy' question) or between labour-intensive and capital-intensive techniques in each sector provided these can be specified. In each case, the choice is made in terms of efficiency criteria, where 'efficiency' is defined in terms of an activity's net contribution to the objective function. A further argument in favour of the technique is the derivation of shadow prices which can be used in project analysis to calculate social as opposed to private profitability.

Planning development using linear programming techniques is not beyond the capabilities of many LDCs and a number of interesting models for the larger LDCs have already been applied. A great deal of resources, however, become tied up in these exercises and the question is whether the same or better results could not be achieved by putting those resources to alternative uses. Analysis of the linear programming technique itself, and the way that models applied to LDCs work, have also thrown up a number of very awkward problems.

The main problem arises from the fact that many important relationships in the economies of LDCs are not linear; the single 'optimal' solution of the linear programming problem is therefore somewhat spurious. Introduction of non-linear relationships is possible up to a point (see Kendrick, 1971), but there is a limit to how far we can go in this direction and each change in the original (linear) statement of the problem will affect the 'optimal' solution and therefore also the derivation of shadow prices.

The single optimal solution is also sensitive to the choice of objective function (see Adelman, 1966); since there are often no strong grounds for preferring one function to another and since writing the function in a linear form often violates reality, this raises further problems with the optimal solution and its associated shadow prices. Some economists, notably Bruno (1966) and Weisskopf (1971) have tried to play down the difficulties by treating the objective function as an arbitrary device for tracing out the efficiency frontier of the economy in response to changes in the economy's constraints; for example, by increasing the volume of foreign aid which an economy can expect to receive, the balance of payments constraint is progressively relaxed so that the 'make or buy' problem is increasingly resolved in favour of imports; the model therefore selects those sectors where domestic production must cease and this, in turn, means that the order in which they leave the 'optimal' solution is a measure of comparative disadvantage with the most efficient sectors leaving last.

These and related experiments are certainly very useful, but it would be a bold planner indeed who took the results at face value. A good development plan requires that planners take cognizance of informal as well as formal constraints on the operation of the plan; only the latter kind of constraint can be entered into the model itself so that the need for judgement cannot be avoided. Furthermore, experimenting with different values for the constraints in a linear programming framework is not all that different to experimenting with final bills of goods in an input–output framework; in both cases the planner is faced with a 'menu' of possibilities from which he must choose according to his judgement.

Economy-wide optimization models do, however, have an enduring fascination and enormous efforts have been made in recent years to improve their flexibility. Chenery (1971) and others have explored ways of increasing the possibility of substitution in these models and, although the data required for implementation are not yet available for most LDCs, at least many of the technical problems have been conquered. The introduction of substitution possibilities, whether in production, consumption, or between factors, helps to remove the knife-edge problem which programming models suffer from, while at the same time giving greater stability to the shadow prices in the related dual solution. For a brilliant exposition of linear programming models, both static and dynamic, the interested reader can turn to the survey by Taylor (1975).

17.7 CONCLUSIONS

In this section, an effort is made to draw together the threads, not only of this chapter, but also of the rest of the book. The reason why the author has combined input–output analysis with the economics of developing countries in one book is because he believes that the former has a key role to play in understanding the latter. Much analysis of LDCs needs to be on an economy-wide basis (e.g. development planning) and this suggests the need for a macro-economic approach; most macro-models, however, are so highly aggregated that they must perforce assume a degree of resource mobility which is just not present in LDCs. The only answer seems to be input–output analysis, which is 'macro' in terms of its coverage and yet 'micro' in terms of its approach. The input–output literature has grown rapidly in the last thirty years and yet in at least two respects it must be classified as deficient; first, insufficient attention (compared with that given to national accounts, for example) has been given to problems of table construction and methodology; and, secondly, input–output analysis of LDCs has not been adequately modified to take account of their special economic problems. The first difficulty has meant that the construction of tables in LDCs has usually been a very protracted affair, leading to a sense of despondence among those responsible; the second has helped to perpetuate a myth that input–output analysis is only appropriate for DCs.

In an effort to overcome the first deficiency, the author has devoted almost two-thirds of the book (Chapters 1–11) to problems of construction and methodology. The reader who has persevered with those chapters and who then finds himself responsible for constructing or interpreting input–output tables should have little trouble in negotiating the traps into which inexperienced researchers in this field tend to fall. The last six chapters of the book, by contrast, are concerned with applications of input–output analysis suitable for LDCs; although these models have been taken or modified from the current literature on developed economies, the author knows of no other book where they are all brought together in one place and it is hoped that in this way, LDCs will never again produce input–output tables for which no use can be found.

NOTES

1 In the Moroccan input–output study, with which the author was involved, a questionnaire was designed with this purpose in mind, but it was unfortunately not adopted because of a shortage of time.

References

Adelman, I. and Sparrow, F. T. (1966). 'Experiments with linear and piece-wise linear dynamic programming models', in Adelman, I. and Thorbecke, E. (eds.), *The Theory and Design of Economic Development*. Baltimore: Johns Hopkins University Press.

Adelman, I. and Morris, C. T. (1973). *Economic Growth and Social Equity in Developing Countries*. Stanford: Stanford University Press.

Adelman, I. and Robinson, S. (1977). *Income Distribution Policies in Developing Countries, A Case Study of Korea*. Stanford: Stanford University Press.

Ahluwahlia, M. (1974). 'Income inequality: some dimensions of the problem,' in Chenery, H. et al., *Redistribution With Growth*. London: OUP.

Aitchison, J. and Brown, J. A. C. (1957). *The Lognormal Distribution*. Cambridge: CUP.

Allen, R. I. G. (1974). 'Some experiments with the RAS method of input–output coefficients.' *Bulletin of the Oxford University Institute of Economics and Statistics*, **36**, pp. 215–228.

Allen, R. I. G. and Lecomber, J. R. C. (1975). 'Some tests on a generalised version of RAS', in Allen, R. I. G. and Gossling, W. F. (eds.), *Estimating and Projecting Input–Output Coefficients*. London: Input–Output Publishing Co.

Almon, C. (1970). 'Investment in input–output models and the treatment of secondary products,' in Carter, A. and Bródy, A. (eds.), *Contributions to Input–Output Analysis*, Vol. II. Amsterdam: North-Holland.

Almon, C., Buckler, M. B., Horwitz, L. M. and Reinhold, T. C. (1974). *1985 Interindustry Forecasts of the American Economy*. Lexington, Mass.: D. C. Heath.

Ara, K. (1959) 'The aggregation problem in input–output analysis.' *Econometrica*, **27**, pp. 257–262.

Armstrong, A. G. (1975). 'Technology assumptions in the construction of U.K. input–output tables,' in Allen, R. I. G. and Gossling, W. F. (eds.), *Estimatimg and Projecting Input–Output Coefficients*. London: Input–Output Publishing Co.

Bacharach, M. (1970). *Biproportional Matrices and Input-Output Change*. Cambridge: CUP.

Balassa, B. (1965). 'Tariff protection in industrial countries: an evaluation.' *Journal of Political Economy*, **73**, pp. 717–724.

Balassa, B. and Schydlowsky, D. M. (1968). 'Effective tariffs, domestic cost of foreign exchange, and the equillibrium exchange rate.' *Journal of Political Economy*, **76**, pp. 348–360.

Balderston, J. B. and Whitin, T. M. (1954). 'Aggregation in the input–output model,' in Morgenstern, O. (ed.), *Economic Activity Analysis*. New York: Wiley.

Barker, T. (1975). 'Some experiments in projecting intermediate demand', in Allen, R. I. G. and Gossling, W. F. (eds.), *Estimating and Projecting Input–Output Coefficients*. London: Input–Output Publishing Co.

Behrman, J. R. and Adams, F. G. (1978). *Econometric Modeling of World Commodity Policy*. New York: Lexington.

Bergsman, J. and Manne, A. S. (1966). 'An almost consistent intertemporal model for India's fourth and fifth plans', in Adelman, I. and Thorbecke, E. (eds.), *The Theory and Design of Economic Development*. Baltimore: Johns Hopkins Press.

Bhagwati, J. (1964). 'The pure theory of international trade: a survey.' *Economic Journal*, **74,** pp. 1–84.

Bhagwati, J. (1978). *Anatomy and Consequences of Exchange Control Regimes*. Cambridge, Mass.: Ballinger.

Bhagwati, J. and Srinivasan, T. (1978). 'Shadow prices for project selection in the presence of distortions.' *Journal of Political Economy*, **86,** pp. 97–116.

Blin, J.-M. and Cohen, C. (1977). 'Technological similarity and aggregation in input–output systems: a cluster-analytic approach.' *Review of Economics and Statistics*, **60,** pp. 82–91.

Blitzer, C. (1975). 'Employment and human capital formation', in Blitzer, C., Clark, P. and Taylor, L. (eds.), *Economy-Wide Models and Development Planning*. Oxford: OUP.

Blitzer, C., Clark, P. and Taylor, L. (1975). *Economy-Wide Models and Development Planning*. Oxford: OUP.

de Boer, P. M. C. (1976). 'On the relationship between production functions and input–output analysis with fixed value shares.' *Weltwirtschaftliches Archiv*, Band 112, pp. 754–759.

de Boer, P. M. C. (1979). 'Effects of relative price changes on input–output ratios—an empirical study for the Netherlands.' Paper presented to the Seventh International Conference on Input–Output Techniques, Innsbruck, April, 1979.

Bródy, A. (1970). *Proportions, Prices and Planning*. Amsterdam: North-Holland.

Brown, A. A. and Licari, J. A. (1977). 'Price formation models and economic efficiency', in Abouchar, A. (ed.), *The Socialist Price Mechanism*. Durham, North Carolina: Duke University Press.

Brown, D. M. and Giarratini, F. (1979). 'Input–output as a simple econometric model: a comment.' *Review of Economics and Statistics*, **61,** pp. 621–623.

Brown, J. A. C. and Stone, R. (1962). 'Output and investment for exponential growth in consumption.' *Review of Economic Studies*, **29,** pp. 241–245.

Bruno, M. (1966). 'A programming model for Israel', in Adelman, I. and Thorbecke, E. (eds.), *The Theory and Design of Economic Development*. Baltimore: Johns Hopkins Press.

Bruno, M. (1971). 'Optimal patterns of trade and development', in Chenery, H. (ed.), *Studies in Development Planning*. Cambridge: Harvard University Press.

Bruno, M., Dougherty, C. and Fraenkel, M. (1972a). 'Dynamic input–output, trade and development', in Carter, A. P. and Bródy, A. (eds.), *Applications of Input–Output Analysis*, Vol. II. Amsterdam: North-Holland.

Bruno, M. (1972b). 'Domestic resource costs and effective protection—Clarification and synthesis.' *Journal of Political Economy*, **80,** pp. 16–33.

Bruno, M. (1975). 'Planning models, shadow prices and project evaluation', in Blitzer, C., Clark, P. and Taylor, L. (eds.), *Economy-Wide Models and Development Planning*. Oxford: OUP.

Bulmer-Thomas, V. (1976). 'The structure of protection in Costa Rica—a new approach to calculating the effective rate of protection.' *Journal of Economic Studies*, **3,** pp. 13–28.

Bulmer-Thomas, V. (1977a). 'An Input–Output Planning Model for Costs Rica', unpublished D. Phil. Thesis, Oxford.

Bulmer-Thomas, V. (1977b). 'A model of inflation for central America.' *Bulletin of the Oxford Institute of Economics and Statistics*, **39,** pp. 319-332.

Bulmer-Thomas, V. (1978a). 'Income, Expenditure and the Balance of Payments in Scotland—an Input–Output Approach', Fraser of Allander Institute, Research Monograph, No. 6.

Bulmer-Thomas, V. (1978b). 'The valuation of transactions in input–output tables.' *Journal of Economic Studies*, **5**, pp. 1–19.

Bulmer-Thomas, V. (1978c). 'Trade, structure and linkages in Costa Rica.' *Journal of Development Economics*, **5**, pp. 73–86.

Bulmer-Thomas, V. (1979). 'Export promotion v. import substitution in the Central American common market.' *Journal of Economic Studies*, **6**, pp. 182–203.

Burdekin, R. (1978a). *The construction of the 1973 Scottish input–output tables*. IBM (UK) Scientific Centre.

Burdekin, R. and Scowen, R. S. (1978b). 'Computers and the construction of economic models.' *The Computer Journal*, **22**, pp. 3–10.

Burdekin, R. and Al-Ali, H. M. (1978c). *An analysis of some aspects of the Scottish economy using input–output techniques*. IBM (UK) Scientific Centre.

Bureau of Labour Statistics (U.S. Department of Labour) (1979). 'Capital Stock Estimates for Input–Output Industries: Methods and Data.' Bulletin 2034, Washington.

Carter, A. (1963). 'Incremental flow coefficients for a dynamic input–output model with changing technology', in Barna, T. (ed.), *Structural interdependence and Economic Development*. London: Macmillan.

Carter, A. (1970). *Structural Change in the American Economy*. Cambridge, Mass.: Harvard University Press.

Central Statistical Office (CSO) (1973). *Input–Output Tables for the United Kingdom*, 1968. London: HMSO.

Central Statistical Office (1976). *Input–Output Tables for the United Kingdom, 1972*. London: HMSO.

Chakravarty, S. (1969). *Capital and Development Planning*. Cambridge, Mass.: MIT Press.

Chenery, H. and Watanabe, T. (1958). 'International comparisons of the structure of production.' *Econometrica*, **26**, pp. 487–521.

Chenery, H. B. and Clark, P. (1959). *Interindustry Economics*. New York: Wiley.

Chenery, H. (1960). 'Pattern of industrial growth.' *American Economic Review*, **50**, pp. 624–654.

Chenery, H. (1961). 'Comparative advantage and development policy.' *American Economic Review*, **51**, pp. 18–51.

Chenery, H. and Taylor, L. (1968). 'Development patterns: among countries and over time.' *Review of Economics and Statistics*, **50**, pp. 391–416.

Chenery, H. and Raduchel, W. (1971). 'Substitution in planning models', in Chenery, H. (ed.), *Studies in Development Planning*. Cambridge, Mass.: Harvard University Press.

Clark, P. B. (1970). *Planning Import Substitution*. Amsterdam: North-Holland.

Corden, M. (1966). 'The structure of a tariff system and the effective protective rate.' *Journal of Political Economy*, **74**, pp. 221–237.

Corden, M. (1971). *The Theory of Protection*. Oxford: OUP.

Courbis, R. and Pommier, C. (1979). *Construction d'un Tableau d'Échanges Inter-Industriels et Inter-Régionaux de l'Économie Française*. Paris: Economica.

Czamanski, S. and Malizia, E. E. (1969). 'Applicability and limitations in the use of national input–output tables for regional studies.' *The Regional Science Association Papers*, **23**, pp. 65–77.

Dar Al-Handasah (1977). 'Étude d'identification et d'évaluation des possibilités d'investissements industriels.' Rapport No. 2, Plan de L'enquête Industrielle, Rabat.

Dar Al-Handasah (1979). Étude d'identification et d'évaluation des possibilités d'investissements industriels, élaboration du tableau entrées-sorties 1975, Vols. 1–3, Beirut.

Deaton, A. S. (1974). 'A reconsideration of the empirical implications of additive preferences.' *Economic Journal*, **84**, pp. 338–348.

Diamond, J. (1975). 'Inter-industry indicators of employment potential.' *Applied Economics*, **7**, pp. 265–273.

Diaz-Alejandro, C. (1965). 'On the import-intensity of import substituting industrialisation', Kyklos.

Dieckheuer, G., Schumann, J. and Meyer, U. (1979). 'Simultaneous determination of sectoral production quantities and prices in a dynamic input–output model—demonstrated for the Federal Republic of Germany.' Paper presented to the Seventh International Conference, on Input–Output Techniques, Innsbruck, April, 1979.

Diewert, W. E. (1971). 'An application of the Shephard duality theorem: a generalized Leontief production function.' *Journal of Political Economy*, **79,** pp. 481–507.

Domar, E. (1957). *Essays in the Theory of Economic Growth.* Oxford: OUP.

Dorfman, R., Samuelson, P. and Solow, R. (1958). *Linear Programming and Economic Analysis.* New York: McGraw-Hill .

Drábek, Z. (1980). 'Input–output price models and their use in inter-country comparisons.' Discussion Paper No. 80—26, Dept. of Economics, University of British Columbia.

van Driel, G. J., Hartog, J. A. and van Ravenzwaaij, C. (1980). *Limits to the Welfare State.* Boston: Martinus Nijhoff.

Eckaus, R. S. and Parikh, K. S. (1968). *Planning for Growth: Multisectoral, Intertemporal Models Applied to India.* Cambridge, Mass.: MIT Press.

Edwards, E. O. (ed.) (1974). *Employment in Developing Nations.* New York: Columbia University Press.

Evans, W. D. and Hoffenberg, M. (1952). 'The interindustry relations study for 1947.' *Review of Economics and Statistics*, **34,** pp. 97–142.

Fisher, W. (1958). 'Criteria for aggregation in input–output analysis.' *Review of Economics and Statistics*, **40,** pp. 250–260.

Fisher, W. H. (1975a). 'Ex ante as a supplement or alternative to RAS in updating input–output coefficients', in Allen, R. I. G. and Gossling, W. F. (eds.), *Estimating and Projecting Input–Output coefficients.* London: Input–Output Publishing Co.

Fisher, W. H. and Chilton, C. H. (1975b). 'Developing ex ante input–output flow and capital coefficients', in Gossling, W. F. (ed.), *Capital Coefficients and Dynamic Input–Output Models.* London: Input–Output Publishing Company.

Fraser of Allander Institute, The Scottish Council Research Institute and IBM United Kingdom Scientific Centre (1978). 'Input–Output Tables for Scotland, 1973.' Edinburgh: Scottish Academic Press.

Friedlander, D. (1961). 'A technique for estamating a contingency table, given the marginal totals and some supplementary data.' *Journal of the Royal Statistical Society*, **124,** pp. 412-420.

Geary, R. C. (1973). 'A method of estimating the elements of an intèr-industry matrix, knowing the row and column totals.' *Economic and Social review*, **4,** pp. 477–485.

Gerking, S. D. (1976). 'Estimation of stochastic input–output models.' *Studies in Applied Regional Science*, vol. 3. Leiden: Martinus Nijhoff Social Sciences Division.

Gerking, S. D. (1979). 'Input–output as a simple econometric model: a reply.' *Review of Economics and Statistics*, **61,** pp. 623–626.

Ghosh, A. and Sengupta, A. K. (1979a). 'Income Distribution and production structure in an input–output framework.' Paper presented to the Seventh International Conference on Input–Output Techniques, Innsbruck, April, 1979.

Ghosh, A. (1979b). 'Input–output models for planning in a mixed economy—a new approach.' Paper presented to the Seventh International Conference on Input–Output Techniques, Innsbruck, April, 1979.

Green, M. J. (1975). 'Investment matrices for the United Kingdom; their structure and use in forecasting', in Gossling, W. F. (ed.), *Capital Coefficients and Dynamic Input–Output Models.* London: Input–Output Publishing Co.

Hadley, G. (1961). *Linear Algebra.* Reading, Mass.: Addison-Wesley.

Harrigan, F., McGilvray, J. and McNicoll, I. H. (1980). 'A comparison of national and regional technical structures.' *Economic Journal*, **90,** pp. 795–810.

Hatanaka, M. (1952). 'A note on consolidation within a Leontief system.' *Econometrica*, **20,** pp. 301–303.

Hawkins, D. and Simon, H. A. (1949). 'Note: some conditions of macroeconomic stability.' *Econometrica*, **17**, pp. 245–248.

Hazari, B. R. and Krishnamurthy, J. (1970). 'Employment implications of India's industrialisation: analysis in an input–output framework.' *Review of Economics and Statistics*, **52**, pp. 181–186.

Henry, E. W. (1973a). 'A note on the logarithmic transformation of the RAS.' *Economic and Social Review*, **4**, pp. 487–492.

Henry, E. W. (1973b). 'Relative efficiency of RAS versus least squares methods of updating input–output structures, as adjudged by application to Irish data.' *Economic and Social Review*, **5**, pp. 7–29.

Hicks, J. R. (1965). *Capital and Growth*. Oxford: OUP.

Hirschman, A. (1958). *The Strategy of Economic Development*. New Haven: Yale University Press.

Hoover, E. (1971). *An Introduction to Regional Economics*. New York: Alfred A. Knopf.

IBGE (1979). *Matriz de Relações Intersetoriais Brazil 1970*, Rio de Janeiro.

International Labor Organization (ILO) (1972). *Employment, Incomes and Equality—a Strategy for Increasing Productive Employment in Kenya*. Geneva: ILO.

International Monetary Fund (1977). *Balance of Payments Manual*. New York.

International Monetary Fund (1979). *Balance of Payments Yearbook*. New York.

Isard, W. et al. (1960). *Methods of Regional Analysis: An Introduction to Regional Science*. Cambridge, Mass.: MIT Press.

Isard, W. (1951). 'International and regional input–output analysis: a model of a space economy.' *Review of Economics and Statistics*, **33**, pp. 318–328.

Isard, W. and Langford, T. (1971). *Regional Input–Output Study: Recollections, Reflections and Diverse Notes on the Philadelphia Experience*. Cambridge, Mass.: MIT Press.

Jarvin Emerson, M. (1976). 'Interregional trade effects in static and dynamic input–output models', in Polenske, K. R. and Skolka, J. V. (eds.), *Advances in Input–Output Analysis*. Cambridge, Mass.: Ballinger.

Jensen, R. C. and McGaurr, D. (1976). 'Reconciliation of purchases and sales estimates in an input–output table.' *Urban Studies*, **13**, pp. 59–65.

Johansen, L. (1978). 'On the theory of dynamic input–output models with different time profiles of capital construction and finite life-time of capital equipment.' *Journal of Economic Theory*, **19**, pp. 513–533.

Jones, L. P. (1976). 'The measurement of Hirschmanian linkages.' *Quarterly Journal of Economics*, **90**, pp. 323–333.

Jones, R. (1956–7). 'Factor proportions and the Hecksher-Ohlin model.' *Review of Economic Studies*, **24**, pp. 1–10.

Kendrick, D. and Taylor, L. (1971). 'Numerical methods and nonlinear optimizing models for economic planning', in Chenery, H. (ed.), *Studies in Development Planning*. Cambridge, Mass.; Harvard University Press.

Khang, C. (1973). 'Factor substitution in the Theory of effective protection: a general equilibrium analysis.' *Journal of International Economics*, **3**, pp. 227–244.

Kmenta, J. (1971). *Elements of Econometrics*. New York: Macmillan.

Komiya, R. and Uchida, T. (1963). 'The labour coefficient and the size of establishment in Two Japanese industries', in Barna, T. (ed.), *Structural Interdependence and Economic Development*. London: Macmillan.

Kossov, V. (1970). 'The theory of aggregation in input–output models', in Carter, A. P. and Bródy, A. (eds.), *Contributions to Input–Output Analysis*, Vol. I. Amsterdam: North-Holland.

Krishnamurty, J. (1975). 'Indirect employment effects of investment', in Bhalla, A. S. (ed.), *Technology and Employment in Industry*. Geneva: ILO.

Krueger, A. (1966). 'Some economic costs of exchange control: the Turkish case.' *Journal of Political Economy*, **74**, pp. 466–480.

Kuyvenhoven, A. (1976). 'Sector appraisal where trade opportunities are limited', in Polenske, K. and Skolka, J. (eds.), *Advances in Input–Output Analysis*. Cambridge, Mass.: Ballinger.

Kuyvenhoven, A. (1978). *Planning with the Semi-Input–Output Method.* Leiden: Martinus Nijhoff.

Kuznets, S. (1955). 'Economic growth and income inequality.' *American Economic Review*, **45,** pp. 1–28.

Kuznets, S. (1963). 'Quantitative aspects of the economic growth of nations: VIII. distribution of income by size.' *Economic Development and Cultural Change*, **11,** pp. 1–80.

Lall, S. (1973). 'Transfer pricing by multinational manufacturing firms.' *Bulletin of the Oxford University Institute of Economics and Statistics*, **35,** pp. 173–196.

Landau, L. (1971). 'Saving functions for Latin America', in Chenery, H. (ed.), *Studies in Development Planning*. Cambridge, Mass.: Harvard University Press.

Laumas, P. S. (1976). 'The weighting problem in testing the linkage hypothesis.' *Quarterly Journal of Economics*, **90,** pp. 308–312.

Lecomber, J. R. C. (1964). 'A generalisation of RAS.' Cambridge, Department of Applied Economics, Growth Project Paper No. 196.

Lecomber, J. R. C. (1975). 'A critique of methods of adjusting, updating and projecting matrices', in Allen, R. I. G. and Gossling, W. F. (eds.), *Estimating and Projecting Input–Output Coefficients.* London: Input–Output Publishing Co.

Lee, T. H. (1971). *Intersectoral Capital Flows in the Economic Development of Taiwan, 1895–1960*. Ithaca: Cornell University Press.

Leontief, W. W. (1951). *The Structure of the American Economy, 1919–39*. Cambridge, Mass.: Harvard University Press.

Leontief, W. (1953). 'Interregional theory', in Leontief, W. (ed.), *Studies in the Structure of the United States Economy*. New York, OUP.

Leontief, W. (1966). 'Domestic production and foreign trade: the American capital position re-examined,' *in Input–Output Economics*, Oxford: Oxford University Press.

Leontief, W. (1970). 'The dynamic inverse', in Carter, A. and Bródy, A. (eds.), *Contributions to Input–Output Analysis*, Vol. I. Amsterdam: North-Holland.

Lewis, W. Arthur (1966). *Development Planning: The Essentials of Economic Policy*. New York: Harper and Row.

Little, I., Scitovsky, T. and Scott, M. (1970). *Industry and Trade in Some Developing Countries.* Oxford: OUP.

Little, I. and Mirrlees, J. (1974). *Project Appraisal and Planning for Developing Countries.* London: Heinemann.

Livesey, D. A. (1976). 'A minimal realization of the Leontief dynamic input–output model', in Polenske, K. R. and Skolka, J. V. (eds.), *Advances in Input–Output Analysis.* Cambridge, Mass.: Ballinger.

Lluch, C., Powell, A. and Williams, R. (1977). *Patterns in Household Demand and Saving.* Oxford: OUP.

Lynch, R. G. (1979). 'An assessment of the RAS method for updating input–output tables.' Paper presented to the Seventh International Conference on Input–Output Techniques, Innsbruck, April, 1979.

McGilvray, J. (1977). 'Linkages, key sectors and development strategy', in Leontief, W. (ed.), *Structure, System and Economic Policy*. Cambridge: CUP.

Malinvaud, E. (1956). 'Aggregation problems in input–output models', in Barna, T. (ed.), *The Structural Interdependence of the Economy*. New York: Wiley.

Manne, A. S. (1963). 'Key sectors of the Mexican economy', in Manne, A. S. and Markowitz, H. M. (eds.), *Studies in Process Analysis: Economy-Wide Production Capabilities*. New York: Wiley.

Manne, A. S. (1966). 'Key sectors of the Mexican economy, 1962–1972', in Adelman, I. and Thorbecke, E. (eds.), *The Theory and Design of Economic Development*. Baltimore: Johns Hopkins Press.

Mathur, P. N. (1977). 'A study of sectoral prices and their movement in the British economy in an input–output framework', in Leontief, W. (ed.), *Structure, Systems and Economic Policy*. Cambridge: CUP.

Maton, J. and Garzuel, M. (1978). 'Redistribution of income, patterns of consumption and employment: a case study for Malaysia.' Working Paper No. 71, ILO, Geneva.

Matuszewski, T., Pitts, P. R. and Sawyer, J. A. (1964). 'Linear programming estimates of changes in input–output coefficients.' *Canadian Journal of Economic and Political Science*, **30**, pp. 203–210.

Meade, J. (1952). 'External economies and diseconomies in a competitive situation.' *Economic Journal*, **62**, pp. 54–67.

de Melo, J. and Robinson, S. (1979). 'Income distribution and trade policy in a multisector planning model.' Paper presented to the Seventh International Conference on Input–Output Techniques, Innsbruck, April, 1979.

Metzler, L. A. (1950). 'A multiple region theory of income and trade.' *Econometrica*, **18**, pp. 329–354.

Middlehoek, A. J. (1970). 'Tests of the marginal stability of input–output coefficients', in Carter, A. P. and Bródy, A. (eds.), *Applications of Input–Output Analysis*, Vol. II. Amsterdam: North-Holland.

Miernyk, H. et al. (1970). *Stimulating Regional Economic Development*. Lexington, Mass.: D. C. Heath.

Miernyk, W. H. (1977). 'The projection of technical coefficients for medium-term forecasting', in Gossling, W. F. (ed.), *Medium-Term Dynamic Forecasting*. London: Input–Output Publishing Co.

Minhas, B. S. (1962). 'The homohypallagic production function, factor intensity reversals and the Hecksher-Ohlin theorem.' *Journal of Political Economy*, **70**, pp. 138–156.

Miyazawa, K. (1976). *Input–Output Analysis and the Structure of Income Distribution*. Berlin: Springer-Verlag.

Morawetz, D. (1974). 'Employment implications of industrialisation in developing countries: a survey.' *Economic Journal*, **84**, pp. 491–542.

Morimoto, Y. (1970). 'On aggregation problems in input–output analysis.' *Review of Economic Studies*, **37**, pp. 119–126.

Morimoto, Y. (1971). 'A note on weighted aggregation in input–output analysis.' *International Economic Review*, **12**, pp. 138–143.

Morley, S. and Smith, G. (1970). 'On the measurement of import substitution.' *American Economic Review*, **60**, pp. 728–735.

Morrison, W. I. and Thumann, R. E. (1979). 'A Lagrangean multiplier approach to the solution of a special constrained matrix problem.' Paper presented to the Seventh International Conference on Input–Output Techniques, Innsbruck, April, 1979.

Moses, L. (1955). 'The stability of interregional trading patterns and input–output analysis'. *American Economic Review*, **45**, pp. 803–832.

Naya, S. (1967). 'Natural resources, factor mix and factor reversals in international trade.' *American Economic Review*, **57**, papers and proceedings, pp. 561–570.

Neudecker, H. (1970). 'Aggregation in input–output analysis: an extension of Fisher's methods.' *Econometrica*, **38**, pp. 921–926.

O'Connor, R. and Henry, E. W. (1975). *Input–Output Analysis and its Applications*. London: Charles Griffin.

Oswald, A. (1977). 'Time in Input–Output Models', Fraser of Allander Institute, Discussion Paper No. 1.

Ozaki, I. (1970). 'Economies of scale and input–output coefficients', in Carter, A. and Brody, A., *Applications of Input–Output Analysis*, Vol. II. Amsterdam: North-Holland.

Paelinck, J. and Waelbroeck, J. (1963). 'Étude empirique sur l'évolution de coefficients "input–output".' *Economie Appliquée*, **16**, pp. 81–111.

Panchamukhi, V. R. (1975). 'Linkages in industrialization: a study of selected developing countries in Asia.' *Journal of Development Planning*, **8**, pp. 121–165.

Parikh, A. (1979). 'Forecasts of technology matrices using the RAS method.' Paper presented to the Seventh International Conference on Input–Output Techniques, Innsbruck, April, 1979.

Paukert, F., Skolka, J. and Maton, J. (1974). 'Redistribution of income, patterns of consumption and employment: a case study for the Philippines.' Paper presented to the Sixth International Conference on Input–Output Techniques, Vienna, April, 1974.

Paukert, F., Skolka, J. and Maton, J. (1979). 'Income distribution by size, structure of the economy and employment: a comparative study for four Asian Countries.' Paper presented to the Seventh International Conference on Input–Output Techniques, Innsbruck, April, 1979.

Pearson, S. R. (1976). 'Net social profitability, domestic resource costs and effective rate of protection.' *Journal of Development Studies*, **12,** pp. 320–333.

Pyatt, G. and Roe, A. R. with Lindley, R. M., Round, J. I. and others (1977). *Social Accounting for Development Planning; with Special Reference to Sri Lanka.* Cambridge: CUP.

Pyatt, G. and Round, J. (1979). 'Accounting and fixed price multipliers in a social accounting framework.' *Economic Journal*, **89,** pp. 850–873.

Rabih, S. (1979). 'Commercial Policy and Its Effects on Manufacturing Industry in Less Developed Countries: a Case Study of Sudan, 1966–1976', unpublished Ph.D. Thesis, Queen Mary College, University of London.

Radhakrishna, R. and Sarma, A. (1979). 'Analysis of sectoral price movements in a developing economy: effects of movement in agricultural prices and production on industrial prices, demand pattern and income distribution.' Paper presented to the Seventh International Conference on Input–Output Techniques, Innsbruck, April, 1979.

Raj, K. N. (1975). 'Linkages in industrialization and development strategy: some basic issues.' *Journal of Development Planning*, **8,** pp. 106–119.

Rasmussen, P. (1957). *Studies in Intersectoral Relations.* Amsterdam: North-Holland.

Richardson, H. (1972). *Input–Output and Regional Economics.* London: Weidenfeld and Nicolson.

Riedel, J. (1975). 'Factor proportions, linkages and the open developing economy.' *Review of Economics and Statistics*, **57,** pp. 487–494.

Riedel, J. (1976). A balanced-growth version of the linkage hypothesis: a comment.' *Quarterly Journal of Economics*, **90,** pp. 319–322.

Riefler, R. and Tiebout, C. M. (1970). 'International input–output: an empirical California-Washington model.' *Journal of Regional Science*, **10,** pp. 135–152.

Robinson, S. (1976). 'Income distribution within groups, among groups, and overall: a technique of analysis.' Discussion Paper No. 65, Princeton University, Princeton.

Robinson, S. and Kubo, Y. (1979). 'Sources of industrial growth and structural change: a comparative analysis of eight countries.' Paper presented to the Seventh International Conference on Input–Output Techniques, Innsbruck, April, 1979.

Samuelson, P. (1951). 'Abstract of a theorem concerning substitution in open Leontief systems', in Koopman, T., *Activity Analysis of Production and Allocation.* New York: Wiley.

Sandee, J. (1960). *A Demonstration Planning Model for India.* New York: Asia Publishing House.

Schaffer, W. A. and Chu, K. (1969). 'Non-survey techniques for constructing regional interindustry models.' *Papers and Proceedings of the Regional Science Association*, **23,** pp. 83–101.

Scitovsky, T. (1954). 'Two concepts of external economies.' *Journal of Political Economy*, **62,** pp. 143–151.

Scott, M., MacArthur, J. D. and Newbery, D. (1976). *Project Appraisal in Practice.* London: Heinemann Educational Books.

Scowan, R. (1977). 'On Grossing-Up', Working Paper No. 30, Scottish Input–Output Project, Fraser of Allander Institute (Mimeo).

Seers, D. (1966). 'The use of a modified input–output system for an economic program in Zambia', in Adelman, I. and Thorbecke, E. (eds.), *The Theory and Design of Economic Development*. Baltimore: Johns Hopkins Press.

Sekerka, B., Kyn, O. and Hejl, L. (1970). 'Price systems computable from input–output coefficients', in Carter, A. and Bródy, A. (eds.), *Contributions to Input–Output Analysis*, Vol. I. Amsterdam: North-Holland.

Sen, A. K. (1972). 'Control areas and accounting prices: an approach to economic evaluation.' *Economic Journal*, **82,** pp. 486–501.

Sen, A. K. (1973). *On Economic Inequality*. New York, Morton.

Seton, F. (1973). 'Shadow wages in Chile', in Eckaus, R. S. and Rosenstein-Rodan, P. N. (eds.), *Analysis of Development Problems: Studies of the Chilean Economy*. Amsterdam: North-Holland.

Shishido, S. and Oshizaka, A. (1976). 'Inventory adjustment in a quarterly input–output model for Japan', in Polenske, K. R. and Skolka, J. V. (eds.), *Advances in Input–Output Analysis*. Cambridge, Mass.: Ballinger.

Si-kang, C. and Shin-wei, S. (1979). 'A non-linear input–output model in physical units and its application in China.' Paper presented to the Seventh International Conference on Input–Output Techniques, Innsbruck, April, 1979.

Simpson, D. and Tsukui, J. (1965). 'The fundamental structure of production.' *Review of Economics and Statistics*, **47,** 1965.

Squire, L. and Van der Tak, H. E. (1975). *Economic Analysis of Projects*. Baltimore: John Hopkins Press.

Srinivasan, T. N. (1975). 'The foreign trade sector in planning models', in Blitzer, C., Clark, P. and Taylor, L. (eds.), *Economy-Wide Models and Development Planning*. Oxford: OUP.

Stewart, F. and Streeten, P. (1972). 'Little-Mirrlees methods and project appraisal.' *Bulletin of the Oxford University Institute of Economics and Statistics*, **34,** pp. 75–92.

Stewart, F. (1977). *Technology and Underdevelopment*. London: Macmillan.

Stone, R. (1961). *Input–Output and National Accounts*. Paris: OECD.

Stone, R. (1962). 'Multiple classifications in social accounting.' *Bulletin de l'Institut International de Statistique*, **39,** pp. 215–233.

Stone, R. (1978). 'The disaggregation of the household sector in the national accounts.' Paper presented to the World Bank Conference on Social Accounting Methods in Development Planning, Cambridge, U.K., April, 1978.

Stone, R. *et al.* (1963). *Input–Output Relationships 1954–66*. Vol. 3 of a Programme for Growth, Cambridge, Department of Applied Economics, London: Chapman and Hall.

Su, T. T. (1970). 'A note on regional input–output models.' *Southern Economic Journal*, **37,** pp. 325–327.

Sutcliffe, R. (1971). *Industry and Underdevelopment*. London: Addison-Wesley.

Syrquin, M. (1976). 'Sources of industrial growth and change—an alternative measure.' Unpublished paper presented to European Meeting of the Econometric Society, Helsinki, 1976.

Szal, R. and Robinson, S. (1977). 'Measuring income inequality', in Frank, C. R. and Webb, R. (eds.), *Income Distribution: Policy Alternatives in Developing Countries*. Washington: Brookings Institute.

Tatemoto, M. and Ichimura, S. (1959). 'Factor proportions and foreign trade: the case of Japan.' *Review of Economics and Statistics*, **41,** pp. 442–446.

Taylor, L. (1975). 'Theoretical foundations and technical implications', in Blitzer. C., Clark, P. and Taylor, L. (eds.), *Economy-Wide Models and Development Planning*. Oxford: OUP.

Taylor, L. and Lysy, F. (1979a). 'Vanishing income redistributions: Keynesian clues about model surprises in the short run.' *Journal of Development Economics*, **6,** pp. 11–30.

Taylor, L. (1979b). *Macro Models for Developing Countries*. New York: McGraw-Hill.

Taylor, P. (1979). 'Estimation of price effects on input–output coefficients.' Paper

presented to the Seventh International Conference on Input–Output Techniques, Innsbruck, April, 1979.
Theil, H. (1957). 'Linear aggregation in input–output analysis.' *Econometrica*, **25,** pp. 111–122.
Tilanus, C. B. (1966). *Input–Output Experiments, The Netherlands 1948—61.* Rotterdam: Rotterdam University Press.
Tinbergen, J. (1965). 'International, national, regional and local industries', in Caves, R. E., Johnson, H. G. and Kenen, P. B. (eds.), *Trade, Growth and the Balance of Payments.* Amsterdam: North-Holland.
Tinbergen, J. (1967). *Development Planning.* London: World University Library.
Tyler, W. G. (1976). *Manufactured Export Expansion and Industrialization in Brazil.* Tubingen: J. C. B. Mohr (Paul Siebeck).
United Nations (1968). 'A System of National Accounts', Series F, No. 2, Rev. 3, New York.
United Nations (1973). 'Input–Output Tables and Analysis', Series F, No. 14, Rev. 1, New York.
United Nations (1975). 'Towards a system of social and demographic statistics', Studies in Methods, Series F, No. 18, New York.
Waugh, F. (1950). 'Inversion of the Leontief matrix by a power series.' *Econometrica*, **18,** pp. 142–154.
Weisskopf, R. and Figueroa, A. (1976). 'Traversing the social pyramid: a comparative review of income distribution in Latin America.' *Latin American Research Review*, **11.**
Weisskopf, T. E. (1971). ''Alternative patterns of import substitution in India', in Chenery, H. (ed.), *Studies in Development Planning.* Cambridge, Mass.: Harvard University Press.
Yamane, T. (1967). *Elementary Sampling Theory.* Englewood Cliffs, N.J.: Prentice-Hall.
Yates, F. (1960). *Sampling Methods for Censuses and Surveys.* London: Charles Griffin, 3rd ed.
Yotopoulos, P. and Nugent, J. (1973). 'A balanced growth version of the linkage hypothesis: a test.' *Quarterly Journal of Economics*, **87,** pp. 157–171.

Author Index

Subject Index